Autodesk Maya 2012:
A Comprehensive Guide

CADCIM Technologies

525 St. Andrews Drive
Schererville, IN 46375, USA
(www.cadcim.com)

Contributing Author

Sham Tickoo

Professor
Purdue University Calumet
Hammond, Indiana, USA

CADCIM Technologies

Autodesk Maya 2012: A Comprehensive Guide
Sham Tickoo

ISBN: 978-1-932709-99-5

NOTICE TO THE READER

www.cadcim.com

Online Training Program Offered by CADCIM Technologies

CADCIM Technologies provides effective and affordable virtual online training on various software packages including Computer Aided Design and Manufacturing (CAD/CAM), computer programming languages, animation, architecture, and GIS. The training is delivered 'live' via Internet at any time, any place, and at any pace to individuals, students of colleges, universities, and CAD/CAM training centers. The main features of this program are:

Training for Students and Companies in a Class Room Setting

Highly experienced instructors and qualified Engineers at CADCIM Technologies conduct the classes under the guidance of Prof. Sham Tickoo of Purdue University Calumet, USA. This team has authored several textbooks that are rated "one of the best" in their categories and are used in various colleges, universities, and training centers in North America, Europe, and in other parts of the world.

Training for Individuals

The cost effective and time saving initiative of CADCIM Technologies strives to deliver the training in the comfort of your home or work place, thereby relieving you from the hassles of traveling to training centers.

Training Offered on Software Packages

We provide basic and advanced training on the following software packages:

CAD/CAM/CAE: CATIA, Pro/ENGINEER Wildfire, SolidWorks, Autodesk Inventor, Solid Edge, NX, AutoCAD, AutoCAD LT, Customizing AutoCAD, EdgeCAM, ANSYS

Computer Programming: C++, VB.NET, Oracle, AJAX, and Java

Animation and Styling: Autodesk 3ds Max, Autodesk 3ds Max Design, Autodesk Maya, and Autodesk Alias Design

Architecture, Civil, and GIS: Autodesk Revit Architecture, AutoCAD Civil 3D, Autodesk Revit Structure, and Autodesk Map 3D

For more information, please visit the following link:

http://www.cadcim.com

Note

The free teaching and learning resources, mentioned in the cover page of this textbook, are available only for those who buy the textbook from our website, **www.cadcim.com** or the university/college bookstores. We need proof of purchase when you request the technical support from us.

Table of Contents

Chapter 4: Polygon Primitives

Chapter 5: Shading and Texturing

Chapter 6: UV Mapping

Chapter 7: Modeling

Chapter 8: Lighting

Chapter 9: Animation - I

Chapter 10: Animation - II

Chapter 11: Paint Effects

Chapter 12: Rendering

Chapter 13: Particle System

Chapter 14: Introduction to nParticles

Chapter 15: Fluids

Chapter 16: Hair and Fur

Preface

Autodesk Maya 2012

Welcome to the world of Autodesk Maya 2012. Autodesk Maya 2012 is a powerful, integrated 3D modeling, animation, visual effects, and rendering software developed by Autodesk Inc. This integrated node based 3D software finds its application in developing films, games, and design projects. A wide range of 3D visual effects, computer graphics, and character animation tools make it an ideal platform for 3D artists. The intuitive user interface and workflow tools of Maya 2012 have made the job of design visualization specialists a lot easier.

Autodesk Maya 2012: A Comprehensive Guide textbook covers all features of Autodesk Maya 2012 in a simple, lucid, and comprehensive manner. It aims at harnessing the power of Autodesk Maya 2012 for 3D artists and designers. This textbook will help you transform your imagination into reality with ease. Also, it will unleash your creativity, thus helping you create realistic 3D models, animation, and visual effects. It caters to the needs of both the novice and advanced users of Maya 2012 and is ideally suited for learning at your convenience and at your pace.

The salient features of this textbook are as follows:

- **Tutorial Approach**

  The author has adopted the tutorial point-of-view and the learn-by-doing theme throughout the textbook. This approach will guide the users through the process of creating the models, adding textures, and animating them in the tutorials.

- **Real-World Models as Projects**

  The author has used about 25 real-world modeling and animation projects as tutorials in this textbook. This will enable the readers to relate the tutorials to the real-world models in the animation and visual effects industry. In addition, there are about 30 exercises that are also based on the real-world animation projects.

- **Tips and Notes**

  Additional information related to various topics is provided to the users in the form of tips and notes.

The first page of every chapter summarizes the topics that will be covered in that chapter. This will help the users to easily refer to a topic.

• **Self-Evaluation Test, Review Questions, and Exercises**
Every chapter ends with a Self-Evaluation test so that the users can assess their knowledge of the chapter. The answers to the Self-Evaluation Test are given at the end of the chapter. Also, the Review Questions and Exercises are given at the end of each chapter that can be used by the Instructors as test questions and exercises.

• **Heavily Illustrated Text**
The text in this book is heavily illustrated with about 500 diagrams and screen captures.

Symbols Used in the Text

The author has provided additional information to the users about the topic being discussed in the form of notes.

Special information and techniques are provided in the form of tips that helps in increasing the efficiency of the users.

This symbol indicates the new command or tool introduced in Autodesk Maya 2012.

This symbol indicates the existing command or tool that has been enhanced in Autodesk Maya 2012.

Free Companion Website

It has been our constant endeavor to provide you the best textbooks and services at affordable price. In this endeavor, we have come out with a free companion website that will facilitate the process of teaching and learning of Autodesk Maya 2012. If you purchase this textbook from our website (www.cadcimtech.com), you will get access to the companion website.

To access the files, you need to register by visiting the **Resources** section at *www.cadcim.com*. The following resources are available for the faculty and students in this website:

Faculty Resources

• **Technical Support**
You can get online technical support by contacting *techsupport@cadcim.com*.

• **Instructor Guide**
Solutions to all review questions and exercises in the textbook are provided to help the faculty members test the skills of the students.

- **PowerPoint Presentations**

  The contents of the book are arranged in powerpoint slides that can be used by the faculty for their lectures.

- **Part Files**

  The part files used in illustration, examples, and exercises are available for free download.

- **Rendered Images**

  If you do an exercise or tutorial, you can compare your rendered output with the one provided in the CADCIM website.

If you are a faculty member, please contact the publisher at *sales@cadcim.com* or the author at *stickoo@purduecal.edu* or *tickoo525@gmail.com* to access the website that contains the teaching resources.

Student Resources

- **Technical Support**

  You can get online technical support by contacting *techsupport@cadcim.com*.

- **Part Files**

  The part files used in illustrations and examples are available for free download.

- **Rendered Images**

  If you do an exercise or tutorial, you can compare your rendered output with the one provided in the CADCIM website.

Chapter *1*

Exploring Maya Interface

Learning Objectives

After completing this chapter, you will be able to:

• *Start Autodesk Maya 2012*
• *Work with menu sets and icons in Autodesk Maya*
• *Understand various terms related to Maya interface*
• *Work with tools in Autodesk Maya*

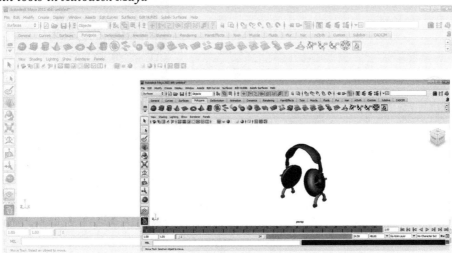

INTRODUCTION TO Autodesk Maya

Welcome to the world of Autodesk Maya. The word "Maya" stands for imagination; thus this textbook will unleash the imaginative power within you. In other words, it will help you turn your imagination into reality. Also, it will help you learn methods to work in Maya. Although Maya is quite a vast software to deal with, yet all major tools used in Autodesk Maya 2012 have been covered in this book. This chapter will make you aware of the Maya interface.

STARTING Autodesk Maya 2012

To start Autodesk Maya 2012, choose **Start > All Programs > Autodesk > Autodesk Maya 2012 > Autodesk Maya 2012** from the taskbar menu, refer to Figure 1-1; the default screen of Maya will be displayed with its different components.

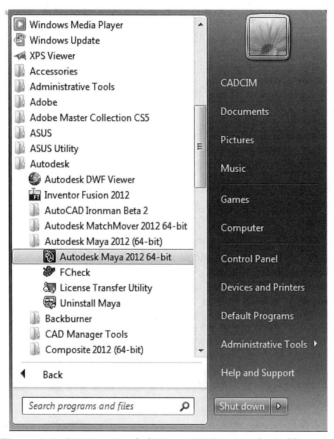

Figure 1-1 Starting Autodesk Maya 2012 using the taskbar menu

Alternatively, you can start Autodesk Maya 2012 by double-clicking on its shortcut icon displayed on the desktop of your computer. This icon is automatically created on installing Autodesk Maya 2012 on a computer. Double-click on the icon; three windows namely, the main Maya window, the **Output Window,** and the **Essential Skills Movies** window will be displayed on the screen. The **Output Window**, as shown in Figure 1-2, displays the render time and the other calculations made while rendering. The **Essential Skills Movies** window, as shown in Figure 1-3, provides access to some video tutorials that are helpful in learning the basic interface of the software.

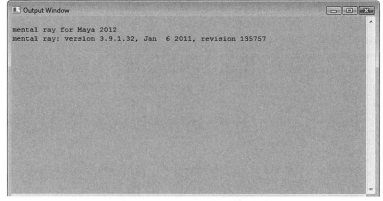

*Figure 1-2 The **Output Window***

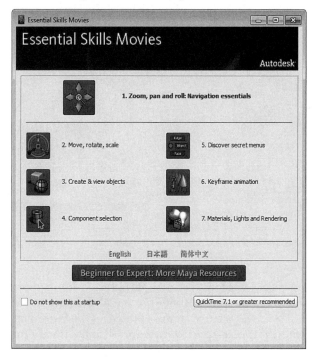

*Figure 1-3 The **Essential Skills Movies** window*

 Note
*For viewing the video tutorials, you need to have Quick Time 7.1 or later installed on your system. To play any video tutorial in the **Essential Skills Movies** window, choose the corresponding button from the window; the video tutorial will be displayed in a separate window. However, if you do not want to play the tutorials, choose the cross button on the upper right corner of the **Essential Skills Movies** window. You can also choose the **Do not show this at startup** check box so that this window does not appear the next time you start Maya 2012.*

Autodesk Maya 2012 SCREEN COMPONENTS

Autodesk Maya screen consists of viewports, title bar, menu bar, status line, shelf, toolbar, and so on. All these components will be discussed later in this chapter. When you start Autodesk Maya 2012 for the first time, the **persp** panel is displayed by default, as shown in Figure 1-4. Panel is the part or the work area where you can create your 3D scene. Panels are also known as viewports or views. In this textbook, panels will be referred to as viewports. Every viewport has a grid placed in the center. A grid is the intersection of lines which are perpendicular to each other in the X-Y plane. The center of the grid is intersected by two dark lines. The point of intersection of these two dark lines is known as the origin. The origin is an arbitrary point, which is used to determine the location of the objects. At the origin, the X, Y, and Z coordinates are at 0, 0, and 0 positions, respectively. Note that, in Maya, the X, Y, and Z axes are displayed in red, green, and blue colors, respectively.

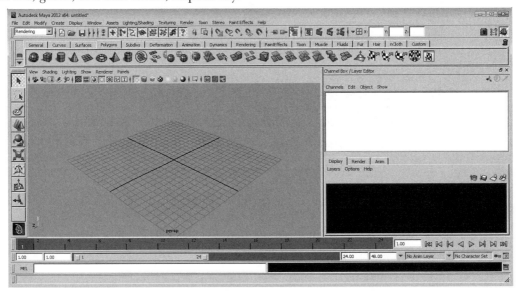

Figure 1-4 *The default screen of Autodesk Maya 2012*

Autodesk Maya 2012 screen is divided into four viewports: top, front, side, and persp. These viewports are classified into two categories, orthographic and perspective. The orthographic category comprises of top, front, and side viewports and the perspective category comprises of the persp viewport. The orthographic viewport displays the 2-dimensional (2D) view of the objects created in it, whereas the perspective viewport displays the 3-dimensional (3D) view of the objects created. Every viewport can be recognized easily by its name, which is displayed at the bottom of each viewport. To view the four viewports simultaneously, choose the Four-view button from the toolbox. Figure 1-5 shows the screen displaying various components of the Maya interface.

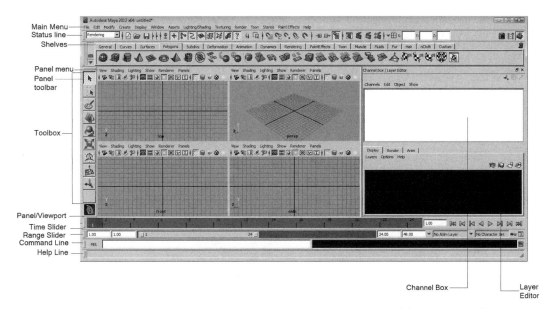

Figure 1-5 Screen displaying various components of the Maya interface

Every viewport has its own panel menubar that allows you to access the tools and functions related to that specific viewport. The axis direction indicator located at the lower left corner of the viewport guides you to the X, Y, and Z coordinates. Similarly, every viewport in Maya has a default camera applied to it through which the viewport scene is visible. The name of the camera is displayed at the bottom of each viewport. In other words, the name of the viewport is actually the name of the camera of that particular viewport.

The title bar, which lies at the top of the screen, displays the name of the software, the name of the file, and the location where this file is saved. A Maya file is saved with the *.mb* extension. The three buttons on the extreme right of title bar are used to minimize, maximize, and close the Autodesk Maya 2012 window, respectively. Various components of this window are discussed next.

 Tip: *To toggle between single viewport and four viewport views, move the cursor over one of the viewport and press the SPACEBAR key.*

Main Menubar

The main menubar is displayed just below the title bar. In Maya, the pull-down menus comprise of various tools. These pull-down menus are known as menusets. Each menuset corresponds to a particular module in Maya interface, refer to Figure 1-6. The modules are located on the extreme left of the status line.

Various types of modules available in Maya are **Animation**, **Polygons**, **Surfaces**, **Dynamics**, **Rendering**, **nDynamics**, and **Customize**. These modules help in grouping the related features and tools together. On selecting a particular module, the menus in the menubar change accordingly. On invoking a menu in the menubar, a pull-down menu will be displayed, as shown in Figure 1-6. On the right of some options in these pull-down menus, there are two types of demarcations, arrows and option boxes, refer to Figure 1-6. When you click on an option box, a dialog box will be displayed. You can use this dialog box to set the options for that particular tool or menu item. On clicking the arrow, the corresponding submenu will be displayed.

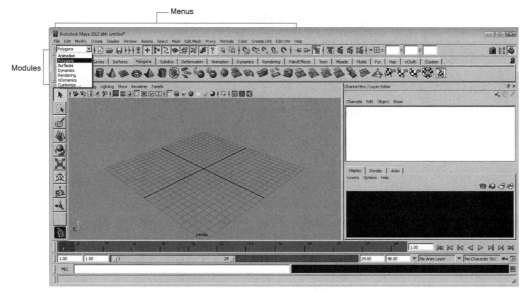

Figure 1-6 *Screen displaying modules and menu sets*

 Tip: *You can also select different modules using the hotkeys that are assigned to them. The default hotkeys are F2 (Animation), F3 (Polygons), F4 (Surfaces), F5 (Dynamics), and F6 (Rendering).*

Status line

The status line is located below the main menubar. It begins with the menu selector drop-down list from which modules are selected. The menuset on the right of the main menubar changes as per the module selected. The status line consists of different graphical icons. The graphical icons are further grouped and these groups are separated by black vertical lines with either a box or an arrow symbol in the middle. These vertical lines are known as collapsers, as shown in Figure 1-7. You can click on a collapser with a box symbol to hide a particular group on the status line. On doing so, the corresponding group will hide and the box will change to an arrow symbol. Similarly, if you click on a collapser that has an arrow symbol in the middle, the particular group will display all the tools grouped in that collapsers group icon. Various groups separated by collapsers are discussed next.

Figure 1-7 *The collapsers*

Menu Selector Group

The menu selector group of the status line is used to select different modules such as **Animation**, **Polygons**, **Surfaces**, **Dynamics**, and **nDynamics** from the drop-down list, as shown in Figure1-8. For example, select the **Rendering** module from the drop-down list; all commands related to it will be displayed in the menus of the main menubar. When you switch between various modules, the menus on the right will change, while those on the left will remain intact.

Figure 1-8 *The menu set drop-down list*

Scene File Group

This group is used to perform different file related operations, refer to Figure 1-9. The tools in this group are discussed next.

Figure 1-9 *The file group*

Create a new scene

The **Create a new scene** button is used to open a new scene. To open a new scene, choose the **Create a new scene** button from the status line; the **Warning: Scene Not Saved** message box will be displayed with the message **Save changes to the untitled scene?**, as shown in Figure 1-10. Choose the **Save** button to save the scene. Choose the **Don't Save** button to open a new scene without saving the changes made in the current scene. Choose the **Cancel** button to cancel the saving procedure.

Figure 1-10 *The* **Warning: Scene Not Saved** *message box*

Open a scene

The **Open a scene** button is used to open a file created earlier. To open an existing file, choose this button from the status line; the **Open** dialog box will be displayed, as shown in Figure 1-11. In this dialog box, specify the location of the file that you want to open and then choose the **Open** button; the selected file will open in the Maya interface. This dialog box is divided into different sections and some of them are discussed next.

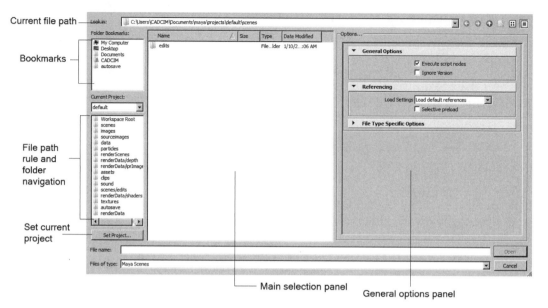

Current file path

Bookmarks

File path
rule and
folder
navigation

Set current
project

Main selection panel

General options panel

Figure 1-11 *The **Open** dialog box*

Folder Bookmarks
The bookmarks section is used to access the computer folders. You can also rearrange the default position of the folders in this section by dragging them up and down using the left mouse button.

Set project
This section is used to set a new project by replacing the current project. On choosing this button, a new window named **Set Project** is displayed. You will learn about this window later in this book.

Save the current scene

The **Save the current scene** button is used to save the current scene. To save the current scene, choose the **Save the current scene** tool; the **Save** dialog box will be displayed. Enter a name for the new file in the **File name** text box, specify the location to save the current scene, and then choose the **Save as** button to save the current scene. Autodesk Maya 2012, provides you with various options that can be used while saving a file. These options are given on the right side of the dialog box in the **Options** section.

Selection Mode Group

The selection mode group shown in Figure 1-12 is used to select objects or the components of objects from the viewport. This group comprises of three buttons that are discussed next.

Figure 1-12 *The selection mode group*

Select by hierarchy and combinations

 The **Select by hierarchy and combinations** button is used to select groups of objects or parts of a group.

Select by object type

The **Select by object type** button is used to select objects such as geometry, cameras, lights, and so on.

Select by component type

The **Select by component type** button is used to select the components of an object, such as vertices or faces. You can also select the control vertices of the NURBS surfaces using this button.

Tip: *To switch between the object and component modes, press the F8 key.*

Selection Masks Group

The selection masks group comprises of a group of selection filters that help you select objects or their components in the viewport, as shown in Figure 1-13. The selection mask helps you decide which filters/icons should be displayed in the viewport. You can select the required object from a group by using these filters/icons. Various filters/icons in the individual selection masks group are discussed next.

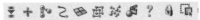

Figure 1-13 The selection masks group

Set the object selection mask

The **Set the object selection mask** button is used to switch all selection icons on or off. To do so, choose the **Set the object selection mask** button from the status line; a flyout will be displayed, as shown in Figure 1-14. Select the **All objects on** option from the flyout to make all selection icons on or select the **All objects off** option to switch off all selection icons from the menu.

Figure 1-14 Flyout displayed on choosing
the Set the object selection mask button

Note
If the All objects off option is chosen, you cannot select any object in the viewport.

Select handle objects

 The **Select handle objects** button allows you to select IK handles and selection handles. You will learn more about this tool in the later chapters.

Select joint objects

 The **Select joint objects** button is used to select only the joints of the objects while animating or rigging them.

Select curve objects

 The **Select curve objects** button is used to select only the curves in the viewport.

Select surface objects

 The **Select surface objects** button is used to select only the surfaces in the viewport.

Select deformations objects

 The **Select deformations objects** button is used to select the lattices and other deformers while animating an object.

Select dynamic objects

 The **Select dynamic objects** button is used to select the particles or dynamic objects in the viewport.

Select rendering objects

 The **Select rendering objects** button is used to select the lights and cameras in the viewport.

Select miscellaneous objects

 The **Select miscellaneous objects** button is used to select miscellaneous objects such as locators and dimensions in the viewport.

Lock / Unlock current selection

 The **Lock / Unlock current selection** button is used to lock the manipulators to the selected object. Select an object in the viewport and invoke the **Lock/ Unlock current selection** tool from the status line; the manipulators will be locked to the object.

Highlight Selection mode

 The **Highlight Selection mode** button is used to turn off the automatic display of components.

Snap Group

The snap group comprises of different snap tools, as shown in Figure 1-15. The snap tools are used to snap the selected objects to specific points in a scene. The tools in this group are discussed next.

Figure 1-15 *The snap tools group*

Snap to grids

 The **Snap to grids** button is used to snap the cursor to the active grid along the X, Y, and Z axes.

Snap to curves

The **Snap to curves** button is used to snap the cursor to the curve in the viewport. For example, to snap a curve on a cube, choose **Create > NURBS Primitives > Cube** from the main menubar and then click in the viewport; a cube will be created. Next, choose **Create > EP Curve Tool** from the main menubar and then create a curve in the top viewport. Next, Choose the **Move Tool** from the toolbox and align the cube over the curve. Choose the **Snap to curves** button from the status line. Press the middle mouse button over the cube and drag it; the cube will move over the curve while remaining snapped to the curve, refer to Figure 1-16.

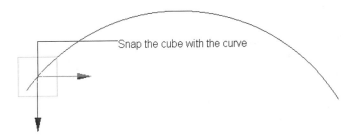

Snap the cube with the curve

Figure 1-16 *The cube snapped to the curve*

Snap to points

 The **Snap to points** button helps to snap the vertex of one object to another. For example, to snap a cube to the vertices of a polygonal plane, choose **Create > Polygon Primitives > Plane > Option Box** from the main menubar; the **Polygons Plane Tool** settings window will be displayed. Now, set the **Width divisions** and **Height divisions** to **10**, and then click in the viewport to make a plane. Next, create a cube in the viewport, as discussed earlier. Next, select the cube and choose the **Snap to points** button from the status line; the cube will snap to the vertices of the polygonal plane.

Tip: *You can also use the shortcut keys to perform particular snap functions. For example, press x (lower case) for* **Snap to grids**, *c (lower case) for* **Snap to curves** *and v (lower case) for the* **Snap to points** *functions.*

Snap to view planes

 The **Snap to view planes** button is used to snap the selected object to the view plane of the viewport.

Make the selected object live

 The **Make the selected object live** button is used to make the selected object live On choosing this button, the selected object will freeze in its place, and then you can create a curve on its surface. To do so, choose the **Make the selected object** live button from the status line. Alternatively, select an object on which you want to create a curve. Next, choose **Modify > Make Live** from the main menubar; the selected object will become a live object. Then, choose **Create > EP Curve Tool** from the main menubar and click on the surface of the object to create a curve on it. You can create various objects such as a bamboo basket by using the **Make Live** option.

Note
*Only NURBS surfaces, meshes, and construction planes can be made live by using the **Make the selected object live** tool.*

Input and Output Connections Group

This part of the status line helps you control various objects. The objects with input connections are affected or controlled by other objects, whereas the objects with output connections affect or control other objects.

Inputs to the selected object

 The Inputs to the selected object button is used to edit all input connections for the selected object such that the selected object gets influenced by another object.

Outputs from the selected object

 The **Outputs from the selected object** button helps you to select and edit any object that is influenced by the selected object.

Construction history on/off

 The **Construction history on/off** button is a toggle tool that is used to record the construction history. The construction history is used in case you want to track the changes made on an object at a later stage. Sometimes, the construction history may make a particular file size heavy. To decrease the file size, it is recommended to turn off the **Construction history on/off** toggle button.

Render Controls Group

This group of the status line helps you access all render controls in Maya. The tools in this group are discussed next.

Open Render View

 The **Open Render View** button is used to display the last rendered view. Choose the **Open Render View** button from the status line; the **Render View** window will be displayed with the last rendered scene.

Render the current frame (Maya Software)

 The **Render the current frame (Maya Software)** button is used to render the selected viewport at the current frame. Choose the **Render the current frame (Maya Software)** button from the status line; the **Render View** window and the **Output Window** will be displayed. The **Render View** window will show the rendered view of the selected scene, as shown in Figure 1-17, whereas the **Output Window** will display all the rendering calculations made for rendering the active scene, as shown in Figure 1-18.

Figure 1-17 The **Render View** window

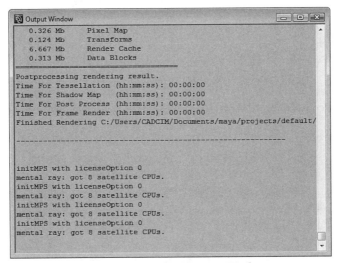

Figure 1-18 The **Output** Window

IPR render the current frame (Maya Software)

The **IPR render the current frame (Maya Software)** button is used to render the current frame. Here, **IPR** stands for Interactive Photorealistic Rendering. This tool helps you adjust the lighting or the shading attributes of the rendered scene and then update it as per the requirement. To render the current frame, choose this button from the status line; the **Render View** window will be displayed. Now, press the left mouse button and drag it in the **Render View** window to set the selection for IPR rendering. As a result, Maya will render the selected part only. In other words, it will help you visualize your scene dynamically. Now, make changes in the color or lightning attribute of the scene using the attribute editor; the selected part will be rendered automatically.

Display Render Settings window (Maya Software)

 The **Display Render Settings window (Maya Software)** button is used to set the parameters for rendering. On choosing this button, the **Render Settings** dialog box will be displayed, as shown in Figure 1-19. This dialog box comprises of all controls needed for rendering. These controls help you adjust the render settings such as resolution, file options, ray tracing quality, and so on.

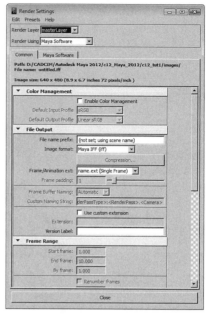

Figure 1-19 The **Render Settings** *dialog box*

Input Box Group

This group in the status line helps you quickly select, rename, and transform the objects that are created in the viewport. Some of the options in the **Name Selection** field are in hidden modes. To view them, move the cursor over the arrow on the left of the input field and then press and hold the left mouse button on it; a list will be displayed. Now, select the required option from the drop-down list; the corresponding mode will be displayed. By default, the **Absolute transform** mode is displayed in the status line. All these modes are discussed next.

Absolute transform

The **Absolute transform** mode is used to move, rotate, and scale a selected object in the viewport. To do so, invoke the required transformation tool from the status line and enter values in the X, Y and Z edit boxes in the **Absolute transform** area, as shown in Figure 1-20. Now, press ENTER; the selected object will be transformed and moved according to the values entered in the edit boxes. Similarly, you can also rotate an object by invoking the **Rotate Tool** from the toolbox and entering the required values in the edit boxes in the **Absolute transform** area.

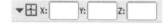

Figure 1-20 The **Absolute transform** *area*

 Note

*The **Absolute transform** mode takes the center of the viewport as a reference for transforming an object.*

Relative transform

The **Relative transform** mode is also used to scale, rotate, and move a selected object in the viewport, refer to Figure 1-21. This mode is similar to the **Absolute transform** mode with the only difference that the **Relative transform** mode takes the last position of the object as a reference point for transforming an object.

*Figure 1-21 The **Relative transform** area*

Rename

The **Rename** mode is used to change the name of a selected object. Select the object from the viewport whose name you want to change; the default name of the selected object will be displayed in the input box in the **Rename** area, as shown in Figure 1-22. Enter a new name for the object in the input box and press ENTER. If more than one object is selected, then on renaming, the name of the last selected object will be changed.

*Figure 1-22 The **Rename** area*

Select by name

You can select an object in the viewport by entering its name in the input box in the **Select by name** area, refer to Figure 1-23. In the input box, enter the name of the object that you want to select in the input box and then press ENTER; the object with the specified name will be selected in the viewport.

*Figure 1-23 The **Select by name** area*

SideBar Buttons Group

This is the last part of the status line. The SideBar buttons control the properties of the objects created in the viewport and the tools required for working with the objects. This group comprises of three buttons that are discussed next.

Show or hide the Attribute Editor

The **Show or hide the Attribute Editor** button helps you control various properties of the objects created in the viewport by using the **Attribute Editor**. Select the object that you have created and choose the **Show or hide the Attribute Editor** button from the status line; the **Attribute Editor** will be displayed, as shown in Figure 1-24. Various tabs in the **Attribute Editor** control different properties of the selected object. The **Attribute Editor** window is discussed later in this chapter.

Show or hide the Tool Settings

The **Show or hide the Tool Settings** button helps you set the properties of the selected tool. On choosing this button, the settings window of the selected tool will be displayed on the left of the viewport, adjacent to the toolbar. For example, if you have chosen the **Move Tool** from the toolbox, then you can control its settings by using the **Tool Settings (Move Tool)** settings window, as shown in Figure 1-25.

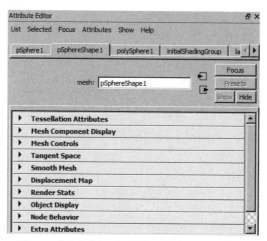

*Figure 1-24 The **Attribute Editor** window*

Show or hide the Channel Box/Layer Editor

The **Show or hide the Channel Box/Layer Editor** button helps you control various properties of the selected object through the **Channel box**. On choosing this button, the **Channel Box/Layer Editor** will be displayed on the right in the viewport, as shown in Figure 1-26. The **Channel Box** is used to control the transformation and the geometrical structure of the selected object. The **Layer Editor** is used when there are many objects in the viewport. Multiple objects can be arranged in the layer editor to simplify the scene.

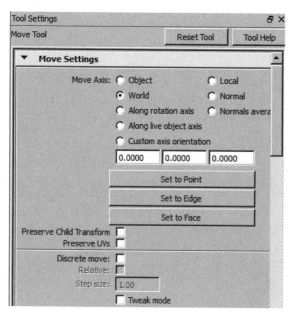

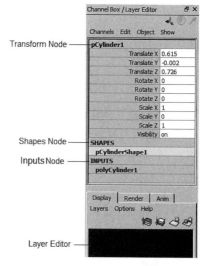

*Figure 1-25 Partial view of the **Tool Settings** (**Move Tool**) settings window*

*Figure 1-26 The **Channel Box/Layer Editor***

Working with Channel Box/Layer Editor

The **Channel Box** and the **Layer Editor** are used for editing the attributes of an object. The **Channel box** consists of all attributes used for editing, and the layer editor is used for creating layers for objects in the scene. To display the **Channel Box/Layer Editor**, choose **Display > UI Elements > Channel Box/Layer Editor** from the main menubar. Alternatively, press the CTRL + a + a keys to open the **Channel Box/Layer Editor**. Select an object for editing its attributes; the attributes of the selected object will be displayed in the **Channel Box/Layer Editor**, refer to Figure 1-26. The **Channel box** is further divided into three parts, which are discussed next.

Transform node

The **Transform** node contains the transformation attributes of the selected object. Select an object from the viewport; the **Transform** node will become active, refer to Figure 1-26. Enter the transform values in different transform parameter edit boxes to transform the object in the viewport. Alternatively, click on an attribute in the **Transform** node; the background of the attribute will change to blue color. Now, move the cursor to the viewport, press and hold the middle mouse button and drag it to make changes in the selected attribute. You can also adjust the values of more than one attribute at a time. To do so, press and hold the SHIFT key and select the attributes that you want to adjust and then move the cursor in the viewport. Now, press and hold the middle mouse button and drag the cursor to make changes in the selected attributes. Choose the **Visibility** attribute to set the visibility of the object. Enter **0** in the **Visibility** edit box to make the visibility of the selected object off. And, enter **1** in the **Visibility** edit box to set the visibility on.

SHAPES node

The **SHAPES** node provides a brief information about an object. It displays the name of the selected object, refer to Figure 1-26. Every object is named in a particular manner. For example, when you create a NURBS sphere in the viewport, it is named as **nurbsSphereShape1**. Here, NURBS indicates that the object has been created using the NURBS primitives; *Sphere* indicates that a sphere has been created; and *Shape1* indicates that this is the first sphere shape created in the workspace.

INPUTS node

The **INPUTS** node is used to modify the geometric structure of an object. Select an object from the viewport; the geometric attributes of the selected object will be displayed in the **INPUTS** node of the **Channel box**, refer to Figure 1-26. Adjust the geometric values as per your requirement.

The layer editor is located below the **Channel box**. To create a new layer in the layer editor, choose **Layers > Create Empty Layer** from the layer editor, as shown in Figure 1-27; a new layer will be created. To add an object to the layer, select the object in the viewport and then press and hold the right mouse button over the empty layer; a flyout will be displayed.

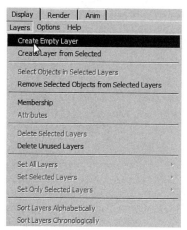

Figure 1-27 Creating a new layer
in layer editor

Choose **Add Selected Object** from the flyout; the selected object will be added to the layer. The layer editor is mainly used when there are multiple objects in a scene. You can also change the name and color of layers by using the layer editor. To do so, double-click on the name of a layer; the **Edit Layer** dialog box will be displayed, as shown in Figure 1-28. Enter the name of the layer in the **Name** text box. You can select the display option of the object from the **display type** drop-down list. If you select the **Normal** option from this list, the object will be displayed in its object mode and will be selectable. If you select the **Template** option from the drop-down list, the object will be displayed in the wireframe mode and the object will not be selectable. Similarly, if you select the **Reference** option, the object will be displayed in the shaded mode and will not be selectable. You can also set the visibility of an object by selecting the **Visible** check box. The **Color** palette located at the bottom of the dialog box enables you to select a color for the layer to give it a distinct identity as compared to other layers.

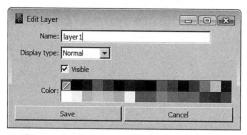

Figure 1-28 The **Edit Layer** dialog box

Note
To edit the components of the channel box first scale the object in the viewport and then, choose
Window > General Editors > Channel Control *from the main menubar.*

Shelf Area

The **Shelf** area is located below the status line, as shown in Figure 1-29. It helps you access various tools in Maya easily and quickly. These tools help you create and edit any object in the viewport. You can also create a new shelf with the required options and also modify the current shelf. To do so, press and hold the left mouse button over the **Menu of items to modify the shelf** option, refer to Figure 1-29; a flyout will be displayed, as shown in Figure 1-30. Various options in this flyout are discussed next.

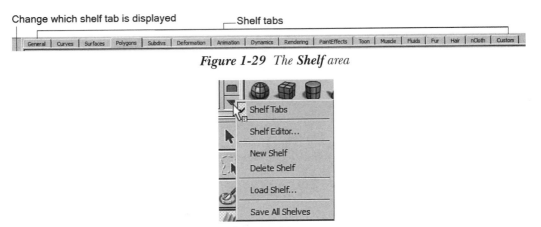

Figure 1-29 The Shelf area

*Figure 1-30 Flyout displayed on choosing the **Menu of items to modify the shelf** option*

Shelf Tabs

The shelf tabs are located below the main menubar. Each shelf tab consists of a complete set of tools and commands to perform a certain operation. You can customize the shelf tabs.

Shelf Editor

The **Shelf Editor** helps you edit a shelf and its properties. To display the **Shelf Editor**, press and hold the left mouse button over the **Menu of items to modify the shelf** area, a flyout will be displayed, refer to Figure 1-30. Choose the **Shelf Editor** option from the flyout; the **Shelf Editor** dialog box will be displayed in the viewport, as shown in Figure 1-31. Alternatively, you can choose **Window > Settings/Preferences > Shelf Editor** from the main menubar to display the **Shelf Editor** dialog box. In the **Shelf Editor** dialog box, you can change the name and position of shelves and shelf contents. You can also create a new shelf and its contents using this dialog box.

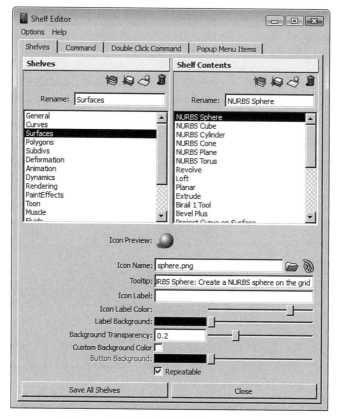

Figure 1-31 The **Shelf Editor** *dialog box*

New Shelf

The **New Shelf** command helps you add a new shelf to the existing **Shelf** area. To add a new shelf, press and hold the left mouse button over the **Menu of items to modify the shelf** option; a flyout will be displayed, refer to Figure 1-30. Select **New Shelf** from the flyout; the **Create New Shelf** dialog box will be displayed, as shown in Figure 1-32. Enter a name for the new shelf and choose the **OK** button; a new shelf will be created in the shelf area, as shown in Figure 1-33.

Figure 1-32 The **Create New Shelf**
dialog box

Figure 1-33 A new shelf added to the shelf area

Delete Shelf

The **Delete Shelf** option is used to delete a shelf from the shelf area. To do so, select the shelf that you want to delete. Next, choose the **Menu of items to modify the shelf** option from the shelf area and then choose the **Delete Shelf** option from the flyout displayed. On doing so, the **Confirm** message box will be displayed, as shown in Figure 1-34. Choose the **OK** button to delete the selected shelf.

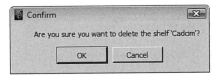

Figure 1-34 *The* **Confirm** *message box*

Load Shelf

The **Load Shelf** option is used to display the predefined shelves. To do so, select the shelf that you want to load. Next, choose the **Menu of items to modify the shelf** option from the shelf area and then choose the **Load Shelf** option from the flyout displayed. On doing so, the **Open** dialog box will be displayed. You can use the options in this dialog box to display the predefined shelves.

Save all Shelves

The **Save all Shelves** tool helps you save the shelves, so that you can use them later while working in Maya.

Toolbox

The toolbox is located on the left of the viewport. It comprises of the most commonly used tools in Maya. In addition to the common commands, the toolbox has several other options/commands that will help you change the interface. Various tools in the toolbox are discussed next.

Select Tool

The **Select Tool** is used to select the objects created in the viewport. To select an object, invoke the **Select Tool** from the toolbox and click on an object in the viewport; the object will be selected. On invoking this tool, the manipulators will not be activated.

Lasso Tool

The **Lasso Tool** is used to select an object by using a free form marquee tool. This tool is very much similar to the **Select Tool**. To select an object, invoke the **Lasso Tool**; the cursor will change to a rope knot. Next, press and hold the left mouse button and drag the cursor in the viewport to create a selection area around the object. Then, release the left mouse button; the object inside the dragged area will be selected. To adjust the properties of the **Lasso Tool**, make sure that the **Lasso Tool** is invoked, and then choose the **Show or hide the Tool Settings** button from the status line; the **Lasso Tool** settings window will be displayed. Adjust the **Lasso Tool** properties from the **Lasso Tool** settings window as per your requirement.

Paint Selection Tool

This tool is used to select various components of an object. To do so, invoke the **Select Tool** from the toolbox and select an object in the viewport. Next, press and hold the right mouse button over the selected object; a marking menu will be displayed. Choose **if the object is NURBS, it will be Control Vertex** from the marking menu to make the vertex component of the object active. Now, choose the **Paint Selection Tool** from the toolbox; the cursor will change to the paint brush. Next, press and hold the left mouse button and drag the cursor over the object to select the vertex.

You can also increase the size of the **Paint Selection Tool** cursor. To do so, press and hold the b key on the keyboard. Next, press and hold the middle mouse button in the viewport and drag the cursor to adjust the size of the brush.

Move Tool

The **Move Tool** is used to move an object from one place to another in the workspace. To do so, invoke the **Move Tool** from the toolbox; the cursor will change to an arrow with a box at its tip. Select the object in the workspace that you want to move. You can move the selected object in the X, Y, and Z direction by using the handles/manipulators over the object. You can also adjust the properties of the **Move Tool** by choosing the **Show or hide the Tool Settings** button from the status line or by double-clicking on the **Move Tool** itself.

Rotate Tool

The **Rotate Tool** is used to rotate the selected object in the viewport. To do so, choose the **Rotate Tool** from the toolbox; the icon will change to an arrow with a box at its tip. Select the object that you want to rotate. You can rotate the selected object in the viewport using the circular rings formed on the object. The properties of the **Rotate Tool** can be adjusted by choosing the **Show or hide the Tool Settings** button from the status line or by double-clicking on the tool.

Scale Tool

The **Scale Tool** is used to scale the selected object in the viewport. To do so, choose the **Scale Tool** from the toolbox and select the object in the viewport that you want to scale. You can scale the selected object in the viewport by moving the handles/manipulators on the object. Each handle scales the object in different axis. You can also scale the object uniformly by moving the yellow cube in the center of the handle/manipulator. You can adjust the properties of the **Scale Tool** by choosing the **Show or hide the Tool Settings** button from the status line or by double-clicking on the tool.

Note
While rotating, moving, or scaling an object, different colored handles are displayed. These handles indicate different areas. You can use this color scheme while working with three transform tools as well. The red, green, and blue colors represent the X, Y, and Z axes, respectively.

Universal Manipulator

The **Universal Manipulator** tool can perform the functions of the **Move**, **Scale**, and **Rotate** tools simultaneously. To use this tool, select an object from the viewport and choose the **Universal Manipulator** tool; the selected object will be surrounded by a number of manipulators or handles to scale or rotate the object, as shown in Figure 1-35. Select the scale or rotate manipulator; an edit box will be displayed on the selected manipulator. Enter the required value in the edit box to transform the object and press ENTER; the selected object will transform accordingly.

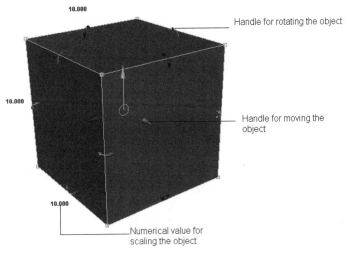

Handle for rotating the object

Handle for moving the object

Numerical value for scaling the object

*Figure 1-35 The **Universal Manipulator** tool handles*

Soft Modification Tool

The **Soft Modification Tool** helps you deform a geometry in such a way that the deformation is widest at the center which gradually decreases towards the end. For example, choose **Create > Polygon Primitives > Sphere** from the main menubar to create a polygon sphere. Next, choose the **Soft Modification Tool** from the toolbox and click on the polygon sphere; the **Soft Modification Tool** manipulator will be displayed, thus creating a colored area on the sphere. Now, move the manipulator to deform the geometry of the sphere.

Show Manipulator

The **Show Manipulator** tool helps you display the object-specific manipulator.

Current Tool Display

The **Current Tool Display** tool displays the last used or the currently selected tool.

Time Slider and Range Slider

The **Time Slider** and the **Range Slider**, as shown in Figure 1-36, are located at the bottom of the viewport. These two sliders control the frames in animation. The time slider comprises of the frames that are used for animation. There is an input box on the time slider called **Set the current time**, which indicates the current frame of animation. The playback range controls at the end of the **Time Slider** let you set the keys for animation of the selected object in the viewport. The keys in the time slider are displayed as red lines.

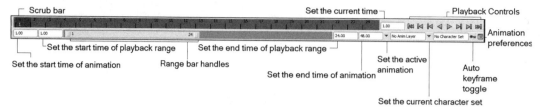

Figure 1-36 The time slider and the range slider

The **Time Slider** displays the range of frames available in your animation. In the **Time Slider**, you will find one grey box, known as scrub bar, and it is used to move back and forth in the active range of frames available for animation. The playback controls at the extreme right of the current frame help you control animation. The **Range Slider** located below the time slider is used to adjust the range of animation playback. The **Range Slider** shows the start and end time of the active animation. The edit boxes both on the left and right of the range slider direct you to the start and end frames of the selected range. The length of the range slider can be altered using these edit boxes. At the right of the **Set the end time of the animation** input box is the **Set the active animation layer** button. This feature gives you access to all the options needed to create and manipulate the animation layers. This option helps you blend multiple animations in a scene, which has been explained in detail in Chapter 9.

Set the current character set located on the right of the range slider. It is used to gain automatic control over the character animated object. There are two buttons on the extreme right of the range slider: **Auto keyframe toggle** and **Animation Preferences**. These buttons are discussed next.

Tip: *You can set the keys for animation by choosing **Animate > Set key** from the main menubar or by pressing the 's' key.*

Auto keyframe toggle

 The **Auto keyframe toggle** button is used to set the keyframes. This button sets the keyframe automatically whenever an animated value is changed. Its color turns red when it is on.

Animation preferences button

 The **Animation preferences** button is used to modify the animation controls. On choosing this button, the **Preferences** dialog box will be displayed, as shown in Figure 1-37. In the **Preferences** dialog box, select the **Time Slider** option from the **Categories** list menu on the left; various options will be displayed on the right of the dialog box. You can set the animation controls in the **Time Slider** and **Playback** area of the **Preferences** window. Choose the **Save** button to save the changes.

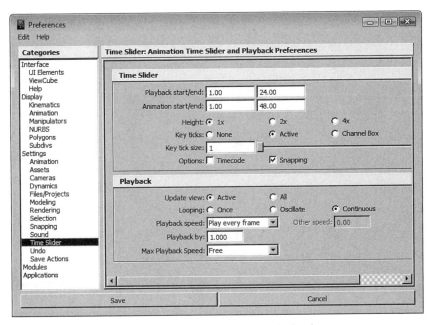

*Figure 1-37 The **Preferences** dialog box*

Command Line

The **Command Line** is located below the **Range slider**. It is used to work in Maya interface by using the MEL script or the Python script. The MEL and Python scripts are the scripting languages used in Maya. Choose the **MEL** button to switch between the two scripts. The **MEL** button is located above the **Help Line**.

> **Note**
> *MEL stands for MAYA Embedded Language. The **MEL** command is a group of text strings that are used to perform various functions in Maya.*

The **Command Line** also displays messages from the program in a grey box on the right. At the extreme left of the **Command Line**, there is an icon for the **Script Editor**. The **Script Editor** is used to enter complex and complicated **MEL** scripts into the scene.

Help Line

The **Help Line** is located at the bottom of the **Command Line**. It provides a brief description about the selected tool or the active area in the Maya interface.

Panel Menu

The **Panel Menu** is available in every viewport, as shown in Figure 1-38. The commands or options in the **Panel Menu** control all the actions performed in the workspace. The **Panel Menu** comprises of six menus, which are discussed next.

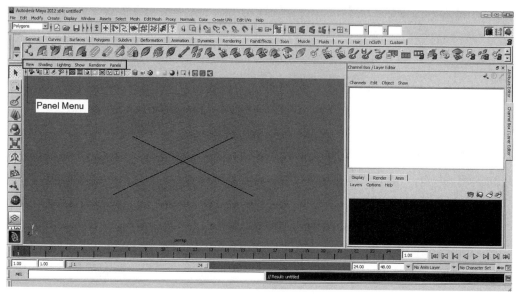

*Figure 1-38 The **Panel Menu***

View

The **View** menu is used to view the object in the viewport from different angles using different camera views.

Shading

This menu helps you use various shading modes in Maya such as wireframe, smooth shade all, flat shade all, X-ray, and so on. You can also use the **Wireframe on Shaded** option in this menu for working comfortably in the shaded mode.

Lighting

This menu helps you use different presets of lights in Maya.

Show

This menu is used to hide or unhide a particular group of objects in the viewport.

Renderer

This menu is used to render the view in the selected panel. You can also set the color texture resolution and the bump texture resolution for high quality rendering using the options in this menu.

Panels

Shortcut: CTRL+SHIFT+m

This menu is used to switch the active viewport to a different view.

Panel Toolbar

This toolbar, as shown in Figure 1-39, is located just below the **panel menu** of all viewports. This toolbar comprises of the most commonly used tools present in the panel menu. These tools are discussed next.

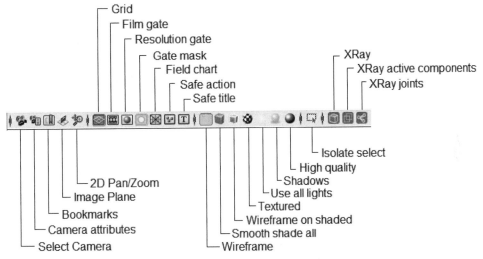

Figure 1-39 The **Panel** toolbar

Select camera

The **Select camera** button is used to select the current camera in the selected viewport. You can also select the current camera in a scene by choosing **View > Select Camera** from the **Panel menu**. To switch between different viewports, right-click on the **Select camera** tool; a flyout will be displayed, as shown in Figure 1-40. Now, from this flyout, you can choose the viewport that you want to switch to.

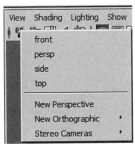

Figure 1-40 The flyout displayed on invoking the **Select Camera** tool

Camera attributes

The **Camera attributes** button is used to display the attributes of the camera in the active viewport. The attributes are displayed on the right of the viewport in the attribute editor. You can also view the attributes by choosing **View > Camera Attribute Editor** from the panel menu.

Bookmarks

The **Bookmarks** button is used to set the current view as a bookmark. You can set a view in the viewport and then invoke the **Bookmarks** button; the set view is bookmarked for further reference. Press and hold the right mouse button over the tool; a flyout with a list of bookmarks created will be displayed. You can also edit existing bookmark by choosing the **Edit Bookmarks** option from this flyout. On doing so, the **Bookmark Editor** dialog box of the active viewport will be displayed, as shown in Figure 1-41. You can change the name and other attributes of the selected bookmark from this dialog box.

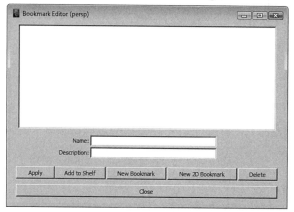

*Figure 1-41 The **Bookmark Editor** dialog box*

Image Plane

The **Image Plane** button is used to add an image to the active viewport. On choosing the **Image Plane** button, the **Open** dialog box will be displayed. In the **Open** dialog box, choose the image plane that you want to insert in the active viewport; the image plane will be inserted in the viewport. You can also set the image to the active viewport by choosing **View > Image Plane > Import Image** from the **Panel menu**.

2D Pan/Zoom

The **2D Pan/Zoom** tool is used to pan or zoom the scene. Using this tool, you can create a new bookmark in Maya. To do so, right-click on the tool icon, a flyout will be displayed. Choose the **Create 2D Bookmark** option to add a new bookmark and choose the **Edit 2D Bookmark** option to edit the already created bookmark. Choose the **Ignore 2D Pan/Zoom** option to toggle between the zoomed view and the full screen view.

Grid

The **Grid** button is used to display grid in the viewport. Invoke this button by choosing **Show > Grid** from the **Panel menu**. In addition, you can set the attributes for the grid in the viewport by using this tool. To display grid, press and hold the right mouse button on the **Grid** tool in the **Panel** toolbar; a flyout will be displayed. Choose **Grid Options** from the flyout; the **Grid Options** dialog box will be displayed, as shown in Figure 1-42. Next, you can set the grid attributes in this dialog box as per your requirement.

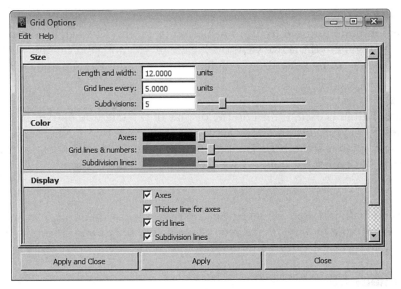

Figure 1-42 *The* **Grid Options** *dialog box*

Film gate

The **Film gate** button is used to toggle the display of film gate border on or off in the active viewport. You can also choose **View > Camera Settings > Film Gate** from the **Panel menu** to display the film gate border in the active viewport.

Resolution gate

The **Resolution gate** button is used to toggle the display of the resolution gate border on or off in the active viewport. The resolution sets the area in the viewport that will be rendered. You can also choose **View > Camera Settings > Resolution Gate** from the **Panel menu** to set the **Resolution Gate** in the active viewport.

Gate mask

The **Gate mask** button is used to turn on the display of the gate mask border. It changes the color and opacity of the area that lies outside the **Film Gate** or the **Resolution Gate**. The gate mask will only work when you have the **Film Gate** or the **Resolution Gate** applied to the active viewport. You can also choose **View > Camera Settings > Gate Mask** from the **Panel menu** to set the gate mask in the active viewport.

Field chart

The **Field chart** button is used to turn on the display of the field chart border. On choosing the **Field Chart** button, a grid is displayed that represents twelve standard cell animation field sizes. The **Field chart** tool should be used only when the render resolution is set to NTSC dimensions. You can also invoke this tool by choosing **View > Camera Settings > Field Chart** from the **Panel menu**.

Safe action

The **Safe action** button is used to turn on the display of the safe action border. This tool is used to set the region in the active viewport for TV production. You can also invoke this tool by choosing **View > Camera Settings > Safe Action** from the **Panel menu**.

Safe title

The **Safe title** button is used to turn on the display of the safe title border. It is also used to set the region for TV production in the active viewport. This tool should be used only when the render resolution is set to NTSC or PAL dimensions. You can also invoke this button by choosing **View > Camera Settings > Safe Title** from the **Panel menu**.

Wireframe

The **Wireframe** button is used to toggle the wireframe display on or off. You can also choose **Shading > Wireframe** from the **Panel menu** to switch to the wireframe mode. Alternatively, press 4 from the keyboard to turn on the wireframe mode.

Smooth shade all

The **Smooth shade all** button is used to set the display to smooth shade. You can also choose **Shading > Smooth Shade All** from the **Panel menu** to switch to smooth shade mode. Alternatively, press 5 from the keyboard for the smooth shade mode.

Wireframe on shaded

The **Wireframe on shaded** button is used to switch the mode of all objects in the viewport to wireframe. You can also invoke this tool by choosing **Shading > Wireframe on Shaded** from the **Panel menu**.

Textured

The **Textured** button is used to set the hardware texturing display of the objects in the viewport. You can also choose **Shading > Hardware Texturing** from the **Panel menu** to toggle on the textures on the objects in the viewport. Alternatively, press 6 from the keyboard to switch to the textured mode.

Use all lights

The **Use all lights** button is used to illuminate objects by using all lights in the viewport. Alternatively, choose **Lighting > Use All Lights** from the **Panel menu** or press 7.

Shadows

The **Shadows** tool is used to display the hardware shadow maps. Alternatively, choose **Lighting > Shadows** from the **Panel menu**.

High quality

The **High quality** tool is used to toggle on the high quality interactive shading in the active viewport itself. On choosing this button, the objects in the viewport will show all the after render effects in the active viewport itself.

Isolate select

The **Isolate select** button is used to display only the selected object in the viewport. To do so, select an object in the viewport and choose the **Isolate Select** button from the **Panel** toolbar. Alternatively, choose **Show > Isolate Select** from the **Panel menu** or press SHIFT + i.

XRay

The **XRay** button is used to make the objects in the viewport semi-transparent. You can also choose **Shading > X-Ray** from the **Panel menu** to switch to the X-Ray mode.

XRay active components

The **XRay active components** button is used to display the active components over the top of other shaded objects. You can also invoke this tool by choosing **Shading > X-Ray Active Components** from the **Panel menu**.

XRay Joints

The **XRay Joints** button is used to display the skeleton joints over the top of other objects in the shaded mode. You can also choose this tool by selecting **Shading > X-Ray Joints** from the **Panel menu**.

Note
Your system should have a good quality graphic card to support high quality settings.

HOTKEYS

By default, every tool has its own shortcut key in Maya. Unlike other software, in Maya 2012 you can create your own shortcut keys or even change default shortcuts. To do so, choose **Window > Settings / Preferences > Hotkey Editor** from the main menubar; the **Hotkey Editor** dialog box will be displayed, as shown in Figure 1-43. Choose the required options from the **Categories** and **Commands** list menus to assign a shortcut key. Choose the **List All...** button in this dialog box to access all mapped and unmapped keys; the **List Hotkeys** window will be displayed, as shown in Figure 1-44. At the lower part of the **Hotkey Editor** dialog box, you can enter a brief description of all commands or shortcuts that you have created. You can also use the **Hotkey Editor** dialog box to know about the commands that are used while writing the MEL script.

HOTBOX

Hotbox, as shown in Figure 1-45, helps you access menu items in a viewport. The hotbox is very useful when you work in the expert mode or the full screen mode. It helps you access the menu items and tools by using cursor in the workspace. To access a command, press and hold the SPACEBAR key; the hotbox will be displayed. Now, you can choose the option that you need to work with from the hotbox. The hotbox is divided into five distinct zones, East, West, North, South, and Center zone, refer to Figure 1-45.

Note
You can use the hotbox to increase the workspace. But you should do it only after you have established a workflow for yourself. In the beginning, you should use the main menubar at the top of the screen instead of using the hotbox, as it reduces the possibility of confusion in finding a command at a later stage.

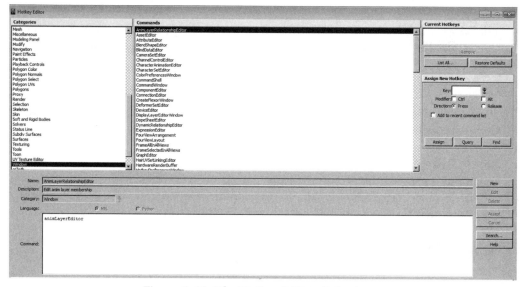

*Figure 1-43 The **Hotkey Editor** dialog box*

WORKING WITH THE GRAPH EDITOR

Main menubar:	Window > Animation Editors > Graph Editor

The **Graph Editor** helps you edit keyframes in an animation. The **Graph Editor** is used to edit the animation curves. It also provides information of all the objects that are animated in the form of graphs. The animated attributes in your scene are represented by curves known as animation curves in the **Graph Editor**. These curves are used to fine-tune your animation.

Alternatively, choose **Window > Animation Editors > Graph Editor** from the main menubar; the **Graph Editor** window will be displayed, as shown in Figure 1-46. The **Graph Editor** is divided into two parts. The left half of the **Graph Editor** displays the hierarchy of the selected objects. The hierarchy lists the animated channels or attributes of the selected objects. The keyframes on the curves are represented as freely moving points, and the animation time moves from left to right on these curves.

Note
*In the **Graph Editor**, the keyframes are indicated by black dots and the animation curves linking the two keyframes are colored.*

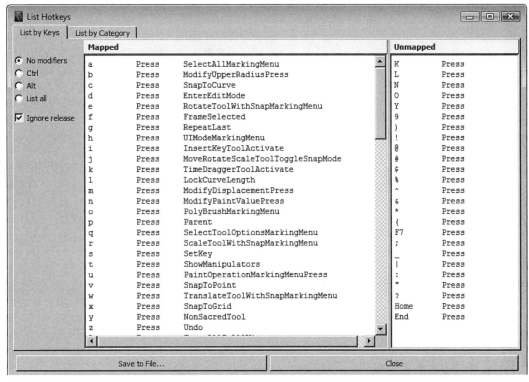

*Figure 1-44 The **List Hotkeys** window*

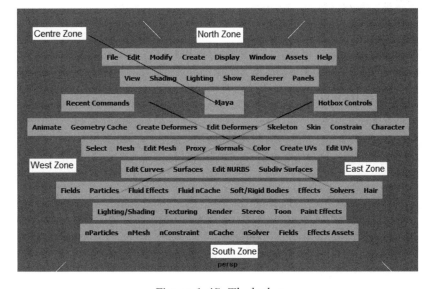

Figure 1-45 The hotbox

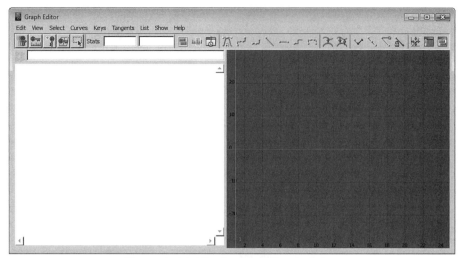

Figure 1-46 The **Graph Editor** window

Tip: *You can use the following shortcuts while working in the **Graph Editor**:*
ALT+LMB+RMB or scroll the MMB to zoom in and out.
SHIFT+ALT+RMB to dolly along Y-axis.
SHIFT+ALT+MMB to track along Y-axis.
SHIFT+MMB to constrain the axis of translation of keyframe.

Self-Evaluation Test

Answer the following questions and then compare them to those given at the end of this chapter:

1. Which of the following combinations of shortcut keys is used to select a menuset?

    (a) h+MMB   (b) h+LMB
    (c) h+RMB   (d) None of these

2. Which of the following shortcut keys is used to switch between the object mode and the component mode?

    (a) F10   (b) F8
    (c) F11   (d) F9

3. IPR can be used only for _____ renderer and _____ rendering.

4. The _____ option helps you select an object by entering its name in the **Name Selection** area.

5. The _____ in the time slider displays the current time.

6. The **Panel menu** has a set of _____ menus.

7. When you switch between modules, all menusets on the menubar change accordingly. (T/F)

8. The keys set for animation are displayed in red color. (T/F)

9. The MEL command is a group of text strings used for performing various actions in Maya. (T/F)

10. The animation time slider moves from left to right in the **Graph Editor**. (T/F)

Review Questions

Answer the following questions:

1. Which of the following tools helps you move the selected objects in a workspace from one place to another?

    (a) **Translate**   (b) **Universal Manipulator**
    (c) **Move**   (d) **Scale**

2. Which of the following combinations of shortcut keys is used to toggle the **Panel** menu on and off ?

    (a) SHIFT+m   (b) CTRL+ SHIFT+m
    (c) SHIFT+N   (d) CTRL+m

3. Which of the following shortcut keys is used to access menu items in a workspace?

    (a) SPACEBAR   (b) BACKSPACE
    (c) INSERT   (d) ESC

4. Hotkeys are also known as _____ keys.

5. The _____ button helps you set keyframes in animation.

6. The user-defined shortcuts can be created by using the_____ .

7. The _____is an arbitrary point, which is used to determine the location of objects.

8. A collapser is used to hide a particular group on the **Status Line**. (T/F)

9. The **Animation Preferences** button is used to modify the animation controls. (T/F)

10. The **Absolute transform** mode is used to move, rotate, and scale a selected object in the viewport. (T/F)

Answers to Self-Evaluation Test
1. b, **2.** b. **3.** Maya software, mental ray, **4. Select by name**, **5.** current time indicator, **6.** six, **7.** T, **8.** T, **9.** T, **10.** T

Chapter 2

Transform Tools in Maya

Learning Objectives

After completing this chapter, you will be able to:

- *Use transform tools*
- *Use manipulators*
- *Use marking menus*

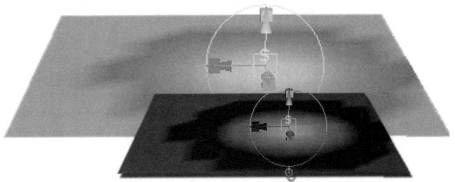

INTRODUCTION

In this chapter, you will learn about the transform tools. These tools are used to position, rotate, and scale objects in Maya. These transforms take place along the X, Y, and Z axes. Additionally, you will learn about changing the pivot points of an object and setting its world space, object space, and local space coordinate axis.

STARTING A NEW FILE IN Autodesk Maya 2012

To start a new file in Maya, choose **File > New Scene** from the main menubar; the **Warning: Scene Not Saved** message box will be displayed, as shown in Figure 2-1. Choose the **Save** button to save the file; choose the **Don't Save** button if you do not want to save the file; or choose the **Cancel** button to cancel it.

Next, invoke the **Preferences** dialog box to restore the default settings of the software. To do so, choose **Window > Settings/Preferences > Preferences** from the main menubar; the **Preferences** dialog box will be displayed in the viewport, as shown in Figure 2-2. Choose **Edit > Restore Default Settings** from the **Preferences** dialog box, and then choose the **Save** button to save the default settings of Maya.

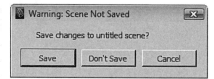

*Figure 2-1 The **Warning: Scene Not Saved** message box*

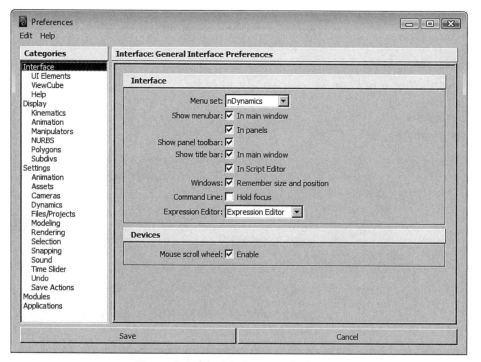

*Figure 2-2 The **Preferences** dialog box*

TRANSFORM TOOLS

Maya creates models by transforming various components of an object using the transform tools (you will learn more about the components of an object in Chapter 3). The transformation process comprises of rotating, scaling, or moving an object. The transforms in Maya are governed by certain tools located in the toolbox, as shown in Figure 2-3. The toolbox is located on the left of the viewport. Various transform tools and their functions are discussed next.

Move Tool

Tool Box:	Move Tool
Keyboard:	W

The **Move Tool** is used to move an object along the X, Y, or Z axis. To use the **Move Tool**, you need to create an object in the viewport. To do so, create a sphere by choosing **Create > Polygon Primitives > Sphere** from the main menubar; the text 'Drag on the grid' will be displayed in the viewport. Next, drag the cursor from one place to the other or click anywhere in the viewport; a sphere will be created. Now, invoke the **Move Tool** from the toolbox and select the object created by clicking on it; the **Move Tool** manipulator will be displayed on the selected object with three color handles, as shown in Figure 2-4. These three color handles are used to move the object in the X, Y, or Z direction. The colors of the handles represent three axes; red represents the X-axis, green represents the Y-axis, and blue represents the Z-axis. At the intersection point of these handles, a cyan box will be displayed that can be used to move the object proportionately in all the three directions. Press and hold the left mouse button over the yellow box and drag the cursor to move the object freely in the viewport. To adjust the default settings of the **Move Tool**, double-click on it in the toolbox; the **Tool Settings (Move Tool)** window will be displayed, as shown in Figure 2-5. Change the settings as per your requirement in this window.

Select Tool
Lasso Tool
Paint Selection Tool
Move Tool
Rotate Tool
Scale Tool
Universal Manipulator Tool
Soft Modification Tool
Show Manipulator Tool
Last Tool Used
Single Perspective View
Four View
Persp/Outliner
Persp/Graph
Hypershade/Persp
Persp/Graph/Hypergraph
Model View

Figure 2-3 *The toolbox*

If the manipulator is not displayed on the object, then you need to set the pivot point of that object. To do so, make sure that the **Move Tool** is invoked and then press the INSERT key; the pivot point will be displayed in the viewport, as shown in Figure 2-6. Move the pivot point to adjust its position. Alternatively, choose **Modify > Center Pivot** from the main menubar; the pivot point will be adjusted to the center of the object. You can also adjust the pivot point by pressing and holding the d key and moving the manipulator.

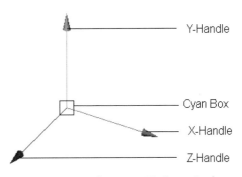

Y-Handle

Cyan Box

X-Handle

Z-Handle

Figure 2-4 *The **Move Tool** manipulator*

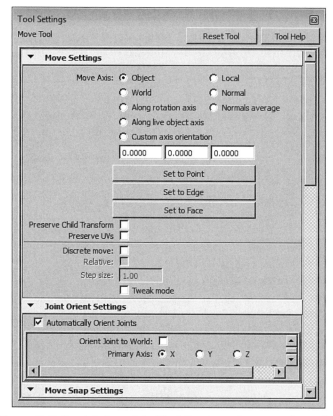

Figure 2-5 Partial view of the **Tool Settings (Move Tool)** window

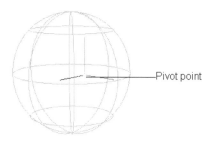

Figure 2-6 The pivot point

Note

A pivot is a point in 3D space that is used as a reference point for the transformation of objects.

Rotate Tool

Tool Box:	Rotate Tool
Keyboard:	e

 The **Rotate Tool** is used to rotate an object along the X, Y, or Z-axis. To rotate an object in the viewport, select the object and invoke the **Rotate Tool** from the toolbox; the **Rotate Tool** manipulator will be displayed on the object, as shown in Figure 2-7. The **Rotate Tool** manipulator consists of three colored rings. The red ring represents the X-axis, whereas the green and blue rings represent the Y and Z axes, respectively. Moreover, the yellow ring around the selected object helps you rotate the selected object in the view axis. On selecting a particular ring, its color changes to yellow. You can change the default settings of the **Rotate Tool** by double-clicking on it in the toolbox. On doing so, the **Tool Settings (Rotate Tool)** window will be displayed, as shown in Figure 2-8. This window contains various tools for rotation. You can change the settings in this window as per your requirement.

Note
The view axis is the view that you see through your computer screen.

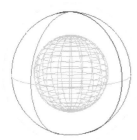

*Figure 2-7 The **Rotate Tool** manipulator*

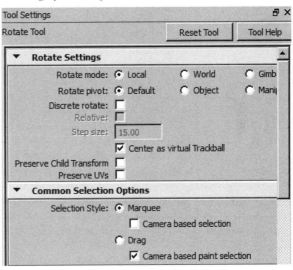

*Figure 2-8 Partial view of the **Tool Settings (Rotate Tool)** settings window*

Scale Tool

Tool Box:	Scale Tool
Keyboard:	r

The **Scale Tool** is used to scale an object along the X, Y, or Z-axis. To scale an object in the viewport, select the object and invoke the **Scale Tool** from the toolbox; the **Scale Tool** manipulator will be displayed on the object, as shown in Figure 2-9.

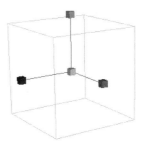

*Figure 2-9 The **Scale Tool** manipulator*

The **Scale Tool** manipulator consists of three boxes. The red box represents the X axis, whereas the green and blue boxes represent the Y and Z axes, respectively. Moreover, the yellow colored box in the center lets you scale the selected object uniformly in all axes. On selecting any one of these colored scale boxes, the default color of the box changes to yellow. You can also adjust the default settings of the **Scale Tool** by double-clicking on it in the toolbox. On doing so, the **Tool Settings (Scale Tool)** window will be displayed, as shown in Figure 2-10. Make the required changes in the **Tool Settings (Scale Tool)** window to adjust the basic parameters of the **Scale Tool**.

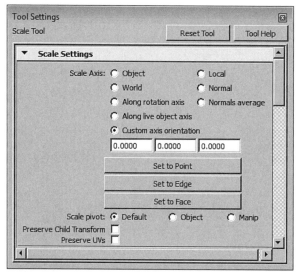

Figure 2-10 *The partial view of the **Tool Settings (Scale Tool)** window*

Before proceeding further, it is recommended to learn about some keyboard shortcuts and their functions. Please refer to the table given below.

Keyboard Shortcut	Function
ALT+MMB+Drag	Helps pan the viewport.
ALT+RMB+Drag	Helps dolly in and out of the viewport. Dolly is similar to zooming in and out.
ALT+LMB+Drag	Helps tumble around in the viewport to see the object from various angles.

Soft Modification Tool

Tool Box: Soft Modification Tool

The **Soft Modification Tool** is a type of deformer that is used to modify a surface by pushing or pulling a group of vertices. To modify a surface, invoke the **Soft Modification Tool** from the toolbox; the **Soft Modification Tool** manipulator will be displayed, as shown in Figure 2-11. On invoking this tool, a colored area is formed at the selection point of the object. The color indicates the extent of deformation. By default, the amount of deformation will be maximum at the center and it gradually decreases as you move outward. The yellow color indicates the greatest amount of deformation. As the color gets darker, the deformation strength decreases.

You can use the manipulators to deform an object. To do so, select an object by using the **Soft Modification Tool**; an "S" symbol will be created at the point of selection. Here "S" symbolizes a special manipulator that can be used to move, rotate, or scale the soft selection. You can also use the **Move** tool to deform the object later by selecting the "S" symbol created on the surface.

To adjust the settings of this tool, choose the **Show or hide the Tool Settings** button from the status line; the **Tool Settings** window will be displayed on the right of the toolbox, as shown in Figure 2-12. Alternatively, double-click on the **Soft Modification Tool** icon in the toolbox.

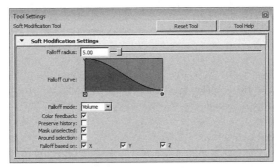

Figure 2-11 The **Soft Modification Tool** *manipulator*

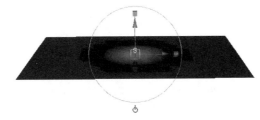

Figure 2-12 The **Tool Settings (Soft Modification Tool)** *window*

Various options in the **Soft Modification Tool** window are discussed next.

Falloff radius
The **Falloff radius** option helps you control the area affecting the deformation in the object.

Falloff curve
The **Falloff curve** option controls the amount of deformation within the area defined by the falloff radius. In other words, the falloff curve helps in determining where the deformation will be more and where it will be less. To apply the deformation, adjust the graph of the **Falloff curve** by clicking over the graph area.

Falloff mode

The **Falloff mode** option is used to determine the deformation type for a selected area of an object. The **Falloff mode** drop-down list has two options, **Volume** and **Surface**. By default, the **Volume** option is selected. As a result, the deformation will be based on the 3D volume of sphere. Here, 3D volume of sphere means the selection area set for the deformation. When you set the **Falloff mode** to **Surface**, the deformation will be based on the profile of the surface. For example, you can separate the upper lip of a character from the lower lip by using the **Surface** option.

Color feedback

The **Color feedback** check box is used to show the deformation on an object through colors. By default, this check box is selected.

Preserve history

The **Preserve history** check box is used to preserve all nodes that were drawn by using the **Soft Modification Tool**.

Mask unselected

The **Mask unselected** check box is used to deform only the selected components. If this check box is cleared, then all components will be deformed.

Around selection

The **Around selection** check box is used to create the radial falloff around each selected vertex. It provides more realistic falloff effect.

Falloff based on

In the **Falloff based on** area, the X, Y, and Z check boxes are selected by default. Therefore, a falloff effect is created in all the three axes. You can clear any check box to view the falloff effect in a specific direction.

Show Manipulator Tool

Tool Box:	Show Manipulator Tool
Keyboard:	t

 The **Show Manipulator Tool** is applied on the selected nodes and attributes. This tool is mainly used to modify the objects using special manipulators.

ATTRIBUTE EDITOR

Main menubar:	Display > UI Elements > Attribute Editor
Keyboard:	Ctrl+a

The **Attribute Editor** provides information about various attributes of a selected object, tool, or the material applied to that particular object. The **Attribute Editor** is used to make changes in the attributes of the selected object. Choose **Display > UI Elements > Attribute Editor** from the main menubar; the **Attribute Editor** window will be displayed on the right of the viewport, as shown in Figure 2-13. The attribute editor comprises of a number of attribute tabs that help you modify an object.

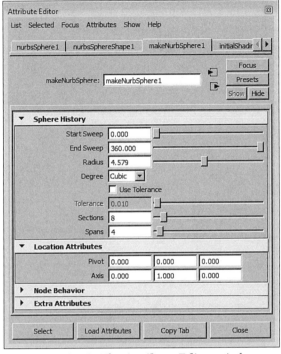

Figure 2-13 The Attribute Editor window

DUPLICATE SPECIAL TOOL

Main menubar:	Edit > Duplicate Special
Keyboard :	Ctrl+Shift + D

The **Duplicate Special** tool is used to create a copy of an object. To create the duplicate copy of an object, select the object in the viewport and choose **Edit > Duplicate Special** from the main menubar; the object will get duplicated at its place. You can also set the properties of the duplicate tool. To do so, choose **Edit > Duplicate Special > Option Box** from the main menubar; the **Duplicate Special Options** dialog box will be displayed, as shown in Figure 2-14. The attributes of the **Duplicate Special Options** dialog box are discussed next.

Geometry type

The **Geometry type** attribute allows you to specify the geometry of the object that will be duplicated. Select the **Copy** radio button to make a copy of the selected object. Select the **Instance** radio button to create an instance of the selected object. All changes made to the object are automatically reflected in the instanced object but there are some limitations that are given next:

1. Instanced lights have zero effect.
2. Instanced objects cannot be deformed.
3. There are certain functions like insert and extrude that cannot be applied to the instanced objects.
4. Hierarchy of instanced objects cannot be created.

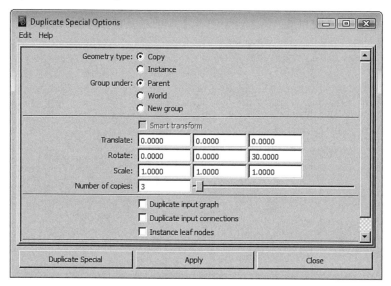

*Figure 2-14 The **Duplicate Special Options** dialog box*

Group under

The **Group under** attribute is used to specify the category under which the selected objects can be grouped. On selecting the **Parent** radio button, the selected objects will be grouped under the lowest common parent in the hierarchy. On selecting the **World** radio button, the selected objects are grouped under the world which is the top level of the hierarchy. On selecting the **New group** radio button, the duplicated objects will create a new group.

Number of copies

You can create n number of duplicates of the selected object by entering the required value in the **Number of copies** edit box or moving the slider next to it. The default value in this edit box is 1.

OUTLINER

| Main menubar: | Window > Outliner |
| Tool Box: | Persp/Outliner |

The **Outliner** is used to display all objects of a scene in a hierarchical manner, as shown in Figure 2-15. The **Outliner** is also known as the scene management editor as it manages all objects in the viewport. An object in the scene can be selected by simply clicking on its name in the **Outliner**. In **Outliner**, the objects

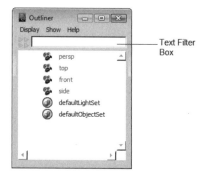

*Figure 2-15 Objects displayed in the **Outliner***

are placed in the order of their creation in the viewport. For example, if you create a cube in the viewport, followed by a sphere and then a cylinder, all these objects will be placed in a hierarchical manner in the **Outliner**, which means the object (cube) created first will be placed first and the object created last (cylinder) will be placed last. To organize the hierarchy manually, choose the MMB and drag and drop one object below another object. To rename an object, double-click on the name of the object. At the top of the **Outliner**, there is an input box known as the **Text Filter Box**. You can use this box to select objects with a particular name. For example, enter *front* in the box and press ENTER; all objects with the name 'front' will be selected in the viewport. By default, there are four cameras in **Outliner** to display four views in Maya. As discussed in the previous chapter, everything that you see in the viewport is seen through the camera view. These cameras are visible in the **Outliner** by default. Each object in the **Outliner** has an icon of its own. When you double-click on any of these icons, the attribute editor will be displayed, where you can change the properties of various objects.

MARKING MENUS

Marking menus are similar to shortcut menus that consist of almost all tools related to an object. There are three different types of marking menus in Maya. The first type of marking menu is used to create default objects in the viewport. To create a default object, press and hold the SHIFT key and then right-click anywhere in the viewport; a marking menu will be displayed, as shown in Figure 2-16. Next, select the object that you want to create from the marking menu.

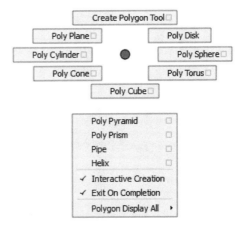

Figure 2-16 Marking menu showing the default objects to be created

The second type of marking menu is used to switch among various components of an object such as vertex, faces, edges, and so on. To display this marking menu, select an object and right-click; a marking menu will be displayed, as shown in Figure 2-17. Now, select the components of the selected object. This marking menu also allows you to add texture to an object. To do so, choose the **Assign New Material** option from this marking menu; the **Material Name** window will be displayed. Choose the required material; the material will be applied to the selected object. This method will be discussed in detail in later chapters.

The third type of marking menu is used to modify a selected object. To do so, select an object, press and hold the SHIFT key and then right-click on the selected object; a marking menu will be displayed, as shown in Figure 2-18.

After invoking the marking menu, drag your cursor to the option that you want to choose; the movement of the cursor will be depicted by a thick grey line trailing behind the cursor, with its one end still attached to the center of the marking menu.

Figure 2-17 *Marking menu displaying components of the selected object*

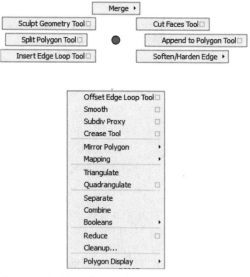

Figure 2-18 *The marking menu displaying various tools for modifying the object*

Self-Evaluation Test

Answer the following questions and then compare them to those given at the end of this chapter:

1. Which of the following tools govern the position transform?

    (a) **Move Tool**   (b) **Rotate Tool**
    (c) **Scale Tool**   (d) **Soft Modification Tool**

2. Which of the following keyboard shortcuts is used to display the **Attribute Editor**?

    (a) CTRL + a   (b) CTRL + a + a
    (c) CTRL + A   (d) CTRL + A + A

3. The **Outliner** is also known as _____.

4. Press the _____ key to invoke the **Show Manipulator Tool**.

5. The _____ displays all objects of a scene in a hierarchical manner.

6. The _____ are shortcut menus that consist of almost all tools related to an object.

7. The manipulators or the handles of the transform tools are colored to make them look more attractive. (T/F)

8. The view axis rotates an object taking the base of the selected view as the reference for rotation. (T/F)

9. The red ring of the **Rotate Tool** manipulator represents the X-axis. (T/F)

10. You can adjust the default settings of the **Scale Tool** by invoking the **Attribute Editor** window. (T/F)

Review Questions

Answer the following questions:

1. When you select an object by using the **Move Tool**, how many manipulators are displayed?

    (a) Two   (b) Four
    (c) Eight   (d) Three

2. If you deform a surface by using the **Soft Modification Tool**, the amount of deformation will be maximum at _____.

3. The _____ is used to scale an object along the X, Y, or Z axis.

4. Choose the _____ colored scale manipulator to scale the object uniformly along all axes.

5. The _____ editor is used to make changes in the attributes of a selected object.

6. The _____ redisplays the geometry being instanced.

7. The dark color in the **Soft Modification Tool** indicates that the deformation is greatest at that point. (T/F)

8. When you use the **Duplicate Special** tool on an object, a new object is created in the viewport irrespective of the original object. (T/F)

9. Creating an instance of an object is similar to copying the object. (T/F)

10. You can apply deformations to the instanced objects. (T/F)

Exercise

Exercise 1

Create the model of the cartoon shown in Figure 2-19 by using the **Sphere** and transform tools. You can view the final rendered image of this model by downloading the *c02_maya_2012_render.zip* file from *http://www.cadcim.com*. The path to download file is as follows:

Textbooks > Animation and Visual Effects > Maya > Autodesk Maya 2012: A Comprehensive Guide
(Expected time: 15 min)

Figure 2-19 Model for Exercise 1

Answers to Self-Evaluation Test
1. a, **2.** a, **3.** Scene management editor, **4.** t, **5. Outliner**, **6.** marking menus, **7.** F, **8.** T, **9.** T, **10.** F

Chapter 3

NURBS Curves and Surfaces

Learning Objectives

After completing this chapter, you will be able to:

- *Reset the Maya interface*
- *Create NURBS Primitives*
- *Create curves*
- *Create surfaces*

INTRODUCTION

In Maya, there are three different methods of modeling: NURBS, polygon, and subdivision surfaces. To create models by using these methods, you need to have a complete overview of these methods. Before modeling an object, you need to visualize it in 3D terms. Visualization of an object in 3D terms helps you in judging / determining the type of modeling that you need to use for creating the object.

In this chapter, you will learn how to create basic environmental structure by using various modeling methods. You will also learn all tools and techniques for creating a NURBS surface.

RESETTING Autodesk Maya 2012

Main menubar: Window > Settings/Preferences > Preferences

Before starting your work in Autodesk Maya 2012, you need to set the new scene to its default settings. To do so, choose **Window > Settings/Preferences > Preferences** from the main menubar; the **Preferences** dialog box will be displayed. Choose a category from the list of **Categories** on the left of the dialog box; the settings of that particular category will be displayed on the right of the dialog box. Set the parameters and choose the **Save** button. Choose the **Revert to Saved** option from the **Edit** menu in the **Preferences** dialog box to revert the settings used in the previous project. Choose the **Restore Default Settings** option from the **Edit** menu to restore the default settings, as shown in Figure 3-1. Now, choose the **Save** button to save the settings.

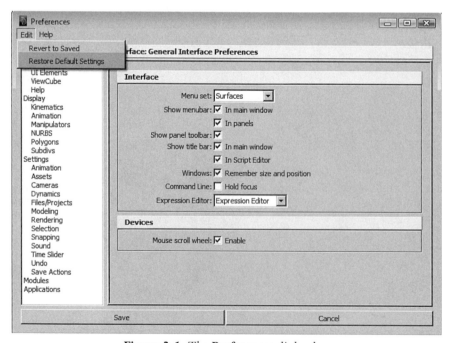

Figure 3-1 The **Preferences** dialog box

Note

If you fail to choose the Restore Default Settings option from the Preferences dialog box, the new scene you create will have the same settings as that of the previous one. As a result, you may not get the desired output.

NURBS PRIMITIVES

In this chapter, you will learn about NURBS curves and NURBS surfaces. NURBS (Non Uniform Rational B-Spline) is a mathematical representation of 3D geometry that can describe any shape accurately. NURBS modeling is basically used for creating curved shapes and lines. You can create cars, animals, characters, and many more high-end 3D objects, using the NURBS modeling.

In Maya, there are default NURBS objects that resemble various geometrical objects. These NURBS objects are grouped together under the NURBS Primitives group in the main menubar. To access the NURBS primitives, choose **Create > NURBS Primitives** from the main menubar; a flyout will be displayed with all the default NURBS primitives in Maya. The creation of different NURBS primitives are discussed next.

Creating a Sphere

Main menubar:	Create > NURBS Primitives > Sphere
Shelf:	Surfaces > NURBS Sphere

A sphere is a solid object and every point on its surface is equidistant from its center, as shown in Figure 3-2. To create a sphere, choose **Create > NURBS Primitives > Sphere** from the main menubar; the instructions to create a sphere will be displayed on the grid. Alternatively, choose the **NURBS sphere** tool from the **Surfaces** shelf. You can create a sphere either dynamically or by entering values using the keyboard. Both the methods are discussed next.

Figure 3-2 The NURBS sphere

Creating a Sphere Dynamically

To create a sphere dynamically, choose **Create > NURBS Primitives > Sphere** from the main menubar; you will be prompted to drag the cursor on the grid to draw the sphere in the viewport. Press and hold the left mouse button, and drag the cursor up or down to define the radius of the sphere. Now, release the left mouse button to get the desired radius; the sphere will be created in all viewports and will be visible in wireframe mode. Press the numeric key 5 to change the display to shaded mode. Alternatively, choose **Shading > Smooth Shade All** from the **Panel menu** to change the display to shaded mode. Press the numeric key 4 or choose **Shading > Wireframe** from the **Panel menu** to revert to the wireframe mode.

Creating a Sphere by Using the Keyboard

To create a sphere by using the keyboard, double-click on the **NURBS Sphere Tool** in the **Surfaces** shelf of the shelf bar; the **NURBS Sphere Tool** property window will be displayed, as shown in Figure 3-3. In this window, set the properties of the sphere by using the keyboard and then click in the viewport; the sphere will be created in all viewports. Alternatively, choose **Create > NURBS Primitives > Sphere > Option Box** from the main menubar to invoke the **NURBS Sphere Tool** window. Choose the **Reset Tool** button at the top of the **NURBS Sphere Tool** property window to reset the settings of the sphere tool. Various properties in this property window are discussed next.

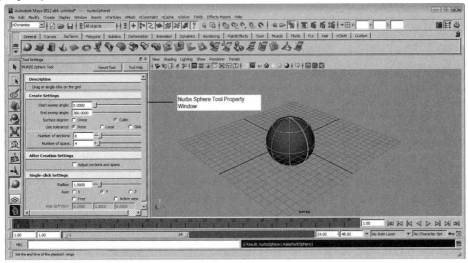

*Figure 3-3 The **NURBS Sphere Tool** property window*

Description Area

The **Description** area gives you information about the method of creation of a sphere in the viewport.

Create Settings Area

The **Create Settings** area of the **NURBS Sphere Tool** property window is used to adjust the parameters of the NURBS sphere. Various options in this area are discussed next.

Start sweep angle and End sweep angle. The **Start sweep angle** and **End sweep angle** edit boxes are used to specify the start and end angles of a sphere. Alternatively, you can move the sliders on the right of these edit boxes to change the values. The values in these edit boxes range from 0 to 360 degrees. You can create the partial parts of a sphere by using the **End Sweep angle** edit box, as shown in Figure 3-4.

Surface degree. The **Surface degree** option is used to create a sphere with a faceted or smooth appearance. This option consists of two radio buttons: **Linear** and **Cubic**. The **Cubic** radio button is selected by default and gives a smooth appearance to the sphere. You can select the **Linear** radio button to give a faceted appearance to the sphere, as shown in Figure 3-5. Note that the number of segments remains the same on the sphere while using any of these two radio buttons.

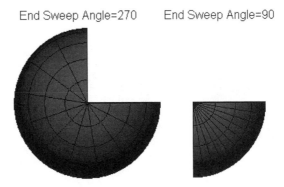

Figure 3-4 *Partial view of the spheres created using the* **End Sweep Angle** *option*

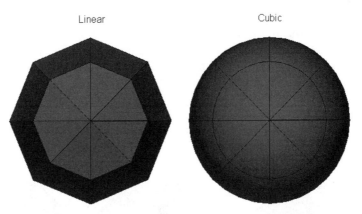

Figure 3-5 *The faceted and smooth appearances of spheres*

Number of sections and Number of Spans. The **Number of sections** and **Number of Spans** edit boxes are used to adjust surface curves on a sphere, as shown in Figure 3-6. More the number of sections or spans on an object, more will be its smoothness. Surface curves are also known as **Isoparms**. You can enter the values directly in these edit boxes to set the number of sections/spans on a NURBS object. Alternatively, you can move the sliders on the right of these edit boxes to change the values.

After Creation Settings

The **After Creation Settings** area is used to adjust the settings of a sphere after it is created in the viewport. To do so, select the **Adjust sections and spans** check box from this area. Now, adjust the parameters of the sphere in the **NURBS Sphere Tool** property window; the change in the parameters will be reflected on the sphere.

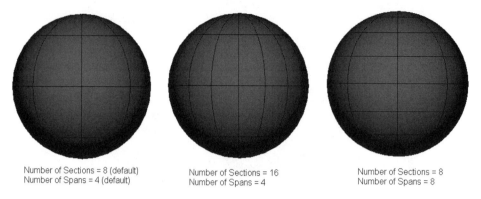

Number of Sections = 8 (default)   Number of Sections = 16   Number of Sections = 8
Number of Spans = 4 (default)   Number of Spans = 4   Number of Spans = 8

Figure 3-6 The number of sections and spans on spheres

Single-click Settings

The **Single-click Settings** area is used to set the radius and axis of formation of the NURBS sphere. The options in this area are discussed next.

Radius. You can set the radius of sphere by entering a value in **Radius** edit box. Alternatively, you can drag the slider on the right of the edit box.

Axis. The **Axis** option has three radio buttons: **X**, **Y**, and **Z**. The **Y** radio button is selected by default. You can use these radio buttons to set axis for creating a NURBS sphere. Figure 3-7 shows the NURBS spheres created on different axes.

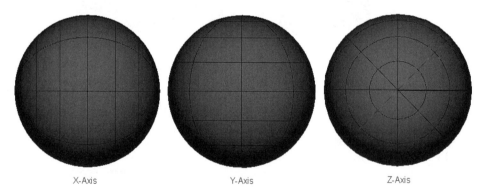

X-Axis   Y-Axis   Z-Axis

Figure 3-7 Spheres created on various axes

Modifying the Names and other Properties of the Sphere

To modify the name and attributes of a sphere in the viewport, you need to invoke the **Channel Box/Layer Editor**. To do so, select a sphere and choose **Display> UI elements > Channel Box/Layer Editor** from the main menubar; the **Channel Box** will be displayed on the left of the viewport, as shown in Figure 3-8. To modify the name of the selected sphere, double-click on the default name of the sphere in the transform node and enter a new name for the sphere. You can also modify the properties of the sphere by expanding the **INPUTS** node. To do so, enter the values in the edit box of sphere parameters in the **Channel Box**; the change will be reflected on the object in the viewport. To dynamically modify the input parameters, select the parameter label in the **Channel Box**, place the cursor in the viewport, press and hold the middle mouse button, and drag it horizontally in the viewport to make the changes.

Creating a Cube

Main menubar:	Create > NURBS Primitives > Cube
Shelf:	Surfaces > NURBS Cube

A cube is a three-dimensional shape with six squares or rectangular sides, as shown in Figure 3-9. To create a NURBS cube, choose **Create > NURBS Primitives > Cube** from the main menubar; the instructions to create cube will be displayed on the grid of the viewport. Alternatively, you can invoke **NURBS Cube** from the **Surfaces** shelf. You can create a cube dynamically or by entering values using the keyboard. Both the methods are discussed next.

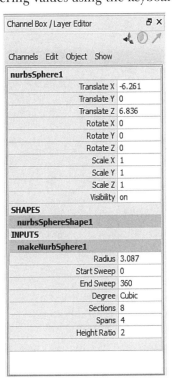

*Figure 3-8 The **Channel Box***

Figure 3-9 The NURBS cube

Creating a Cube Dynamically

To create a cube dynamically, choose **Create > NURBS Primitives > Cube** from the main menubar; you will be prompted to drag the cursor on the grid to draw a cube in the viewport. Press and hold the left mouse button and drag the cursor on the grid to define the base of the cube. Now, release the left mouse button to get the desired base. Next, press and hold the left mouse button again and drag the cursor up to set the height of the cube and then release the left mouse button; the cube will be created in all viewports.

Creating a Cube by Using the Keyboard

To create a cube by using the keyboard, double-click on the **NURBS Cube** tool in the **Surfaces** shelf of the shelf bar; the **NURBS Cube Tool** property window will be displayed on the right of the viewport, as shown in Figure 3-10. In this window, set the properties of the cube by using the keyboard and then click in the viewport; a cube will be created in all viewports. Alternatively, choose **Create > NURBS Primitives > Cube > Option Box** from the main menubar to invoke the **NURBS Cube Tool** property window. Choose the **Reset Tool** button at the top of the **NURBS CubeTool** property window to reset the settings of the cube tool. Various properties in the **NURBS Cube Tool** property window are discussed next.

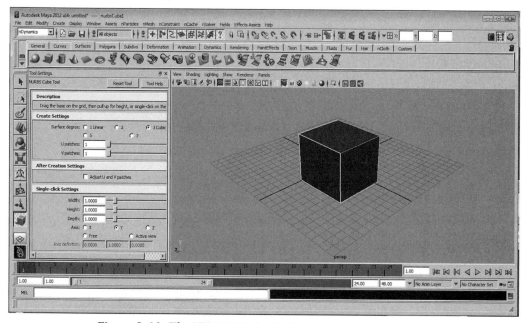

Figure 3-10 *The **NURBS Cube Tool** property window*

Create Settings

The **Create Settings** area of the **NURBS Cube Tool** property window is used to set the parameters of the NURBS Cube. Various options in this area are discussed next.

> **U and V patches**. The **U patches** and **V patches** edit boxes are similar to **Number of sections** and **Number of spans** options in the **NURBS Sphere Tool** property window and are used to create the surface patches on the cube.

Single-click Settings

The **Single-click Settings** area is used to set the width, height, and depth for creating the NURBS cube.

> **Width, Height, and Depth**. You can adjust the width, height, and depth of the NURBS cube by entering values in the **Width**, **Height**, and **Depth** edit boxes, respectively. Alternatively, you can set these values by moving the slider on the right of these edit boxes.

Modifying the Names and other Properties of the Cube

You can modify the name and other properties of the cube using the channel box, as discussed in the NURBS sphere section.

Creating a Cylinder

Main menubar:	Create > NURBS Primitives > Cylinder
Shelf:	Surfaces > NURBS Cylinder

A cylinder is a solid object in which the surface is at an equal distance from the center, as shown in Figure 3-11. To create a cylinder in the viewport, choose **Create > NURBS Primitives > Cylinder** from the main menubar; the instructions to create the cylinder will be displayed on the grid in the viewport. Alternatively, invoke **NURBS Cylinder** from the **Surfaces** shelf. You can create a cylinder either dynamically or by entering values using the keyboard. Both the methods of creating a cylinder are discussed next.

Figure 3-11 The NURBS cylinder

Creating a Cylinder Dynamically

To create a cylinder dynamically, choose **Create > NURBS Primitives > Cylinder** from the main menubar; you will be prompted to drag the cursor on the grid. Press and hold the left mouse button and drag the cursor on the grid to define the base of the cylinder. Next, release the left mouse button to get the desired base. Now, press and hold the left mouse button again, drag the cursor up to set the height of the cylinder and then release the left mouse button; the cylinder will be created in all viewports.

Creating a Cylinder by Using the Keyboard

To create a cylinder by using the keyboard, double-click on the **NURBS Cylinder** tool in the **Surfaces** shelf; the **NURBS Cylinder Tool** property window will be displayed, as shown in Figure 3-12. Set the properties of the cylinder to be created in the viewport using various options available in the **NURBS Cylinder Tool** property window and click in the viewport; a cylinder will be created in all viewports. Alternatively, choose **Create > NURBS Primitives > Cylinder > Option Box** from the main menubar to invoke the **NURBS Cylinder Tool** property window. Choose the **Reset Tool** button at the top of the **NURBS Cylinder Tool** property window to reset the settings of the cylinder. The properties of the **NURBS Cylinder Tool** property window are similar to those discussed in the NURBS sphere section.

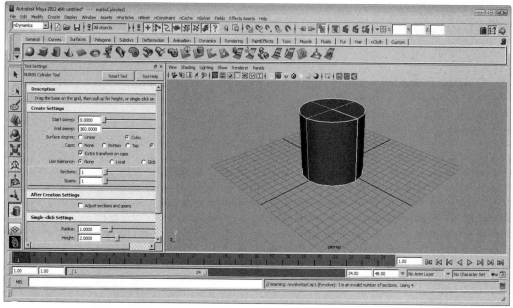

Figure 3-12 The **NURBS Cylinder Tool** *property window*

Modifying the Names and other Properties of the Cylinder

You can modify the name and properties of the cylinder by using the **channel box**, as discussed in the NURBS sphere section.

Creating a Cone

Main menubar:	Create > NURBS Primitives > Cone
Shelf:	Surfaces > NURBS Cone

A cone is an object whose base is a circle and its sides taper up to a point, as shown in Figure 3-13. To create a cone, choose **Create > NURBS Primitives > Cone** from the main menubar. Alternatively, you can create a cone by invoking **NURBS Cone** tool from the **Surfaces** shelf in the shelf bar. You can create a cone either dynamically or by entering values using the keyboard. Both the methods of creating a cone are discussed next.

Creating a Cone Dynamically

To create a cone dynamically, choose **Create > NURBS Primitives > Cone** from the main menubar; you will be prompted to drag the cursor on the grid. Press and hold the left mouse button and drag the cursor on the grid to define the base of the cone. Next, release the left mouse button to get the desired base. Now, press and hold the left mouse button again and drag the cursor up to set the height of the cone. Next, release the left mouse button; the cone will be created in all viewports.

Figure 3-13 *The NURBS cone*

Creating a Cone by Using the Keyboard

To create a cone by using the keyboard, double-click on the **NURBS Cone** tool of the **Surfaces** shelf in the; the **NURBS Cone Tool** property window will be displayed on the right of the viewport, as shown in Figure 3-14. In this window, set the properties of the cone by using the keyboard and then click in the viewport; the cone will be created in all viewports. Alternatively, choose **Create > NURBS Primitives > Cone > Option Box** from the main menubar to invoke the **NURBS Cone Tool** property window. Choose the **Reset Tool** button at the top of the **NURBS Cone Tool** property window to reset the settings of the cone tool. The properties in the **NURBS Cone Tool** property window are similar to those discussed in the NURBS sphere section.

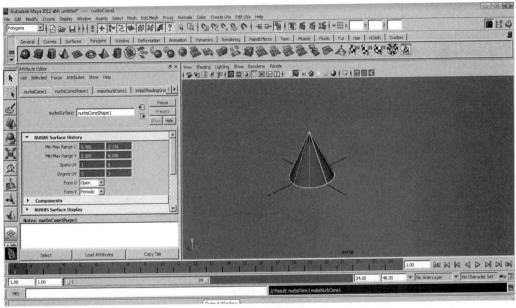

*Figure 3-14 The **NURBS Cone Tool** property window displayed*

Creating a Plane

Main menubar:	Create > NURBS Primitives > Plane
Shelf:	Curves > NURBS Plane

A plane is a two-dimensional flat surface, as shown in Figure 3-15. To create a NURBS plane, choose **Create > NURBS Primitives > Plane** from the main menubar. Alternatively, you can create a plane by invoking **NURBS Plane** from the **Surfaces** shelf. You can create a plane either dynamically or by entering values using the keyboard. Both the methods of creating a plane are discussed next.

Creating a Plane Dynamically

To create a plane dynamically, choose **Create > NURBS Primitives > Plane** from the main menubar; you will be prompted to drag the cursor on the grid. Next, press and hold the left mouse button and drag the cursor on the grid; the plane will be created in all viewports.

Creating a Plane by Using the Keyboard

To create a plane by using the keyboard, double-click on the **NURBS Plane** tool in the **Surfaces** shelf of the shelf bar; the **NURBS Plane Tool** property window will be displayed on the right of the viewport, as shown in Figure 3-16. Next, in this window, set the properties of the plane by using the keyboard and then click in the viewport; the plane will be created in all viewports. Alternatively, choose **Create > NURBS Primitives >**

Figure 3-15 The NURBS plane

Plane > Option Box from the main menubar to invoke the **NURBS Plane Tool** property window. Choose the **Reset Tool** button at the top of the **NURBS Plane Tool** property window to reset the settings of the plane tool. The properties in the **NURBS Plane Tool** property window are similar to those discussed in the NURBS cube section.

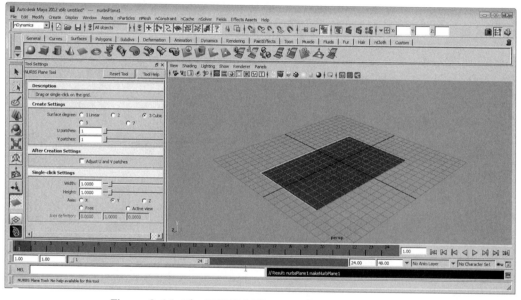

Figure 3-16 The **NURBS Plane Tool** property window

Creating a Torus

Main menubar:	Create > NURBS Primitives > Torus
Shelf:	Surfaces > NURBS Torus

A torus is created by revolving a circular profile around a circular or an elliptical path, as shown in Figure 3-17. To create a NURBS torus, choose **Create > NURBS Primitives > Torus** from the main menubar. Alternatively, you can create a torus by invoking **NURBS Torus** from the **Surfaces** shelf in the shelf bar. You can create a torus either dynamically or by entering values using the keyboard. Both the methods of creating a torus are discussed next.

Creating a Torus Dynamically

To create a torus dynamically, choose **Create > NURBS Primitives > Torus** from the main menubar; you will be prompted to drag the cursor on the grid to create torus in the viewport. Press and hold the left mouse button, drag the cursor on the grid to define the radius of the torus, and then release the left mouse button. Now, press and hold the left mouse button again and drag the cursor to edit the section radius. Next, release the left mouse button; the torus will be created in all viewports.

Figure 3-17 *The NURBS torus*

Creating a Torus by Using the Keyboard

To create a torus by using the keyboard, double-click on the **NURBS Torus** tool in the **Surfaces** shelf of the shelf bar; the **NURBS Torus tool** property window will be displayed on the right of the viewport, as shown in Figure 3-18. In this window, set the properties of the torus by using the keyboard and then click in the viewport to create a torus in all viewports. Alternatively, choose **Create > NURBS Primitives > Torus > Option Box** from the main menubar to invoke the **NURBS Torus Tool** property window. Choose the **Reset Tool** button at the top of the **NURBS Torus Tool** property window to reset the settings of the torus tool. The properties in the **NURBS Torus Tool** property window are similar to those discussed in the **NURBS sphere** section.

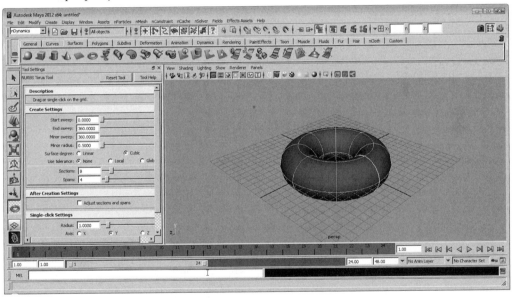

Figure 3-18 *The **NURBS Torus Tool** property window*

Creating a Circle

Main menubar:	Create > NURBS Primitives > Circle
Shelf:	Curves > NURBS Circle

A circle is a closed plane curve in which every point on the curve is equidistant from the center, as shown in Figure 3-19. To create a circle, choose **Create > NURBS Primitives > Circle** from the main menubar. Alternatively, you can create a circle by invoking the **NURBS Circle** tool from the **Curves** shelf in the shelf bar. You can create a circle either dynamically or by entering values using the keyboard. Both the methods of creating a circle are discussed next.

Creating a Circle Dynamically

To create a circle dynamically, choose **Create > NURBS Primitives > Circle** from the main menubar; you will be prompted to drag the cursor on the grid. Press and hold the left mouse button and drag the cursor on the grid and then release the left mouse button; the circle will be created in all viewports.

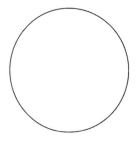

Creating a Circle by Using the Keyboard

Figure 3-19 The NURBS circle

To create a circle by using the keyboard, double-click on **NURBS Circle** tool in the **Curves** shelf; the **NURBS Circle Tool** property window will be displayed, as shown in Figure 3-20. In this window, set the properties of the circle by using the keyboard and then click in the viewport to create a circle in all viewports. Alternatively, choose **Create > NURBS Primitives > Circle > Option Box** from the main menubar to invoke the **NURBS Circle Tool** property window. Choose the **Reset Tool** button at the top of the **NURBS Circle Tool** property window to reset the settings of the circle tool. The properties in the **NURBS Circle Tool** property window are similar to those discussed in the NURBS sphere section.

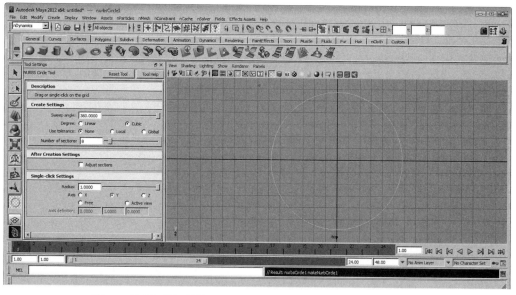

*Figure 3-20 The **NURBS Circle Tool** property window*

Creating a Square

| Main menubar: | Create > NURBS Primitives > Square |
| Shelf: | Curves > NURBS Square |

A square is a four-sided regular polygon with equal sides, as shown in Figure 3-21. To create a square, choose **Create > NURBS Primitives > Square** from the main menubar. Alternatively, you can create a square by invoking **NURBS Square** from the **Curves** shelf in the shelf bar. You

can create a square either dynamically or by entering values
by using the keyboard. Both the methods of creating a
square are discussed next.

Creating a Square Dynamically

To create a square dynamically, choose **Create > NURBS
Primitives > Square** from the main menubar; you will
be prompted to drag the cursor on the grid. Press and
hold the left mouse button and drag the cursor on the
grid. Next, release the left mouse button; the square will
be created in all viewports.

Figure 3-21 *The NURBS square*

Creating a Square by Using the Keyboard

To create a square by using the keyboard, double-click on the **NURBS Square** tool
in the **Curves** shelf of the shelf bar; the **NURBS Square tool** property window will
be displayed on the right of the viewport, as shown in Figure 3-22. Set the properties
of the square using various options available in the **NURBS Square Tool** property
window and click in the viewport to create a square in all viewports. Alternatively,
Create > NURBS Primitives > Square > Option Box from the main menubar to invoke the
NURBS Square Tool property window. Choose the **Reset Tool** button at the top of the **NURBS
Square Tool** property window to reset the settings of the square tool. The properties in the
NURBS Square Tool property window are similar to those discussed in the **NURBS cube** section.

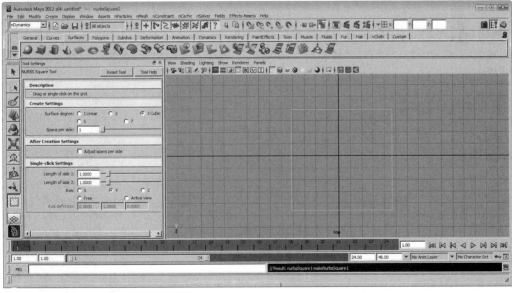

Figure 3-22 *The **NURBS Square Tool** property window*

Interactive Creation

Main menubar:	Create > NURBS Primitives > Interactive Creation

The **Interactive Creation** option is used to create objects dynamically. It is a toggle on/off option in the NURBS primitives submenu. To select this option, choose **Create > NURBS Primitives > Interactive Creation** from the main menubar. The **Interactive Creation** option is selected by default. Therefore, it allows you to edit the object as per your requirement. If you clear this option, you need to modify the object using the channel box.

Exit on Completion

Main menubar:	Create > NURBS Primitives > Exit on Completion

The **Exit on Completion** option is used to end the command of creating tools with the creation of an object in the viewport. To invoke this option, choose **Create > NURBS Primitives > Exit on Completion** from the main menubar. Deselect the option to interactively create multiple primitives of the same type until another tool is invoked.

WORKING WITH NURBS COMPONENTS

Each NURBS object has certain components such as **Isoparm**, **Hull**, **Surface Patch**, **Surface UV**, **Control Vertex**, and **Surface Point**, as shown in Figures 3-23 to 3-28. To view components of the NURBS object, select the NURBS object in the viewport and choose **Display > NURBS** from the main menubar; a cascading menu will be displayed. Choose the component that you want to modify from the cascading menu; the selected component will be displayed in the viewport. Alternatively, press and hold the right mouse button over the object and choose the required component from the marking menu. If you want to move any component in the viewport, you can do so by invoking the **Move Tool**.

CREATING NURBS CURVES

In Maya you can create **NURBS** curves. The following tools are used to create NURBS curves:

CV Curve Tool

Main menubar:	Create > CV Curve Tool

The **CV Curve Tool** is used to sketch the outline of a curve by placing control vertices over it. To create an outline, choose **Create > CV Curve Tool** from the main menubar; the cursor will change to a plus sign. Next, click on different places in the viewport to create a curve and then press ENTER. To edit the properties of a curve, choose **Create > CV Curve Tool > Option Box** from the main menubar; the **CV Curve Tool** property window will be displayed on the right of the viewport, as shown in Figure 3-29. The options in the property window are discussed next.

Curve degree

The **Curve degree** area is used to define the smoothness of a curve. By default, the **3 Cubic** radio button is selected in the **Curve Degree** area. Higher the degree of curve, smoother it will be. So, select the curve degree according to your requirement.

Knot spacing

The **Knot spacing** area is used to define the curve U position for editing knots (points). It is used to distribute the curvature in a better way so that the surface displays a symmetrical texture applied over it.

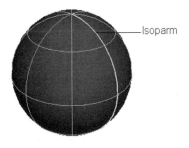

*Figure 3-23 The **Isoparm** component*

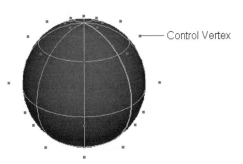

*Figure 3-24 The **Control Vertex** component*

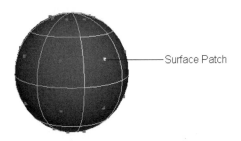

*Figure 3-25 The **Surface Patch** component*

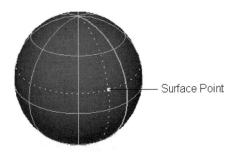

*Figure 3-26 The **Surface Point** component*

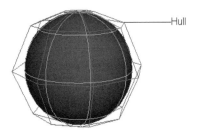

*Figure 3-27 The **Hull** component*

*Figure 3-28 The **Surface UV** component*

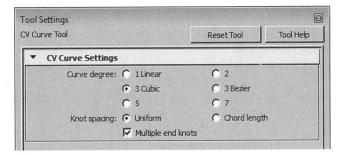

*Figure 3-29 Partial view of the **CV Curve Tool** property window*

> **Tip**. *By default, the **CV Curve Tool** is not present in the **Curves** shelf bar. To add **CV Curve Tool** to the shelf bar, press and hold CTRL+SHIFT and choose **Create > CV Curve Tool** from the main menubar; the **CV Curve Tool** icon will be created in the shelf bar.*

EP Curve Tool

Main menubar:	Create > EP Curve Tool
Shelf:	Curves > Ep Curve Tool

The **EP Curve Tool** is also used to create an outline of a curve by placing edit points on it. To create an outline, choose **Create > EP Curve Tool** from the main menubar; the cursor sign will change to a plus sign. Next, click on different places in the viewport to create a curve. To modify the properties of the curve, choose **Create > EP Curve Tool > Option Box** from the main menubar; the **EP Curve Tool** property window will be displayed. Alternatively, you can invoke the **EP Curve Tool** from the **Curves** shelf of the shelf bar. This tool is placed in the shelf bar by default. Double-click on the icon in the shelf bar; the **EP Curve Tool** property window will be displayed on the left of the viewport. The options in the **EP Curve Tool** property window are similar to those discussed in the **CV Curve Tool** property window.

> **Note**
> *The process of creating a curve using **EP Curve Tool** is different from that of using the **CV Curve Tool**. In both the cases, if **3 cubic** is selected as the curve degree, then the curve created using the **CV Curve Tool** will create a smooth curve on creating the fourth segment, whereas in case of **EP curve Tool**, a smooth curve will be created in the third segment.*

Pencil Curve Tool

Main menubar:	Create > Pencil Curve Tool
Shelf:	Curves > Pencil Curve Tool

The **Pencil Curve Tool** works similar to the brush tool in other software. The **Pencil Curve Tool** is used to create an outline for creating a NURBS surface. To create an outline, choose **Create > Pencil Curve Tool** from the main menubar; the cursor will change to a pencil sign. Next, press and hold the left mouse button and drag the cursor in the viewport to create a curve. To set the properties of the curve, choose **Create > Pencil Curve Tool > Option Box** from the main menubar; the **Pencil Curve Tool** property window will be displayed. Alternatively, you can invoke the **Pencil Curve Tool** from the Curves shelf of the shelf bar. By default, this tool is displayed in the shelf bar. Double-click on the icon in the shelf bar; the **Pencil Curve Tool** property window will be displayed. The options in the **Pencil Curve Tool** are similar to those discussed in the **CV Curve Tool** property window.

Arc Tools

Main menubar:	Create > Arc Tools
Shelf:	Curves > Three Point Circular Arc

The **Arc Tools** are used to create arc curves by specifying points in the viewport. In Maya, there are two types of arc tools: **Three Point Circular Arc** and **Two Point Circular Arc**. To create an arc curve, choose **Create > Arc Tools** from the main menubar; a cascading menu will be displayed. Choose **Two Point Circular Arc** from the cascading menu to create an arc by defining the start and end points of the curve. Similarly, choose the **Three Point Circular Arc** from the cascading menu to create an arc by defining the start point, the curve point, and the endpoint.

CREATING SURFACES

The product designers give special importance to product styling and providing a unique shape to components. Generally, this is done to make the product look more attractive and presentable. Most of the times, the shape of the product is managed using the surface modeling techniques. Surface models are three-dimensional models with no thickness and no mass properties. You can view the tools that are used to create various surfaces by selecting the **Surfaces** menuset from the **Module** drop-down list in the status line. Next, invoke the **Surfaces** menu to display all the surfacing methods in Maya. To change this drop-down menu to a floating menu, click on the line, refer to Figure 3-30. Maya provides a number of tools to create complex three-dimensional surface models, which are discussed next.

Figure 3-30 *Surfaces floating menu*

Revolve Tool

Main menubar:	Surfaces > Revolve

The revolved surfaces are created by revolving a profile curve about a revolution axis. The axis of revolution depends on the pivot point of an object. To create a revolved surface, choose **Create > EP Curve Tool** from the main menubar and then create a profile curve in the Front viewport, as shown in Figure 3-31. Select the profile curve and choose **Surfaces > Revolve** from the main menubar; the profile curve will rotate about its pivot point, thus creating a revolved surface, as shown in Figure 3-32. You can also set the properties of the revolved model. To do so, choose **Surfaces > Revolve > Option Box** from the main menubar; the **Revolve Options** dialog box will be displayed, as shown in Figure 3-33. The options in this dialog box are discussed next.

Figure 3-31 The NURBS curve created by
using the **EP Curve** tool

Figure 3-32 The NURBS curve created
after using the **Revolve** tool

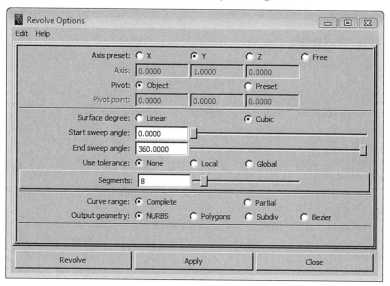

Figure 3-33 The **Revolve Options** dialog box

Axis preset

The options in the **Axis preset** area are used to set the axis on which the curve will rotate. Select the required radio button to set the axis of rotation of the curve. The default axis is Y. You can also select the **Free** radio button to enter the value of the axis manually.

Axis Area

The **Axis** area is inactive by default. If you select the **Free** radio button, the **Axis** area will get activated. You can specify the axis about which you want to revolve the NURBS curve in the viewport.

Pivot Area

The **Pivot** area has two radio buttons: **Object** and **Preset**. The **Object** radio button is selected by default and is used to revolve an object at the default pivot location (0, 0, 0). Select the **Preset** radio button to specify the pivot point.

Surface degree Area

The **Surface degree** area has two radio buttons: **Linear** and **Cubic**. If you select the **Linear** radio button, the surface will be formed with edgy facets. If you select the **Cubic** radio button, the edgy facets of the surface will be converted to smooth.

Start sweep angle and End sweep angle

You can specify the start and end sweep angle values in the respective edit boxes to define the degree of rotation of a curve. By default, the values in the **Start sweep angle** and **End sweep angle** edit boxes are 0 and 360, respectively. You can adjust the slider next to these edit boxes to change values as per your requirement.

Use tolerance Area

The **Use tolerance** area is used to define the accuracy of the NURBS surface that is formed by using the **Revolve** method. There are three radio buttons in this area: **None**, **Local**, and **Global**. By selecting the **None** radio button, you can make changes in the number of segments of the NURBS surface. More the number of segments, more will be the smoothness of the NURBS surface.

Segments

The **Segments** area is used to set the number of segments in the revolved surface. More the number of segments, more will be the smoothness of the surface. To do so, either enter the value in the input box or drag the slider at right side of the **Segments** area. The default value is 8.

Curve range Area

There are two radio buttons in the **Curve range** area: **Complete** and **Partial**. The **Complete** radio button is selected by default; therefore, the entire profile curve will be rotated about the pivot point. To create a revolved surface by revolving a part of profile curve about its pivot point, select the **Partial** radio button from the **Curve range** area. Next, select the curve in the viewport and choose **Display > UI Elements > Channel Box/Layer Editor** from the main menubar; the **Channel Box/Layer Editor** will be displayed. Next, choose **subCurve1** from the **OUTPUTS** node to set the curve range for rotation; the **subCurve1** options will be displayed in the **Channel Box**. Set the **Min Value** and **Max** values of the **subCurve1** option in the **Channel Box**. You can also edit the NURBS curve by using the **Show Manipulator Tool** from the toolbox. To do so, select the NURBS curve in the viewport and invoke the **Show Manipulator Tool**. Next, drag the **Curve Segment Manipulator** to set the partial curve range, as shown in Figure 3-34. Next, choose the **Revolve** tool to create the NURBS surface.

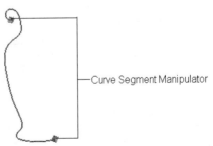

*Figure 3-34 Dragging the **Curve** Segment Manipulator*

Output geometry Area

The **Output geometry** area is used to define the type of geometry to be created using NURBS curve. The radio buttons in this area are used to convert the NURBS curve into four different types of geometry, **NURBS**, **Polygons**, **Subdiv**, and **Bezier** (Subdiv refers to Subdivision surfaces). Select the required geometry to set the type of output geometry.

Loft Tool

Main menubar:	Surfaces > Loft

Loft is the creation of surface between two or more drawn entities. The **Loft tool** is used to skin a surface along a number of NURBS curves. While using this tool, at least two profile curves are required to create a NURBS surface. To create a NURBS surface by using this tool, create three curves, as shown in Figure 3-35, using any of the curve tools discussed earlier. Next, press and hold the SHIFT key and select the curves from the viewport. Now, create the NURBS surface and choose **Surfaces > Loft** from the main menubar; the lofted surface will be created in the viewport, as shown in Figure 3-36. To set the properties of the lofted surface created, choose **Surfaces > Loft > Option Box** from the main menubar; the **Loft Options** dialog box will be displayed, as shown in Figure 3-37. The options in the **Loft Options** dialog box are discussed next.

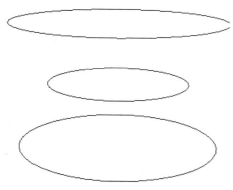 

Figure 3-35 *The NURBS curves before applying the* ***Loft*** *tool*

Figure 3-36 *The lofted surface created after applying the* ***Loft*** *tool*

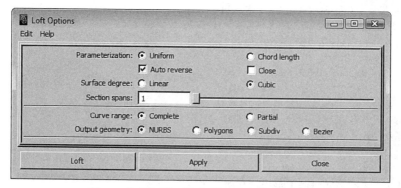

Figure 3-37 *The* ***Loft Options*** *dialog box*

Parameterization Area

The radio buttons in the **Parameterization** area are used to modify the parameters of the lofted surface. Select the **Uniform** radio button to set the number of control points uniformly along the curve. Select the **Chord length** radio button to parameterize the curve such that its value is proportional to the chord length. The **Auto reverse** check box is selected by default and is used to create a NURBS surface in the reverse order of selection of NURBS curves. Select the **Close** check box to close the open ends of the NURBS surface, as shown in Figures 3-38 and 3-39.

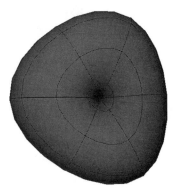

Figure 3-38 *Surface created with the **Close** check box cleared*

Figure 3-39 *Surface created with the **Close** check box selected*

Surface degree Area

The **Surface degree** area is used to specify smoothness on a NURBS surface. The **Cubic** radio button is selected by default; therefore, smoothness is added to the NURBS surface. If you select the **Linear** radio button, less smoothness will be applied to the NURBS surface. For example, to check the working of this radio button, choose **Create > CV Curve Tool** from the main menubar and create NURBS curves in the viewport, as shown in Figure 3-40. Next, select the **Linear** or **Cubic** radio button from the **Surface degree** area in the **Loft Option** dialog box; the NURBS surfaces will be displayed, as shown in Figures 3-41 and 3-42.

Figure 3-40 *NURBS curves for creating a surface*

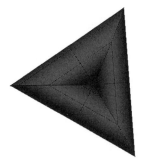
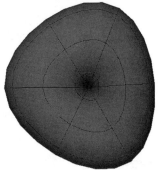

Figure 3-41 *Surface created on selecting the **Linear** radio button*

Figure 3-42 *Surface created on selecting the **Cubic** radio button*

Section spans

The **Section spans** edit box is used to specify the number of sections or segments on the NURBS surface. To do so, enter a value in the edit box to specify the number of sections in the NURBS surface. Alternatively, adjust the slider on the right of the **Section spans** edit box. More the number of sections, more will be the smoothness of the NURBS surface.

Output geometry Area

The options in the **Output geometry** area are used to specify the type of outputs of the NURBS surface. Select the required radio button to get the output surface as **NURBS**, **Polygons**, **Subdiv**, or **Bezier**. After setting the options in the **Loft Options** dialog box, choose the **Loft** button to convert the NURBS curves to NURBS surface. Alternatively, choose the **Apply** button to create a NURBS surface. The function of the **Loft** and the **Apply** buttons is quite similar. On choosing the **Loft** button, the loft command is applied to the NURBS curves and the **Loft Options** dialog box gets closed. On the other hand, on choosing the **Apply** button, the loft command is applied to the NURBS curves without closing the dialog box. Choose the **Close** button to close the **Loft Options** dialog box without applying the loft command to the NURBS curve.

Planar Tool

Main menubar:	Surfaces > Planar

The **Planar** tool is used to create a NURBS surface with all the vertices lying on the same plane. In order to create a NURBS surface using this tool, the curve should form a close loop and should at least have three sides. To create a NURBS surface using this tool, create a close curve using any curve tool. Next, invoke the **Move** tool from the toolbox. Next, choose **Surfaces > Planar** from the main menubar; a NURBS surface will be created. To set the properties of the NURBS surface, choose **Surfaces > Planar > Option Box** from the main menubar; the **Planar Trim Surface Options** dialog box will be displayed, as shown in Figure 3-43. The options in the dialog box are discussed next.

*Figure 3-43 The **Planar Trim Surface Options** dialog box*

Degree Area

The options in the **Degree** area are used to add smoothness to the edges of the surface created. The **Cubic** radio button is selected by default. As a result, a planar surface with smooth edges is created. Select the **Linear** radio button to create a planar surface with rough edges.

Curve range Area

The options in the **Curve range** area are used to set curves for creating a planar surface. The **Complete** radio button is selected by default and is used to display manipulators on the planar surface. Select the **Complete** radio button to create a planar surface along the selected curve. Next, invoke the **Show Manipulator Tool** from the toolbox and edit the resulting planar surface along a part of the input curve.

Output geometry Area

The **Output geometry** area specifies the type of geometry to be created. Select the **NURBS** radio button to set the output geometry as NURBS. Select the **Polygons** radio button to set the output geometry as polygon.

Extrude Tool

Main menubar:	Surfaces > Extrude

The **Extrude** tool is used to extrude a particular object by sweeping its profile curve along the path curve. Note that to extrude a surface, two curves are required: a profile curve and a path curve. The profile curve gives shape to a surface, whereas the path curve defines the path on which the shape will sweep to create a surface. To create an extruded surface, select the two curves created in the viewport using the SHIFT key. The first curve selected will act as the profile curve, whereas the second curve will act as the path curve. Now, choose **Surfaces > Extrude** from the main menubar to extrude the surface. You can use this method to create objects such as curtains, parts of a vehicle, and so on. To adjust the properties of the **Extrude** tool, choose **Surfaces > Extrude > Option Box** from the main menubar; the **Extrude Options** dialog box will be displayed, as shown in Figure 3-44. The options in this dialog box are discussed next.

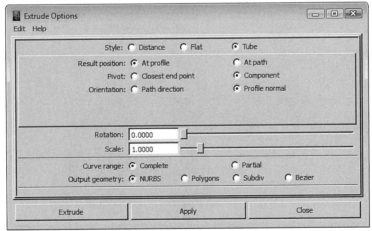

Figure 3-44 *The Extrude Options dialog box with the Tube radio button selected*

Style Area

The **Style** area comprises of three radio buttons: **Distance**, **Flat**, and **Tube**. The **Tube** radio button is selected by default and is used to maintain a cross-section along the path, with the reference vector remaining tangent to the path. Select the **Distance** radio button to extrude the profile in a straight line. On selecting the **Distance** radio button, several other options will get activated. Select the **Flat** radio button to maintain the orientation path of the profile curve.

Result position Area

The **Result position** area is used to set the position at which the extruded surface will be created. By default, the **At profile** radio button is selected and therefore the position of the extruded surface is set along the profile curve. You can select the **At path** radio button to set the position of the extruded surface along the path curve.

Pivot Area

The **Pivot** area is used to set the pivot point of an extruded surface. There are two radio buttons in this area: **Closest end point** and **Component**. By default, the **Closest end point** radio button is selected. As a result, an extruded surface is created close to the center of the bounding box of the profile curves. Select the **Component** radio button to create an extruded surface along the components of the profile curve. Note that the **Pivot** area is activated only when the **Tube** radio button is selected in the **Style** area. Figure 3-45 shows a profile curve and a path curve to create an extruded surface. Figures 3-46 and 3-47 show extruded surfaces created on selecting the **Closest end point** and **Component** radio buttons, respectively.

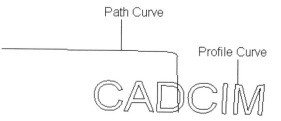

Figure 3-45 *The profile curve and the path curve for creating an extruded surface*

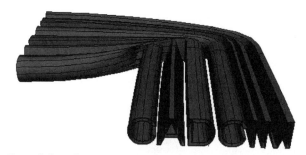

Figure 3-46 *Extruded surface created on selecting the **Closest end point** radio button*

Figure 3-47 *Extruded surface created on selecting the Component radio button*

Orientation Area

The **Orientation** area is used to set the orientation of an extruded surface. This option is available only when the **Tube** radio button is selected in the **Extrude Options** dialog box. Select the **Path direction** radio button to extrude the profile curve along the direction of path curve. By default, the **Profile normal** radio button is selected. As a result, the surface is extruded such that the path curve is created normal to the profile curve.

Rotation

In Maya, you can create a twisted surface by rotating the profile curve while it is being extruded along the path curve. To do so, specify the angle of rotation in the **Rotation** edit box of the **Extrude Options** dialog box.

Scale

If you need to scale the profile while extruding it along the path curve, specify the scale factor in the **Scale** edit box.

Curve range and Output geometry Areas

The options in the **Curve range** and **Output Geometry** areas are the same as discussed in the revolved surface section. On selecting the **Distance** radio button from the **Style** area, some other options are displayed, as shown in Figure 3-48. These options are discussed next.

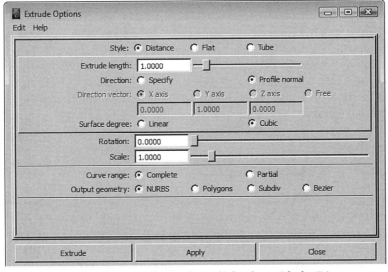

*Figure 3-48 The **Extrude Options** dialog box with the **Distance** radio button selected*

Extrude length Area

You can specify the distance value by which the object will be extruded in this area.

Direction Area

There are two radio buttons in the **Direction** area: **Specify** and **Profile normal**. The **Profile normal** option sets the direction of the path to normal, whereas **Specify** lets you set the direction for creating the surface in a particular axis. For example, if you select the X-axis, the extrusion will be in the X-direction only.

Surface degree Area

The **Surface degree** area helps you give smoothness or sharpness to the surface created. This option comprises of two parts: **Linear** and **Cubic**. The **Linear** option creates sharp edges near the isoparms, whereas the **Cubic** option creates smooth surfaces.

Birail Tool

Main menubar:	Surfaces > Birail

The **Birail** tool works similar to the **Extrude** tool. This tool lets you create surfaces using one or two profile curves along two path curves. You can create complex NURBS surfaces using this tool. Maya has three different types of birails: **Birail 1 Tool**, **Birail 2 Tool**, and **Birail 3+ Tool**. Before creating a NURBS surface using different birail types, the following points should be kept in mind:

1. The profile curves and the path curves must touch each other and have continuity with their respective positions.

2. All profile curves should have the same number of CVs.

3. All path curves should also have the same number of CVs.

4. Press V to snap the vertex of the profile curve and the path curve together.

5. If the profile curve and path curve do not have the same number of CVs, you will have to draw the curve again.

Boundary Tool

Main menubar:	Surfaces > Boundary

In Maya, you can use the **Boundary** tool to restrict the formation of a surface to a limit. This tool creates a NURBS surface by filling the space between boundary curves. It is not necessary for the curves to have a closed loop, but they should intersect with each other at some point. To use this tool, create four NURBS curves in the viewport, as shown in Figure 3-49. Press and hold the SHIFT key and select all curves in the viewport. You can select the curves in any order but it is preferable to select them in opposite pairs to maintain continuity. Now, choose **Surfaces > Boundary** from the main menubar to create the NURBS surface. To set the properties of the **Boundary** tool, choose **Surfaces > Boundary > Option Box** from the main menubar; the **Boundary Options** dialog box will be displayed, as shown in Figure 3-50. The properties in this dialog box are similar to those discussed in other surfacing methods earlier.

Square Tool

Main menubar:	Surfaces > Square

The **Square** tool is used to create a NURBS surface from the intersecting NURBS curves.

With this tool, the surface is created by filling the region defined by four intersecting curves. This tool is similar to the **Boundary** tool with the only difference that in the **Boundary** tool, you can select curves in any order, whereas in the **Square** tool, you need to select them in the clockwise or counterclockwise direction. To use this tool, create four intersecting NURBS curves in the viewport. Next, press and hold the SHIFT key and select the curves either in clockwise or counterclockwise direction. Now, choose **Surfaces > Square** from the main menubar; the NURBS surface will be created.

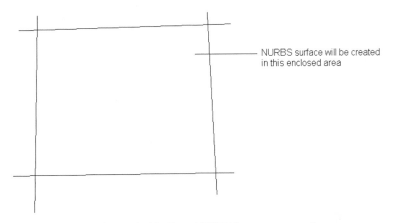

Figure 3-49 *Four NURBS curves created*

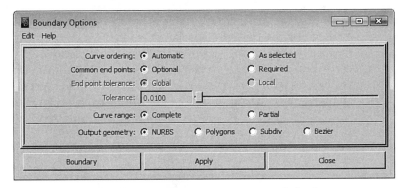

Figure 3-50 *The **Boundary Options** dialog box*

Bevel Tool

Main menubar:	Surfaces > Bevel

The **Bevel** tool uses a three-dimensional edge effect applied on curves to create a NURBS surface. This tool helps you extrude the curve. The resulting surface has some open area that can be filled by using the planar method. To create a surface by using the **Bevel** method, create a NURBS circle in the top viewport, as shown in Figure 3-51. Next, select the circle in the viewport and choose **Surfaces > Bevel** from the main menubar; a beveled surface will be created, as shown in Figure 3-52. To set the properties of the beveled surface, choose **Display > UI Elements > Channel Box/Layer Editor** from the main menubar; the channel box will be displayed on the right of the viewport. Choose **bevel1** in the **INPUTS** node of the **Channel box** to make changes in the beveled surface, as shown in Figure 3-53.

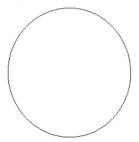

Figure 3-51 *A NURBS circle created in the top viewport*

Figure 3-52 *The **Bevel** method applied on the NURBS circle*

INPUTS	
bevel1	
Width	0.1
Depth	0.1
Extrude Depth	1
Corner Type	Circular
Bevel Shape Type	Straight Cut

Figure 3-53 *The **bevel1** settings area in the INPUTS node*

Bevel Plus Tool

Main menubar:	Surfaces > Bevel Plus

The **Bevel Plus** tool is the advance version of the **Bevel** tool. This tool has a higher degree of control over the NURBS surface than the regular **Bevel** tool. To create a surface by using this tool, create a NURBS circle in the top viewport, as shown in Figure 3-54. Next, select the NURBS curve in the viewport and choose **Surfaces > Bevel Plus** from the main menubar; a beveled surface will be created, as shown in Figure 3-55. To edit the beveled surface, choose **Display > UI Elements > Channel Box/Layer Editor** from the main menubar; the channel box will be displayed on the right of the viewport. Next, choose **bevelPlus1** in the **INPUTS** node of the channel box. The properties of the **bevelPlus1** will be displayed. You can now edit the properties of the beveled surface in this window, as shown in Figure 3-56.

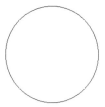

Figure 3-54 *A NURBS circle created in the top viewport*

Figure 3-55 *The beveled surface created using the **Bevel Plus** method*

bevelPlus1	
Bevel Inside	off
Width	0.1
Depth	0.1
Extrude Depth	0.25

Figure 3-56 *The **bevelPlus1** settings area in the INPUTS node*

You can also create the beveled text by using the **Bevel Plus** method. To do so, choose **Create > Text > Option Box** from the main menubar; the **Text Curves Options** dialog box will be displayed, as shown in Figure 3-57. By default, **Maya** is displayed in this edit box. Enter the text that you want to display in the viewport in the edit box. You can also set the font of the text. To do so, choose the arrow shaped button on the right of the **Font** edit box; the **Select Font** dialog box will be displayed, as shown in Figure 3-58. Set font, font style, size, and other font attributes in this dialog box and choose the **OK** button. Next, choose the **Create** button from the **Text Curves Options** dialog box; the text will be displayed in wireframe mode, as shown in Figure 3-59. Next, select the text in the viewport and choose **Surfaces > Bevel Plus** from the main menubar; now the text in the wireframe mode will change to the NURBS surface, as shown in Figure 3-60.

Figure 3-57 The **Text Curves Options** *dialog box*

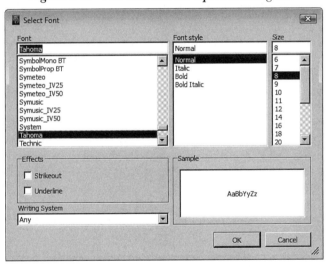

Figure 3-58 The **Select Font** *dialog box*

Figure 3-59 *Text displayed in the wireframe mode*

Figure 3-60 The **Bevel Plus** *method applied on the NURBS surface*

TUTORIALS

Tutorial 1

In this tutorial, you will create the 3D model of a wine glass, as shown in Figure 3-61, using the curve tools and the surface methods. **(Expected time: 15 min)**

The following steps are required to complete this tutorial:

a. Set a project folder.
b. Create a profile curve for the wine glass.
c. Create the wine glass by revolving the profile curve.
d. Change the background color of the final output at rendering.
e. Render the model.
f. Save the model.

Setting the Project Folder

Before starting a new file, it is recommended that you set the project folder. Setting a project folder helps you keep all files of a project in an organized manner. You need to follow the steps given below to set the project folder:

Figure 3-61 The wine glass

1. Open the Windows File Browser and browse to the *Documents* folder. In this folder, create a new folder with the name *Maya_Tutorials*.

2. Start Autodesk Maya 2012, by double-clicking on its icon in the desktop. If the application is already running, you need to restore the default settings of Maya. To do so, choose **Window > Setting /Preferences > Preferences** from the main menubar; the **Preferences** dialog box is displayed. Choose **Edit > Restore Default Settings** from it. Next, choose the **Save** button to close the dialog box.

3. Choose **File > Project Window** from the main menubar, the **Project Window** dialog box is displayed. In this dialog box, choose the **New** button. As a result, the **Current Project** and **Location** text boxes are enabled. Now, type *c03_tut1* in the **Current Project** text box. Next, click the folder icon next to the **Location** text box and browse to the *\Documents\Maya_Tutorials* folder. Then, choose the **Accept** button; *Documents\ Maya_Tutorials\c03_tut1* will become the current project folder.

Creating a Profile Curve for the Wine Glass

In this section, you need to create a profile curve for the wine glass by using the **CV Curve Tool**.

1. Choose the **Four View** button from the toolbox to switch over to four views. Move

the cursor on the Front viewport and then press the SPACEBAR key to maximize this viewport.

2. Choose **Create > CV Curve Tool > Option Box** from the main menubar; the **CV Curve Tool** property window is displayed. Select the **3 Cubic** radio button from this property window.

3. Create a profile curve for the wine glass by using the **CV Curve Tool**, as shown in Figure 3-62.

Create the wine glass by revolving the profile curve

In this section, you need to apply the **Revolve** tool to the profile curve to create the wine glass.

1. Activate the Perspective viewport and select the profile curve in the viewport. Choose the **Surfaces** module from the menuset drop-down list in the status line.

2. Choose **Surfaces > Revolve** from the main menubar; the profile curve rotates at 360-degrees and the wine glass is created, refer to Figure 3-61.

 Note
*Before applying the **Revolve** command to the selected curve, adjust the pivot point to the center of the curve from where the new surface will be created.*

Figure 3-62 The profile curve for the wine glass

Changing the Background Color of the Final Output at Rendering

In this section, you need to change the background color of the rendered output from black to white.

1. Choose **Window > Outliner** from the main menubar. Next, double-click on the left of the **persp** camera icon; the **Attribute Editor** is displayed.

2. Expand the **Environment** attribute tab, as shown in Figure 3-63. Move the **Background Color** attribute slider to right. As a result, the background color turns into white.

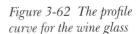

*Figure 3-63 The **Environment** attribute tab*

Rendering the Model

In this section, you need to render the wine glass.

1. Activate the Perspective viewport.

2. Activate the **Rendering** menuset from the status line. Choose **Render > Render Current Frame** from the main menubar; the **Render View** window is displayed, showing the final rendered output. Alternatively, invoke the **Render the current frame (Maya Software)** tool from the status line to display this window with the final rendered output, as shown in Figure 3-64.

Figure 3-64 *The rendered view of the wine glass*

Saving the File

In this section, you need to save the wine glass model that you have created.

1. Choose **File > Save Scene** from the main menubar; the **Save As** dialog box is displayed.

   As the project folder is already set, by default the path *\Documents\Maya_Tutorials\c03_tut1\ scenes* is displayed in **Look In** text box of the dialog box.

2. Enter **c03_tut1** in the **File name** text box and then select **Maya Binary** from the **Files of type** drop-down list. Next, choose the **Save As** button.

You can view the final rendered image of the model by downloading the *c03_Maya_2012_render.zip* file from *http://www.cadcim.com*. The path of the file is as follows:

Textbooks > Animation and Visual Effects >Maya > Autodesk Maya 2012 : A Comprehensive Guide

Tutorial 2

In this tutorial, you will create the 3D model of a tea cup, as shown in Figure 3-65, using the curve tools and the surface methods.   **(Expected time: 30 min)**

The following steps are required to complete this tutorial:

a.   Create a project folder.
b.   Create a profile curve.
c.   Create the cup using the revolve tool.
d.   Create crease in the tea cup.
e.   Create the handle of the tea cup.
f.   Render the final output.
g.   Save the model.

Creating the Project Folder

Before starting a new file, it is recommended that you create the project folder.

1.   Create a project with the name *c03_tut2* in the folder *Maya_Tutorials* as discussed in Tutorial 1.

Figure 3-65 The tea cup

Creating a Profile Curve for the Tea Cup

In this section, you need to create a profile curve for the tea cup by using the **CV Curve Tool**.

1.   Activate the Front viewport and choose **Create > CV Curve Tool** from the main menubar.

2.   Create a profile curve by using the **CV Curve Tool**, as shown in Figure 3-66.

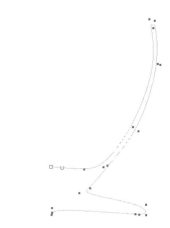

Figure 3-66 The profile curve for the tea cup

Creating the Tea cup using the Revolve tool

In this section, you need to apply the **Revolve** method to the profile curve created for the tea cup.

1.   Activate the Top viewport and select the profile curve from the viewport.

2.   Invoke the **Move Tool** and press and hold the D key to set the pivot point of the profile curve. Next, move the manipulator to set the pivot point, as shown in Figure 3-67.

3.   Activate the Perspective viewport and select the profile curve in the viewport. Then,

choose **Surfaces > Revolve** from the main menubar; the tea cup is created in the wireframe mode.

4. Press 5 to view the cup in the smooth shade. Alternatively, choose **Shading > Smooth Shade All** from the **Panel menu** to view the cup in the smooth shade, refer to Figure 3-68.

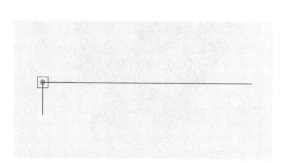

Figure 3-67 Position of the new pivot point   *Figure 3-68 The **Revolve** method applied on the profile curve*

Creating Crease in the Tea Cup

Next, you need to reshape the tea cup to give it the required shape.

1. Activate the Perspective viewport and select the tea cup. Next, press and hold the right mouse button over the tea cup; a marking menu is displayed. Choose **Isoparm** from the marking menu (for marking menu, refer to Chapter 1).

2. Choose the vertical isoparm on the tea cup, and press and drag the selected isoparm to the left of the tea cup; a dotted impression of the isoparm is created, as shown in Figure 3-69.

3. Activate the **Surfaces** menuset from the status line. Choose **Edit Curves > Insert Knot** from the main menubar; a new isoparm is created, as shown in Figure 3-70.

Figure 3-69 Dotted impression of the isoparm   *Figure 3-70 A new isoparm created*

4.   Repeat steps 1, 2, and 3 to increase the number of isoparms, as shown in Figure 3-71.

5.   Press and hold the right mouse button on the tea cup and choose **Control Vertex** from the marking menu. Next, press and hold the SHIFT key and select the vertices, as shown in Figure 3-72.

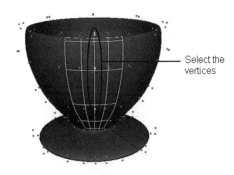

Figure 3-71 Isoparms created

Figure 3-72 Vertices selected to make crease in the cup

6.   Choose the **Move Tool** from the toolbox and move the selected vertices to the center of the cup. Next, activate the side viewport and move the selected vertices in the Y direction; a crease is created in the tea cup, as shown in Figure 3-73.

Now, you need to duplicate the creased part of the cup to create the remaining parts of the cup.

7.   Activate the Perspective viewport. Press and hold the right mouse button on the tea cup and choose **Isoparm** from the marking menu. Next, select the isoparms from the creased part of the cup, as shown in Figure 3-74.

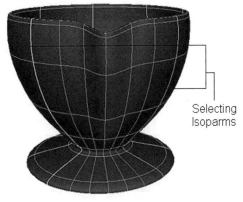

Figure 3-73 Crease created in the cup

Figure 3-74 Selecting isoparms

8. Choose **Edit NURBS > Detach Surfaces** from the main menubar; the selected part is separated from the remaining part of the cup, as shown in Figure 3-75.

Note

For better understanding of this tutorial, the parts of the cup have been marked as A, B, C, and D, as shown in Figures 3-75 and 3-79.

9. Delete part 'B' from the scene, refer to Figure 3-75. Activate the top viewport. Press and hold the D key and move the manipulator to adjust the pivot point to the center, as shown in Figure 3-76.

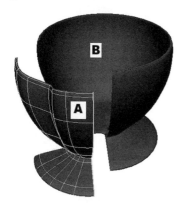

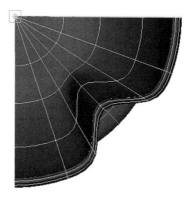

Figure 3-75 The creased part separated from the cup

Figure 3-76 Pivot point set to the center

10. Activate the perspective viewport and select part 'A' of the cup. Choose **Edit > Duplicate Special > Option Box** from the main menubar; the **Duplicate Special Options** dialog box is displayed. Set the properties of the cup in this dialog box, as shown in Figure 3-77.

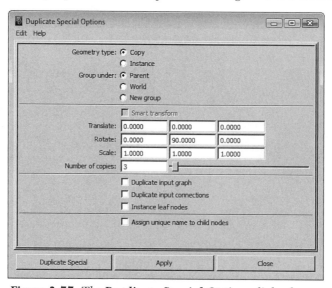

*Figure 3-77 The **Duplicate Special Options** dialog box*

11. Choose the **Duplicate Special** button from this dialog box to duplicate the selected object in the viewport; the basic shape of the cup is created, as shown in Figure 3-78.

Note

*On applying the **Duplicate Special** command to an object, the object will rotate, scale, and move with reference to its pivot point. So, you need to check the pivot point each time you duplicate an object.*

12. Press and hold the SHIFT key and select the parts 'A' and 'B' of the cup, as shown in Figure 3-79. Choose **Edit NURBS > Attach Surfaces > Option Box** from the main menubar to attach the surfaces; the **Attach Surfaces Options** dialog box is displayed. Set the parameters in this dialog box, as shown in Figure 3-80, and then choose the **Attach** button; the selected parts get attached.

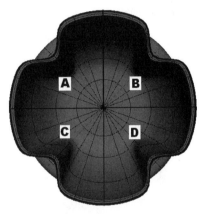

Figure 3-78 The basic shape of the cup   *Figure 3-79 Four parts of the cup*

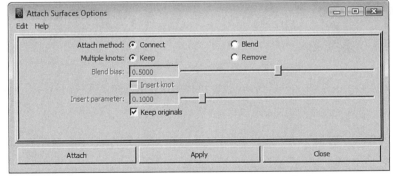

*Figure 3-80 The **Attach Surfaces Options** dialog box*

13. Similarly, join parts C and D. Next, join the remaining two parts.

Note

*The **Attach Surfaces** option joins only two NURBS surfaces at a time.*

Creating the Handle of the Cup

In this section, you need to create the handle of the cup by using the **CV Curve Tool**.

1. Activate the Front viewport. Choose **Create > CV Curve Tool** from the main menubar and draw the profile curve, as shown in Figure 3-81.

2. Activate the Top viewport. Choose **Create > NURBS Primitives > Circle** from the main menubar and draw a circle in the viewport.

3. Select the NURBS circle from the viewport. Choose **Display > UI Elements > Channel Box/Layer Editor** from the main menubar; the **Channel Box/layer editor** is displayed. Choose the **makeNurbCircle1** tab from the **INPUTS** node and set the **Radius** value to **0.5**.

4. Select the NURBS circle from the viewport. Press and hold the SHIFT key and then select the profile curve. Next, choose **Surfaces > Extrude** from the main menubar; the extruded surface is created, refer to Figure 3-82. Next, select the extruded surface and open the channel box. Select the **extrude1** tab from the **Channel box**; the options of the **extrude1** tab are displayed. Press and release the **Closest End** option of the **Use Component Pivot** attribute; a flyout is displayed. Choose the **Component Pivot** option from the flyout.

Figure 3-81 *The profile curve for the handle*   *Figure 3-82* *The **Extrude** tool applied to the profile curve*

5. Invoke the **Move Tool** and adjust the handle with the cup to get the final image, as shown in Figure 3-83.

Rendering the Scene

In this section, you need to render the scene to get the final output.

1. Activate the Perspective viewport. Set the view angle of the tea cup by using the middle mouse button and the ALT key.

2. Choose the **Render the current frame (Maya Software)** button from the status line to render the scene; the final rendered view is shown in Figure 3-84.

Saving the Model

In this section, you need to save the cup model that you have created.

1. Choose **File > Save Scene** from the main menubar; the **Save As** dialog box is displayed.

Figure 3-83 Final image of the cup

As the project folder is already set, by default the path *\Documents\Maya_Tutorials\c03_tut2\ scenes* is displayed in **Look In** text box of the dialog box.

2. Enter **c03_tut2** in the **File name** text box and then select **Maya Binary** from the **Files of type** drop-down list. Next, choose the **Save As** button.

You can view the final rendered image of the model by downloading the *c03_Maya_2012_render.zip* file from *http://www.cadcim.com*. The path of the file is as follows:

Textbooks > Animation and Visual Effects >Maya > Autodesk Maya 2012 : A Comprehensive Guide

Figure 3-84 The final rendered view

Tutorial 3

In this tutorial, you will create the 3D model of a house, as shown in Figure 3-85, using the curve tools and the surface methods.   **(Expected time: 45 min)**

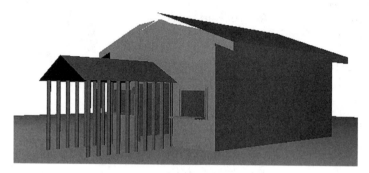

Figure 3-85 *3D model of a house*

The following steps are required to complete this tutorial:

a.   Create a project folder.
b.   Create the front and back sides of the house.
c.   Create roof and side walls.
d.   Create door and window frames.
e.   Extend the roof of the house.
f.   Create a shade over the door.
g.   Save the file.

Creating the Project Folder

Before starting a new file, it is recommended that you create the project folder.

1.   Create a project with the name *c03_tut3* in the folder *Maya_Tutorials* as discussed in Tutorial 1.

Creating the Front and Back Sides of the House

In this section, you need to create the front and back sides of the model of the house by using the **EP Curve Tool**.

1.   Activate the Front viewport. Choose **Create > EP Curve Tool > Option Box** from the main menubar; the **EP Curve Tool** property window is displayed. Set the parameters in the **EP Curve Settings** area, as shown in Figure 3-86.

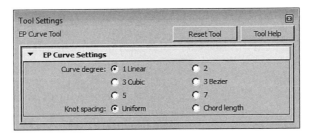

Figure 3-86 The **EP Curve Settings** *area*

2. Activate the Front viewport. Create curves by using the **EP Curve Tool**, as shown in Figure 3-87. Make sure the start point and the endpoint of the NURBS curve are snapped to each other. To do so, press and hold the v key while connecting the endpoint to the start point. Alternatively, invoke the **Snap to points** tool from the status line to snap the endpoint to the start point.

3. Similarly, create the profile curves for doors and windows in the Front viewport using the **EP Curve Tool**, as shown in Figures 3-88 and 3-89.

4. Select the profile curves for the door and the house by using the SHIFT key. Choose **Edit > Duplicate** from the main menubar; the selected parts are duplicated. Next, invoke the **Move Tool** from the toolbox and activate the Perspective viewport. Move the duplicated parts to the back, as shown in Figure 3-90.

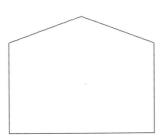

Figure 3-87 *Profile curves for creating a house*

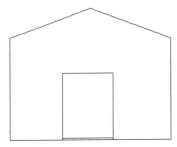

Figure 3-88 *Profile curve for the house and the door*

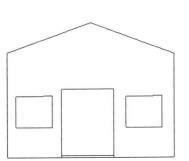

Figure 3-89 *Complete profile curve in the Front viewport*

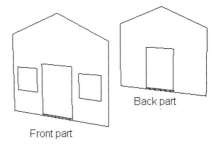

Figure 3-90 *The front and back parts of the house*

5. Press and hold the SHIFT key and select the curves of the front part. Activate the **Surfaces** menuset from the status line. Next, choose **Surfaces > Planar** from the main menubar to get the final output. Press 5 to change it to the shaded mode, as shown in Figure 3-91.

6. Similarly, create the NURBS surface for the back part of the house, as shown in Figure 3-92.

Note

If the door area is not created on applying the planar surface type, move the door curve in the upward direction, so that it does not intersect with other curves.

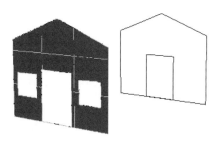

Figure 3-91 *The **Planar** method applied to the front part*

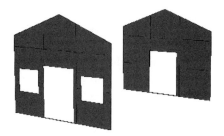

Figure 3-92 *The **Planar** method applied to both parts*

Creating the Roof and the Side Walls

In this section, you need to create the roof and the side walls of the house model by using the **Loft** tool.

1. Choose **Display > UI Elements > Channel Box/Layer Editor** from the main menubar; the **Channel Box/layer editor** is displayed. Next, create two layers by choosing the **Create a new layer** button, refer to Figure 3-93. Name the layers as **wireframe** and **mesh**.

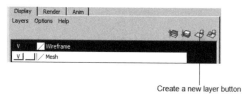

Figure 3-93 *Creating new layers*

2. Now, you need to add a surface object to the **mesh** layer and NURBS curves to the **wireframe** layer. To do so, select the NURBS surface created in the viewport and press and hold the right mouse button over the **mesh** layer in the layer editor; a flyout is displayed. Choose **Add Selected Objects** from the flyout, as shown in Figure 3-94. Similarly, add the NURBS curves from the viewport to the **wireframe** layer.

Figure 3-94 *Choosing the* ***Add Selected*** ***Objects*** *option from the flyout*

3. Click on the **V** option corresponding to the **wireframe** layer to hide the curves in it. The **V** option in the **Layer Editor** is used to set the visibility of a layer on/off. Now, activate the Perspective viewport and choose the front part of the model. Next, press and hold the right mouse button on the front part of the model and choose **Trim Edge** from the marking menu, as shown in Figure 3-95.

4. Press SHIFT and select the back part of the house. Next, press and hold the right mouse button over the back part of the house and choose **Trim Edge** from the marking menu, as discussed in the previous step. Select the edges from the front and back parts of the house by using the SHIFT key, as shown in Figure 3-96.

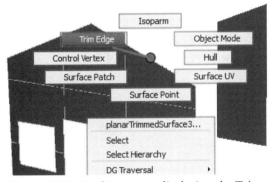

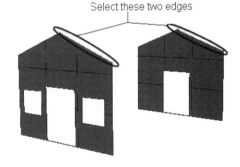

Figure 3-95 *Marking menu displaying the* ***Trim*** ***Edge*** *option*

Figure 3-96 *Selecting the edges of the house*

5. Choose **Surfaces > Loft** from the main menubar; the half part of the roof is created, as shown in Figure 3-97.

6. Similarly, create another part of the roof and the side walls of the house by using the **Loft** method to get the final output. Figure 3-98 shows the house with complete walls and roof.

7. Add the side walls and the roof of the house to the **mesh** layer in the **Layer Editor**, as discussed earlier.

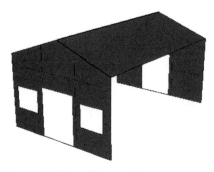

Figure 3-97 *Half part of the roof created*   **Figure 3-98** *House with complete walls and roof*

Creating Frames for Doors and Windows

In this section, you need to create frames for doors and windows by using the **Extrude** tool.

1. Hide the objects of the **mesh** layer and unhide the objects of the **wireframe** layer. Activate the Top viewport. Choose **Create > CV Curve Tool > Option Box** from the main menubar; the **CV Curve Tool** property window is displayed. Select the **1 Linear** radio button in the **Curve degree** attribute area of this window. Next, create the profile curve for the frame, as shown in Figure 3-99. Choose **Modify > Center Pivot** from the main menubar to set the pivot point of the frame to the center.

2. Activate the Perspective viewport. Choose **Edit > Delete by Type > History** from the main menubar to delete the history of the surfaces created earlier. Next, press and hold the right mouse button over the front door curve and choose **Edit Point** from the marking menu, as shown in Figure 3-100.

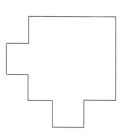

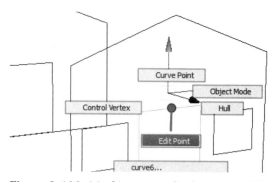

Figure 3-99 *The profile curve created for the frame*   **Figure 3-100** *Marking menu displaying the Edit Point option*

Note
*Maya is a node-based software. It keeps the track of each action performed in the software. Sometimes, the use of the NURBS curves for creating a surface does not yield the desired result. In such a case, choose **Edit > Delete by type > History** from the main menubar to delete the history. On deleting the history of scene objects, the child objects in the viewport will not keep the track of their parent objects and will form an independent identity which can be used again.*

3. Select the lower right edit point from the door curve, and then choose **Edit Curves >
Detach Curves** from the main menubar; the curves are detached into two parts, as shown
in Figure 3-101.

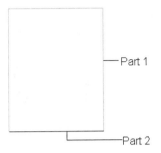

Figure 3-101 *The door curves detached*

4. Next, select the profile curves of frames. Press SHIFT and select Part 1 of the door curves,
refer to Figure 3-101. Choose **Surfaces > Extrude** from the main menubar; the NURBS
surface for the door frame is created. You can decrease the thickness of the frame by
scaling the profile curve of frames.

5. Select the door frame and choose **Window > Attribute Editor** from the main menubar.
Choose the **extrude1** attribute tab from the **Attribute Editor** and set the parameters in it,
as shown in Figure 3-102. After setting the parameters, the NURBS surface for the frame
is displayed, as shown in Figure 3-103.

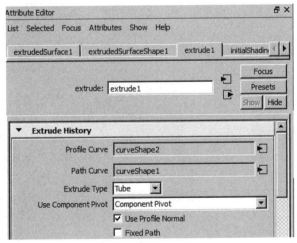

Figure 3-102 *Partial view of the **extrude1** attribute tab
in the **Attribute Editor***

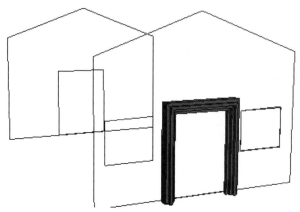

Figure 3-103 *The NURBS surface created for the door frame*

6. Activate the Front viewport and then choose **Create > EP Curve Tool** from the main menubar. Now, create the curve for the window frame, as shown in Figure 3-104.

7. Invoke the **Move Tool** from the toolbox and then move the profile curve of the window to the window area. Select the profile curve for the frame. Press and hold the SHIFT key and select the curve for the frame. Next, choose **Surfaces > Extrude** from the main menubar to get the output, as shown in Figure 3-105.

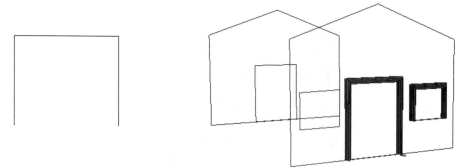

Figure 3-104 *Profile curve for the window frame*   ***Figure 3-105*** *Frame for the window*

8. Select the window frame and press CTRL+d to duplicate the frame. Next, invoke the **Move Tool** from the toolbox again to move the duplicate frame to another part of the window, as shown in Figure 3-106.

9. Activate the Perspective viewport. Duplicate the door frame and move it to the back to create the frame for the back door, as shown in Figure 3-107. Choose **Display > UI Elements > Channel Box/Layer Editor** from the main menubar to display the **Channel Box/Layer Editor**. In the **Channel Box**, enter -1 in the **Scale Z** edit box.

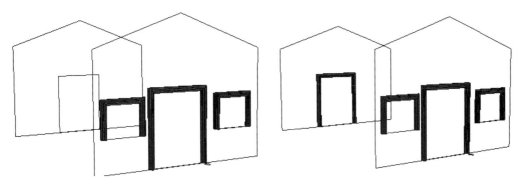

Figure 3-106 *Window frames*   *Figure 3-107* *Back door frame*

Extending the Roof of the House

In this section, you need to extend the roof of the house and add thickness to it by using the **Loft** tool.

1. Make the objects in the **mesh** layer visible by using the **Layer Editor**. Set the **wireframe** layer to invisible mode in the **Layer Editor**. Next, press the SHIFT key and select both parts of the roof. Now, choose **Edit NURBS > Attach Surfaces > Option Box** from the main menubar; the **Attach Surfaces Options** dialog box is displayed in the viewport. Set the required parameters in this dialog box, as shown in Figure 3-108, and then choose the **Attach** button; both parts of the roof get attached.

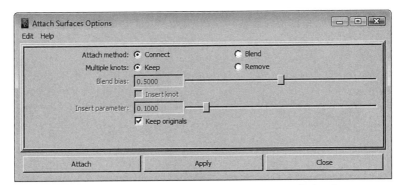

Figure 3-108 *The* ***Attach Surfaces Options*** *dialog box*

2. Select the roof and choose **Edit > Delete by Type > History** from the main menubar to delete the history of the roof. Choose **Edit NURBS > Extend Surfaces > Option Box** from the main menubar; the **Extend Surface Options** dialog box is displayed. Set the parameters in the **Extend Surface Options** dialog box, as shown in Figure 3-109, and then choose the **Extend** button to set the extended roof, as shown in Figure 3-110.

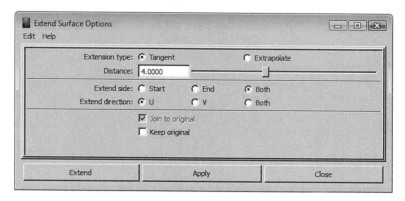

Figure 3-109 The **Extend Surface Options** *dialog box*

3. Make a duplicate of the roof, as discussed earlier. Select the Roof 1 shown in Figure 3-111. Next, press and hold the right mouse button and choose **Isoparm** from the marking menu, as shown in Figure 3-112. Next, press SHIFT and select the Roof 2. Release the SHIFT key, press and hold the right mouse button over the Roof 2 and choose **Isoparm** from the marking menu. Select the isoparms on the Roof 1 and the Roof 2, refer to Figure 3-112. Next, choose **Surfaces > Loft** from the main menubar; a surface is created between the selected isoparms. Similarly, close all sides of the roof to get the output shown in Figure 3-113.

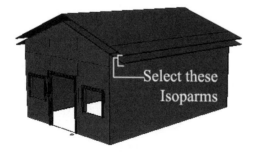

Figure 3-110 Extended roof

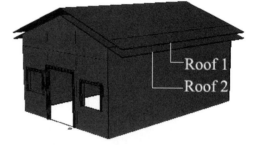

Figure 3-111 Duplicate of the roof

Figure 3-112 Selecting the Isoparms

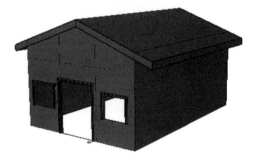

Figure 3-113 Final roof created

4. Activate the Top viewport. Choose **Create > NURBS Primitives > Plane** from the main menubar. Next, adjust the plane in the perspective viewport to get the output shown in Figure 3-114.

5. Activate the Top viewport. Choose **Create > Polygon Primitives > Cube** from the main menubar to create the base of the window. Now, drag the cursor on the grid and then pull it up to specify the height of the cube. Use the **Move Tool** to move and the **Scale Tool** to scale the window base, as shown in Figure 3-115.

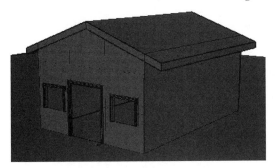

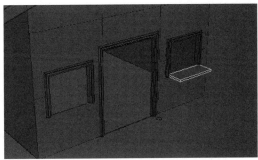

Figure 3-114 *The adjusted plane*   *Figure 3-115* *Window base*

6. Select the base of the window and press CTRL+d to make a duplicate of the base of the window. Next, invoke the **Move Tool** from the toolbox and place the duplicate window below another window.

Creating the Shade over the Door

In this section, you need to create the shade over the door area and the pillar for the support of the shade by using the **Loft** and **Revolve** tools, respectively.

1. Activate the Front viewport. Choose **Create > EP Curve Tool** from the main menubar and then draw the curve for the shade of the door, as shown in Figure 3-116.

2. Activate the Perspective viewport. Select the curve for the shade of the door. Press CTRL+d to make a duplicate of the curve. Invoke the **Move Tool** from the toolbox and drag the blue manipulator to move the selected curve to the required location, as shown in Figure 3-117.

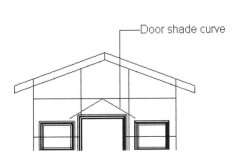

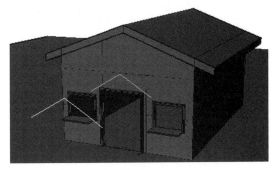

Figure 3-116 *Door shade curve*   *Figure 3-117* *Duplicating the door shade curve*

3. Select both the NURBS curves by using the SHIFT key. Choose **Surfaces > Loft** from the main menubar to create the shade over the door. Adjust the shade to get the final output, as shown in Figure 3-118.

4. Activate the Top viewport. Choose **Create > NURBS Primitives > Circle** from the main menubar. Press the left mouse button and drag the cursor on the grid to draw a circle, as shown in Figure 3-119.

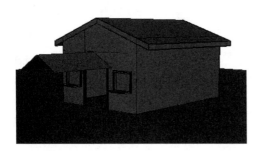

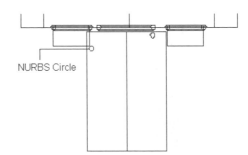

Figure 3-118 The door shade created

Figure 3-119 The NURBS circle for creating the pillar

5. Activate the Perspective viewport and adjust the NURBS circle with the plane. Press CTRL+d to make a duplicate of the circle. Invoke the **Move Tool** and move the duplicate circle to the door shade, as shown in Figure 3-120.

6. Select the two NURBS circles and then choose **Surfaces > Loft** from the main menubar to create the pillar for the door shade, as shown in Figure 3-121.

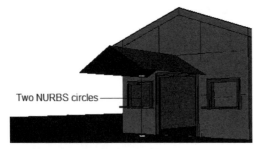

Figure 3-120 Two NURBS circles selected

Figure 3-121 The pillar support for the door shade

7. Select the pillar surface in the perspective viewport. Choose **Modify > Center Pivot** from the main menubar to align the pivot point to the center of the object.

8. Activate the Top viewport and press CTRL+d to duplicate the surface. Now, move the pillar surface to the place shown in Figure 3-122. Next, press SHIFT+d seven times to place the seven pillars in a row at equal distance from each other, as shown in Figure 3-123.

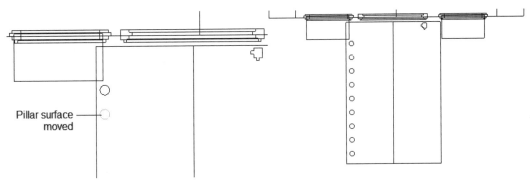

Figure 3-122 *Duplicate of the pillar surface*   **Figure 3-123** *Pillars aligned in a row*

9. Repeat the previous step to create multiple pillars on the other side of the door shade. The final model of the house is shown in Figure 3-124.

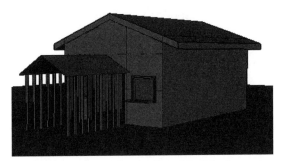

Figure 3-124 *The final model of the house*

Saving the File

In this section, you need to save the house model that you have created.

1. Choose **File > Save Scene** from the main menubar; the **Save As** dialog box is displayed.

   As the project folder is already set, by default the path *\Documents\Maya_Tutorials\c03_tut3\ scenes* is displayed in **Look In** text box of the dialog box.

2. Enter **c03_tut3** in the **File name** text box and then select **Maya Binary** from the **Files of type** drop-down list. Next, choose the **Save As** button.

You can view the final rendered image of the model by downloading the *c03_Maya_2012_render.zip* file from *http://www.cadcim.com*. The path of the file is as follows:

Textbooks > Animation and Visual Effects >Maya > Autodesk Maya 2012 : A Comprehensive Guide

Self-Evaluation Test

Answer the following questions and then compare them to those given at the end of this chapter:

1. A _____ is an object whose base is a circle and its sides taper to a point.

2. A _____ is a closed plane curve in which every point is equidistant from its center.

3. You can reset the options in Maya by using the _____ dialog box.

4. NURBS stands for _____.

5. The default NURBS objects in Maya are grouped together under _____.

6. You can use the _____ node to rename an object.

7. You can switch from the wireframe mode to the object mode by pressing 4 on the keyboard. (T/F)

8. A cube is a two-dimensional shape with six square or rectangular sides. (T/F)

9. A square is a six-sided regular polygon with six equal sides and six right angles. (T/F)

10. The **Boundary** tool helps you create a surface by filling the boundary curve. (T/F)

Review Questions

Answer the following questions:

1. Which of the following is not a component of NURBS object?

    (a) **Isoparm**   (b) **Vertex**
    (c) **Hull**   (d) **Surface patch**

2. Which of the following tools works similar to the brush tool in other software?

    (a) **EP Curve Tool**   (b) **CV Curve Tool**
    (c) **Pencil Curve Tool**   (d) **Arc Tool**

3. _____ is a four-sided regular polygon with equal sides.

4. Which of the following keys are required to adjust the centre pivot of an object?

    (a) SPACEBAR   (b) HOME

    (c) CTRL   (d) INSERT

5. The _____ tool is used to create a sphere with faceted or a smooth appearance.

6. _____ is the addition of surface between two or more specified drawn entities.

7. The _____ option is used to create a sphere with a faceted or a smooth appearance.

8. The _____ is a solid object in which the surface is at an equal distance from the center.

9. The **Square** tool helps you create a surface from the intersecting NURBS curves. (T/F)

10. The NURBS curves, which are used to create the NURBS surfaces by using the **Loft** tool, should have curves with equal number of vertices. (T/F).

Exercises

Exercise 1

Create the model of an apple, as shown in Figure 3-125. You can view the final rendered image of this model by downloading the *c03_maya_2012_render.zip* file from *http://www.cadcim.com*. The path of file is as follows:

Textbooks > Animation and Visual Effects > Maya > Autodesk Maya 2012: A Comprehensive Guide
(Expected time: 15 min)

Figure 3-125 Model of an apple

Exercise 2

Create the model of a Lantern, as shown in Figure 3-126. You can view the final rendered image of this model by downloading the *c03_maya_2012_render.zip* file from *http://www.cadcim. com*. The path of the file is mentioned in Exercise 1.   **(Expected time: 15 min)**

Figure 3-126 Model of a lantern

Exercise 3

Create the model of a table, as shown in Figure 3-127. You can view the final rendered image of this model by downloading the *c03_maya_2012_render.zip* file from *http://www.cadcim.com*. The path of the file is mentioned in Exercise 1.   **(Expected time:15 min)**

Figure 3-127 Model of Table

Exercise 4

Create the model of a castle, as shown in Figure 3-128. You can view the final rendered image of this model by downloading the *c03_maya_2012_render.zip* file from *http://www.cadcim.com*. The path of the file is mentioned in Exercise 1. **(Expected time:30 min)**

Figure 3-128 *Model of a castle*

Exercise 5

Create the model of a candle stand, as shown in Figure 3-129. You can view the final rendered image of this model by downloading the *c03_maya_2012_render.zip* file from *http://www.cadcim.com*. The path of the file is mentioned in Exercise 1.   **(Expected time: 15 min)**

Figure 3-129 *Model of a candle stand*

Answers to Self-Evaluation Test
1. cone, **2.** sphere, **3. Preferences**, **4.** Non uniform rational B-Spline, **5.** NURBS Primitives, **6.** shapes, **7.** F, **8.** F, **9.** F, **10.** T

Chapter 4

Polygon Primitives

Learning Objectives

After completing this chapter, you will be able to:

- *Create polygon primitives*
- *Edit polygon surfaces*

INTRODUCTION

In this chapter, you will learn to create polygon surfaces. A polygon is made up of flat surface with n number of sides. Each side of a polygon is called a face. Each face can be further classified into edges and vertices. By modifying a face, an edge, or a vertex of an object, you can create a new object depending on your requirement. The creation of a polygon is more rigid than that of a NURBS object because NURBS object has a more pliable and sculptural surface.

POLYGON PRIMITIVES

In Maya, polygon primitives are classified into various objects. These objects are grouped under the **Polygon Primitives** in the main menubar. The method of creating different polygon primitives is discussed next.

Creating a Sphere

Main menubar:	Create > Polygon Primitives > Sphere
Shelf:	Polygons > Sphere

A sphere is a solid object and every point on its surface is equidistant from its centre, as shown in Figure 4-1. The sphere can be created dynamically or by entering the values using the keyboard. Both these methods are discussed next.

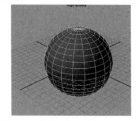

Figure 4-1 A polygon sphere

Creating a Sphere Dynamically

To create a sphere dynamically, choose **Create > Polygon Primitives > Sphere** from the main menubar; you will be prompted to drag the cursor on the grid to draw the sphere in the viewport. Press and hold the left mouse button, and drag the cursor up or down to define the radius of the sphere. Now, release the left mouse button to get the desired radius; the sphere will be created in all viewports and will be visible in the wireframe mode. Press the numeric key 5 to change the display to shaded mode. Alternatively, choose **Shading > Smooth Shade All** from the **Panel menu** to change the display to shaded mode. Press the numeric key 4 or choose **Shading > Wireframe** from the **Panel menu** to revert to the wireframe mode.

Creating a Sphere by Using the Keyboard

To create a sphere by using the keyboard, choose **Create > Polygon Primitives > Sphere > Option Box** from the main menubar; the **Polygon Sphere Tool** property window will be displayed on the left of the viewport, as shown in Figure 4-2. In this window, set the properties of the sphere by using the keyboard and then click in the viewport; the sphere will be created in all viewports. Choose the **Reset Tool** button at the top of the **Polygon Sphere Tool** window to reset the settings of the sphere. The properties given in this window are the same as those of other polygon primitives discussed in Chapter 3.

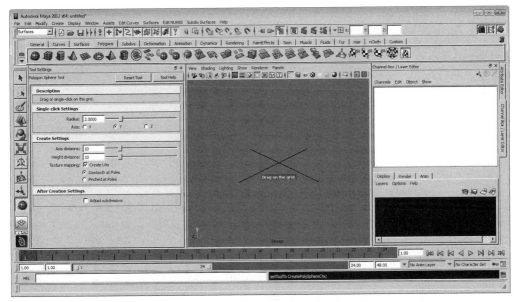

Figure 4-2 The **Polygon Sphere Tool** *window*

Creating a Cube

Main menubar:	Create > Polygon Primitives > Cube
Shelf:	Polygons >Cube

A cube is a three-dimensional shape with six squares or rectangular faces, as shown in Figure 4-3. A cube can be created dynamically or by entering values using the keyboard. Both these methods are discussed next.

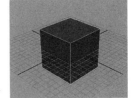

Creating a Cube Dynamically

To create a cube dynamically, choose **Create >Polygon > Primitives > Cube** from the main menubar; you will be prompted to

Figure 4-3 *A polygon cube*

drag the cursor on the grid to draw a cube in the viewport. Press and hold the left mouse button, and drag the cursor on the grid to define the base of the cube. Now, release the left mouse button to get the desired base. Next, press and hold the left mouse button again and drag the cursor up to set the height of the cube and then release the left mouse button; the cube will be created in all the viewports.

Creating a Cube by Using the Keyboard

To create a cube by the using the keyboard, choose **Create > Polygon Primitives > Cube > Option Box** from the main menubar; the **Polygon Cube Tool** window will be displayed on the left of the viewport, as shown in Figure 4-4. In this window, set the properties of the cube by using the keyboard and then click in the viewport; the cube will be created in all viewports. Choose the **Reset Tool** button at the top of the **Polygon Cube Tool** window to reset the settings of the cube. The properties in the **Polygon Cube Tool** property window are the same as those of other polygon primitives discussed in Chapter 3.

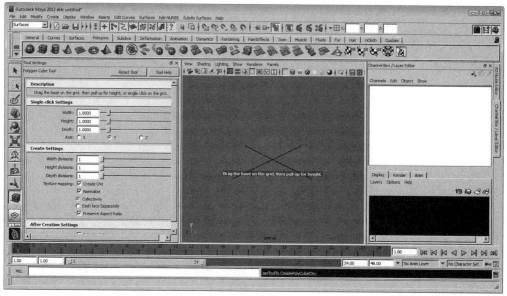

*Figure 4-4 The **Polygon Cube Tool** window*

Note

*By default, polygon primitives are displayed in the wireframe mode. Press 5 on the keyboard to change the mode to shaded. Alternatively, choose **Shading > Smooth Shade All** from the **Panel menu**. You can also switch back to the wireframe mode by pressing 4 on the keyboard or by choosing **Shading > Wireframe** from the **Panel menu**.*

Creating a Prism

Main menubar:	Create > Polygon Primitives > Prism
Shelf:	Polygons >Prism

A prism is a semi-regular polyhedron created by combining n-sided polygons and n number of squares, as shown in Figure 4-5. You can create a prism dynamically and by using the keyboard. Both these methods are discussed next.

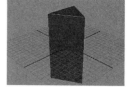

Creating a Prism Dynamically

Figure 4-5 A polygon prism

To create a prism dynamically, choose **Create > Polygon Primitives > Prism** from the main menubar; you will be prompted to drag the cursor on the grid to define the base of the prism. Press and hold the left mouse button and drag the cursor; the base of the prism is created. Release the left mouse button. Again, press and hold the left mouse button and drag the cursor up to set the height of the prism, and then release the left mouse button. Again, press and hold the left mouse button to set the thickness of the polygon prism. The polygon prism will be created in all viewports. By default, it will be visible in the wireframe mode. Press 5 on the keyboard to change it to the shaded mode. Alternatively, choose **Shading > Smooth Shade All** from the **Panel menu** to switch to the shaded mode.

Creating a Prism by Using the Keyboard

To create a prism by using the keyboard, choose **Create > Polygon Primitives > Prism > Option Box** from the main menubar; the **Polygon Prism Tool** window will be displayed on the left of the viewport, as shown in Figure 4-6. In this window, set the properties of the prism by using the keyboard and then click in the viewport; the prism will be created in all viewports. Choose the **Reset Tool** button at the top of the **Polygon Prism Tool** window to reset the settings of the prism. The properties in this window are the same as those of other polygon primitives discussed in Chapter 3.

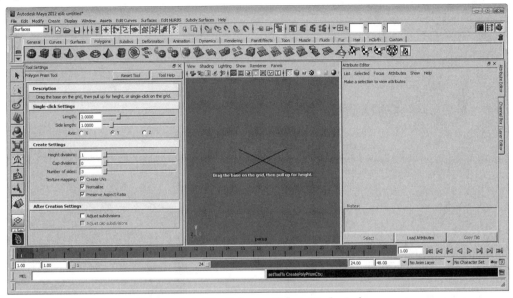

Figure 4-6 The Polygon Prism Tool window

Modifying the Name and other Parameters of a Prism

You can modify the name and other parameters of a prism in the viewport. To do so, select the prism and choose **Display > UI Elements > Channel Box / Layer Editor** from the main menubar. The **Channel Box /Layer Editor** will be displayed on the right of the viewport, as shown in Figure 4-7. Click on the **pPrism1** name in the **INPUTS** node and rename it. To modify the properties of the prism, expand the **INPUTS** node; various options will be displayed. Enter the required values in the edit boxes; the changes will be dynamically reflected on the prism in the viewport. Alternatively, select the parameter of the prism that you want to change; the corresponding parameter will be highlighted in the viewport. Now, press and hold the middle mouse button and drag the cursor horizontally to change that particular parameter.

Creating a Pyramid

Main menubar:	Create > Polygon Primitives > Pyramid
Shelf:	Polygons >Pyramid

A pyramid is a geometric shape with a polygonal base and a point called apex. The base and the apex are connected through triangular faces, as shown in Figure 4-8. You can create a pyramid dynamically or by entering values using the keyboard. Both the methods are discussed next.

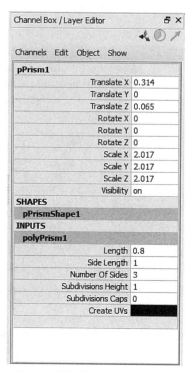

Figure 4-7 **The Channel Box/**
Layer Editor

Figure 4-8 A polygon
pyramid

Creating a Pyramid Dynamically

To create a pyramid dynamically, choose **Create > Polygon Primitives > Pyramid** from the main menubar; you will be prompted to drag the cursor on the grid to define the base of the pyramid. Press and hold the left mouse button and drag the cursor; the base of the pyramid is created. Release the left mouse button. Next, press and hold the left mouse button and drag the cursor up to set the height of the pyramid, and then release the left mouse button. Again, press and hold the button to set the thickness of the polygon pyramid. The polygon pyramid will be created in all viewports. By default, it will be visible in the wireframe mode. Press 5 on the keyboard to change it to the shaded mode. Alternatively, choose **Shading > Smooth Shade All** from the **Panel menu** to switch to the shaded mode.

Creating a Pyramid by Using the Keyboard

To create a pyramid by using the keyboard, choose **Create > Polygon Primitives > Pyramid > Option Box** from the main menubar; the **Polygon Pyramid Tool** window will be displayed on the left of the viewport, as shown in Figure 4-9. In this window, set the properties of the pyramid by using the keyboard and then click in the viewport; the pyramid will be created in all viewports. Choose the **Reset Tool** button at the top of the **Polygon Pyramid Tool** window to reset the settings of the pyramid. The properties in the **Polygon Pyramid tool** property window are the same as those of other polygon primitives discussed in Chapter 3.

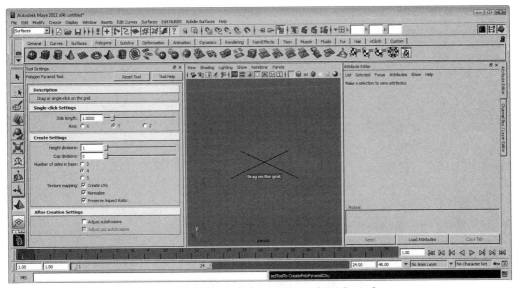

Figure 4-9 The **Polygon Pyramid Tool** *window*

Creating a Pipe

Main menubar:	Create > Polygon Primitives > Pipe
Shelf:	Polygons > Pipe

A pipe is similar to a hollow cylinder. But unlike a cylinder, the top and bottom portions of a pipe are open, as shown in Figure 4-10. You can create a pipe either dynamically or by entering values using the keyboard. Both the methods are discussed next.

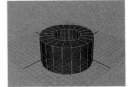

Figure 4-10 A polygon pipe

Creating a Pipe Dynamically

To create a pipe dynamically, choose **Create > Polygon Primitives > Pipe** from the main menubar; you will be prompted to drag the cursor on the grid to define the base of the pipe. Press and hold the left mouse button and drag the cursor; the base of the pipe is created. Release the left mouse button. Next, press and hold the left mouse button and drag the cursor up to set the height of the pipe, and then release the left mouse button. Again, press and hold the left mouse button to set the thickness of the polygon pipe. The polygon pipe will be created in all viewports. By default, it will be visible in the wireframe mode. Press 5 on the keyboard to change it to the shaded mode. Alternatively, choose **Shading > Smooth Shade All** from the **Panel menu** to switch to the shaded mode.

Creating a Pipe by Using the Keyboard

To create a pipe by using the keyboard, choose **Create > Polygon Primitives > Pipe> Option Box** from the main menubar; the **Polygon Pipe Tool** window will be displayed on the left of the viewport, as shown in Figure 4-11. In this window, set the properties of the pipe by using the keyboard and then click in the viewport; the pipe will be created in all the viewports. Choose the **Reset Tool** button at the top of the **Polygon Pipe Tool** window to reset the settings of the pipe. The properties in this window are the same as those of other polygon primitives discussed in Chapter 3.

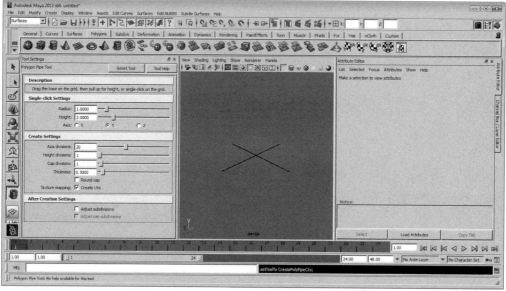

*Figure 4-11 The **Polygon Pipe Tool** window*

Creating a Helix

Main menubar:	Create > Polygon Primitives > Helix
Shelf:	Polygons >Helix

A helix is a three-dimensional curve that lies on a cylinder or a cone, so that its perpendicular angle remains constant to the axis, as shown in Figure 4-12. You can create a helix dynamically or by entering values using the keyboard. Both the methods are discussed next.

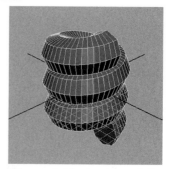

Figure 4-12 A polygon helix

Creating a Helix Dynamically

To create a helix dynamically, choose **Create > Polygon Primitives > Helix** from the main menubar; you will be prompted to drag the cursor on the grid. Press and hold the left mouse button and drag the cursor on the grid to define the diameter of the helix and then release the left mouse button. Again, press and hold the left mouse button and drag the cursor up to set the height of the helix, and then release the left mouse button. Next, press and hold the left mouse button and drag the cursor to set the number of coils in the helix. Release the left mouse button after setting the number of coils. Again, press and hold the left mouse button and drag the cursor to set the section radius; the helix will be created in all viewports.

Creating a Helix by Using the Keyboard

To create a helix by using the keyboard, choose **Create > Polygon Primitives > Helix > Option Box** from the main menubar; the **Polygon Helix Tool** window will be displayed on the left of the viewport, as shown in Figure 4-13. In this window, set the properties of the helix by using the keyboard and then click in the viewport; the helix will be created in all viewports. Choose the **Reset Tool** button at the top of the **Polygon Helix Tool** window to reset the settings of the helix. The properties in this window are the same as of other polygon primitives discussed in Chapter 3.

Tip. *By default, the **Polygon Helix Tool** is not available in the Shelf. But, if the need arises, you can add it to the Shelf. To do so, choose the **Custom Shelf** tab from the Shelf. By default, the **Custom** Shelf tab is empty. This tab can be used to add tools that are frequently used. Press and hold the SHIFT and CTRL keys and choose **Create > Polygon Primitives > Helix** from the main menubar; a helix icon is formed in the **Custom** shelf. Similarly, you can add other tools in the **Custom** Shelf tab for quick reference.*

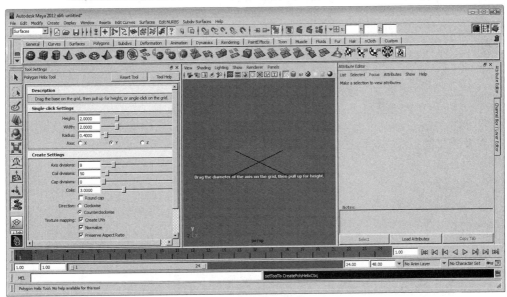

*Figure 4-13 The **Polygon Helix Tool** window*

Creating a Soccer Ball

Main menubar:	Create > Polygon Primitives > Soccer ball
Shelf:	Polygons > Soccer Ball

A soccer ball polygon primitive created in Maya is very much similar to a real-world soccer ball, as shown in Figure 4-14. A soccer ball is formed by an alternate arrangement of hexagons and pentagons. It has total thirty two faces. You can create a soccer ball dynamically or by entering values using the keyboard. Both the methods are discussed next.

Figure 4-14 A soccer ball

Creating a Soccer Ball Dynamically

To create a soccer ball dynamically, choose **Create > Polygon Primitives > Soccer Ball** from the main menubar; You will be prompted to drag the cursor on the grid. Press and hold the left mouse button and drag the cursor on the grid; the soccer ball will be created in all viewports. By default, it will be displayed in the wireframe mode. Press 5 on the keyboard to switch to the shaded mode. Alternatively, choose **Shading > Smooth Shade All** from the Panel menu to switch to the shaded mode.

Creating a Soccer Ball by Using the Keyboard

To create a soccer ball by using the keyboard, choose **Create > Polygon Primitives > Soccer Ball > Option Box** from the main menubar; the **Polygon Soccer Ball Tool,** window will be displayed on the left of the viewport, as shown in Figure 4-15. In this window, set the properties of the soccer ball by using the keyboard and then click in the viewport; the soccer ball will be created in all the viewports. Choose the **Reset Tool** button at the top of the **Polygon Soccer Ball Tool** property window to reset the settings of the soccer ball. The properties in the **Polygon Soccer Ball Tool** window are the same as those of other polygon primitives that have already been discussed in Chapter 3.

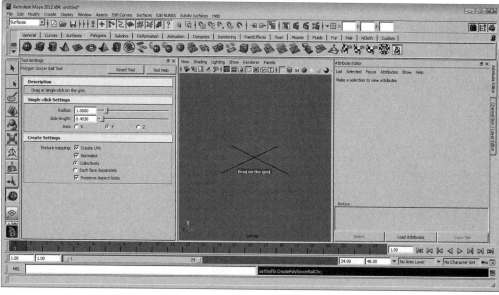

Figure 4-15 *The **Polygon Soccer Ball Tool** window*

Creating a Platonic Solid

Main menubar:	Create > Polygon Primitives > Platonic Solids

A platonic solid is a regular polyhedron with every face being a regular polygon of the same size and shape, as shown in Figure 4-16. You can create a platonic solid dynamically or by entering values using the keyboard. Both the methods are discussed next.

Creating a Platonic Solid Dynamically

To create a platonic solid dynamically, choose **Create > Polygon Primitives > Platonic**

Solids from the main menubar; you will be prompted to drag the cursor on the grid. Press and hold the left mouse button and drag the cursor on the grid; the platonic solid will be created in all viewports and it will be displayed in the wireframe mode. Press 5 on the keyboard to change it to the shaded mode. Alternatively, choose **Shading > Smooth Shade All** from the **Panel menu** to switch to the shaded mode.

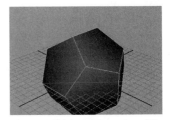

Figure 4-16 A platonic solid

Creating a Platonic Solid by Using the Keyboard

To create a **Platonic Solid** by using the keyboard, choose **Create > Polygon Primitives > Platonic Solids > Option Box** from the main menubar; the **Polygon Platonic Solid Tool** window will be displayed on the left of the viewport, as shown in Figure 4-17. In this window, set the properties of the platonic solid by using the keyboard and then click in the viewport; the platonic solid will be created in all viewports. Choose the **Reset Tool** button at the top of the **Polygon Platonic Solid Tool** window to reset the settings of the platonic solid. The properties in the **Polygon Platonic Solid Tool** window are the same as those of other polygon primitives discussed in Chapter 3.

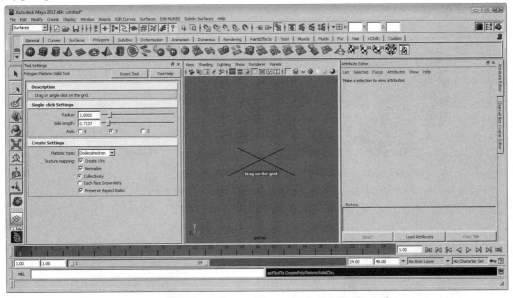

*Figure 4-17 The **Polygon Platonic Solid Tool** window*

Note
The polygon surfaces that have been created in this chapter are composed of components such as edges, vertices, and faces. You can access these components from the marking menus, as shown in Figure 4-18 (for marking menus, refer to Chapter 1).

Tip. *You can use the shortcut keys for displaying or activating various components of an object. For example, press F8 for object mode, F9 for vertex, F10 for edges, F11 for faces, and F12 for UVs.*

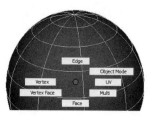

Figure 4-18 *Marking menus for accessing polygon components*

EDITING THE POLYGON SURFACES

In the previous section, you learned to create simple polygon primitives. For creating complex polygon objects, you need to edit the previously created objects. To edit a polygon object, you need to choose the components of a polygon object from the marking menu. To do so, select a polygon object in the viewport and then press and hold the right mouse button over it; the marking menu of the corresponding object will be displayed, consisting of various components of the object, refer to Figure 4-19 through 4-22. To access the various tools for editing the polygon primitives, choose polygon menuset from the status line. Next, choose **Edit Mesh** menu from the main menubar. These editing tools are discussed next.

Figure 4-19 *Vertex faces of the sphere*

Figure 4-20 *Faces of the sphere*

Figure 4-21 *UVs of the sphere*

Figure 4-22 *The sphere in object mode*

Note

1. The face components in the marking menu let you select the faces on the active object. When you move the cursor on a face, the corresponding face will be highlighted in red. Next, when you click over the highlighted face, its color will change to green, which means it is selected now. In this way, you can identify between the selected and the unselected faces.

*2. The **Multi** component allows you to select all components at a time without switching between components. To select all components, press and hold the right mouse button on the selected component, and then choose the **Multi** option from the marking menu. Next, select a face on the object, press and hold the SHIFT key, and then select the next required component.*

Duplicate Face

Main menubar:	Edit Mesh > Duplicate Face

The **Duplicate Face** tool helps you create the duplicate copies of the selected faces. For example, create a polygon cube in the viewport. Select the polygon cube, press and hold the right mouse button over it. Next, choose **Face** from the marking menu; the face component of the polygon cube will be activated. Choose the **Move** tool from the toolbox. Next, select a face on the polygon cube and choose **Edit Mesh > Duplicate Face** from the main menubar; a duplicate copy of the selected face will be created in the viewport.

Bevel

Main menubar:	Edit Mesh > Bevel

The **Bevel** tool helps you to create beveled transition surfaces on a profile curve. This option is used to add smoothness to a sharp object. The bevel option adds fillet to edges by creating new faces on the selected edge. To do so, create a polygon object in the viewport. Now, select the object and right-click on it; the marking menu will be displayed. Choose **Edge** from the marking menu. Now, select any edge on the object and then choose **Edit Mesh > Bevel** from the main menubar; a beveled transition surface will be created on the selected edge. Figure 4-23 shows a polygon cube before using the **Bevel** tool and Figure 4-24 shows the polygon cube after using the **Bevel** tool on all its edges.

*Figure 4-23 A polygon cube before using the **Bevel** tool*

*Figure 4-24 The edges of the polygon cube after using the **Bevel** tool*

To adjust the bevel parameters, choose **Display > UI Elements > Channel Box/Layer Editor** from the main menubar; the **Channel Box / Layer Editor** will be displayed on the right of the viewport. Select the beveled part of the object in the viewport. Next, expand the **pollybevel1** parameter from the **INPUTS** node of the channel box and then set the bevel parameters; the changes will be reflected on the selected object in the viewport. Alternatively, select the beveled object in the viewport. Choose **Window > Attribute Editor** from the main menubar. Next, choose the **polyBevel1** tab from the **Attribute Editor**; the bevel parameters will be displayed in the **Attribute Editor**, as shown in Figure 4-25. Set the parameters as per your requirement.

Cut Faces Tool

Main menubar:	Edit Mesh > Cut Faces Tool

The **Cut Faces Tool** is used to modify a selected object by splitting its faces along a cut line. To use this tool, create a polygonal object in the viewport and choose **Edit Mesh > Cut Faces Tool** from the main menubar. Then, drag the cursor to the selected object in the viewport; the faces of the object will be cut along the cut line.

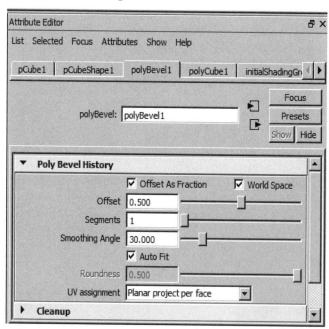

Figure 4-25 Partial view of the various bevel attributes in the Attribute Editor

Insert Edge Loop Tool

Main menubar:	Edit Mesh > Insert Edge Loop Tool

The **Insert Edge Loop Tool** helps in adding segments to the selected object. This tool is different from the **Cut Faces** tool such that the new segment created by using this tool forms a complete ring. In other words, it ends at the same point from where it starts. To use this tool, create a polygon object in the viewport and choose **Edit Mesh > Insert Edge Loop Tool** from the main menubar. Next, click on an edge; a new segment will be created on the selected object, as shown in Figure 4-26. Note that the **Insert Edge Loop Tool** works only with the objects that have quads (quads are faces with four sides). If the sides of a face are more or less than four, then this tool will not work. To set the properties of this tool, choose **Edit Mesh > Insert Edge Loop Tool > Option Box** from the main menubar; the **Insert Edge Loop Tool** property window will be displayed on the left of the viewport, as shown in Figure 4-27. You can set the properties of this tool by using this property window.

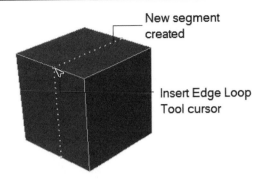

Figure 4-26 *A new segment created using the* *Insert Edge Loop Tool*

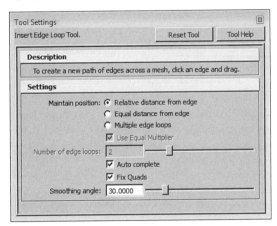

Figure 4-27 *The* *Insert Edge Loop Tool* *property window*

Offset Edge Loop Tool

Main menubar:	Edit Mesh > Offset Edge Loop Tool

The **Offset Edge Loop Tool** works similar to the **Insert Edge Loop Tool** with the only difference that it creates segments on both sides of the edges selected. To use this tool, create a polygon object in the viewport and choose **Edit Mesh > Offset Edge Loop Tool** from the main menubar. Next, click and drag the cursor to the edges to create new segments on both sides of the selected object, as shown in Figure 4-28.

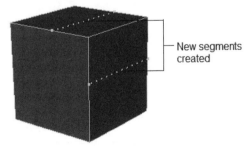

Figure 4-28 *New segments created using the* *Offset Edge Loop Tool*

Add Divisions

Main menubar:	Edit Mesh > Add Divisions

The Add Divisions tool is used to add segments equally on all faces of an object. To do so, select an object in the viewport and choose **Edit Mesh > Add Divisions** from the main menubar; new segments will be created equally on all faces of the selected object.

Merge

Main menubar:	Edit Mesh > Merge

The **Merge** tool is used to merge two or more vertices, faces, edges, or UVs together. To do so, create a polygon object in the viewport and press and hold the right mouse button over it; a marking menu will be displayed. Choose **Vertex** from the marking menu. Now, press and hold the SHIFT key and select the vertices that you want to merge. Next, choose the **Polygon** menuset from the status line. Then, choose **Edit Mesh > Merge** from the main menubar; the selected vertices will merge together. You can also adjust the threshold value of the **Merge** tool. The threshold value is the point at which a particular effect begins to produce. To do so, choose **Edit Mesh > Merge > Option Box** from the main menubar; the **Merge Vertices Options** dialog box will be displayed in the viewport, as shown in Figure 4-29. Set the threshold value in the **Threshold** edit box. More is the threshold value, more easily the polygon components will merge together, even if they are at a distance.

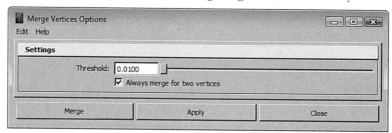

*Figure 4-29 The **Merge Vertices Options** dialog box*

Merge To Center

Main menubar:	Edit Mesh > Merge To Center

The **Merge To Center** tool works similar to the **Merge** tool. The only difference is that the **Merge To Center** tool is used to merge vertices together to the center of all the selected vertices.

Merge Vertex Tool

Main menubar:	Edit Mesh > Merge Vertex Tool

The **Merge Vertex Tool** is used to merge two vertices together by dragging one vertex toward the other vertex. To do so, select an object in the viewport and press and hold the right mouse button over it; a marking menu will be displayed. Choose **Vertex** from the marking menu. Next, choose **Edit Mesh > Merge Vertex Tool** from the main menubar; the **Merge Vertex Tool** will be activated. Now, select a vertex and drag the selected vertex to the nearby vertex, with which you want to merge it. When you drag the cursor from one vertex to the other, a red line appears between the two vertices, indicating that these two points will merge together, as shown in Figure 4-30. You can also use the **Merge Vertex Tool** for merging the selected vertex to the target vertex or to the center of the two vertices. To do so, choose **Edit Mesh > Merge Vertex Tool > Option Box** from the main menubar; the **Merge Vertex Tool** property window will be displayed on the right of the window. Now, you can select the required radio button from this window to perform the respective action.

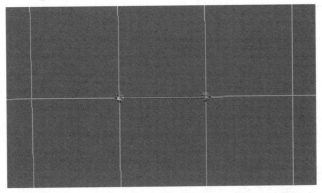

Figure 4-30 The red line indicating that the two vertices will be merged

Chamfer Vertex

Main menubar:	Edit Mesh > Chamfer Vertex

The **Chamfer Vertex** tool is used to replace a vertex with a flat polygon face. To do so, create a polygon object in the viewport and press and hold the right mouse button over it; a marking menu will be displayed. Choose **Vertex** from the marking menu; the vertex component will be activated on the selected object. Select a vertex from the object. Next, choose **Edit Mesh > Chamfer Vertex** from the main menubar; a new polygon face will be created at the place of the selected vertex, as shown in Figure 4-31.

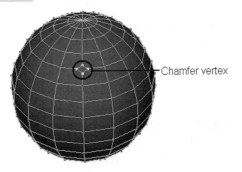

Chamfer vertex

Figure 4-31 A new face created using the Chamfer Vertex tool

Smooth

Main menubar:	Mesh > Smooth

The **Smooth** option is used to make a polygonal object smooth by adding segments to it. To do so, create a polygonal object in the viewport and then choose **Mesh > Smooth** from the main menubar; the selected polygonal object will be smoothened.

SUBDIVISION SURFACES

Subdivision surfaces are used to divide an object into regions of greater detail. These surfaces exhibit characteristics of both the polygons and NURBS surfaces. The subdivision surfaces are mainly used to model smooth objects with comparatively less control vertices.

To model an object, it is advisable to start with polygons. After getting the basic shape, it should be converted into a subdivision surface to get greater details with comparatively less control vertices. In other words, a subdivision surface allows you to take the original polygonal model and produce an approximation of the surface by adding vertices and subdividing the existing polygons.

The subdivision surfaces have some default shapes such as sphere, cube, cylinder, cone, plane, and torus. You can access these shapes from the main menubar or the shelf. Choose **Create > Subdiv Primitives** from the main menubar or choose the **Subdivs** shelf from the shelf bar to access the subdivision surfaces.

The process of creating all subdivision surfaces is the same as discussed under the NURBS surfaces and polygon surfaces sections in Chapter 3. To modify a NURBS surface, choose **Display > Subdiv Surfaces** from the main menubar; various components of the subdivision surfaces will be highlighted. Now, you can modify them as per your requirement.

TUTORIALS

Tutorial 1

In this tutorial, you will create the model of an umbrella, as shown in Figure 4-32, using the polygon primitive objects and NURBS curves.   **(Expected time: 15 min)**

The following steps are required to complete this tutorial:

a.   Create a new project.
b.   Create the upper part of the umbrella.
c.   Make the stick of the umbrella.
d.   Render the final output.
e.   Save the model.

Creating the Project Folder

Before starting a new file, it is recommended that you create the project folder.

1.   Create a project with the name *c04_tut1* in the folder *Maya_Tutorials* as discussed in Tutorial 1 of Chapter 3.

Figure 4-32   The model of an umbrella

Creating the Upper Part of the Umbrella

In this section, you will use the polygon primitive sphere to create the upper part of the umbrella.

1.   Choose **Create > Polygon Primitives > Sphere > Option Box** from the main menubar; the **Polygon Sphere Tool** property window is displayed on the left of the viewport. Alternatively, you can choose **Polygon Sphere** from the shelf bar and then double-click on the sphere icon in the shelf to invoke this property window. Enter the required values in the property window, as shown in Figure 4-33.

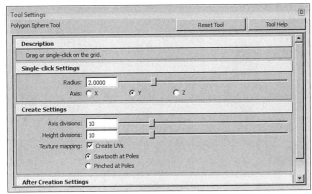

Figure 4-33 The *Polygon Sphere Tool* window

2. Activate the Front viewport. Select the sphere and then press and hold the right mouse button; a marking menu is displayed. Choose **Face** from the marking menu; the face component of the sphere polygon is activated. Press 5 to switch to the shaded mode. Next, select the faces on the lower part of the sphere, as shown in Figure 4-34, and then press the DELETE key to delete the selected faces.

3. Activate the Top viewport. Press and hold the right mouse button and choose **Edge** from the marking menu. Select the edges in the center of the sphere, as shown in Figure 4-35, and then press the DELETE key to delete them.

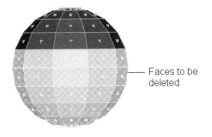

Faces to be deleted

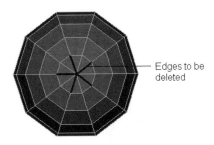

Edges to be deleted

Figure 4-34 Selecting the faces to be deleted

Figure 4-35 Selecting the edges to be deleted

4. Choose **Edit Mesh > Insert Edge Loop Tool** from the main menubar and insert the segments into circular segments of the sphere, as shown in Figure 4-36.

5. Repeat step 5 to get the final segment arrangement, as shown in Figure 4-37.

6. Activate the Perspective viewport and select the edges, as shown in Figure 4-38. Similarly, select the other edges on the sphere.

7. Choose the **Scale Tool** from the toolbox and scale all the selected edges to get the output, as shown in Figure 4-39.

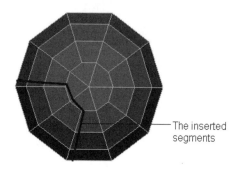

Figure 4-36 *The inserted segments*

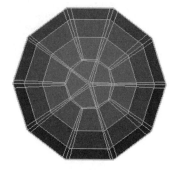

Figure 4-37 *The sphere after inserting all segments*

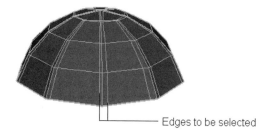

Figure 4-38 *Edges to be selected*

Figure 4-39 *Scaled edges*

8. Choose the **Move Tool** from the toolbox. Press and hold the right mouse button and choose **Vertex** from the marking menu. Next, select the centermost vertex, as shown in Figure 4-40. Next, move the vertex upward in the Y axis to create the tip of the umbrella, as shown in Figure 4-41.

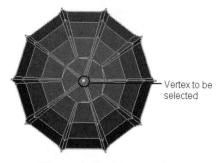

Figure 4-40 *Selecting the vertex*

Figure 4-41 *Tip of the umbrella created*

Creating the Stick of the Umbrella

1. Activate the Front viewport. Choose **Create > CV Curve Tool** from the main menubar and then create a profile curve for the umbrella stick, as shown in Figure 4-42.

2. Activate the Top viewport. Choose **NURBS Circle** from the **Curves** shelf. Next, double-click on the circle icon in the shelf; the **NURBS Circle Tool** property window is displayed on the right of the viewport. Set the value in the **Radius** spinner to **0.05**.

3. Draw the NURBS circle in the viewport and adjust it with the profile curve, as shown in Figure 4-43.

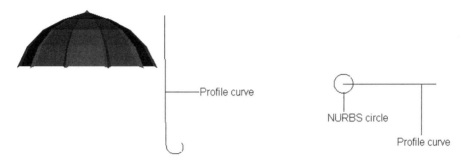

Figure 4-42 Profile curve for the umbrella stick

Figure 4-43 The NURBS circle and the profile curve

4. Activate the Perspective viewport. Invoke the **Move Tool** from the toolbox. Select the NURBS circle. Next, press and hold the SHIFT key and select the profile curve of the umbrella stick. Choose the **Surfaces** menuset from the status line. Next, choose **Surfaces > Extrude** from the main menubar; the umbrella stick gets extruded.

5. Select the umbrella stick and open the **Channel box**. Next, select the **extrude1** attribute from the **Channel box**; the attributes related to the **extrude1** attribute are displayed. Next, from the **Attribute Editor**, set **Fixed Path** to **on** and the **Use component Pivot** option to **Component Pivot**. The umbrella stick gets its final shape, as shown in Figure 4-44.

6. Invoke the **Move Tool** from the toolbox and adjust the umbrella stick under the umbrella by using the move tool manipulators, as shown in Figure 4-45.

Figure 4-44 The umbrella stick created

Figure 4-45 The umbrella after adjusting the stick

7. Select the **Polygons** module from the menu set drop-down list in the status line. Select the upper part of the umbrella and choose **Mesh > Smooth** from the main menubar to make the umbrella smooth.

Rendering the Final Output

1. Activate the Perspective viewport, if it is not already activated.

2. Choose the **Render the current frame (Maya Software)** tool from the status line; the final output is displayed, as shown in Figure 4-46.

Figure 4-46 *The umbrella after rendering*

Saving the File

In this section, you need to save the umbrella model that you have created.

1. Choose **File > Save Scene** from the main menubar; the **Save As** dialog box is displayed.

   As the project folder is already set, by default the path *\Documents\Maya_Tutorials\c04_tut1\ scenes* is displayed in **Look In** text box of the dialog box.

2. Enter **c04_tut1** in the **File name** text box and then select **Maya Binary** from the **Files of type** drop-down list. Next, choose the **Save As** button.

You can view the final rendered image of the model by downloading the *c04_Maya_2012_render. zip* file from *http://www.cadcim.com*. The path of the file is as follows:

Textbooks > Animation and Visual Effects > Maya > Autodesk Maya 2012: A Comprehensive Guide

Tutorial 2

In this tutorial, you will create the model of an umbrella, as shown in Figure 4-32, using the polygon primitive objects and NURBS curves.   **(Expected time: 45 min)**

Figure 4-47 *The model of a skateboard*

The following steps are required to complete this tutorial:

a. Create the project folder.
b. Create the board.
c. Create the axle.
d. Create tyres.
e. Save the model.

Creating the Project Folder

Before starting a new file, it is recommended that you create the project folder.

1. Create a project with the name *c04_tut2* in the folder *Maya_Tutorials* as discussed in Tutorial 1 of Chapter 3.

Creating the Board

In this section, you need to create the board of the skateboard using the **Cube** primitive tool.

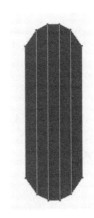

1. Activate the Perspective viewport and choose **Create > Polygon Primitives > Cube > Option Box** from the main menubar; the **Polygon Cube Tool** property window is displayed. Set the **Width divisions** to **5** and create a cube in the viewport.

2. Choose **Shading > Wireframe on Shaded** from the **Panel menu** to show the segments on the model created in the viewport.

3. Activate the Top viewport. Press and hold the right mouse button on the cube to display a marking menu and then choose **Vertex** from the marking menu. Now, using the **Move Tool**, adjust the vertices on the cube, as shown in Figure 4-48.

Figure 4-48 The vertices adjusted

4. Activate the Front viewport and drag the lower vertices upward to reduce the thickness of the cube. Next, press and hold the right mouse button on the cube to display a marking menu and choose **Object Mode** from the marking menu to set the cube to the object mode.

5. Choose **Polygons** from the menuset in the status line. Next, choose **Edit Mesh > Insert Edge Loop Tool** from the main menubar and create two new segments on the cube in the front viewport, as shown in Figure 4-49.

6. Similarly, activate the Top viewport and create two new segments on the cube, as shown in Figure 4-50.

7. Invoke the **Move Tool** from the toolbox. Select the cube and choose **Mesh > Smooth** from the main menubar; the cube is smoothened.

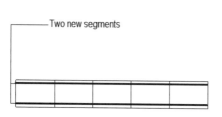

Figure 4-49 Two new segments created in the front viewport

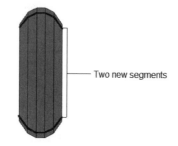

Figure 4-50 Two segments created in the top viewport

Creating the Axle Part

In this section, you need to create the axle part using the **Polygon Cube** primitive tool and other edit mesh options.

1. Choose **Create > Polygon Primitives > Cube > Option Box** from the main menubar; the **Polygon Cube Tool** property window is displayed. Set the values of the following parameters in the window and then create a cube in the viewport:

    Width: **0.5**   Height: **0.5**   Width divisions: **5**

2. Activate the Front viewport. Next, press and hold the right mouse button on the cube created for making the axle and choose **Vertex** from the marking menu displayed. Now, using the **Move Tool**, adjust the vertices on the cube to get the result shown in Figure 4-51.

    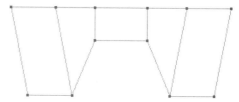

    Figure 4-51 The adjusted vertices

3. Activate the Side viewport and drag the vertices on the right toward the left side. Reduce the width of the cube proportionate to the size of the board.

4. Activate the Front viewport and choose **Edit Mesh > Insert Edge Loop Tool** from the main menubar. Using this tool, insert four new segments, as shown in Figure 4-52.

    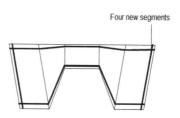

    Figure 4-52 Four new segments inserted in the front viewport

5. Select the cube and choose **Mesh > Smooth** from the main menubar; the selected object is smoothened.

6. Choose **Create > Polygon Primitives > Cylinder > Option Box** from the main menubar; the **Polygon Cylinder Tool** property window is displayed. Set the values of the following parameters in the window and create a cylinder in the front viewport.

    Radius: **0.03**   Height: **0.2**   Axis divisions: **10**

7. Choose **Display > UI Elements > Channel Box/Layer Editor** from the main menubar; a **Channel box** is displayed. In the **Channel Box/ Layer Editor** window, enter **38** as **Rotate Z** value and press the ENTER key.

    Next, invoke the **Move Tool** from the toolbox and align the cylinder in both Front and Side viewports, as shown in Figures 4-53 and 4-54.

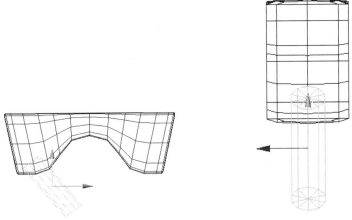

Figure 4-53 *The cylinder rotated and aligned in the front viewport*

Figure 4-54 *The cylinder rotated and aligned in the side viewport*

8. Choose **Create > Polygon Primitives > Cylinder > Option Box** from the main menubar; the **Polygon Tool** property window is displayed. Set the values of the following parameters in the window and create a cylinder in the Front viewport.

    Radius: **0.08**   Height: **0.15**   Axis: **Z**
    Axis divisions: **10**

9. Press and hold the right mouse button on the cylinder to display a marking menu and choose **Face** from the marking menu; the face component is activated.

10. Select the face marked as 1, refer to Figure 4-55. Choose **Edit Mesh > Extrude** from the main menubar; the selected face is extruded. Similarly, extrude the face marked as 2.

11. Press and hold the right mouse button on the cylinder and choose **Vertex** from the marking menu displayed; the vertex component gets activated. Adjust the vertices of the cylinder to get the desired shape, as shown in Figure 4-56.

12. Activate the Perspective viewport. Press and hold the right mouse button over the cylinder and choose **Face** from the marking menu displayed; the face component gets activated. Extrude the top and bottom faces of the cylinder; the shape of the cylinder is modified, as shown in Figure 4-57.

13. Press and hold the right mouse button over the cylinder and choose **Object Mode** from the marking menu displayed; the cylinder switches to the object mode. Choose **Edit Mesh >**

Insert Edge Loop Tool from the main menubar and add new segments to the cylinder, as shown in Figure 4-58.

14. Select the cylinder and choose **Mesh > Smooth** from the main menubar; the cylinder gets smoothened.

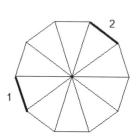

Figure 4-55 *Faces to be selected*

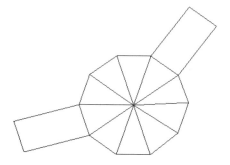

Figure 4-56 *The vertices adjusted*

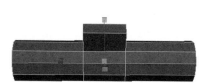

Figure 4-57 *The cylinder after extrusion*

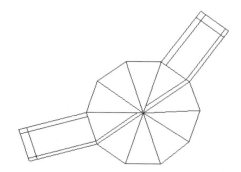

Figure 4-58 *New segments added to the cylinder*

15. Choose the **Move Tool** from the toolbox and align the three components of the axle, as shown in Figures 4-59 and 4-60.

16. Select all the three components of the axle and choose **Mesh > Combine** from the main menubar; the components are combined together.

Figure 4-59 *The axle components aligned in the front viewport*

Figure 4-60 *The axle components aligned in the side viewport*

17. Choose **Display > UI Elements > Channel Box/Layer Editor** from the main menubar; a **Channel box** is displayed on the right in the viewport. In the **Channel Box/ Layer Edito**r window, set **90** as **Rotate Y** value and then press the ENTER key.

Creating Tyres

In this section, you need to create tyres for the skateboard using the torus polygon primitive.

1. Choose **Create > Polygon Primitives > Torus > Option Box** from the main menubar; the **Polygon Torus Tool** property window is displayed on the right of the viewport. In this window, enter the values of the following parameters and then create a torus in the perspective viewport:

    Radius: **0.07**   Section radius: **0.05**

2. Using the **Move Tool** and the **Rotate Tool** from the toolbox, align the torus with the axle, as shown in Figure 4-61.

3. Select the torus and then press CTRL + d; a duplicate copy of the torus is created. Invoke the **Move Tool** from the toolbox and align the duplicate torus to the other end of the axle, as shown in Figure 4-62.

Figure 4-61 The torus aligned to one end of the axle in the front viewport

Figure 4-62 The duplicate torus aligned to another end of the axle

4. Select the axle and the torus by using the **Move Tool** and then choose **Mesh > Combine** from the main menubar; the selected components will combine to form a single mesh.

5. Choose **Modify > Center Pivot** from the main menubar; the pivot point of the combined mesh is centralized. Next, press CTRL + d on the keyboard to make a duplicate of the selected mesh.

6. Invoke the **Move Tool** and align the combined mesh with the skateboard, as shown in Figure 4-63.

Figure 4-63 The combined mesh aligned to the skateboard

Saving the Model

In this section, you need to save the skateboard model that you have created.

1. Choose **File > Save Scene** from the main menubar; the **Save As** dialog box is displayed.

    As the project folder is already set, by default the path *Documents\Maya_Tutorials\c04_tut2* *scenes* is displayed in **Look In** text box of the dialog box.

2. Enter **c04_tut2** in the **File name** text box and then select **Maya Binary** from the **Files of type** drop-down list. Next, choose the **Save As** button.

You can view the final rendered image of the model by downloading the *c04_Maya_2012_render.zip* file from *http://www.cadcim.com*. The path of the file is as follows:

Textbooks > Animation and Visual Effects > Maya > Autodesk Maya 2012: A Comprehensive Guide

Self-Evaluation Test

Answer the following questions and then compare them to those given at the end of this chapter:

1. Which of the following geometric shapes is formed by connecting a polygonal base and an apex?

    (a) **Prism**   (b) **Pyramid**
    (c) **Sphere**   (d) **Cube**

2. Which of the following shortcuts can be used to display an object in the object mode?

    (a) **F8**   (b) **F9**
    (c) **F10**   (d) **F11**

3. The _____ is used to merge two vertices together by dragging one vertex toward another vertex.

4. A _____ is similar to a hollow cylinder.

5. A helix is a continuous and uniform turn of constant radius that is generally of _____ degrees.

6. All the faces of a _____ solid are equal.

7. The **Insert Edge Loop Tool** is used to create beveled transition surfaces on a profile curve. (T/F)

8. The face components in the marking menu let you select faces on the active object. (T/F)

9. The **Smooth** option is used to make a polygonal object smooth by adding segments to it.

10. Subdivision surfaces divide an object into regions of greater detail. (T/F)

Review Questions

Answer the following questions:

1. Which of the following tools is used to add smoothness to a sharp edge?

   (a) **Extrude**   (b) **Duplicate face**
   (c) **Bevel**   (d) **Revolve**

2. Which of the following primitives is formed by an alternate arrangement of hexagons and pentagons?

   (a) **Prism**   (b) **Helix**
   (c) **Soccer ball**   (d) **Sphere**

3. The _____ face option is used to create the duplicate copy of a selected face.

4. The _____ tool is used to add segments on both sides of a selected edge.

5. The function of the **Merge To Center** tool is similar to the _____ tool.

6. The _____ tool is used to replace a vertex with a flat polygon face.

7. A _____ is a three-dimensional curve that lies on a cylinder or a cone such that the perpendicular angle is constant to the axis.

8. The **Merge** tool is used to merge two or more vertices or UVs together. (T/F)

9. The **Channel box** of the **Subdivision Primitives** does not have the INPUTS node. (T/F)

10. The **Merge Vertex Tool** can be used to merge a selected vertex to a target vertex or to the center of vertices. (T/F)

Exercises

Exercise 1

Create the model of a see saw, as shown in Figure 4-64, using the polygon primitive modeling techniques. You can view the final rendered image of this model by downloading the *c04_maya_2012_render.zip* file from *http://www.cadcim.com*. The path of file is as follows: *Textbooks > Animation and Visual Effects > Maya > Autodesk Maya 2012: A Comprehensive Guide*
                                                                  (**Expected time: 30 min**)

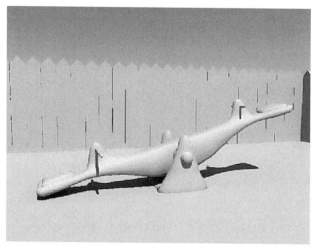

Figure 4-64 *Model of a see saw*

Exercise 2

Create the model of a clock, as shown in Figure 4-65, using the polygon modeling technique. You can view the final rendered image of this model by downloading the *c04_maya_2012_render.zip* file from *http://www.cadcim.com*. The path of the file is same as mentioned in Exercise 1.   (**Expected time: 30 min**)

Figure 4-65 *Model of a clock*

Answers to Self-Evaluation Test
1. b, **2.** a, **3. Merge Vertex Tool**, **4.** Pipe, **5.** 360, **6.** Platonic, **7.** F, **8.** T, **9.** T, **10.** T

Chapter 5

Shading and Texturing

Learning Objectives

After completing this chapter, you will be able to:
- *Navigate in the Hypershade window*
- *Use shaders*
- *Apply textures and colors to objects*

INTRODUCTION

In the earlier chapters, you learned about modeling NURBS and polygon primitives. By default, all objects were created in grey color. Grey is the default color of Lambert shader in Maya. In this chapter, you will learn how to give a realistic look to the objects by adding textures to them. For example, while creating a brick wall, you first need to apply texture to it to give it basic color and look. Next, you need to apply the bump attribute of the same texture on the wall. On doing so, the darker area of the texture will generate bumpiness to the surface on rendering.

WORKING IN THE HYPERSHADE WINDOW

Main menubar: Window > Rendering Editors > Hypershade

The **Hypershade** window consists of options to create, edit, and connect together the rendering nodes such as textures, materials, and lights. To choose the window, choose **Window > Rendering Editors > Hypershade** from the main menubar; the **Hypershade** window will be displayed, as shown in Figure 5-1. The **Hypershade** window has different sections that are discussed next.

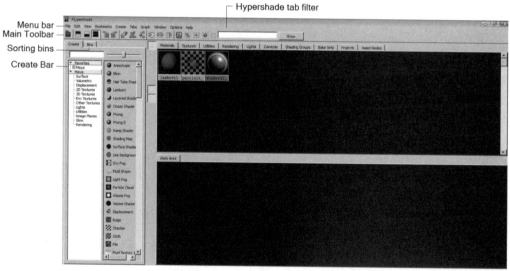

Figure 5-1 The **Hypershade** window

Create Bar

The **Create Bar** panel is located on the left of the **Work Area** in the **Hypershade** window, refer to Figure 5-1. This panel comprises of different types of nodes, which help to create different rendering effects. These nodes are divided into two categories: Maya and mental ray. These categories are further divided into sections. On selecting these categories, their respective nodes will be displayed in the panel on the right. Scroll through this panel to select the required node. Each category in the **Create Bar** panel is further divided into various groups such as surface, lights, volumetric, environment, and many more. You can also search the nodes by their respective names in the **Hypershade** window. To do so, enter the name of the required node in the search area, as shown in Figure 5-2. The render node with that particular name will be displayed in the node list. To increase or decrease the size of node icons, scrub the slider bar left and right, refer to Figure 5-2. On moving the slider to the right, the size of the icon will increase, and on moving it to left, the size of the icon will decrease. The Create Bar panel is discussed in detail later in this chapter.

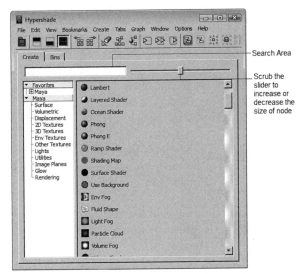

Figure 5-2 The Create Bar panel

Hypershade Top Tabs

The Hypershade top tabs are located at top of the Work Area (Upper Tab), refer to Figure 5-1. The **Hypershade** window contains nine tabs, each of which corresponds to various objects present in the viewport. For example, the **Materials** tab contains all materials that can be applied to a scene; the **Lights** tab contains lights that can be used in the scene, and so on.

Work Area

The white part of the **Hypershade** window is known as the **Work Area**, refer to Figure 5-1. This area is divided into two tabs and it displays the shading network for a selected node. A shading network is an arrangement of different nodes that affect the final look of the surface on which the material is applied.

Hypershade Main Toolbar

The **Hypershade** main toolbar, located just below the **Hypershade** menubar, has different buttons, as shown in Figure 5-3. These buttons are used to control shading and texturing in the **Hypershade** window and they are discussed next.

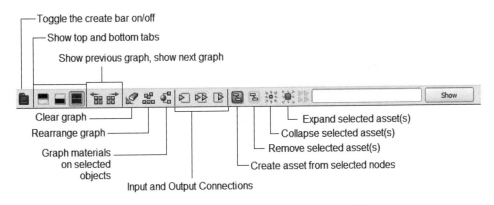

*Figure 5-3 The **Hypershade** main toolbar*

Create Bar On/Off

 This is the first button of the **Hypershade** main toolbar. It is a toggle button and is used to display or hide the Create Bar.

Show Top and Bottom Tabs

This area of the **Hypershade** main toolbar comprises of three buttons. These buttons are used to switch between two different views in the **Hypershade** window.

Show top tabs only
Choose this button to display only the top tab of the **Work Area** in the **Hypershade** window.

Show bottom tabs only
Choose this button to display only the bottom tab of the **Work Area** in the **Hypershade** window.

Show top and bottom tabs
Choose this button to display the default view of the **Hypershade** window, if it has been changed. This button is chosen by default.

Show Previous Graph, Show Next Graph Area

This area of the **Hypershade** main toolbar consists of two buttons: **Show Previous Graph** and **Show Next Graph**. As the name indicates, these buttons help you switch between two graphs. These buttons work similar to the forward and backward buttons in the web browser. You can switch from one graph to another using the **Hypershade** menubar.

Show Previous Graph
This button helps you move to the previous graph.

Show Next Graph
This button helps you move to the next graph.

Clear Graph
This button of the Hypershade main toolbar is used to clear the current layout in the **Hypershade** window. To do so, choose **Graph > Clear Graph** from the **Hypershade** menubar.

 Tip. *The **Show Previous Graph** and **Show Next Graph** buttons are extremely useful for adjusting camera in the viewport.*

Rearrange Graph

 This button of the **Hypershade** main toolbar is used to rearrange nodes in the current layout such that all nodes and networks are displayed properly in a defined manner. To invoke this tool, choose **Graph > Rearrange Graph** from the **Hypershade** menubar.

Graph Materials on Selected Objects

 This button of the Hypershade main toolbar is used to display the **Hypershade** layout of the selected nodes or the shading networks of the selected objects. To invoke this tool, choose **Graph > Graph Materials on Selected Objects** from the **Hypershade** menubar.

Input and Output Connections Area

This area of the Hypershade main toolbar displays the input and output connections of the selected nodes. You can invoke the tools given in this area by choosing **Graph > Input and Output Connections** from the **Hypershade** menubar.

 Input Connections

This button is used to display the input connection of the selected node. This connection is automatically created by the Maya software depending upon the type of node selected.

 Input and Output Connections

This button is used to display both the input and output connections of the selected node.

 Output Connections

This button is used to display the output connection of the selected node.

Containers

This area of the **Hypershade** main toolbar comprises of four tools that control the working of containers. The containers help you work efficiently in the Work Area of the **Hypershade** window. For example, if a complex shading network is used many times within a scene, each shading network can be grouped into one container to make the Work Area simpler.

Hypershade Tab Toolbar

The **Hypershade tab toolbar** is located on the right of the Create Bar, refer to Figure 5-1. This toolbar is used to control the positioning of shader icons. You can also choose the tools in the **Hypershade tab toolbar** from the **View** menu in the **Hypershade** window. To do so, choose **View** from the **Hypershade** menubar; a flyout will be displayed. Choose the desired option from the flyout. Various tools in the **Hypershade tab toolbar** are shown in Figure 5-4 and are discussed next.

View as icons

 You can choose the **View as icons** button to display shader balls as icons. On choosing this button, names of shader balls will be displayed at the bottom of shader in the Upper Tab of the Work Area.

View as list

 You can choose the **View as list** tool to display names of various shader balls in the form of a list in the Upper Tab of the **Work Area**.

View as small/medium/large/extra large swatches

 You can choose these buttons in the **Hypershade** window to resize the icons in the Upper Tab of the **Work Area**. The size of shader icons changes according to the size of the ball.

 Note

*The **Hypershade tab toolbar** is not active by default. To activate it, select the **lambert1** shader ball from the Work Area (Upper Tab).*

Sort by name

 You can choose the **Sort by name** button to arrange shaders alphabetically (A-Z) in the **Work Area** (Upper Tab).

Sort by type

 You can choose the **Sort by type** tool to arrange shaders according to shader types. For example, on choosing this button, the **Blinn** shaders will be grouped together in one group and the **Anisotropic** shaders will be grouped together under another group. Apart from grouping and arranging similar types of shaders, you can also use this tool to arrange the types of shaders alphabetically.

Figure 5-4 The Hypershade tab toolbar

Sort by time

You can choose the **Sort by time** button to arrange shaders according to the time of their creation (oldest to newest). This means that the shader created first will be displayed first, then the next, and so on.

Sort in reverse order

 You can choose the **Sort in reverse order** button to reverse the arrangement of shaders in the **Hypershade** window, irrespective of their sequence of placement in the Work Area (Upper Tab) of the **Hypershade** window.

Exploring the Create Tab

As you know that the **Create Tab** is located on the left of the **Hypershade** window. It comprises of various sections that are used to create different shading and texturing effects. Among these sections, the **Surface** section comprises of all shaders/nodes that are required to apply texture to an object. The **Surface** section is discussed next.

Surface

The **Surface** section is the first section that you come across while navigating in the **Create Tab**. By default, all shaders/nodes of this section are displayed in the create bar. The **Surface** section is mainly used to define the physical appearances of objects. If any shader is missing in the **Surface** section, choose **Create > Materials** from the **Hypershade** menubar; a flyout will be displayed. This flyout displays all shaders in Maya. The shaders in the **Surface** section are discussed next.

Lambert

The **Lambert** shader is mainly used to create unpolished surfaces. This shader diffuses and scatters light evenly across an object created in the viewport, thus giving it an unpolished appearance. It has no specular highlighting properties. Figure 5-5 shows a sphere with the **Lambert** shader applied to it.

Phong

The **Phong** shader is used to give shininess to an object, as shown in Figure 5-6. A phong surface reflects light, thus creating a specular highlight on the object which drops off sharply on the surface. The **Phong** shader has certain characteristics such as diffusion and specularity that can be used to create smooth light reflecting surfaces. For example, you can create plastics, glass, ceramics, and most of the metals by using the **Phong** shader.

*Figure 5-5 The **Lambert** shader applied to a sphere*

*Figure 5-6 The **Phong** shader applied to a sphere*

Phong E

The **Phong E** shader is the modified form of the **Phong** shader. This shader has a better control over specular settings because it adjusts the glossiness of a surface in the viewport. Therefore, the **Phong E** shader takes less time in rendering as compared to the **Phong** shader. Figure 5-7 shows the **Phong E** shader applied to a sphere.

Blinn

The **Blinn** shader is mainly used to create shiny and metallic surfaces. This shader is also used to simulate metallic surfaces. Figure 5-8 shows the **Blinn** shader applied to a sphere. It is similar to **Phong** shader with the only difference that it has circular specularity.

*Figure 5-7 The **Phong E** shader applied to a sphere*

*Figure 5-8 The **Blinn** shader applied to a sphere*

Anisotropic

The **Anisotropic** shader is used to create deformed surfaces such as foil wrapper, wrapped plastic, hair, or brushed metal. The properties of the **Anisotropic** shader change according to direction of the object in the viewport. Due to this property, elliptical or anisotropic highlights are created, as shown in Figure 5-9. Some of the examples of the objects created by applying the **Anisotropic** shader are CDs, feather, and utensils.

Layered Shader

The **Layered Shader** is used when multiple materials are needed to be applied to the surface of an object. Figure 5-10 shows an object with **Layered Shader** applied to it. It helps in creating a surface with distinct look and style. In this shader, different textures and shades are blended together to give the surface of an object a realistic look. The **Layered Shader** takes more time in rendering.

*Figure 5-9 The **Anisotropic** shader applied to an object*

*Figure 5-10 The **Layered shader** applied to an object*

Follow the steps given below to apply the **Layered Shader** on an object.

1. Choose **Window > Rendering Editors > Hypershade** from the menubar; the **Hypershade** window will be displayed.

2. Choose the **Layered Shader** from the left of the **Hypershade** window; the **layeredShader1** will be created in the Work Area (Upper Tab).

3. Choose the **Lambert** and **Anisotropic** shaders from the **Create** panel; the **lambert2** and **anisotropic1** shaders will be created in the **Work Area** (Upper Tab). Double-click on the **layeredShader1** shader in the **Work Area** (Upper Tab); the **Attribute Editor** will be displayed, as shown in Figure 5-11.

4. Press and hold the middle mouse button over the **lambert2** shader in the **Hypershade** window and drag it to the green swatch in the **Layered Shader Attributes** area of the **Attribute Editor**.

5. Similarly, add the **anisotropic1** shader to the green swatch in the **Layered Shader Attributes** area of the **Attribute Editor**

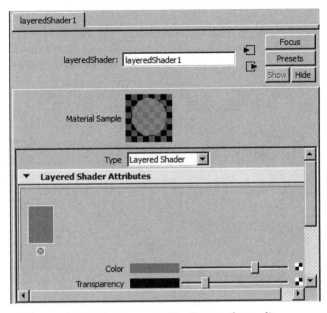

*Figure 5-11 The **Layered Shader** attribute editor*

6. Choose the cross box under the green swatch to delete swatch from the **Layered Shader Attributes** area.

7. Now, double-click on the **lambert2** shader and adjust transparency of the **lambert2** shader from the **Common Material Attributes** area of the **Attribute Editor**. Next, choose the grey color box from the **Color** attribute; the **Color History** palette will be displayed. Select the required color for shader from this palette and then click anywhere outside.

8. Finally, select the object in the viewport and then press and hold the right mouse button over the **layeredshader1** shader in the **Hypershade** window. Next, choose **Assign Material To Selection** from the marking menu; the **layeredshader1** shader will be applied to the object.

 Note
*The transparency level in the **Lambert** shader will help you see the effect of shader layer under it.*

Ocean Shader
The **Ocean Shader** is used to create realistic ocean . It can also be used to stimulate waves with different patterns in viewport. To use this shader, choose **Create > Polygon Primitives > Plane > Option Box** from the main menubar; the **Polygon Plane Tool** property window will be displayed on the left of the viewport. In the **Create Settings** area, set the **Width divisions** and **Height divisions** value to 20 each, and then create a plane in the viewport. Next, choose **Window > Rendering Editors > Hypershade** from the main menubar; the **Hypershade** window will be displayed. Choose the **Ocean Shader** from the right of the **Hypershade** window; the **oceanShader1** will be created in the **Work Area** (Upper Tab). Select the plane in the viewport and press and hold the right mouse button over the

oceanShader1 in the **Hypershade** window; a marking menu will be displayed. Choose **Assign Material to Selection** from the marking menu; the material will be applied to the plane in the viewport. Choose **Render the current frame (Maya Software)** from the status line to render the scene. You will get an effect similar to the one shown in Figure 5-12.

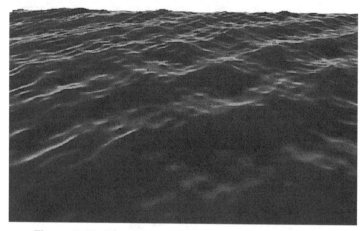

*Figure 5-12 The plane rendered using the **Ocean Shader***

You can also set the properties of the **Ocean Shader** to modify the wavelengths and other attributes related to waves. To do so, select a plane in the viewport and then press and hold the right mouse button over it; a marking menu will be displayed. Choose **Material Attributes** from the marking menu; the **Attribute Editor** will be displayed on the right of the viewport. Expand the **Common Material Attributes** area from the **Attribute Editor**. This area shows the general attributes of an ocean, mainly the colors that can be applied to the ocean, as shown in Figure 5-13. You can set the attributes of ocean in this area based on your requirement. Next, expand the **Ocean Attributes** area. On expanding this area, three more attributes will be displayed, namely **Wave Height**, **Wave Turbulence**, and **Wave Peaking**. The **Wave Height** attribute is used to specify the height of the waves relative to their wavelengths, the **Wave Turbulence** attribute is used to give variation in the movement of the waves while animating at different frequencies, and the **Wave Peaking** attribute is used to set the depth of the crests in the wavelengths.

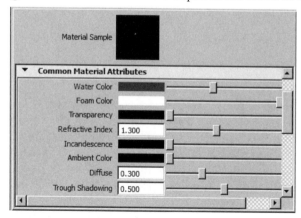

*Figure 5-13 The **Common Material Attributes** area*

Note
*If you apply the **Ocean shader** to an object and then play the animation, the shader will
animate automatically. Additionally, while using the **Ocean Shader**, you always need to apply
general lighting to brighten the scene.*

Ramp Shader

The **Ramp Shader** shader is used to apply additional control over the color of
shader with respect to change in light and direction of the object in the viewport.
All attributes related to colors in this shader are controlled by ramps. Ramps are
known as gradients and are used to create smooth transitions among different colors.
Follow the steps given below to apply the **Ramp Shader** to an object in the viewport:

1. Invoke the **Hypershade** window and choose the **Ramp Shader** from the **Create** area.
    Next, double-click on the **rampshader1** in the **Work Area** (Upper Tab); the properties of
    the **Ramp Shader** will be displayed in the **Ramp Shader** attribute editor, as shown in
    Figure 5-14.

2. Click on the color box on the right of the **Selected Color** attribute to create a new color
    node. Select the circular handle on top of the new color node to adjust it, as shown in
    Figure 5-15.

3. To add a color to the new color node, select the circular handle and choose the color from
    the color box on the right of the **Selected Color** attribute.

4. To add a map to a particular color node, select the handle (refer to Figure 5-15 for handle)
    and choose the checker button on the right of the **Selected Color** attribute; the **Create
    Render Node** window will be displayed.

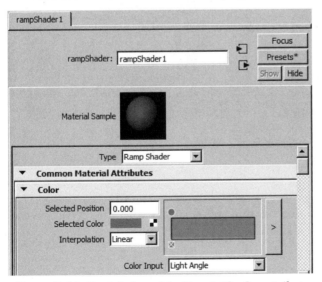

Figure 5-14 *Partial view of the* ***Ramp Shader*** *attribute
editor*

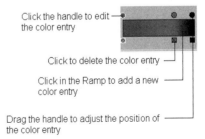

Figure 5-15 *The* ***Color*** *area of the*
Color *attribute*

5. Choose the **Mountain** texture from the **Create Render Node** window. Select object in the viewport, press and hold the right mouse button on the ramp shader in the **Hypershade** window, and choose the **Assign Material To Selection** option from the marking menu; the object after applying the **Ramp Shader** will appear, as shown in Figure 5-16.

 Tip. *The ramps in the* ***Ramp Shader*** *can be used to control particle effects.*

 Note
You can also assign different effects to an object by changing the ***Interpolation*** *and* ***Color Input*** *attributes in the* ***Ramp Shader*** *attribute editor.*

Shading Map

The **Shading Map** shader is used to apply a non-photorealistic effect on an object in the viewport, as shown in Figure 5-17. This shader works in accordance with the basic shaders, **Phong** and **Blinn**. When you apply this shader to an object, first the color of the basic shader is applied to the object and then this color is replaced by the **Shading Map** shader, thus creating a non-photorealistic effect on it. The hue and brightness of the original color affects the mapping on the object. To apply the **Shading Map** shader to an object, choose **Shading Map** from the **Create** area in the **Hypershade** window. Next, select the object in the viewport, press and hold the right mouse button over the **Shading Map** shader, and choose the **Assign Material To Selection** option from the flyout menu; the **Shading Map** shader will be applied to the object in the viewport.

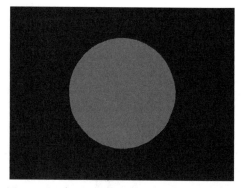

Figure 5-16 Ball with the ***Ramp*** *shader applied to it*

Figure 5-17 The ***Shading Map*** *shader type*

Use Background

The **Use Background** shader is used to merge the object created in the viewport to the image applied in the background such that the object seems to be a part of the background itself.

 Note
You can also rename a shader created in the ***Hypershade*** *window. To do so, press and hold the CTRL key and double-click over the shader in the* ***Hypershade*** *window; an input box displaying the default name of the shader will be displayed. Type a new name for the shader in the input box and press ENTER.*

Shader Attributes

Each shader in the **Hypershade** window is governed by many attributes. To view these attributes, double-click on a shader in the **Work Area** (Upper Tab) of the **Hypershade** window; all attributes of the corresponding shader will be displayed on the right of the viewport in the **Attribute Editor** window, as shown in Figure 5-18.

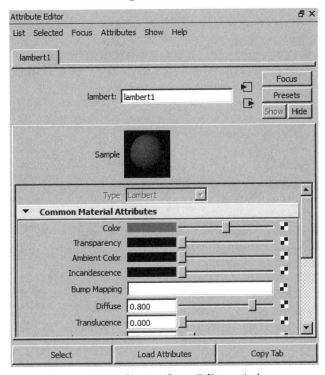

*Figure 5-18 The **Attribute Editor** window*

Common Material Attributes

The **Common Material Attributes** area consists of general attributes of an object. These attributes are discussed next.

Color

The **Color** attribute is used to assign a color to a shader. To do so, click on the color box on the right of the **Color** attribute; the **Color History** palette will be displayed, as shown in Figure 5-19. Choose a color from the **Color History** palette and then click anywhere outside the palette; the shader will display the color selected from this window. Next, adjust the brightness of the color of shader by dragging the slider available on the right of the **Color** attribute.

*Figure 5-19 The **Color History** palette*

You can also apply a map instead of a particular color on a shader. To do so, choose the checker button on the right of the slider bar; the **Create Render Node** window will be displayed, as shown in Figure 5-20. You can choose either the **File** or **PSD File** button to apply maps or textures other than the default one in the **Create Render Node** window. The **File** button allows you to add images as maps and textures, whereas the **PSD File** button allows you to add the Photoshop file as maps and textures. If you choose the **File** button from the **Create Render Node** window, the **File Attributes** area will be displayed in the **Attribute Editor**. Choose the folder button on the right of the **Image Name** attribute; the **Open** window will be displayed. Choose the JPEG file from the location on the disk and then choose the **Open** button. Similarly, add the PSD texture by choosing the **PSD File** button from the **Create Render Node** window.

Transparency

The **Transparency** shader attribute is used to make an object transparent. To set the transparency of an object, adjust the slider on the right of the **Transparency** attribute in the **Attribute Editor**. You can also apply a transparency map to an object. To do so, choose the checker button on the right of the **Transparency** attribute; the **Create Render Node** window will be displayed, refer to Figure 5-20. Choose the required map from default maps and textures in the **Create Render Node** window and then choose the **Close** button. The lighter area in the material map will become transparent and the darker area will become opaque.

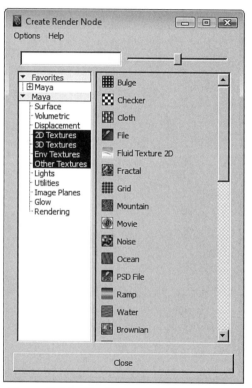

 Note
While applying transparency map to an object, the black and white part of the image acts as the transparency map.

Ambient Color

The **Ambient Color shader** attribute is used to add depth to an object by specifying the ambience level. By using this attribute, you can increase or decrease the effect of

*Figure 5-20 The **Create Render Node** window*

ambient light in the scene (you will learn about the ambient light in later chapters). To vary the effect of ambient color, drag the slider on the right of the **Ambient Color** attribute. Figure 5-21 shows the uppermost sphere with **Ambient Color** set to **Black**, the middle sphere with **Ambient Color** set to **Medium Gray**, and the bottommost sphere with **Ambient Color** set to **White**.

Figure 5-21 *The spheres showing the effect of the **Ambient Color** attribute*

Incandescence

The **Incandescence** attribute is used to self-illuminate an object such that the object creates a self-illuminating effect around it. For example, you can use the **Incandescence** shader attribute to illuminate a bulb or tube light. Figure 5-22 shows the difference between a normal sphere (left) and a sphere with the **Incandescence** attribute (right) applied to it.

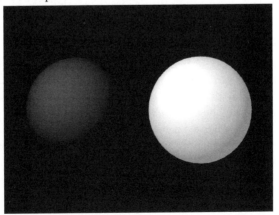

Figure 5-22 *Spheres showing the effect of the **Incandescence** attribute*

Bump Mapping

The **Bump Mapping** attribute is used to add highlights and shadows to an object on rendering. This attribute does not alter the surface of the object, but it shows roughness on the surface on rendering. To apply bump map to an object, choose the checker button on the right of the **Bump Mapping** attribute; the **Create Render Node** window will be displayed, refer to Figure 5-20. Select the map or texture to which you want to apply the bump and then choose the **Close** button. Render the object to see the bump effect. Figure 5-23 shows the object after applying different types of bump effects.

No Bump Map   Bulge Texture   Grid Texture
                     Bump Map   Bump Map

Figure 5-23 Object after applying different bump effects

Diffuse

The **Diffuse** attribute is used to apply metallic attribute to a surface. Also, it controls the distribution of light on the surface of an object. Higher the **Diffuse** value, more is the illumination on the surface when light falls on it. Similarly, lower the **Diffuse** value, more is the light absorbed by that particular surface, resulting into a darker area, especially while making a metallic surface.

Special Effects

The **Special Effects** area is used to set the parameters of special effects to an object. These special effects are visible only when the object is rendered. This area consists of only the **Glow Intensity** attribute to add glow effect on the edges of objects. The glow effect is discussed next.

Glow Intensity

The **Glow Intensity** attribute is used to add glow on the edges of an object, as shown in Figure 5-24. To add glow intensity to an object, enter the required value in the **Glow Intensity** input box, or drag the slider on the right of the **Glow Intensity** attribute. Next, choose the **Render the Current Frame (Maya Software)** button from the status line to render and adjust the glow based on your requirement. If you want that the source object remains hidden and the glow is displayed only on rendering an object, then select the **Hide Source** check box from the **Special Effects** attribute area. You can also add a light glow source to an object. To do so, choose the checker button on the right of the **Glow Intensity** attribute; the **Create Render Node** window will be displayed. Choose the **Glow** option on the left of the window; the **Glow** attribute tab will appear, as shown in Figure 5-25. Choose the **Optical FX** button from the **Glow** attribute tab; the **Optical FX** feature will be added to the object (you will learn more about the **Optical FX** and its attributes in later chapters). Now, render the scene to see the final effect.

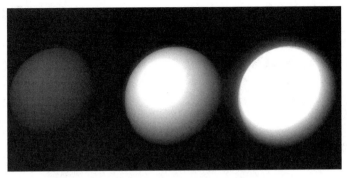

Figure 5-24 Spheres with different glow intensity

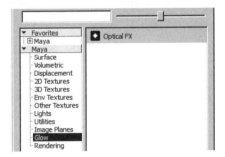

*Figure 5-25 Partial view of the **Glow** effect attribute tab*

Matte Opacity

The **Matte Opacity** attribute is used to composite or merge two layers in a scene. For compositing the layers, this attribute mainly uses alpha channels (you will learn more about alpha channels in later chapters). The **Matte Opacity** area consists of **Matte Opacity Mode**. This drop-down list contains the **Black Hole**, **Solid Matte**, and **Opacity Gain** options.

TUTORIALS

Tutorial 1

In this tutorial, you will apply texture to a box, as shown in Figure 5-26, using the shaders in the **Hypershade** window.   **(Expected time: 15 min)**

The following steps are required to complete this tutorial:

a. Set a project folder.
b. Download the texture file.
c. Create a polygon cube.
d. Create the cube material using the **Hypershade** window.

Figure 5-26 Model for Tutorial 1

e. Change the background color of the final output at rendering and render the object.

f. Save the scene.

Setting the Project Folder

Before starting a new file, it is recommended that you set the project folder.

1. Set a project with the name *c05_tut1* in the folder *Maya_Tutorials*.

Downloading the Texture File

In this section, you need to download the texture file.

1. Download the *c05_maya_2012_tut.zip* file from *http://www.cadcim.com*. The path of the file is as follows:

    Textbooks > Animation and Visual Effects > Maya> Autodesk Maya 2012: A Comprehensive Guide

2. Extract *cubetexture.jpg* from *sourceimages* folder at the location *Documents\ Maya_Tutorials\ c05_tut1*.

Creating a Cube

In this section, you need to create a cube using polygon primitives.

1. Open the **Auotdesk Maya 2012** software. By default, the Perspective viewport is displayed. Choose the **Four View** button from the toolbox to switch over to four views. Move the cursor on the Front viewport and then press the SPACEBAR key to maximize this viewport.

2. Choose **Create > Polygon Primitives > Cube > Option Box** from the main menubar; the **Polygon Cube Tool** settings window is displayed. Alternatively, double-click on the polygon cube icon in the **Polygons** shelf bar to display the **Polygon Cube Tool** settings window. Enter values in the **Polygon Cube Tool** settings window to set the properties of the polygon cube, as shown in Figure 5-27.

 Tip. *Press the numeric key 5 to change the display to the shaded mode, and press the numeric key 4 to change the display to the wireframe mode.*

3. Move the cursor and press the left mouse button to create a polygon cube in the viewport. Next, choose **Shading > Smooth Shade All** from the **Panel menu** to change the polygon cube from the wireframe mode to the shaded mode. Press the F key to zoom into the selected object.

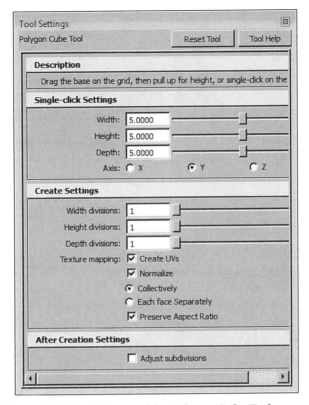

Figure 5-27 *Partial view of the **Polygon Cube Tool** settings window*

Creating the Cube Material Using the Hypershade Window

In this section, you need to create material for the cube in the **Hypershade** window and apply it to the polygon cube.

1. Choose **Window > Rendering Editors > Hypershade** from the main menubar to invoke the **Hypershade** window.

2. Choose the **Lambert** shader from the **Create** panel area in the **Hypershade** window; the **Lambert** shader named **lambert2** appears in the **Work Area** (Upper Tab). Next, press the CTRL key and double-click on the **lambert2** shader to rename the lambert shader; the **Rename node** dialog box is displayed. Enter **box** as the new name of the lambert shader and choose the **OK** button.

3. Select the polygon cube in the viewport. In the **Hypershade** window, press and hold the right mouse button on the **box** shader and choose the **Assign Material To Selection** option from the marking menu, as shown in Figure 5-28; the **box** shader is applied on the polygon cube.

Figure 5-28 Choosing **Assign Material To Selection** *from the marking menu*

4.   Double-click on the **box** shader; the attributes of the **box** shader are displayed in the **Attribute Editor** on the right of the viewport.

5.   In the **Attribute Editor**, click on the color swatch next to the **Color** attribute; the **Color History** palette is displayed. Next, enter the **HSV** values in the **Color History** palette, as shown in Figure 5-29. Click anywhere outside the palette to exit it. You can also apply a texture file on the polygon cube. To do so, follow the steps given next.

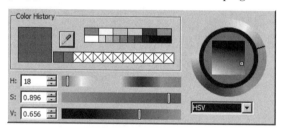

Figure 5-29 The **Color History** *palette*

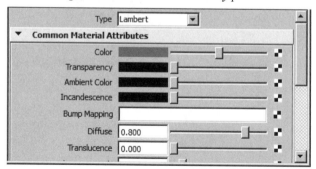

Figure 5-30 The checker button on the right of the **Color** attributes

6.   Invoke the **Hypershade** window, as discussed earlier. Double-click on the **box** shader; the attributes of the **box** shader are displayed in the **Attribute Editor**.

7.   Choose the checker button on the right of the **Color** attributes, refer to Figure 5-30; the **Create Render Node** window is displayed, as shown in Figure 5-31.

8. Choose the **File** button from the **Create Render Node** window, refer to Figure 5-31.

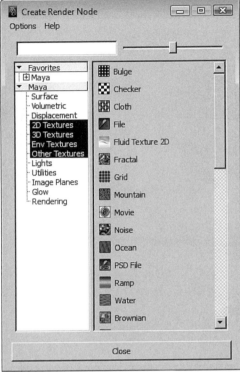

Figure 5-31 *The Create Render Node window*

9. Choose the folder button on the right of the **Image Name** attribute in the **File Attributes** area of the **Attribute Editor**, as shown in Figure 5-32; the **Open** dialog box is displayed. Next, open the downloaded file from *sourceimages*.

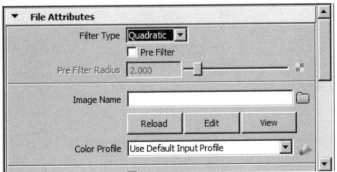

Figure 5-32 *The **File Attributes** area of the **Attribute Editor***

10. Press the numeric key 6 to view the material of the object in the viewport. The texture appears to be stretched on the object, as shown in Figure 5-33.

11. Select the cube in the viewport, if it is not already selected. Next, choose **Edit UVs > Unitize** from the main menubar. Note that the **Unitize** option is used to place the complete texture over the face of an object. Figure 5-34 shows the textured cube after the **Unitize** option is applied on it.

Figure 5-33 The default material applied on the cube

*Figure 5-34 The **Unitize** option applied on the cube*

Changing the Background Color of the Final Output at Rendering and Rendering the Object

In this section, you need to change the default background color from black to white using the **persp** camera in the outliner.

1. Choose **Window > Outliner** from the main menubar; the **Outliner** window is displayed. Double-click on the icon of the **persp** camera; the attributes of the **persp** camera are displayed in the **Attribute Editor**.

2. Expand the **Environment** attribute area in the **Attribute Editor**. Adjust the background color to white by moving the slider bar to the right of the **Background Color** color swatch, as shown in Figure 5-35.

*Figure 5-35 The **Environment** attribute area of the Attribute Editor*

3. Choose the **Render the Current Frame (Maya Software)** button from the status line; the cube is rendered and appears as shown in Figure 5-36.

    You will notice that the cube becomes dark on rendering, refer to Figure 5-36. You need to decrease the darkness of the image.

4. Open the **Hypershade** window and double-click on the **box** shader. Next, move the **Ambient Color** slider to right to increase the effect. Now, render the polygon cube again to get the final output, as shown in Figure 5-37.

Figure 5-36 *The final output*

Figure 5-37 *The final rendered cube after increasing the ambient color*

Saving the Scene

In this section, you need to save the model that you have created.

1. Choose **File > Save Scene** from the main menubar; the **Save As** dialog box is displayed.

    As the project folder is already set, by default the path *\Documents\Maya_Tutorials\c05_tut1\ scenes* is displayed in **Look In** text box of the dialog box.

2. Enter **c05_tut1** in the **File name** text box and then select **Maya Binary** from the **Files of type** drop-down list. Next, choose the **Save As** button.

You can view the final rendered image of the model by downloading the *c05_Maya_2012_render. zip* file from *http://www.cadcim.com*.

Tutorial 2

In this tutorial, you will apply blinn shader to a glass, as shown in Figure 5-38.

(Expected time: 20 min)

Figure 5-38 *Blinn shader applied to glass*

The following steps are required to complete this tutorial:

a.   Create a project folder.
b.   Create a revolved surface.
c.   Create the blinn material using the **Hypershade** window.
d.   Render the scene.
e.   Save the file.

Creating the Project Folder
Before starting a new file, it is recommended that you create the project folder.

1.   Create a project with the name *c05_tut2* in the folder *Maya_Tutorials*.

Creating a Surface Using Profile Curve
In this section, you will create a surface using the profile curve.

1.   Activate the Front viewport. Next, choose **Create > EP Curve Tool > Option Box** from the main menubar; the **EP Curve Tool** window is displayed. Select the **5** radio button. Next, create a profile curve in the viewport, as shown in Figure 5-39.

2.   Activate the Perspective viewport. Next, select the **Surfaces** module from the module drop-down list in the status line.

3.   Choose **Surfaces > Revolve** from the main menubar; the profile curve rotates at 360 degrees. As a result, a glass is created, as shown in Figure 5-40.

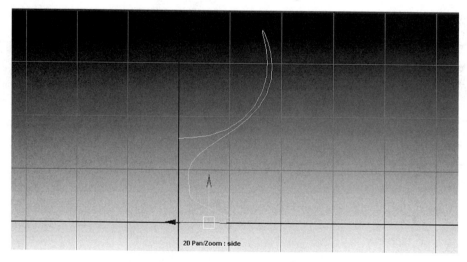

Figure 5-39 *Profile curve of the glass*

Figure 5-40 *The model of glass created*

Creating the Blinn Material Using the Hypershade Window

In this section, you need to create material for the glass in the **Hypershade** window and apply it to the glass.

1. Choose **Window > Rendering Editors > Hypershade** from the main menubar to open the **Hypershade** window.

2. Choose the **Blinn** shader from the **Create Panel** area in the **Hypershade** window; the **Blinn** shader named **Blinn1** appears in the work area. Next, press the CTRL key and double-click on **Blinn1** to rename the shader; the **Rename node** dialog box is displayed. Enter **Glass** as the new name of the blinn shader and choose the **OK** button.

3. Select the glass geometry in the viewport. In the **Hypershade** window, press and hold the right mouse button on the **glass** shader and choose the **Assign Material to selection** option from the marking menu displayed; the glass shader is applied to the glass.

4. Double-click on the **glass** shader in the **Hypershade** window; the attributes of the **glass** shader are displayed in the **Attribute Editor** placed on the right of the viewport.

5. In the **Attribute Editor**, click on the color swatch next to **Color** attribute in the **Common Material Attributes** area; the **Color History** Palette is displayed. Next, enter the **H,S,**and **V** values in the **Color History** Palette, as shown in Figure 5-41. Click anywhere outside the palette to exit it.

Figure 5-41 *The **Color History** Palette*

6. Choose the color swatch next to the **Transparency** attribute. Change the **HSV** values in the **Color History** palette as follows:

    H: **0**   S: **0**   V: **0.484**.

7. In the **Specular Shading** area, set the parameters as follows:

    Eccentricity: **0.450**   Reflectivity: **0.450**

8. In the **Raytrace Options** area, select the **Refractions** check box and set the parameters as follows:

    Refractive Index: **1.500**   Refraction Limit: **6**

Rendering the Scene

In this section, you will render the scene using **mental ray**.

1. Choose the **Display Render Settings** window button. Select **mental ray** from **Render Using** drop-down list. In the **Quality** tab, set **Quality Presets** to **Production**. Next, in the **Raytracing** area, select the **Raytraycing** check box and set the parameters as follows:

    Reflections: **10**   Refractions: **10**   Max Trace Depth: **20**.

    Close the **Render Settings** window.

2. Place a plane below the glass. Apply the **Lambert** shader and change the color of the plane. Next, render the scene. Choose the **Render the Current frame (Maya Software)** button from the status line; the final rendered scene is shown in Figure 5-42.

Figure 5-42   *The rendered scene*

Saving the Scene

In this section, you need to save the model that you have created.

1. Choose **File > Save Scene** from the main menubar; the **Save As** dialog box is displayed.

    As the project folder is already set, by default the path *\Documents\Maya_Tutorials\c05_tut2\ scenes* is displayed in **Look In** text box of the dialog box.

2. Enter **c05_tut2** in the **File name** text box and then select **Maya Binary** from the **Files of type** drop-down list. Next, choose the **Save As** button.

You can view the final rendered image of the model by downloading the *c05_Maya_2012_render. zip* file from *http://www.cadcim.com*.

Tutorial 3

In this tutorial, you will apply texture to a hut, as shown in Figure 5-43. You can use the hut model created in Tutorial 3 of Chapter 3.   **(Expected time: 45 min)**

The following steps are required to complete this tutorial:

a. Set a project folder.
b. Download the texture file.
c   Apply texture to hut.
d   Apply texture to ground, railings, and path.
e. Apply texture to background.
f. Save the scene.

Figure 5-43 *The textured scene of a hut*

Setting the Project Folder

Before starting a new file, it is recommended that you set the project folder.

1.   Set a project with the name *c05_tut3* in the folder *Maya_Tutorials*.

Downloading the Texture File

In this section, you need to download the texture file.

1.   Download the *c05_maya_2012_tut.zip* file from *http://www.cadcim.com*. The path of the file is as follows:

     Textbooks > Animation and Visual Effects > Maya> Autodesk Maya 2012: A Comprehensive Guide

2.   Extract *huttexture.jpg* to *sourceimages* folder at the location *\Documents\ Maya_Tutorials\ c05_tut3*.

Applying Texture to the Hut

In this section, you need to apply texture to the hut model in the viewport using the **Hypershade** window.

1.   Activate the Perspective viewport; the scene is displayed without texture, as shown in Figure 5-44. Choose **Window > Rendering Editors > Hypershade** from the main menubar; the **Hypershade** window is displayed.

2.   Choose the **Lambert** shader from the **Create** area. Press CTRL and then double-click on the **lambert2** shader; the **Rename node** dialog box is displayed. Enter **brickwall** in the text box and press ENTER; the **lambert2** shader is renamed as **brickwall**. Double-click on the **brickwall** shader; the brickwall attributes are displayed in the **Attribute Editor**.

Figure 5-44 The scene without texture

3.   Choose the checker button on the right of the **Color** attribute in the **Common Material Attributes** area of the **Attribute Editor**, as shown in Figure 5-45; the **Create Render Node** window is displayed. Choose the **File** button from the **Create Render Node** window; the **File Attributes** area is displayed in the **Attribute Editor**, as shown in Figure 5-46.

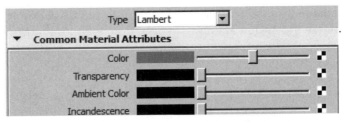

*Figure 5-45 The **Common Material Attributes** area*

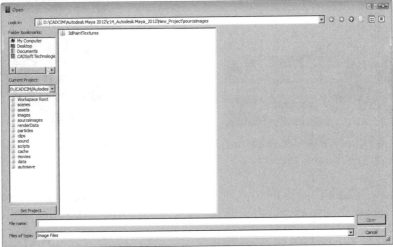

*Figure 5-46 The **File Attributes** area*

4. Choose the **Open** button on the right of the **Image Name** attribute in the **File Attributes** area in the **Attribute Editor**; the **Open** dialog box is displayed. Next, select the *brickwall.jpg* and then choose the **Open** button.

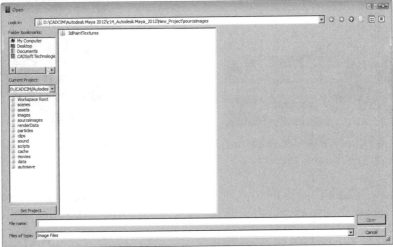

*Figure 5-47 The **Open** dialog box*

5. Press and hold the SHIFT key and then select all walls of the hut in the viewport. Choose **Show > Isolate Select > View Selected** from the panel menu; only the selected objects are displayed in the viewport, as shown in Figure 5-48.

6. In the **Hypershade** window, press and hold the right mouse button over the **brickwall** shader and choose the **Assign Material To Selection** option from the marking menu, as shown in Figure 5-49. The brick texture is applied to all walls of the hut. Press the numeric key 6 to make the texture visible, as shown in Figure 5-50.

7. Choose **Show > Isolate Select > View Selected** from the panel menu; whole scene becomes visible in the viewport. In the **Hypershade** window, choose the **Lambert** shader from the **Create** area and rename the shader to **rooftexture**, as discussed earlier.

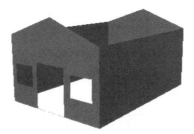

Figure 5-48 Selected objects displayed in the viewport

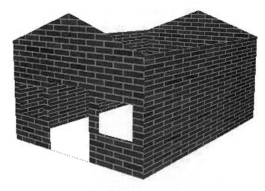

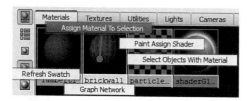

*Figure 5-49 Choosing the **Assign Material To***   *Figure 5-50 The brick texture applied on walls*
Selection option from the marking menu

8. Select the roof of the hut from the viewport. Then, choose **Show > Isolate Select > View Selected** from the panel menu; only the roof is displayed in the viewport, as shown in Figure 5-51.

9. Choose the **Open** button on the right of the **Image Name** attribute in the **File Attributes** area in the **Attribute Editor**; the **Open** dialog box is displayed. Next, select the *rooftexture.jpg* and then choose the **Open** button.

10. Again, select the roof of the hut from the viewport and activate the **Hypershade** window. Next, press and hold the right mouse button over the **rooftexture** shader and then choose the **Assign Material To Selection** option from the marking menu to get the final output, as shown in Figure 5-52.

Figure 5-51 Roof displayed in the viewport *Figure 5-52 Roof texture applied to the roof*

11. Choose **Show > Isolate Select > View Selected** from the panel menu; whole scene becomes visible in the viewport.

12. Select the door and window frames of the hut from the viewport. Then, choose **Show > Isolate Select > View Selected** from the panel menu; only doors and windows become visible in the viewport, as shown in Figure 5-53.

13. Activate the **Hypershade** window and then choose the **Lambert** shader from the **Create** area; a new lambert shader is created. Rename the new **Lambert** shader to **Frames**, as discussed earlier.

14. Double-click on the **Frames** shader; the attributes of the **frames** shader are displayed in the **Attribute Editor**. Locate the *frames.jpg* file in the **Hut scene** project folder and assign it to the **Frames** shader, as discussed earlier. Next, press the SHIFT key and select frames and windows in the viewport.

15. Again, activate the **Hypershade** window, press and hold the right mouse button over the **Frames** shader and then choose the **Assign Material To Selection** option; the material is applied to the selected object. After applying the texture, the frames of the hut appear, as shown in Figure 5-54.

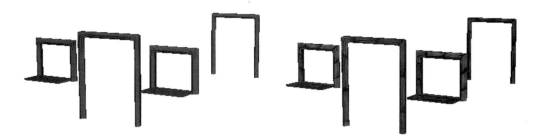

Figure 5-53 Door, window, and window base displayed in the viewport *Figure 5-54 Texture applied to frames*

16. Choose **Show > Isolate Select > View Selected** from the **Panel menu**; whole scene becomes visible in the viewport.

Applying Textures to Ground, Railings, and Path

In this section, you need to apply texture to ground, railings, and path in the viewport using the **Hypershade** window.

1. Select the ground in the scene. Next, choose **Show > Isolate Select > View Selected** from the **Panel menu**; only the ground becomes visible in the viewport, as shown in Figure 5-55.

2. Choose **Window > Rendering Editors > Hypershade** from the main menubar, if it is not already chosen. Next, choose the **Lambert** shader from the **Create** area; a lambert shader is displayed in the **Work Area** (Upper Tab). Rename the lambert shader to **ground**, as discussed earlier.

3. Double-click on the **Ground** shader; the attributes of the **Ground** shader are displayed in the **Attribute Editor**. Locate the *ground.jpg* file from the **Hut scene** project folder and assign it to the **Ground** shader, as discussed earlier.

4. Select the ground from the viewport. Activate the **Hypershade** window, press and hold the right mouse button over the **Ground** shader and then choose the **Assign Material To Selection** option from the marking menu; the texture is applied to the ground, as shown in Figure 5-56.

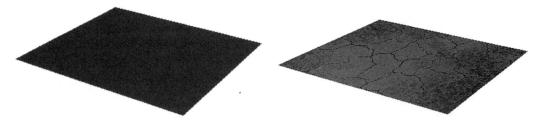

Figure 5-55 Ground displayed in the viewport   *Figure 5-56 Texture applied to the ground*

5. Choose **Show > Isolate Select > View Selected** from the panel menu; whole scene becomes visible in the viewport.

6. Select the path in the viewport. Choose **Show > Isolate Select > View Selected** from the panel menu; only the path becomes visible in the viewport, as shown in Figure 5-57.

7. Choose **Window > Rendering Editors > Hypershade** from the main menubar. Next, choose the **Lambert** shader from the **Create** area to create a lambert shader. Rename the newly created lambert shader to **path**.

8. Choose the **Open** button on the right of the **Image Name** attribute in the **File Attributes** area in the **Attribute Editor**; the **Open** dialog box is displayed. Next, select the *path.jpg* and then choose the **Open** button.

9. Again, select the path in the viewport. Activate the **Hypershade** window, press and hold

the right mouse button over the **path** shader and then choose the **Assign Material To Selection** option from the marking menu in the **Hypershade** window. The texture is applied to the path in the scene, as shown in Figure 5-58.

Figure 5-57 Path displayed in the viewport   *Figure 5-58 Texture applied to the path*

10. Choose **Show > Isolate Select > View Selected** from the panel menu; whole scene becomes visible in the viewport.

11. Select railings in the viewport using the SHIFT key. Then, choose **Show > Isolate Select > View Selected** from the panel menu; only railings are displayed in the viewport, as shown in Figure 5-59.

Figure 5-59 Railings displayed in the viewport

12. Choose **Window > Rendering Editors > Hypershade** from the main menubar. Next, choose the **Lambert** shader from the **Create** area to create a lambert shader. Rename the newly created lambert shader to **railings**.

13. Double-click on the **Railings** shader; the attributes of the **railings** shader are displayed in the **Attribute Editor**. Locate the *railing.jpg* file in the **Hut scene** project folder and assign it to the **railings** shader.

14. Again, select railings in the viewport. Activate the **Hypershade** window, press and hold the right mouse button over the **railings** shader and then choose the **Assign Material To Selection** option from the marking menu in the **Hypershade** window. The texture is applied to railings, as shown in Figure 5-60.

15. Now, press SHIFT and select railings in the viewport. Choose **Create UVs > Cylindrical Mapping** from the **Polygons** menu set in the status line to cylindrically map texture to railings (you will learn more about mapping in the later chapters).

16. Choose **Show > Isolate Select > View Selected** from the panel menu; the complete textured scene becomes visible in the viewport, as shown in Figure 5-61.

Figure 5-60 *Railing texture applied to railings*

Figure 5-61 *Complete textured scene*

Applying Texture to Background

In this section, you will apply a background image to the scene to create an environment to merge the hut model in it.

1. Activate the **Hypershade** window and choose **Lambert** from the **Create** panel; a new lambert shader is created in the Work Area (Upper Tab) of the **Hypershade** window. Rename the shader created to **background**.

2. Double-click on the **background** shader; the attributes of the **background** shader are displayed in the **Attribute Editor**. Locate the *background.jpg* file in the **Hut scene** project folder and then assign it to the **background** shader.

3. Select the background plane from the viewport. Activate the **Hypershade** window, press and hold the right mouse button over the **background** shader and then choose the **Assign Material To Selection** option; the texture is applied to the background, as shown in Figure 5-62.

Figure 5-62 *Fully textured scene with background*

4. Choose **Panels > Perspective > camera1** from the **Panel menu**; the camera view is displayed. Choose the **Render the current frame (Maya Software)** button from the status line to render the scene. The final rendered scene is shown in Figure 5-63.

Saving the Scene

In this section, you need to save the model that you have created.

1. Choose **File > Save Scene** from the main menubar; the **Save As** dialog box is displayed.

   As the project folder is already set, by default the path *\Documents\Maya_Tutorials\c05_tut3\ scenes* is displayed in **Look In** text box of the dialog box.

2. Enter **c05_tut3** in the **File name** text box and then select **Maya Binary** from the **Files of type** drop-down list. Next, choose the **Save As** button.

You can view the final rendered image of the model by downloading the *c05_Maya_2012_render. zip* file from *http://www.cadcim.com*.

Figure 5-63 The final rendered scene

Tutorial 4

In this tutorial, you will create the model of a bulb and then apply multiple textures on it. The final output will be as shown in Figure 5-64.   **(Expected Time: 20 min)**

Figure 5-64 *The final rendered image*

The following steps are required to complete this tutorial:

a.   Create a project folder.
b.   Create a model of bulb.
c.   Apply chrome texture on the bottom of the bulb.
d.   Apply texture on the glass portion of the bulb.
e.   Apply lights and render the scene.
f.   Save the scene.

Creating the Project Folder

Before starting a new file, it is recommended that you create the project folder.

1.   Create a project with the name *c05_tut4* in the folder *Maya_Tutorials*.

Creating the Model of Bulb

In this section you need to create two profile curves using **EP curve** to create a bulb in the Front viewport.

1.   Select the profile curve in the Perspective viewport, refer to Figure 5-65. Next, choose the **Surfaces Module** from the module drop-down list in the status line.

2.   Choose **Surface > Revolve** from the main menubar; the profile curve rotates at 360 degrees. As a result, a bulb is created in the viewport, as shown in Figure 5-66.

Figure 5-65 The curve of bulb

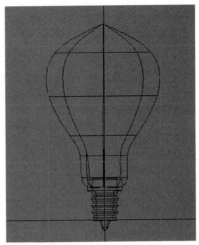

Figure 5-66 The bulb created using the *Revolve* tool

Applying the Chrome Texture to Bottom of the Bulb

In this section, you need to make the chrome texture and apply it on the bottom of the bulb.

1. Choose **Window > Rendering Editors > Hypershade** from the main menubar to invoke the **Hypershade** window.

2. Choose the **Blinn** shader from the **Create** tab in the **Hypershade** window; the **Blinn** shader named **Blinn1** appears in the **Work Area** tab. Next, press the CTRL key and double-click on the **Blinn1** shader; the **Rename node** dialog box is displayed. Enter **Chrome** as the new name of the shader in this dialog box and choose the **OK** button; the shader is renamed to **Chrome**.

3. Select the bottom part of the bulb in the viewport. In the **Hypershade** window, press and hold the right mouse button on the **Chrome** shader and choose **Assign material to Selction** from the marking menu; the **Chrome** shader is applied to the curve.

4. Double-click on the **Chrome** shader; the attributes of **Chrome** shader are displayed in the **Attribute Editor** on the right of the viewport.

5. In the **Attribute Editor**, choose the checker button on the right of the **Reflected Color** attribute in the **Specular Shading** area, refer to Figure 5-67.

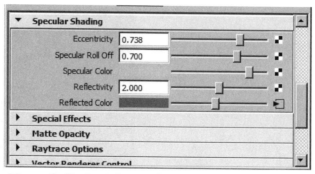

*Figure 5-67 Partial view of the **Specular Shading** area*

6. Choose the **Env Ball** option from the **Create Render Node** window, as shown in Figure 5-68.

7. In the **Environment Ball Attributes** area, choose the checker box button on the right of the image option; the **Create Render Node** window is displayed. Choose **Stucco** from the **Create Render Node** window, as shown in the Figure 5-69.

*Figure 5-68 The **Create Render Node** window*

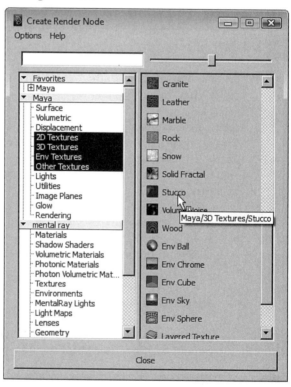

*Figure 5-69 Selecting **Stucco** from the **Create Render** node window*

8. In **Stucco Attributes** area of **Stucco Attribute Editor**, set the parameters as follows:

Shaker: **40.00**   Channel 1 HSV: **0, 0, 0.4**
Channel 2 HSV: **0, 0, 1.00**

 Note
The **Stucco** *shader is a color map. It randomly mixes two colors as channel 1 and 2 to create a final combination of colors as cloud or stain.*

Applying texture the Glass Portion

In this section, you need to apply texture the glass portion of the bulb and add glow to it.

1. Choose the **Lambert** shader from the **Hypershade** window. You need to rename it to **Bulb**. To do so, press CTRL and double click on it; a **Rename node** dialog box is displayed. Type **Bulb** in the **Enter new name** text box and choose the **OK** button to close the dialog box. Next, assign the texture to the glass portion of the bulb.

2. In the **Bulb** shader attributes, set the attributes as follows:

Color (H, S, V): **(46, 1, 1)**   Incandesence (H, S, V):   **(60, 0.451, 0.902)**

3. In **Special Effects** area, enter **0.147** as the value of **Glow Intensity**.

Adding Light and Rendering the Scene

In this section, you need to add lights to the scene and render it by using mental ray renderer.

1. Before rendering the scene, create one **directional light** in the Front viewport. To do so, choose **Rendering** from module drop-down list in the main menu bar. Next, choose **Create > Lights > Directional Light** from the status line. As a result, a directional light will be created on the grid. Set the translation and rotation parameters of directional light in the **Channel/Layer Box Editor** as follows:

Translate X: **0**   Translate Y: **2.49**   Translate Z: **-2.94**

Rotate X: **-123.2**   Rotate Y: **0**   Rotate Z: **0**

2. Set the **Intensity** and **Color** attribute of light in the attribute editor as follows:

Intensity: **1.2**   Color (H, S, V): **65, 0.658, 0.975**

3. Choose the **Display Render Settings** button on the status line; the **Render Settings** window is displayed. Choose **mental ray** from the **Render Using** drop-down list; **mental ray** settings are displayed.

4. In the **Render Settings** window, choose the **Indirect Lighting** tab. In the **Global**

Illumination area, select the **Global Illumination** check box. In **Final Gathering** area, select the **Final Gathering** check box to enable **Final gathering** while rendering.

5. Render the bulb. The final rendered image will appear as shown in Figure 5-64.

Saving the Scene

In this section, you need to save the model that you have created.

1. Choose **File > Save Scene** from the main menubar; the **Save As** dialog box is displayed.

    As the project folder is already set, by default the path *\Documents\Maya_Tutorials\c05_tut4\ scenes* is displayed in **Look In** text box of the dialog box.

2. Enter **c05_tut4** in the **File name** text box and then select **Maya Binary** from the **Files of type** drop-down list. Next, choose the **Save As** button.

You can view the final rendered image of the model by downloading the *c05_Maya_2012_render. zip* file from *http://www.cadcim.com*.

Self-Evaluation Test

Answer the following questions and then compare them to those given at the end of this chapter:

1. Which of the following numeric keys is pressed to view the object in shaded mode.

    (a) 1   (b) 6
    (c) 4   (d) 3

2. The _____ **Color** attribute is used to add depth to an object.

3. The _____ shader is used to apply multiple materials to the surface of an object.

4. The _____ **Map** shader is used to apply a non-photorealistic effect on an object.

5. The **Hypershade** main toolbar is located below the _____.

6. The _____ shader attribute is used to add depth to an object by specifying the ambience level.

7. The **Transparency** shader is used to make an object opaque. (T/F)

8. The **Lambert** shader is mainly used to create polished surfaces. (T/F)

9. The **Ambient Color** shader attribute is used to add depth to an object by specifying the ambience level. (T/F)

10. The **Ocean** shader is used to create the effect of a realistic ocean. (T/F)

Review Questions

Answer the following questions:

1. The _____ button is used to arrange shader balls according to the time of their creation (oldest to newest).

2. When you double-click on any of the shader swatches, its related attributes appear in the _____.

3. The _____ drop-down list is used to select the **Black hole**, **Solid Matte**, and **Opacity Grain** options.

4. The _____ button is used to arrange shader balls alphabetically (A-Z).

5. The _____ connections are created automatically by Maya, depending upon the type of node selected.

6. The properties of the **Anisotropic** shader change according to the direction of the object it is applied on. (T/F)

7. The **Clear Graph** tool is used to rearrange nodes in the current layout such that all nodes and networks are displayed properly in the **Hypershade** window. (T/F)

8. The **View as icons** button is used to display the default name of shader balls as icons. (T/F)

9. The lower dark part of the **Hypershade** window is known as Work Area. (T/F)

10. The **Show bottom tabs** button is used to display only the lower part of the two tabs in the **Hypershade** window. (T/F)

Exercises

Exercise 1

Create a house model, as shown in Figure 5-71, and then apply UV textures on it to get the final output, as shown in Figure 5-72. You can view the final rendered image of this model by downloading the *c05_maya_2012_render.zip* file from *http://www.cadcim.com*. The path of file is as follows:

Textbooks > Animation and Visual Effects > Maya > Autodesk Maya 2012: A Comprehensive Guide
                                                              (Expected time: 30 min)

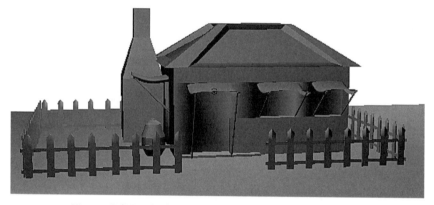

Figure 5-71 *The house model before applying the texture*

Figure 5-72 *The house model after applying the texture*

Exercise 2

Create a model, as shown in Figure 5-73, and then apply UV textures on it to get the final output, as shown in Figure 5-74. You can view the final rendered image of this model by downloading the *c05_maya_2012_render.zip* file from *http://www.cadcim.com*. The path of the file is mentioned in Exercise 1. **(Expected time: 30 min)**

Figure 5-73 *The house model before applying the texture*

Figure 5-74 *The house model after applying the texture*

Exercise 3

Create a scene and then apply UV textures on it to get the final output, as shown in Figure 5-75. You can view the final rendered image of this model by downloading the *c05_maya_2012_render. zip* file from *http://www.cadcim.com*. The path of the file is mentioned in Exercise 1.

(Expected time: 30 min)

Figure 5-75 *Model of a study table after applying texture*

Chapter 6

UV Mapping

Learning Objectives

After completing this chapter, you will be able to:
- *Use different UV mapping techniques in Maya*
- *Learn about the UV Texture Editor*
- *Use tools and options in the UV Texture Editor window*

UV MAPPING TECHNIQUES

UV mapping is one of the most important techniques used in Maya. It is mainly used in applying and unwrapping texture to an object. It helps in adding details to the model. This technique is used to apply different types of textures on a model. Therefore, it is important to use the mapping space efficiently to minimize seams and distortions in a model. The look of your model depends on the way you project and arrange the UVs. In this chapter, you will learn to use the tools and techniques needed to create good UV maps.

There are six types of UV mapping used in Maya.

1.   Planar Mapping
2.   Cylindrical Mapping
3.   Spherical Mapping
4.   Automatic Mapping
5.   Create UVs based on the camera
6.   Base plane texturing tool

These types of UV mappings are discussed next in detail.

Planar Mapping

Main menubar:	Create UVs > Planar Mapping

The Planar Mapping is used to create UVs on a polygonal object through a plane. This is the most commonly used technique applied on objects with a flat surface. When you apply this technique to an object, the projection manipulator handles are displayed on that object, as shown in Figure 6-1. You can adjust the manipulators to set the planar mapping. You can also apply the planar mapping on some specific faces of an object. To do so, select a polygonal object from the viewport, press and hold the right mouse button over it, and then choose **Face** from the marking menu; the face option will be activated. Now, you can select the face on which you want to apply the planar mapping. After selecting the face, choose **Create UVs > Planar Mapping** from the main menubar; the planar map will be applied on the selected face.

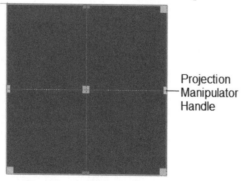

Projection
Manipulator
Handle

Figure 6-1 *The planar mapping projection manipulators*

You can also adjust the properties of the planar mapping. To do so, choose **Create UVs > Planar Mapping > Option Box** from the main menubar; the **Planar Mapping Options** dialog box will be displayed, as shown in Figure 6-2. The options in this dialog box are discussed next.

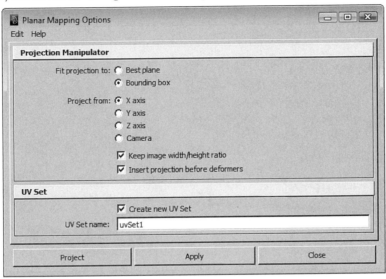

Figure 6-2 The **Planar Mapping Options** *dialog box*

Projection Manipulator Area

This area is used to set the projection of planar mapping on the selected object in the viewport. Various options in this area are discussed next.

Fit projection to

The **Fit projection to** parameter is used to fit the mapping projection manipulator on the selected object. On selecting the **Best plane** radio button from this area, the planar mapping manipulator will be positioned on the selected face of the polygonal object. On selecting the **Bounding box** radio button, the planar mapping manipulator will be positioned on the bounding box of the selected polygonal object.

Project from

The **Project from** parameter is used to project the planar mapping manipulator on a particular axis. You can select the **X axis**, **Y axis**, **Z axis**, or **Camera** radio button to set the projection of planar mapping on the selected object in the viewport. If you select the **Keep image width/height ratio** check box, the width to height ratio will remain same and the projected image will not distort.

UV Set Area

The **UV Set** area is used to create a UV set for the projection created on the selected object in the viewport. To create a new UV set for the planar mapping projection, select the **Create new UV Set** check box from the **UV Set** area; the **UV Set name** text box will be activated. In this text box, enter a name for the **UV set** and choose the **Project** button from this dialog box; a new UV set with the specified name will be created.

Tip: *You can also apply the planar mapping on an object by using the marking menus. To do so, select the object from the viewport, press and hold the SHIFT key, and then right-click on the object; a marking menu will be displayed. Choose* **Mapping > Planar Map** *from the marking menu; the planar mapping will be applied on the selected object.*

Cylindrical Mapping

Main menubar:	Create UVs > Cylindrical Mapping

The Cylindrical Mapping is used to create UVs on a polygonal object by creating a cylindrical projection around the object. This technique works best for the objects that can be enclosed completely in a cylindrical projection area. To apply cylindrical mapping, create an object in the viewport and then choose **Window > Rendering Editors > Hypershade** from the main menubar; the **Hypershade** window will be displayed. Next, apply a checker texture on the selected object (refer to Chapter 5 for Textures). Note that the checker texture helps you judge how the texture will appear in the final render. If the checkers in the checker map stretch, the texture will also stretch in the final render. Next, select the object from the viewport and choose **Create UVs > Cylindrical Mapping** from the main menubar; the cylindrical mapping manipulators will be projected on the object, as shown in Figure 6-3. You can now use these manipulators to adjust the cylindrical mapping as per your need. You can also change the default settings of the cylindrical mapping. To do so, choose **Create UVs > Cylindrical Mapping > Option Box** from the main menubar; the **Cylindrical Mapping Options** dialog box will be displayed, as shown in Figure 6-4. In this dialog box, set values of the required parameters as per your need and then choose the **Project** button.

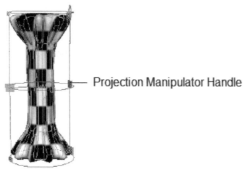

Projection Manipulator Handle

Figure 6-3 The cylindrical mapping projection manipulators

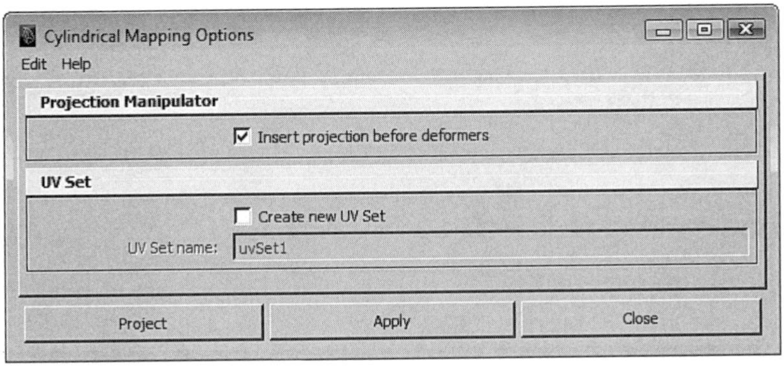

Figure 6-4 *The **Cylindrical Mapping Options** dialog box*

Spherical Mapping

Main menubar: Create UVs > Spherical Mapping

The Spherical Mapping is used to create UVs on a polygonal object by creating a spherical projection around the selected object/mesh. This technique works best with the objects that are spherical in shape and can be enclosed completely in a spherical projection area. To apply the spherical mapping on an object, select the object in the viewport and choose **Windows > Rendering Editors > Hypershade** from the main menubar. Next, apply a color shader on the selected object (refer to Chapter 5 for applying shaders). Again, select the object in the viewport, press and hold the SHIFT key, and then the right mouse button; a marking menu will be displayed. Choose **Mapping > Spherical Mapping** from the marking menu; the spherical mapping manipulators will be displayed on the selected object, as shown in Figure 6-5. You can adjust these mapping manipulators to set the mapping coordinates. You can also change the default settings of the spherical mapping. To do so, choose **Create UVs > Spherical Mapping > Option Box** from the main menubar; the **Spherical Mapping Options** dialog box will be displayed, as shown in Figure 6-6. Set the required parameters in the dialog box and choose the **Project** button.

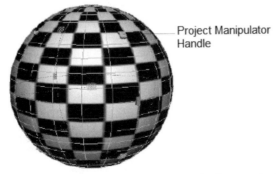

Project Manipulator
Handle

Figure 6-5 *The spherical mapping projection manipulators*

Figure 6-6 *The **Spherical Mapping Options** dialog box*

Automatic Mapping

Main menubar:	Create UVs > Automatic Mapping

The Automatic mapping is used to unwrap a polygon to create the texture coordinates. This type of mapping is mainly used for complex objects, in which other mapping techniques cannot be applied. You can also use the automatic mapping technique for the objects that are hollow and projected outward. The method of applying the automatic UV mapping technique is similar to other mapping techniques. On applying this technique, a number of projection planes of different colors are created around the polygonal object, refer to Figure 6-7. The color of a projection plane indicates the projection orientation of the object.

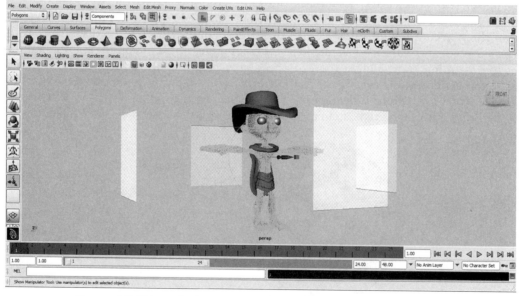

Figure 6-7 *The projection planes with the automatic UV mapping applied*

For example, the light blue color of the projection plane indicates that the projection face is oriented away from the polygonal object, whereas the dark blue color of the projection plane indicates that this plane is facing towards the polygonal object. You can also change the default settings of the automatic UV mapping. To do so, choose **Create UVs > Automatic Mapping > Option Box** from the main menubar; the **Polygon Automatic Mapping Options** dialog box will be displayed, as shown in Figure 6-8. The options in this dialog box are discussed next.

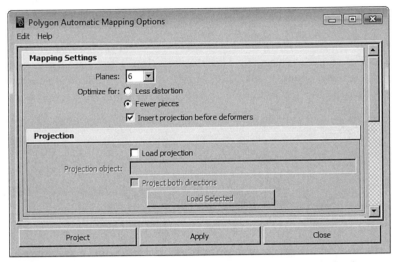

Figure 6-8 The **Polygon Automatic Mapping Options** *dialog box*

Mapping Settings Area
The options in this area are discussed next.

Planes
This option is used to specify the number of projection planes for the automatic UV mapping. You can specify the number of projection planes in the **Planes** drop-down list. Higher is the value specified for the number of projection planes, more will be the number of shells created in the **UV Texture Editor**. The **UV Texture Editor** will be explained in detail later in this chapter. Shells are different parts of the 2D texture coordinates created from a 3D model in the **UV Texture Editor**. Figure 6-9 shows the projection planes created with the value **4** selected in the **Planes** drop-down list and Figure 6-10 shows the projection planes created with the value **8** selected in the **Planes** drop-down list.

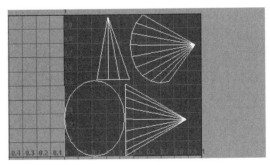
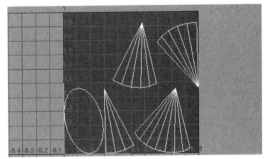

Figure 6-9 Projection planes created with the value *4* selected in the **Planes** drop-down list

Figure 6-10 Projection planes created with the value *8* selected in the **Planes** drop-down list

Optimize for

The **Optimize for** parameter is used to set the optimization of the automatic UV mapping projection. By default, the **Fewer pieces** radio button is selected as the **Optimize for** parameter in the **Polygon Automatic Mapping Options** dialog box. As a result, the projection planes that are not ideal for texture mapping are created and can result in the formation of larger shells, as shown in Figure 6-11. Select the **Less distortion** radio button to project all planes in the **UV Texture Editor** at equal distance, as shown in Figure 6-12. Select the **Insert projection before deformers** check box, if it is not already selected, before applying any texture to the object. It prevents the texture from being deformed while the object is being animated in the viewport.

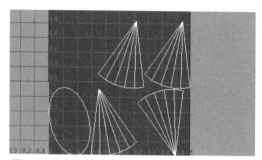
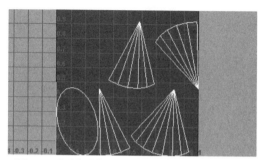

Figure 6-11 *Planes projected using the* **Fewer pieces** *radio button*

Figure 6-12 *Planes projected using the* **Less distortion** *radio button*

Create UVs Based On Camera

Main menubar:	Create UVs > Create UVs Based On Camera

Create UVs Based On Camera is used to create UVs on a polygonal object based on the current camera view. In this type of projection, UVs are created on the object based on faces visible on the view plane. To create UVs using this technique, select a polygonal object from the viewport, press and hold the right-mouse button on it, and then choose **Face** from the marking menu; the **face** selection mode will be activated. Now, select the face on which you want to apply the UVs. After selecting the faces, choose **Create UVs > Create UVs Based On Camera** from the main menubar; the UVs will be created on the selected faces.

Best Plane Texturing Tool

Main menubar:	Create UVs > Best Plane Texturing Tool

In Maya 2012, you can project UVs on a plane according to vertices of the selected face. To do so, choose **Create UV's > Best Plane Texturing Tool** from the main menubar and press ENTER. On doing so, you will be prompted to select the vertices to be projected. Select the vertices of the faces to be mapped and press ENTER; the selected vertices will be projected as UVs in the **UV Editor**.

UV TEXTURE EDITOR

Main menubar:	Window > UV Texture Editor Edit UVs > UV Texture Editor

The **UV Texture Editor** window, as shown in Figure 6-13, is used to edit UV texture coordinates. The options in this window are used to view and edit the 2D texture coordinates of an object in the viewport. Use the middle mouse button and the ALT key to move in the **UV Texture Editor** window. Similarly, use the ALT key and the right mouse button to zoom in and zoom out of the editor area.

To view the UV coordinates of a cube, create a cube in the viewport and choose **Windows > UV Texture Editor** from the main menubar; the **UV Texture Editor** window will be displayed with the UV texture coordinates for the cube primitive, refer to Figure 6-13. In this window, all tools are grouped together in the **UV Texture Editor** toolbar and are discussed next.

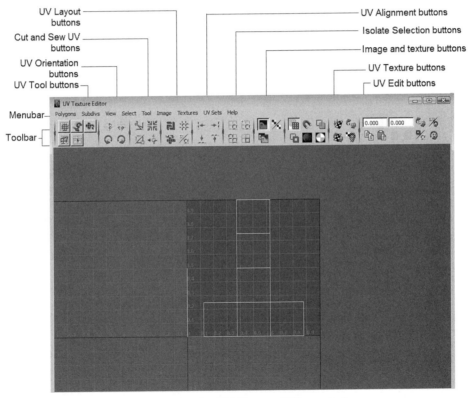

Figure 6-13 The **UV Texture Editor** window

UV Tool Buttons

The tools/options in the **UV tool** buttons group of the **UV Texture Editor** window are used to select and move the UVs of the selected object. These tools are discussed next.

UV Lattice Tool

UV Texture Editor menubar: Tool > UV Lattice Tool

 The **UV Lattice Tool** is used to create a lattice around UVs for deforming the 2D texture coordinates, as shown in Figure 6-14. To deform the UVs of an object using this tool, select the object in the viewport and then choose **Window > UV Texture Editor** from the main menubar; the 2D UV coordinates of the selected object will be displayed in the **UV Texture Editor** window. Next, choose **Tool > UV Lattice Tool** from the **UV Texture Editor** menubar; the **UV Lattice Tool** will be activated. Now, press and hold the right mouse button in the **UV Texture Editor** area; a marking menu will be

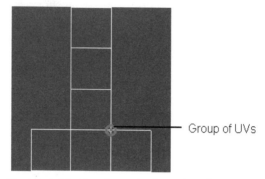

Group of UVs

Figure 6-14 Creating a lattice using the UV Lattice Tool

displayed. Choose **UV** from the marking menu; all UVs will be activated in the viewport. Now, press and hold the left mouse button over the selected UVs and deform the 2D coordinates by moving the selected UVs as per your requirement.

Move UV Shell Tool

UV Texture Editor menubar: Tool > Move UV Shell Tool

 The Move **UV Shell Tool** is used to select and move a particular shell. To move a shell, choose **Tool > Move UV Shell** Tool from the UV Texture Editor menubar. Now, select a 2D texture coordinate in the **UV Texture Editor** window; the move manipulator will be displayed on the selected 2D coordinate, as shown in Figure 6-15. Select and move the manipulator to adjust the UV shells. Now, press and hold the right mouse button in the **UV Texture Editor** window; a marking menu will be displayed.

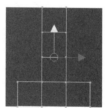

Figure 6-15 The move manipulator

Choose UV from the marking menu and select one of the UVs on the 2D texture coordinate. Next, press CTRL and hold the right mouse button anywhere in the UV texture editor window; a marking menu will be displayed. Choose the **To Shell** option from the marking menu; the complete shell will be selected. Now, you can adjust the selected shells as per your requirement.

UV Smudge Tool

UV Texture Editor menubar: Tool > UV Smudge Tool

 The **UV Smudge Tool** is used to move the UVs of the selected shell. To move the UVs, select a UV on the object in the viewport. Next, choose **Tool > UV Smudge Tool** from

the **UV Texture Editor** menubar; a circle will be displayed around the cursor, as shown in Figure 6-16. Press and hold the left mouse button and drag the circular cursor over the selected UV in the **UV Texture Editor** window to reposition the UVs of the selected shell.

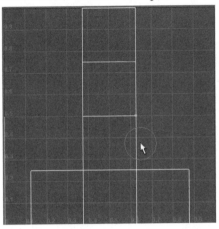

Figure 6-16 Moving UVs using the UV Smudge Tool

Select Shortest Edge Path Tool

The **Select Shortest Edge Path** Tool is used to select the shortest path between the two selected vertices. To do so, invoke this tool from the **UV Texture Editor** toolbar in the **UV Texture Editor** window. Now, press and hold the right mouse button in the **UV Texture Editor** area; a marking menu will be displayed. Choose **UV** from the marking menu. Now, select any two UVs from the 2D texture coordinate; the shortest edge between the two selected vertices will be highlighted in dull orange color.

Smooth UV Tool

UV Texture Editor menubar:	Tool > Smooth UV Tool

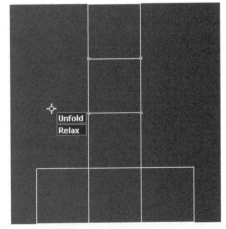

The **Smooth UV Tool** is used to relax or unfold the selected 2D UV coordinates in the **UV Texture Editor** window. To apply this tool, select the UVs that you want to unfold or relax and choose **Tool > Smooth UV Tool** from the **UV Texture Editor** menubar; the **Unfold** and **Relax** slider areas will be displayed in the **UV Texture Editor window**, as shown in Figure 6-17. Press and hold the left mouse button in the slider area, and then unfold or relax the selected UVs as per your requirement.

Figure 6-17 The Unfold and Relax slider areas

UV Orientation Buttons

The tools in the UV orientation buttons group are used to modify the orientation of the selected UVs. These tools are discussed next.

Flip selected UVs in U direction

UV Texture Editor menubar: Polygons > Flip

The **Flip selected UVs in U direction** tool is used to flip the selected UVs in the U direction. To flip UVs in the U direction, select the UVs to be flipped from the **UV Texture Editor** window and then choose **Polygons > Flip > Option Box** from the **UV Texture Editor** menubar; the **Flip UVs Options** dialog box will be displayed. Select the **Horizontal** radio button from the **Settings** area and choose the **Apply and Close** button from the dialog box; the selected UVs will flip in the U direction.

Flip selected UVs in V direction

UV Texture Editor menubar: Polygons > Flip

The **Flip selected UVs in V direction** tool is used to flip the selected UVs in the direction. To flip UVs in the V direction, select the UVs to be flipped from the **UV Texture Editor** window and choose **Polygons > Flip > Option Box** from the **UV Texture Editor** menubar; the **Flip UVs Options** dialog box will be displayed. Select the **Vertical** radio button from the **Settings** area and choose the **Apply and Close** button from the dialog box; the selected UVs will flip in the V direction.

Rotate selected UVs counterclockwise

UV Texture Editor menubar: Polygons > Rotate

The **Rotate selected UVs counterclockwise** tool is used to rotate the selected UVs by 90 degrees in the counterclockwise direction. To rotate UVs by 90 degrees, select the UVs to be rotated from the **UV Texture Editor** window. Then, choose **Polygons > Rotate** from the **UV Texture Editor** menubar; the selected UVs will rotate by 90 degrees in the counterclockwise direction. Alternatively, you can invoke the **Rotate selected UVs counterclockwise** tool from the **UV Texture Editor** toolbar; the UVs will rotate by an angle of 90 degrees in the counterclockwise direction. You can also change the rotation angle of UVs. To do so, choose **Polygons > Rotate > Option Box** from the **UV Texture Editor** menubar; the **Rotate UVs Counterclockwise Options** dialog box will be displayed, as shown in Figure 6-18. Next, enter a value in the **Rotation angle** input box or move the slider on its right to change the rotation angle. Next, choose the **Apply** button.

Rotate selected UVs clockwise

UV Texture Editor menubar: Polygons > Rotate

The **Rotate selected UVs clockwise** tool is used to rotate the selected UVs by 90 degrees in the clockwise direction. To rotate UVs clockwise by 90 degrees,, select the UVs to be selected using the **UV Smudge Tool** from the **UV Texture Editor window** and then choose **Polygons > Rotate** selected UV's clockwise from the main menubar; the selected UVs will rotate by 90 degrees in the clockwise direction. Alternatively, you can invoke the **Rotate selected UVs clockwise** tool from the **UV Texture Editor** toolbar; the UVs will rotate by an angle of 90 degrees in the clockwise direction. You can also change the rotation angle of UVs by choosing **Polygons > Rotate > Option Box** from the **UV Texture Editor** menubar; the **Rotate UVs Options** dialog box will be displayed, as shown in Figure 6-18. Next, enter a value in the **Rotation angle** input box or move the slider on its right to change the rotation angle. Next, choose the **Apply** button.

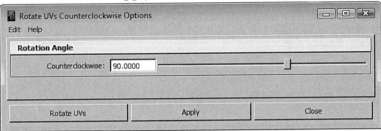

*Figure 6-18 The **Rotate UVs CounterclockwiseOptions** dialog box*

Cut and Sew UV Buttons Group

The tools in this group are used to cut and sew the UV shells. These tools are discussed next.

Separate the UVs along the Selected Edges

UV Texture Editor menubar: Polygons > Cut UV Edges

The **Separate the UVs along the selected edges** tool is used to separate the selected UVs along the selected edges. To do so, select the UVs of an object using the **UV Smudge Tool** from the **UV Texture Editor** toolbar. Next, choose **Polygons > Cut UV Edges** from the **UV Texture Editor** menubar; the UVs will be separated along the selected edges. Alternatively, invoke the **Separate the UVs along the selected edges** tool from the **UV Texture Editor** toolbar to cut the selected UVs.

Separate the selected UV into one for Each connected edge

UV Texture Editor menubar: Polygons > Split UVs

The **Separate the selected UV into one for each connected edge** tool is used to separate the UVs along the edges connected to the selected UV points. To invoke this tool, select the UVs on the selected object and choose **Polygons > Split UVs** from the **UV Texture Editor** menubar; the selected UVs will split. Alternatively, select the UVs of the object using the **UV Smudge Tool** from the **UV Texture Editor** window. Next, invoke the **Separate the selected UV into one for each connected edge** tool from the **UV Texture Editor** toolbar; the UVs will be separated along the edges and the borders will be created.

Sew the Selected Edges or UVs together

UV Texture Editor menubar: Polygons > Sew UV Edges

 The **Sew the selected edges** or **UVs together** tool is used to attach or sew two separate UVs together. To do so, select the UVs from the selected object and choose **Polygons > Sew UV Edges** from the **UV Texture Editor** menubar to sew the selected UVs together. Alternatively, select the UVs that you want to sew from the **UV Texture Editor** window. Next, invoke the **Sew the selected edges** or **UVs together** tool from the **UV Texture Editor** toolbar; the UVs will be attached together. Note that the UVs sewed in this case cannot move together in the **UV Texture Editor** window.

Move and Sew the Selected Edges

UV Texture Editor menubar: Polygons > Move and Sew UV Edges

The **Move and Sew the selected edges** tool works similar to the **Sew the selected edges** or **UVs together** tool, except that the UVs attached in the case of the Move and Sew the selected edges tool can move together in the **UV Texture Editor** window.

UV Layout Buttons Group

The tools in this area are used to arrange the selected UVs in the layout. These tools are discussed next.

Select faces to be moved in UV space

UV Texture Editor menubar: Polygons > Layout

The **Select faces to be moved in UV space** tool is used to arrange the selected UVs in a cleaner layout. To arrange the UVs, select the UVs of the 2D coordinate object from the **UV Texture Editor** window and choose **Polygons > Layout** from the **UV Texture Editor** menubar; the selected UVs will be arranged in a cleaner layout. Alternatively, you can choose the **Layout** tool from the **UV Texture Editor** toolbar to arrange the UVs.

Snap selected UVs to user specified grid

UV Texture Editor menubar: Polygons > Grid

The **Snap selected UVs to user specified grid** tool is used to move the selected UVs to their nearest grid intersection point. To apply this tool, select the UVs of an object from the **UV Texture Editor** window and right click over the **Snap selected UVs to user specified grid** tool from the **UV Texture Editor** toolbar; the **Grid UVs Options** dialog box will be displayed, as shown in Figure 6-19. You can use this dialog box to set the grid size for the UV texture editor. Set the options as per the requirement and invoke the **Apply and Close** button; the selected UVs will move to their nearest grid intersection in the texture space. Alternatively, choose the **Polygons > Grid > Option Box** from the **UV Texture Editor** menubar to move the UVs to their nearest grid intersection point.

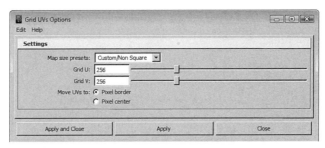

Figure 6-19 *The **Grid UVs Options** dialog box*

Unfold Selected UVs

UV Texture Editor menubar: Polygons > Unfold

The **Unfold Selected UVs** tool is used to unwrap the selected object in the viewport. To unwrap an object, select the UVs of the object from the **UV Texture Editor** window and choose **Polygons > Unfold** from the **UV Texture Editor** menubar. Alternatively, invoke the **Unfold Selected UVs** tool from the **UV Texture Editor** toolbar; the selected UVs will be unwrapped without overlapping each other.

Automatically move UVs for better texture space distribution

UV Texture Editor menubar: Polygons > Relax

The **Automatically move UVs for better texture space distribution** tool is used to spread the selected UVs mesh to get a cleaner UV layout. This tool works similar to the **Unfold** tool and spreads the UV mesh uniformly in the **UV Texture Editor** window. It helps you work better on the 2D texture coordinate.

UV Alignment Buttons Group

The tools in the UV alignment buttons group are used to align the selected UVs in the U and V directions. These tools are discussed next.

Align selected UVs to Minimum U value

UV Texture Editor menubar: Polygons > Align

The **Align selected UVs to minimum U value** tool is used to align the selected UVs vertically to the minimum U value. To align the UVs in this way, select the UVs that you want to align and choose **Polygons > Align > Option Box** from the **UV Texture Editor** menubar; the **Align UVs Options** dialog box will be displayed. Select the **Minimum U value** radio button and then choose the **Apply** button from this dialog box; the selected UVs will be aligned vertically in a straight line. Alternatively, choose the **Align selected UVs to minimum U value** from the **UV Texture Editor** toolbar to align the selected UVs.

Align selected UVs to Maximum U value

UV Texture Editor menubar:	Polygons > Align

The **Align selected UVs to maximum U** value tool is used to align the selected UVs vertically to the maximum U value. To align UVs in this way, select the UVs that you want to align and choose **Polygons > Align > Option Box** from the **UV Texture Editor** menubar; the **Align UVs Options** dialog box will be displayed. Select the **Maximum U value** radio button and then choose the **Apply** button from this dialog box; the selected UVs will be aligned vertically in a straight line. Alternatively, choose the **Align selected UVs to maximum U** value from the **UV Texture Editor** toolbar to align the selected UVs.

Align selected UVs to Minimum V value

UV Texture Editor menubar:	Polygons > Align

The **Align selected UVs to minimum V** value tool is used to align the selected UVs horizontally to the minimum V value. To align UVs in this way, select the UVs to align and choose **Polygons > Align > Option Box** from the **UV Texture Editor** menubar; the **Align UVs Options** dialog box will be displayed. Select the **Minimum V value** radio button and then choose the **Apply** button from this dialog box; the selected UVs will be aligned horizontally in a straight line. Alternatively, choose the **Align selected UVs** to **minimum V value** from the **UV Texture Editor** toolbar to align the selected UVs.

Align selected UVs to Maximum V value

UV Texture Editor menubar:	Polygons > Align

The **Align selected UVs to maximum V** value tool is used to align the selected UVs horizontally to the maximum V value. To do so, select the UVs that you want to align and choose **Polygons > Align > Option Box** from the **UV Texture Editor** menubar; the **Align UVs Options** dialog box will be displayed. Select the **Maximum V value** radio button and then choose the **Apply** button from this dialog box; the selected UVs will be aligned horizontally in a straight line. Alternatively, choose the **Align selected UVs to maximum V** value from the **UV Texture Editor** toolbar to align the selected UVs.

Isolate Selection Buttons Group

The tools in the **Isolate selection** buttons group are used to work on a particular UV independently. You can use these tools to hide the remaining UVs. The tools in this group are discussed next.

Toggle Isolate Select mode

UV Texture Editor menubar:	View > Isolate Select > View Set

The **Toggle isolate select mode** tool is used to toggle between the selected UVs and the isolated UVs in the **UV Texture Editor** window. To do so, select the UVs of the object from the **UV Texture Editor** window and choose **View > Isolate Select > View Set** from the **UV Texture Editor** menubar to switch between the selected UVs and the isolated

UVs. Alternatively, invoke the **Toggle isolate select mode** tool from the **UV Texture Editor** toolbar to switch between the selected UVs and the isolated UVs.

Add Selected UVs to the Isolate Select set

UV Texture Editor menubar: View > Isolate Select > Add Selected

The **Add selected UVs to the isolate select set** tool is used to add the selected UVs to the isolated UVs group. Select the UVs from the 2D object in the **UV Texture Editor** window, as well as, the UVs that you want to add to the isolate select set from the **UV Texture Editor** window. Now, choose **View > Isolate Select > Add Selected** from the **UV Texture Editor** menubar; the selected UVs will be added to the isolate select set. Alternatively, invoke the **Add selected UVs to the isolate select set** tool from the **UV Texture Editor** toolbar to add the selected UVs to the isolated UVs group.

Remove Selected UVs to the Isolate Select set

UV Texture Editor menubar: View > Isolate Select > Remove Selected

The **Remove selected UVs to the isolate select set** tool is used to remove the selected UVs from the isolated UVs group. To do so, select the UVs from the 2D object in the **UV Texture Editor** window as well as the UVs that you want to remove from the isolate select set from the **UV Texture Editor** window. Now, choose **View > Isolate Select > Remove Selected** from the **UV Texture Editor** menubar; the selected UVs will be removed from the isolate select set. Alternatively, invoke the **Remove selected UVs to the isolate select set** tool from the **UV Texture Editor** toolbar to remove the selected UVs from the isolated UVs group.

Remove all UVs of the Selected object from the isolate select set

UV Texture Editor menubar: View > Isolate Select > Remove All

The **Remove all UVs of the selected object from the Isolate select set** tool is used to delete the existing isolated UV set and form a new UV set in the **UV Texture Editor** window. To do so, choose **View > Isolate Select > Remove All** from the **UV Texture Editor** menubar; the existing isolated UV set will be deleted. Alternatively, invoke the **Remove all UVs of the selected object from the isolate select set** tool in the **UV Texture Editor** toolbar to remove the isolated UV set.

Image and Texture Buttons Group

The tools in the image and texture buttons group are used to switch the texture images on/off and adjust their appearances. The tools in this group are discussed next.

Display Image on/off

UV Texture Editor menubar: Image > Display Image

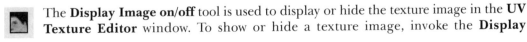

The **Display Image on/off** tool is used to display or hide the texture image in the **UV Texture Editor** window. To show or hide a texture image, invoke the **Display**

Image on/off tool from the **UV Texture Editor** toolbar. Alternatively, choose **Image > Display Image** from the **UV Texture Editor** menubar to invoke this tool.

Toggle filtered image on/off

UV Texture Editor menubar:	Image > Display Unfiltered

The **Toggle filtered image on/off** tool is used to toggle the background image between the hardware rendering pixels and the sharply defined pixels. To show or hide the background image, invoke the **Display Image on/off** tool from the **UV Texture Editor** toolbar. Alternatively, choose **Image > Display Unfiltered** from the **UV Texture Editor** menubar to toggle the background image.

Dim Image on/off

UV Texture Editor menubar:	Image > Dim Image

The **Dim Image on/off** tool is used to reduce the brightness of the background image. Choose **Image > Dim Image** from the **UV Texture Editor** menubar; the brightness of the currently displayed background image in the **UV Texture Editor** window will be reduced. Alternatively, invoke the **Dim Image on/off** tool from the **UV Texture Editor** toolbar to invoke this tool.

Show/Hide the Display Icons Buttons Group

The tools in the **Show/Hide the Display Icons Buttons** group are used to adjust alpha channels and other texture properties. These tools are discussed next.

View grid on/off

UV Texture Editor menubar:	View > Grid

The **View grid on/off** tool is used to show or hide the grid in the **UV Texture Editor** window. Choose **View > Grid** from the **UV Texture Editor** menubar to show or hide the grid. Alternatively, choose the **View grid on/off** button from the **UV Texture Editor** menubar to show or hide the grid.

Pixel snap on/off

UV Texture Editor menubar:	View > Grid

The **Pixel snap on/off** tool is used to snap the selected UVs to pixel boundaries. Choose **Image > Pixel Snap** from the **UV Texture Editor** menubar to snap the selected UVs to the boundaries. Alternatively, choose the **Pixel snap on/off** button from the **UV Texture Editor** toolbar to snap the selected UVs to the boundaries.

Toggle shaded UV display

The **Toggle shaded UV display** tool is a toggle button that is used to provide transparency to the selected UV shells such that you can differentiate between the overlapping UVs in the **UV Texture Editor** window. Invoke this tool from the **UV Texture Editor** toolbar to provide transparency to the selected UV shells.

Toggle the display of texture borders for the active mesh

The **Toggle the display of texture borders for the active mesh** tool is a toggle button that is used to display the texture borders on the UV shells. To do so, invoke this tool from the **UV Texture Editor** toolbar; the border of UV texture coordinates will be displayed with a thick line.

Display RGB Channels

UV Texture Editor menubar:	Image > Display RGB Channels

The **Display RGB Channels** tool is used to display the color channels. To display the channels, choose **Image > Display RGB Channels** from the **UV Texture Editor** menubar; the RGB channels of the selected texture image will be displayed.

Display Alpha Channel

UV Texture Editor menubar:	Image > Display Alpha Channel

The **Display Alpha Channel** tool is used to display the transparency channel. To display the channel, choose **Image > Display Alpha Channel** from the **UV Texture Editor**. As a result, the alpha channels of the selected texture image will be displayed.

UV Texturing Buttons Group

The tools in the UV Texturing Buttons group are used to perform functions such as baking textures, updating texture group, and so on. Texture baking is a method to render multiple materials and shaders including scene lighting, shadows, and complicated materials into a single texture. The tools in this group are discussed next.

UV Texture Editor baking on/off

UV Texture Editor menubar:	Image > UV Texture Editor Baking

The **UV Texture Editor baking on/off** tool is used to bake textures and store them in the virtual memory of the software. Choose **Image > UV Texture Editor Baking** option from the **UV Texture Editor** menubar to bake the textures. Alternatively, invoke the **UV Texture Editor baking on/off** button from the **UV Texture Editor** toolbar to bake the textures and store them in the virtual memory of the software.

Update PSD networks

UV Texture Editor menubar:	Image > Update PSD Networks

The **Update PSD networks** tool is used to update the current PSD network used in the scene. Modify the PSD texture in photoshop and choose **Image > Update PSD Networks** tool from the **UV Texture Editor** menubar to update the PSD network. Alternatively, invoke the **Update PSD Networks** tool from the **UV Texture Editor** toolbar; the PSD network will be updated automatically.

Force editor texture rebake

The **Force editor texture rebake** tool is used to rebake the selected texture.

Use image ratio on/off

UV Texture Editor menubar:	Image > Use Image Ratio

The **Use image ratio on/off** tool is a toggle button that is used to adjust the ratio of the selected image texture in the **UV Texture Editor** window. To use this tool, choose **Image > Use Image Ratio** from the **UV Texture Editor** menubar to adjust the ratio of image texture. Alternatively, invoke the **Use image ratio on/off** button from the **UV Texture Editor** toolbar.

UV Edit Buttons Group

The tools in this group are used to edit the UVs of the selected object. The tools in this area are discussed next.

U Coordinate, V Coordinate

0.000	0.000

The **U Coordinate, V Coordinate** edit boxes are used to set the U and V coordinates of the selected UV shell in the **UV Texture Editor** window. Select the UV shell and enter the UV coordinate values in the corresponding input boxes in the toolbar. Then, press ENTER.

Refresh the current UV values

The **Refresh the current UV values** tool is used to update the UV values of the selected UV shells. On selecting a particular UV, the U and V coordinate values are displayed in the input area. However, on moving the UVs, the values do not change dynamically in the input area. You can invoke the **Refresh the current UV values** tool from the **UV Texture Editor** window to update the UV coordinates.

UV Transformation Entry

The **UV Transformation Entry** tool is used to change the entry mode of the UV coordinates between absolute and relative values. For relative and absolute values, refer to the earlier chapters.

Copy

The **Copy** tool is used to copy colors, UVs, or shaders from the face of an object to the clipboard.

Paste

The **Paste** tool is used to paste colors, UVs, or shaders from a face to the clipboard.

Paste U to selected UVs

The **Paste U to selected UVs** tool is used to paste only the U values to the selected UV points.

Paste V to selected UVs

 The **Paste V to selected UVs** tool is used to paste only the V values to the selected UV points.

Copy/paste faces or UVs

 The **Copy/paste faces or UVs** tool is used to make the **Copy** and **Paste** buttons active in the **UV Texture Editor** toolbar. Invoke the **Copy/paste faces or UVs** tool from the **UV Texture Editor** toolbar; the **Paste U to selected UVs** and **Paste V to selected UVs** tools will be activated.

Cycle UVs

 The **Cycle UVs** tool is used to cycle the U and V values of the selected faces counterclockwise.

TUTORIALS

Tutorial 1

In this tutorial, you will unwrap a polygon cube to create the model of a dice.

(Expected time:15 min)

The following steps are required to complete this tutorial:

a. Set a project folder.
b. Download the texture file.
b. Create a polygon cube.
c. Fit the 2D UV coordinates into the texture.
d. Change the background color of the final output at rendering and render the object.
e. Save the file.

Setting the Project Folder

Before starting a new file, it is recommended that you set the project folder.

1. Set a project with the name *c06_tut1* in the folder *Maya_Tutorials*.

Downloading the Texture File

In this section, you need to download the texture file.

1. Download the *c06_maya_2012_tut.zip* file from *http://www.cadcim.com*. The path of the file is as follows:

    Textbooks > Animation and Visual Effects > Maya> Autodesk Maya 2012: A Comprehensive Guide

2. Extract *dicetexture.jpg* to **sourceimages** folder at the location *\Documents\ Maya_Tutorials\ c06_tut1*.

Creating a Polygon Cube

In this section, you need to create a polygon cube and use the **UV Texture Editor** window to set the 2D texture coordinates.

1. Choose **Create > Polygon Primitives > Cube** from the main menubar and create a cube in the viewport. Press 5 on the keyboard to switch the polygon cube from the wireframe mode to the object mode.

2. Press the F key on the keyboard to zoom in on the polygon cube in the viewport.

Fitting 2D UV Coordinates into the Texture

In this section, you need to apply the dice texture to the polygon cube and fit the 2D UV coordinates into the dice texture.

1. Activate the Perspective viewport. Choose **Window > Rendering Editors > Hypershade** from the main menubar; the **Hypershade** window is displayed.

2. Choose the **Blinn** shader from the **Hypershade** window; a blinn shader ball is created in the work area. Press and hold the CTRL key and double-click on the blinn shader in the **Materials** tab; the **Rename node** dialog box is displayed, as shown in Figure 6-20. Change the name of the blinn shader to **dice** in the **Enter new name** input area and choose the **OK** button.

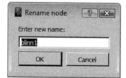

*Figure 6-20 The **Rename**
node dialog box*

3. Double-click on the **dice** shader ball; the **Attribute Editor** displaying the properties of the **dice** shader on the right side of the viewport. This helps you adjust the properties of the **dice** shader. Expand the **Common Material Attributes** tab from the **Attribute Editor**.

4. Click on the checker box beside the **Color** attribute in the **Common Material Attributes** window, as shown in Figure 6-21; the **Create Render Node** window is displayed. Next, choose the **File** button; the **File Attributes** area is displayed in the attribute editor. Choose the open folder icon on the right of the **Image Name** attribute area; the **Open** window is displayed. Open the *dicetexture.jpg* file from */Documents/C06_tut1/sourceimages*.

5. Select the polygon cube from the viewport. Choose from the main menubar to assign the texture to the cube in the viewport. Press and hold the right mouse button over the **dice** shader; a marking menu is displayed. Next, choose the **Assign Material To Selection** option from the marking menu; the dice texture is applied to the polygon cube. Press 6 on the keyboard to view the texture in the viewport, if it is not visible by default. Figure 6-22 shows the polygon cube with the dice texture applied.

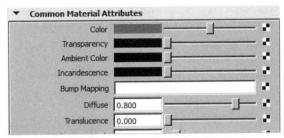

Figure 6-21   *The* ***Common Material Attributes*** *area*

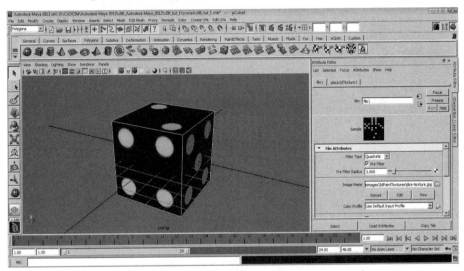

Figure 6-22   *The dice texture applied to the polygon cube*

6.   Select the cube and then choose **Window > UV Texture Editor** from the main menubar; the **UV Texture Editor** window is displayed. Next, choose **View > Grid** from the **UV Texture Editor** menubar; the grids becomes invisible and the texture is displayed, as shown in Figure 6-23.

7.   Press and hold the right mouse button in the empty space of the window; a marking menu is displayed. Choose **UV** from the marking menu and marquee select all UVs of the 2D UV texture coordinate. Now, invoke the **Scale Tool** from the toolbox to scale the selected UVs. Figure 6-24 shows the selected 2D UV texture coordinates after scaling them. The entire dice texture is mapped on to the polygon cube, except the two UVs that are not covered in the V area.

Note
The texture within the 2D UV coordinates in the ***UV Texture Editor*** *will be visible only on the object in the viewport. Scale the UVs of the 2D coordinates in the* ***UV Texture Editor*** *window to fit the texture.*

8.   Press and hold the right mouse button in the empty space of the window; a marking menu is displayed. Next, choose **Edge** from the marking menu. Next, select edge **12** from the

UV Texture Editor window, refer to Figure 6-25. Now, choose **Polygons > Cut UV Edges** from the **UV Texture Editor** main menubar to cut the selected UVs. Select edge **4** from this window and choose **Polygons > Move and Sew UV Edges** from the **UV Texture Editor** main menubar to cut the selected edge; the face corresponding to the selected edge of the 2D texture coordinate is moved and sewed. In this way, the 2D UV coordinate will partially map over the texture, as shown in Figure 6-26.

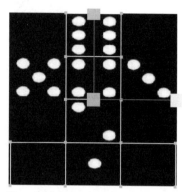

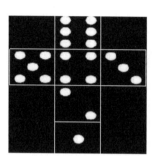

Figure 6-23 The texture

Figure 6-24 The 2D UV texture coordinates after scaling

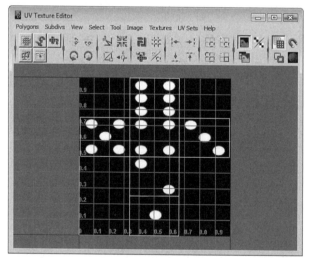

*Figure 6-25 Edge **12** to be selected from the **UV Texture Editor** window*

9. Select edge **13** from the **UV Texture Editor** window, refer to Figure 6-25. Choose **Polygons > Cut UV Edges** from the **UV Texture Editor** main menubar to cut the selected edge. Now, select edge **6**, refer to Figure 6-25, and choose **Polygons > Move and Sew UV Edges** from the main menubar, as shown in Figure 6-26; the face corresponding to the selected edge of the 2D texture coordinate is moved and sewed to match the 2D UV coordinate completely with the texture, as shown in Figure 6-27.

10. Close the **UV Texture Editor** window. Now, you can dolly in the perspective viewport to check if the texture is properly applied on the polygon cube.

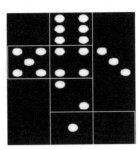

Figure 6-26 *The 2D UV coordinate partially mapped over the texture*

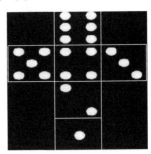

Figure 6-27 *The 2D UV coordinate completely mapped over the texture*

Changing the Background Color of the Output at Rendering

In this section, you need to change the background color of the rendered view.

1. Choose **Window > Outliner** from the main menubar; the **Outliner** window is displayed. Double-click on the **persp** camera in the **Outliner** window; the **Attribute Editor** displaying the properties of the perspective camera is displayed on the right of the viewport.

2. Click on the down arrow of the **Environment** tab to expand the tab. Now, move the **Background Color** slider to change the background color of the environment to white.

3. Choose the **Render the current Frame (Maya Software)** button from the status line to render the scene; the **Render View** window is displayed, as shown in Figure 6-28. This window displays the final output of the textured dice.

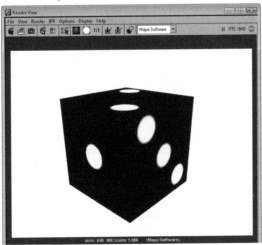

Figure 6-28 *The **Render View** window with the final rendered image*

Saving the Model

In this section, you need to save the dice model that you have created.

1. Choose **File > Save Scene** from the main menubar; the **Save As** dialog box is displayed.

   As the project folder is already set, by default the path *Documents\\Maya_Tutorials\\c06_tut1\\ scenes* is displayed in **Look In** text box of the dialog box.

2. Enter **c06_tut1** in the **File name** text box and then select **Maya Binary** from the **Files of type** drop-down list. Next, choose the **Save As** button.

You can view the final rendered image of the model by downloading the *c06_Maya_2012_render.zip* file from *http://www.cadcim.com*.

Tutorial 2

In this tutorial, you will create a model of an eyeball, as shown in Figure 6-29.

(Expected time:15 min)

The following steps are required to complete this tutorial:

a. Create a project folder.
b. Create a NURBS sphere.
c. Assign material to the sphere.
d. Change the background color of the final output at rendering and render the object.
e. Save the file.

Creating the Project Folder

Before starting a new file, it is recommended that you create the project folder.

1. Create a project with the name *c06_tut2* in the folder *Maya_Tutorials*.

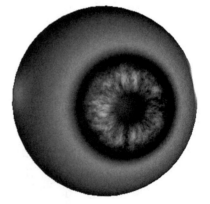

Figure 6-29 Model of an eyeball

Creating the NURBS Sphere

In this section, you need to create the NURBS sphere for eyeball.

1. Choose **Create > NURBS Primitives > Sphere** from the main menubar and click in the viewport to create a NURBS sphere. Press 5 to change the view to shaded mode.

2. Select the sphere. Choose **Display > UI Elements > Channel Box/Layer Editor** from the main menubar; a channel box is displayed on the right of the viewport. Enter **90** in the **Rotate Z** input box of the channel box and press the ENTER key; the sphere rotates by 90 degrees in the Z direction.

Assigning Material to the Sphere

In this section, you need to create a material for the eyeball and then assign it to the NURBS sphere.

1. Choose **Window > Rendering Editors > Hypershade** from the main menubar; the **Hypershade** window is displayed. Select the **Blinn** shader from **Create** area in the **Hypershade** window; the blinn shader is created in **Work Area** of the **Hypershade** window.

2. Press and hold the CTRL key and double-click on the blinn shader; the **Rename node** dialog box is displayed. Change the name of the blinn shader to **eye** in the **Enter new name** input area and choose the **OK** button.

3. Select the sphere in the viewport. Press and hold the right mouse button on the **eye** shader and choose **Assign Material to Selection** from the marking menu in the **Hypershade** window; the **eye** shader is applied to the sphere.

4. Double-click on the **eye** shader from the **Hypershade** window; the **Attribute Editor** with the properties of the **eye** shader is displayed on the right of the viewport.

5. Expand the **Common Material Attributes** tab in the **Attribute Editor** and choose the checker box on the right of the **Color** attribute; the **Create Render Node** window is displayed. Choose the **Ramp** 2D texture from the **Create Render Node** window; a **Ramp** shader is created in the work area of the **Hypershade** window.

6. Select **U Ramp** from the **Type** drop-down list and **Bump** from the **Interpolation** drop-down-list to set the type of ramp shader.

7. Click in the ramp color area to create four nodes. Change the color of the ramp to black and white. To do so, select a node and change its color by using the options in the **Selected Color** attribute below the ramp color area. Next, set appropriate distance between nodes; the initial eyeball material is applied to the NURBS sphere, as shown in Figure 6-30. Press 6 to view the material, as shown in Figure 6-31. Similarly, change the color of other nodes.

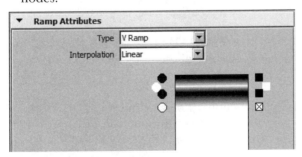

Figure 6-30 *Adjusting the ramp color in the* **Ramp Attributes** *area*

Figure 6-31 *Initial eyeball material applied to the NURBS sphere*

8. Select a circular icon from the **Ramp Attributes** area in the **Attribute Editor**, as shown in Figure 6-32. Next, select the checker box on the right of the **Selected Color** attribute;

the **Create Render Node** window is displayed. Choose **Fractal** from the **Create Render Node** window; the fractal color is applied to the eyeball, as shown in Figure 6-33, and the fractal attributes are displayed in the **Attribute Editor**.

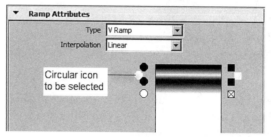

Figure 6-32 Selecting the circular icon from the Ramp Attributes area

9. Expand the **Color Balance** attribute tab and choose the grey color box on the right of the **Default Color** attribute in the **Attribute Editor**; the **Color History** palette is displayed. To specify the color of the fractal attribute, set the **H**, **S**, and **V** values to **191.73**, **0.967**, and **0.779** respectively in the **Color History** palette.

10. Repeat step 9 and enter the **H, S**, and **V** values for **Color Gain** as **199, 1**, and **1** respectively. Similarly, enter the **H, S**, and **V** values for **Color Offset** as **191, 1**, and **1** respectively. The final eyeball after applying the required attributes is shown in Figure 6-34.

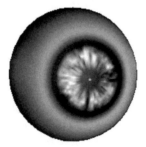

Figure 6-33 Eyeball after applying fractal color

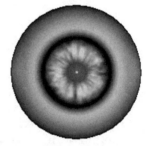

Figure 6-34 The final eyeball

Changing the Background Color of the Final Output at Rendering

In this section, you need to change the background color of the rendered scene and save the file.

1. Choose **Window > Outliner** from the main menubar; the **Outliner** window is displayed. Double-click on the **persp** camera in the **Outliner** window; the attributes of the perspective camera are displayed in the **Attribute Editor**.

2. Expand the **Environment** attribute tab from the **Attribute Editor** and set the **Background Color** to white. Render the eyeball as discussed in the earlier chapters.

Saving the File

In this section, you need to save the eye model that you have created.

1. Choose **File > Save Scene** from the main menubar; the **Save As** dialog box is displayed.

   As the project folder is already set, by default the path *Documents\Maya_Tutorials\c06_tut2** *scenes* is displayed in **Look In** text box of dialog box.

2. Enter **c06_tut2** in the **File name** text box and then select **Maya Binary** from the **Files of type** drop-down list. Next, choose **Save As** button.

You can view the final rendered image of the model by downloading the *c06_Maya_2012_render.zip* file from *http://www.cadcim.com*.

Self-Evaluation Test

Answer the following questions and then compare them to those given at the end of this chapter:

1. Which of the following tools is used to change the position of the selected UVs and their neighboring UVs to a diminishing extent?

   (a) **UV Shell**   (b) **UV Smudge**
   (c) **UV Lattice**   (d) **Flip U**

2. Which of the following mapping techniques is used to map complex objects?

   (a) Planar   (b) Spherical
   (c) Cylindrical   (d) Automatic

3. The **Rotate UVs Counterclockwise** tool is used to rotate the selected UVs by _____ degrees.

4. _____ creates UVs by creating a spherical projection around a polygonal object.

5. You can view and edit the 2D texture coordinate of an object by using the _____ window.

6. Press _____ to show or hide the texture image in the viewport.

7. The **Cycle UVs** tool is used to rotate the U and V values of a selected polygon. (T/F)

8. You can apply Planar Mapping by selecting the face of a particular object. (T/F)

9. Spherical Mapping is mainly used for planar objects. (T/F)

10. The navigation options in **UV Texture Editor** are different from that of the normal viewport area. (T/F)

Review Questions

Answer the following questions:

1. Which of the following is a UV mapping technique used in Maya?

   (a) Planar   (b) Cylindrical
   (c) Spherical   (d) All of these

2. Which of the following tools is used to create a lattice around UVs for deformation?

   (a) **UV Lattice**   (b) **UV Smudge**
   (c) **UV Shell**   (d) **Lattice**

3. You can change the number of projection planes in the _____ UV mapping technique.

4. The _____ tool is used to unwrap the selected UV mesh without overlapping the UVs.

5. _____ is used to creates UVs on a polygonal object by creating a bounding cylinder around it.

6. The _____ tool is used to arrange the UVs in a cleaner layout, based on the settings in the **Layout UVs** option box.

7. You can project the Planar Mapping manipulators in the camera axis. (T/F)

8. Automatic Mapping is mainly used for the objects that are hollow or projected outwards. (T/F)

9. You can map texture on to 2D UV coordinates by scaling UVs in the **UV Texture Editor** window. (T/F)

10. The **Sew UVs** tool is used to attach the UVs along the selected borders, but it cannot be used to move them together in the texture editor window. (T/F)

Exercises

Exercise 1

Create the model shown in Figure 6-35, and apply textures to it. You can view the final rendered image of this model by downloading the *c06_maya_2012_render.zip* file from *http://www.cadcim.com*. The path of file is as follows:

Textbooks > Animation and Visual Effects > Maya > Autodesk Maya 2012: A Comprehensive Guide
(Expected time: 20 min)

Figure 6-35 The toothpaste

Exercise 2

Create the model shown in Figure 6-36 and apply textures to it. You can view the final rendered image of this model by downloading the *c06_maya_2012_render.zip* file from *http://www.cadcim.com*. The path of the file is mentioned in Exercise 1.   **(Expected time: 20 min)**

Figure 6-36 *The scene for Exercise 2*

Answers to Self-Evaluation Test
1. b, **2**. d, **3**. 90, **4**. Spherical mapping, **5**. **UV Texture Editor**, **6**. 6, **7**. F, **8**. T, **9**. F, **10**. F

Chapter 7

Modeling

Learning Objectives

After completing this chapter, you will be able to:
- *Understand NURBS editing techniques*
- *Use the Trim and Sculpt Geometry tools*
- *Use different tessellation methods*

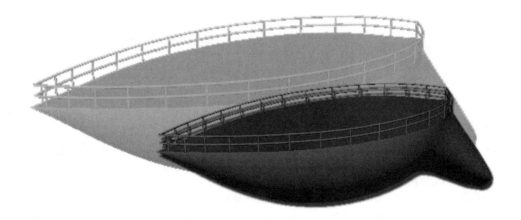

NURBS MODELING

The NURBS (Non uniform Rational B-Spline) modeling is mainly used to do organic modeling. These are mathematical representations of 3D geometry. NURBS modeling can be used to model any simple or complex model using a 2D line, circle, arc, or curve. In the earlier chapters, you have learned about different methods of creating NURBS surfaces. In this chapter, you will learn about various editing techniques used for modifying NURBS surfaces. The tools for modifying the NURBS surfaces are discussed next.

Duplicate NURBS Patches

Main menubar: Edit NURBS > Duplicate NURBS Patches

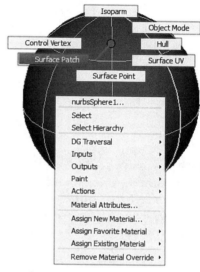

The **Duplicate NURBS Patches** tool is used to make a duplicate NURBS patch from an existing one. To do so, choose **Create > NURBS Primitives > Sphere** from the main menubar and create a NURBS sphere in the viewport. Select the sphere, press and hold the right mouse button over the sphere and choose **Surface Patch** from the marking menu, as shown in Figure 7-1; the surface patch component will be activated on the NURBS sphere. Now, select the surface patch that you want to duplicate. Choose **Edit NURBS > Duplicate NURBS Patches** from the main menubar; a duplicate surface patch will be created. Invoke the **Move** tool from the toolbox and move the duplicate surface patch away from the NURBS sphere. Note that the pivot point of the duplicate surface patch will remain at the same position as does the NURBS sphere. To reset the pivot point to the center of the duplicate patch, choose **Modify > Center Pivot**

Figure 7-1 *Choosing the **Surface Patch** option from the marking menu*

from the main menubar; the pivot point will be reset to its default position automatically.

Project Curve on Surface

Main menubar: Edit NURBS > Project Curve on Surface

The **Project Curve on Surface** tool is used to project a NURBS curve on a NURBS surface. To do so, activate the front viewport and choose **Create > NURBS Primitives > Square** from the main menubar. Now, create a square in the front viewport and choose **Surfaces > Planar** from the main menubar to create a NURBS surface. After creating the NURBS surface, press 5 to switch to the shaded mode. Next, choose **Create > CV Curve Tool** from the main menubar to create a curve, as shown in Figure 7-2. Next, select the NURBS curve, press and hold the SHIFT key and choose NURBS surface. Then, choose **Edit NURBS > Project Curve on Surface** from the main menubar to project the curve on the surface and activate the perspective viewport; the NURBS curve will be projected over the NURBS surface, as shown in Figure 7-3.

Note
The curve will be projected exactly at the same position, as visible through the camera of that particular viewport.

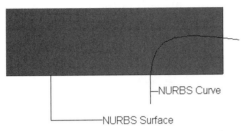

Figure 7-2 NURBS curve created

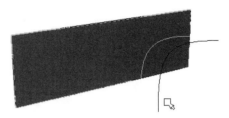

Figure 7-3 NURBS curve projected on the NURBS surface

Intersect Surfaces

Main menubar:	Edit NURBS > Intersect Surfaces

The **Intersect Surfaces** tool is used to create a new segment at the intersection of two NURBS surfaces. To do so, create two surfaces, as discussed earlier, and align them such that they intersect with each other, as shown in Figure 7-4. Select both the surfaces and choose **Edit NURBS > Intersect Surfaces** from the main menubar; the selection handles will be displayed at the intersection point, refer to Figure 7-4. You can now move these handles to align the intersection point anywhere on the NURBS surface.

Figure 7-4 The aligned surfaces and the selection handles

Trim Tool

Main menubar:	Edit NURBS > Trim Tool

The **Trim Tool** is used to trim a particular area from the NURBS surface. To do so, project a curve on the surface as discussed in the **Project Curve on Surface** section. Next, select the NURBS surface and choose **Edit NURBS > Trim Tool** from the main menubar; the NURBS surface will change to the wireframe mode with a dotted outline. Select the part that you want to trim from the surface and press ENTER; the surface will be trimmed. You can also change the settings of the **Trim Tool** as per your requirement. To do so, choose **Edit NURBS > Trim Tool > Option Box** from the main menubar; the **Trim Tool** property window will appear on the left of the viewport, as shown in Figure 7-5. You can select the **Keep** radio button to keep the part that you selected from the NURBS surface and trim the unselected part. Similarly, you can select the **Discard** radio button to trim the selected part from the NURBS surface and keep the deselected part.

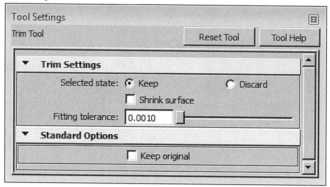

*Figure 7-5 The **Trim Tool** property window*

Untrim Surfaces

Main menubar: Edit NURBS > Untrim Surfaces

The **Untrim Surfaces** tool is used to untrim the trimmed surface. To do so, select the trimmed surface and choose **Edit NURBS > Untrim Surfaces** from the main menubar; the surface changes back to the untrimmed surface.

Attach Surfaces

Main menubar: Edit NURBS > Attach Surfaces

The **Attach Surfaces** tool is used to attach two selected NURBS surfaces. To do so, choose two NURBS surfaces in the viewport, as shown in Figure 7-6. Then, choose **Edit NURBS > Attach Surfaces > Option Box** from the main menubar; the **Attach Surfaces Options** dialog box will be displayed in the viewport, as shown in Figure 7-7. The **Blend** radio button is selected by default in the **Attach method** area of this dialog box. Choose the **Apply** button; the selected surfaces will be connected, as shown in Figure 7-8. You can also select the **Connect** radio button from the **Attach method** area to connect one end of the surface to another end of other surface, as shown in Figure 7-9.

Figure 7-6 The two NURBS surfaces

Note
*The **Attach Surfaces** tool does not attach trimmed surfaces. For attaching two surfaces, they need to be untrimmed.*

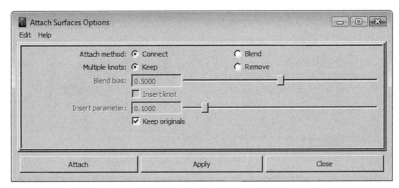

Figure 7-7 The ***Attach Surfaces Options*** *dialog box*

Figure 7-8 *Surfaces blend by using the **Blend** radio button*

Figure 7-9 *Connecting surfaces using the **Connect** radio button*

Attach Without Moving

Main menubar:	Edit NURBS > Attach Without Moving

The **Attach Without Moving** tool is used to attach two NURBS surfaces by selecting their respective isoparms. To do so, create two NURBS surfaces and select one isoparm each from the two surfaces. Now, choose **Edit NURBS > Attach Without Moving** from the main menubar; the two surfaces will be attached along the two isoparms.

Detach Surfaces

Main menubar:	Edit NURBS > Detach Surfaces

The **Detach Surfaces** tool is used to detach the attached NURBS surfaces. To do so, select the isoparm of a surface that is attached to another surface and then choose **Edit NURBS > Detach Surfaces** from the main menubar; the surface will detach from the selected isoparm.

Tip. *You can make changes in the attached surfaces by using the **attachSurface1** tab in the **Attribute Editor**. To do so, choose **Window > Attribute Editor** from the main menubar; the **Attribute Editor** will be displayed. Choose the **attachSurface1** tab from the **Attribute Editor**; the properties of the attached surface will be displayed, as shown in Figure 7-10. You can apply different styles on the surface by using the parameters in the **Attribute Editor**.*

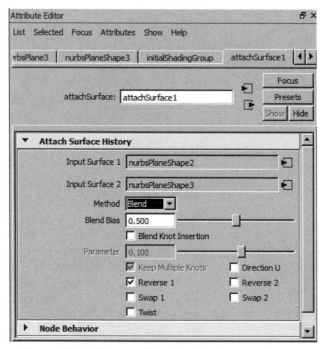

*Figure 7-10 The **attachSurface1** tab properties area*

Align Surfaces

Main menubar: Edit NURBS > Align Surfaces

The **Align Surfaces** tool is used to align selected NURBS surfaces. To do so, select the NURBS surfaces that you want to align. Choose **Edit NURBS > Align Surfaces > Option Box** from the main menubar; the **Align Surfaces Options** dialog box will be displayed, as shown in Figure 7-11. Now, you can try different options in this dialog box to align the selected NURBS surfaces as per your requirement.

Open/Close Surfaces

Main menubar: Edit NURBS > Open/Close Surfaces

The **Open/Close Surfaces** tool is used to open or close the NURBS surfaces. To close an open surface, as shown in Figure 7-12, select the surface and choose **Edit NURBS > Open/ Close Surfaces** from the main menubar; the open surface will be closed, as shown in Figure 7-13. Similarly, select the closed surface in the viewport and choose **Edit NURBS > Open/ Close Surfaces** from the main menubar; the closed surface will change into an open surface.

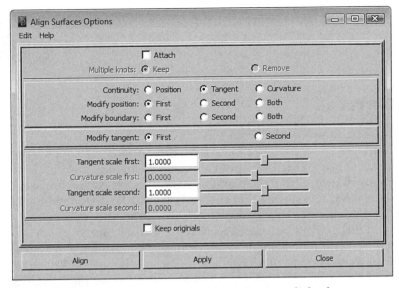

Figure 7-11 *The **Align Surfaces Options** dialog box*

Figure 7-12 *The open NURBS surface*

Figure 7-13 *The closed NURBS surface*

Insert Isoparms

Main menubar:	Edit NURBS > Insert Isoparms

The **Insert Isoparms** tool is used to insert an isoparm on a NURBS surface. To do so, create a NURBS surface and then select it. Next, press and hold the right mouse button on the NURBS surface and choose **Isoparm** from the marking menu; the isoparms will be highlighted on the selected NURBS object. Now, press and hold the left mouse button on any NURBS isoparm and drag the mouse to specify the position for the new isoparm; a yellow dotted line will appear over the NURBS surface, as shown in Figure 7-14. Next, choose **Edit NURBS > Insert Isoparms** from the main menubar; a new isoparm will be inserted in place of the yellow dotted line.

Figure 7-14 *The yellow dotted line displayed on the NURBS surface*

Tip. *To create multiple isoparms, press and hold the SHIFT key over a NURBS isoparm and then drag the mouse; multiple yellow dotted lines will appear on the NURBS surface. Now, choose **Edit NURBS > Insert Isoparms** from the main menubar; As a result, multiple isoparms will be created.*

Extend Surfaces

Main menubar:	Edit NURBS > Extend Surfaces

The **Extend Surfaces** tool is used to extend a NURBS surface. To extend a surface, create a NURBS surface in the viewport. Then, press and hold the right mouse button on the NURBS surface and choose **Isoparm** from the marking menu. Now, select the isoparm that you want to extend from the NURBS surface and choose **Edit NURBS > Extend Surfaces** from the main menubar; the selected surface will be extended. To set the properties of the extended surface, choose **Edit NURBS > Extend Surfaces > Option Box** from the main menubar; the **Extend Surface Options** dialog box will be displayed, as shown in Figure 7-15. Adjust the values in the dialog box to make changes in the working of the **Extend Surfaces** tool. Figures 7-16 and 7-17 show a hut roof before and after applying the **Extend Surfaces** tool. Any change made in the original surface will also be displayed in the offset surface created.

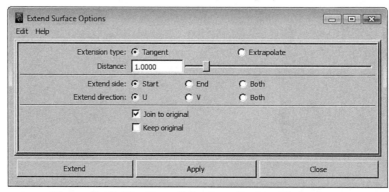

*Figure 7-15 The **Extend Surface Options** dialog box*

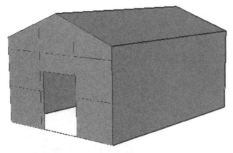

Figure 7-16 *The hut roof before applying the* ***Extend Surfaces*** *tool*

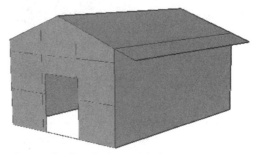

Figure 7-17 *The hut roof after applying the* ***Extend Surfaces*** *tool*

Offset Surfaces

Main menubar: Edit NURBS > Offset Surfaces

The **Offset Surfaces** tool is used to create a copy of the selected surface. To do so, create a NURBS surface in the viewport, select it, and then choose **Edit NURBS > Offset Surfaces** from the main menubar; a copy of the selected surface will be created. To set the properties of the **Offset Surfaces** tool, choose **Edit NURBS > Offset Surfaces > Option Box** from the main menubar; the **Offset Surface Options** dialog box will be displayed, as shown in Figure 7-18. The **Offset distance** option in the dialog box is used to specify the distance of the copied surface from the original surface.

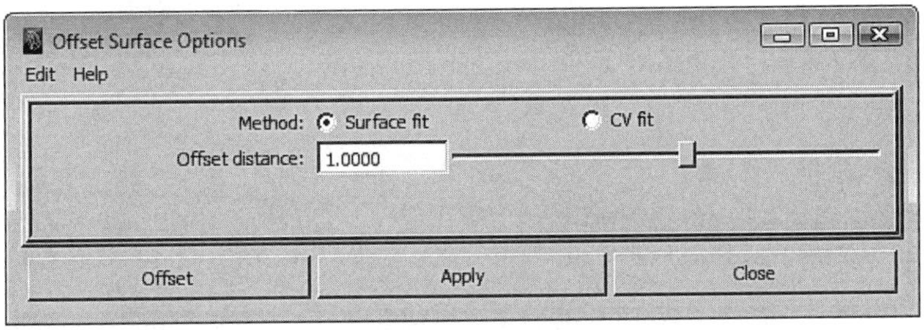

*Figure 7-18 The **Offset Surface Options** dialog box*

Reverse Surface Direction

Main menubar: Edit NURBS > Reverse Surface Direction

The **Reverse Surface Direction** tool is used to reverse or swap the U and V directions of a selected surface. To do so, create a NURBS surface in the viewport, select it, and then choose **Edit NURBS > Reverse Surface Direction > Option Box** from the main menubar; the **Reverse Surface Direction Options** dialog box will be displayed, as shown in Figure 7-19. Select the required radio button from the **Surface direction** area of this dialog box and then choose the **Reverse** button to reverse the surface direction.

*Figure 7-19 The **Reverse Surface Direction Options** dialog box*

Rebuild Surfaces

Main menubar: Edit NURBS > Rebuild Surfaces

The **Rebuild Surfaces** tool is used to rebuild the number of U and V spans on a selected NURBS surface. To do so, select the NURBS surface that you want to rebuild and choose **Edit NURBS > Rebuild Surfaces > Option Box** from the main menubar; the **Rebuild Surface Options** dialog box will be displayed, as shown in Figure 7-20. The options in this dialog box are discussed next.

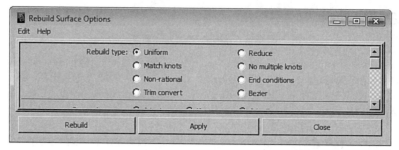

*Figure 7-20 The **Rebuild Surface Options** dialog box*

Rebuild type

You need to specify the **Rebuild type** parameter by choosing any of the following radio buttons:

Uniform

Select the **Uniform** radio button to rebuild the surface with uniform parameterization. On doing so, the number of spans will be entered uniformly on the selected surface.

Reduce

Select the **Reduce** radio button to remove the knots from the NURBS surface.

Match knots

Select the **Match knots** radio button to match the curve degree, knot values, number of spans, and sections of two surfaces.

No multiple knots

Select the **No multiple knots** radio button to remove the extra knots formed while rebuilding a surface.

Non-rational

Select the **Non-rational** radio button to convert a rational surface into a non-rational surface.

End conditions

Select the **End conditions** radio button to rebuild the positioning of the CVs and knots of the surface.

Trim convert

Select the **Trim convert** radio button to convert a trimmed surface into a non-trimmed surface.

Bezier

Select the **Bezier** radio button to rebuild a surface as a bezier surface.

Parameter range

The **Parameter range** parameter is used to specify the U and V parameters to rebuild a surface. There are three different ways to specify the U and V parameters, which are discussed next.

0 to 1

Select the **0 to 1** radio button to specify the U and V parameters from 0 to 1.

Keep

Select the **Keep** radio button to match the U and V parameters with the original surface.

0 to #spans

Select the **0 to #spans** radio button to get the rebuild surface value in integers.

Direction

The **Direction** parameter is used to determine the parametric direction of the surface in the **U**, **V**, or both **U and V** directions.

Keep

The **Keep** parameter is used to ensure that some particular characteristics of the original object or surface are retained while creating a new surface. Select the **Corners, CVs** or the **NumSpans** radio button to retain the corresponding characteristics.

Rebuild Method

Select the **Match Knots** radio button from the **Rebuild type** attribute area to activate this radio button. The **Rebuild method** parameter is used to rebuild the surface by specifying the quality of the new surface. Select the **Classic** radio button to get the surface quality similar to that obtained with the version 5.0 or earlier versions of Maya. Select the **Match** radio button to get a better quality for surfaces having multiple knots at the end.

Number of spans U and Number of spans V

The **Number of spans U** and **Number of spans V** options are used to set the number of spans in the U and V directions of the rebuild surface respectively.

Degree U and Degree V

The **Degree U** and **Degree V** options are used to set the degree of the rebuild surface.

Keep original

The **Keep original** check box is selected to keep the original surface and rebuild a new surface.

Use tolerance

The **Use tolerance** option will be available only on selecting the **Non-Rational** or **Reduce** radio button in the **Rebuild type** area. The tolerance value is used to make the rebuild surface resemble the original surface. Smaller the tolerance value, more the rebuild surface will resemble the original surface.

Output geometry

The **Output geometry** option is used to specify the output type for the rebuild surface. Select the **NURBS**, **Polygons**, or **Subdiv** radio button to specify the output geometry.

Sculpt Geometry Tool

Main menubar:	Edit NURBS > Sculpt Geometry Tool

The **Sculpt Geometry Tool** is used to sculpt an object manually in viewport. On invoking this tool, the cursor sign will change to a brush sign. To sculpt an object, create a NURBS surface in the viewport and choose **Edit NURBS > Sculpt Geometry Tool > Option Box** from the main menubar; the **Sculpt Geometry Tool** property window will be displayed on the left of the viewport, as shown in Figure 7-21.

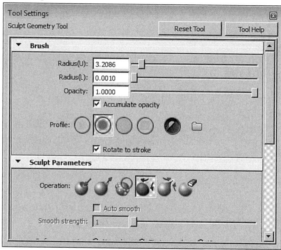

*Figure 7-21 Partial view of the **Sculpt Geometry Tool** window*

 Note

*More the number of segments on an object, better sculpting can be done on it using the **Sculpt Geometry Tool**. You can sculpt an object using five different tools: **Push**, **Pull**, **Smooth**, **Relax**, and **Erase**. All these methods are discussed next.*

Push

The **Push** tool is used to push down a NURBS mesh. To do so, create a NURBS plane in the viewport. Next, choose **Edit NURBS > Sculpt Geometry Tool > Option Box** from the main menubar; the **Sculpt Geometry Tool** property window will be displayed on the left of the viewport, refer to Figure 7-21. Choose the **Push** button in the **Sculpt Parameters** area; the cursor will be modified, as shown in Figure 7-22. Move the cursor over the NURBS plane, press and hold the left mouse button and drag the brush over the plane. Now, move it to sculpt the mesh surface. Figure 7-23 shows a NURBS plane before sculpting and Figure 7-24 shows the NURBS plane sculpted using the **Push** tool.

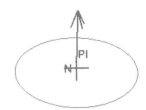

Figure 7-22 The ***Sculpt Geometry Tool*** *cursor*

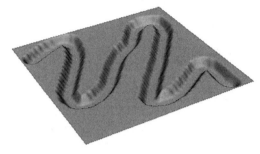

Figure 7-23 The NURBS plane before sculpting

Figure 7-24 The NURBS plane sculpted using the ***Push*** tool

Pull

The **Pull** tool is used to pull the NURBS mesh from the surface. This tool works similar to the **Push** tool and the procedure to apply it on a NURBS plane is same as that of the **Push** tool. Figure 7-25 shows a NURBS plane sculpted using the **Pull** tool.

Figure 7-25 The NURBS plane sculpted using the ***Pull*** tool

Smooth

The **Smooth** tool is used to paint a mesh to give it a smoother look. To use this method, follow the steps as discussed in the **Push** tool, and choose the **Smooth** button from the **Sculpt Parameters** area of the **Sculpt Geometry Tool** property window. Figure 7-26 shows a surface before smoothening and Figure 7-27 shows the surface after smoothening.

Figure 7-26 *Surface before smoothening*   **Figure 7-27** *Surface after smoothening*

Relax

 The **Relax** tool works similar to the **Smooth** tool. It is used to relax the bumps over the surface, thus maintaining the overall shape of the mesh.

Pinch

 The **Pinch** tool is used to pull selected vertices toward each other. It helps in bringing the vertices closer in order to make sharp or well defined creases.

Erase

 The **Erase** method is used to erase the changes made by using the push or pull method on the surface. For example, create a polygonal cylinder in the viewport and paint the surface of the cylinder by choosing the **Push** button, as shown in Figure 7-28. Next, choose the **Erase** button from the **Operation** option of the **Sculpt Parameters** area and erase the required part; you will get the output, as shown in Figure 7-29.

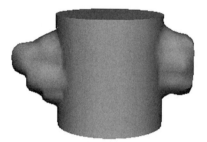

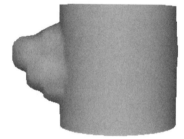

Figure 7-28 *Surface before erasing*   **Figure 7-29** *Surface after erasing*

CONVERTING OBJECTS

In Maya, you can convert object from one form to another form. For example, using this method you can convert a NURBS object to polygonal object and vice-versa. To use this method, select an object in the viewport and choose **Modify > Convert** from the main menubar; a flyout will be displayed. Choose the conversion type from the flyout to specify the output geometry for the selected object. Various options in this flyout are discussed next.

Converting NURBS to Polygons

Main menubar: Modify > Convert > NURBS to Polygons

The **NURBS to Polygons** conversion tool is used to convert a NURBS mesh i~~n~~ a polygonal mesh. To do so, choose **Modify > Convert > NURBS to Polygons > Opti**~~on~~ **Box** from the main menubar; the **Convert NURBS to Polygons Options** dialog box will ~~b~~ displayed in the viewport, as shown in Figure 7-30. You can use this dialog box to set th~~e~~ options for the conversion of the object from NURBS to polygons. The options in the **Conver**~~t~~ **NURBS to Polygons Options** dialog box are discussed next.

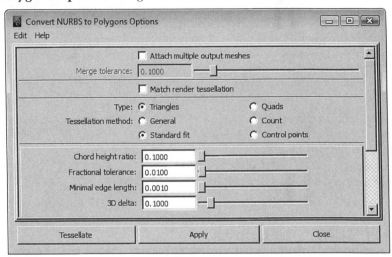

Figure 7-30 The **Convert NURBS to Polygons Options** dialog box

Type

The **Type** parameter is used to set the output of the conversion. If you select the **Triangles** radio button, then three-sided polygons will be created on the surface, as shown in Figure 7-31. If you select the **Quads** radio button, then four-sided polygons will be created on the surface, as shown in Figure 7-32.

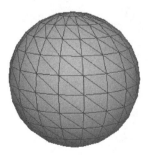

Figure 7-31 Surface created on applying the **Triangles** polygon type

Figure 7-32 Surface created on applying the **Quads** polygon type

...hod

...thod parameter is used to convert a NURBS mesh to a set of polygons. ...our tessellation methods that are discussed next.

...radio button is used to define the number of polygons in the U or in the V ...n selecting this radio button, various options for setting the tessellation are ...Set the attributes as per your requirement.

...d fit

...andard fit tessellation method is the default tessellation method. This method is ...o determine when to stop the tessellation by setting the fractional tolerance value. ...electing this radio button, the options related to it are displayed. Adjust them as per ...r requirement.

...ount

The **Count** tessellation method is used to specify the polygon count in the mesh after the conversion. More the count value, smoother will be the object.

Control Points

The **Control Points** tessellation method is used to create a new mesh while matching its CVs to the original NURBS surface. The resulting polygons will be quads by default.

Converting NURBS to Subdiv

Main menubar:	Modify > Convert > NURBS to Subdiv

The **NURBS to Subdiv** conversion tool is used to convert a NURBS mesh into a subdiv mesh. To do so, select the NURBS object in the viewport and choose **Modify > Convert > NURBS to Subdiv > Option Box** from the main menubar; the **Convert NURBS/Polygons to Subdiv Options** dialog box will be displayed, as shown in Figure 7-33. The options in the **Convert NURBS/Polygons to Subdiv Options** dialog box are discussed next.

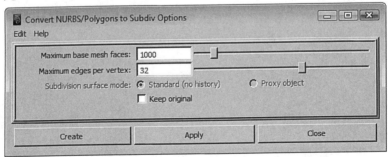

Figure 7-33 The Convert NURBS/Polygons to Subdiv Options dialog box

Maximum base mesh faces

The **Maximum base mesh faces** option is used to set the maximum number of faces that the original surface can have, such that it can be successfully converted into a subdivision surface.

Maximum edges per vertex

The **Maximum edges per vertex** option is used to set the maximum number of edges that each vertex can have in the original surface, such that it can be successfully converted into a subdivision surface.

Keep original

Select the **Keep original** check box to keep the original object, while creating the new subdivision surface.

Note

The options in other tessellation methods are similar to those discussed in the previous topics.

TUTORIALS
Tutorial 1

In this tutorial, you will create the model of a cowboy hat, as shown in Figure 7-34, using the NURBS modeling.   **(Expected time: 15 min)**

Figure 7-34 The model of cowboy hat

The following steps are required to complete this tutorial:

a.   Create a project folder.
b.   Create a NURBS cylinder.
c.   Add details to the hat.

Creating the Project Folder

Before starting a new file, it is recommended that you create the project folder.

1.   Create a project with the name *c07_tut1* in the folder *Maya_Tutorials*.

Creating a NURBS Cylinder

In this section, you need to create a NURBS cylinder to form the basic structure of the cowboy hat.

1. Choose **Create > NURBS Primitives > Cylinder** from the main menubar and click in the active viewport; a cylinder is created in the viewport. Next, choose **Display > UI Elements > Channel Box/Layer Editor** from the main menubar; the channel box/layer editor is displayed on the right in the viewport.

2. Enter a value in the **INPUTS** node of the **Channel box**, as shown in Figure 7-35.

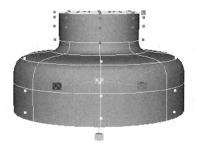

INPUTS	
makeNurbCylinder1	
Radius	4
Start Sweep	0
End Sweep	360
Degree	Cubic
Sections	8
Spans	6
Height Ratio	6

3. Activate the front viewport and press 5 to change it to shaded mode. Press and hold the right mouse button on the NURBS cylinder and choose **Control Vertex** to switch to the vertex mode. Now, select the vertices, as shown in Figure 7-36. Next, invoke the **Scale Tool** from the toolbox and scale the vertices uniformly in the perspective viewport, as shown in Figure 7-37.

*Figure 7-35 The **INPUTS** node*

4. Select the green handle of the **Scale Tool** and scale the selected vertices along the Y axis; the mesh gets modified, as shown in Figure 7-38.

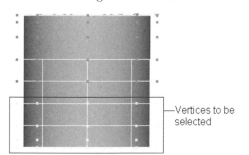

Vertices to be selected

Figure 7-36 Selecting vertices

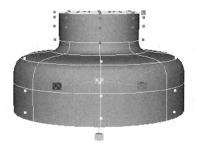

Figure 7-37 Scaling the selected vertices uniformly

Figure 7-38 Scaling the selected vertices along the Y axis

Adding Details to the Hat

In this section, you need to add details to the hat to give it a cowboy hat look.

1. Activate the Top viewport and select the vertices, as shown in Figure 7-39 (vertices to be selected are numbered for your reference). Next, invoke the **Scale Tool** from the toolbox, if it is not already invoked, and scale the selected vertices along the Z axis using the blue handle; the mesh gets scaled, as shown in Figure 7-40.

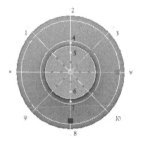

Figure 7-39 *Selecting vertices*

Figure 7-40 *Scaled mesh*

2. Activate the Side viewport and select the vertices, as shown in Figure 7-41 (the vertices to be selected are encircled for your reference). Next, invoke the **Move Tool** and move the vertices along the -Y direction, as shown in Figure 7-42.

Figure 7-41 *Selecting vertices*

Figure 7-42 *The modified mesh after moving the vertices*

3. Press the F8 key to convert the object from the component mode to the object mode. Alternatively, press and hold the right mouse button over the cowboy hat model and choose **Object Mode** from the marking menu.

4. Select the model in the viewport. Then, press and hold the right mouse button over the cowboy hat model and choose **Isoparm** from the marking menu.

5. Activate the Perspective viewport and select an isoparm, as shown in Figure 7-43. Drag the isoparm outward and choose **Edit NURBS > Insert Isoparms** from the main menubar; a new isoparm is created, as shown in Figure 7-44.

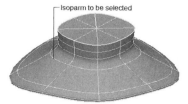

Figure 7-43 *Selecting an isoparm*

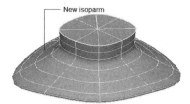

Figure 7-44 *A new isoparm created*

6. Press the F8 key to into enter the object mode. Select the model and choose **Edit > Delete All by Type > History** from the main menubar; the history of all actions performed on the model is deleted.

7. Again, select the model. Next, press and hold the right mouse button on the lower part of the hat and then choose **Control Vertex** from the marking menu. Next, select the vertices of the object in the side viewport, as shown in Figure 7-45 (the vertices to be selected are encircled for your reference). Next, move the vertices up along the Y axis to change the shape of the cowboy hat, as shown in Figure 7-46.

Figure 7-45 *Selecting vertices*   *Figure 7-46* *The modified mesh*

8. Press F8 to enter the object mode. Choose **View > Predefined Bookmarks > Bottom** from the **Panel menu**; the bottom viewport is activated.

9. Insert two new isoparms into the viewport, as shown in Figure 7-47. Press F8 again to switch back to the object mode.

10. Press and hold the right mouse button over the cowboy hat model and choose **Control Vertex** from the marking menu. Next, press and hold the SHIFT key and select the vertices, as shown in Figure 7-48 (vertices to be selected are encircled for your reference).

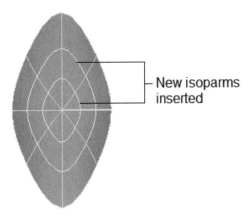

New isoparms
inserted

Figure 7-47 *Inserting two new isoparms*

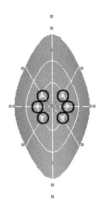

Figure 7-48 *Selecting vertices*

11. Choose **View > Predefined Bookmarks > Perspective** from the **Panel menu**; the Perspective viewport is activated. Invoke the **Move Tool** from the toolbox and move the selected vertices up along the Y axis to get the final output, as shown in Figure 7-49.

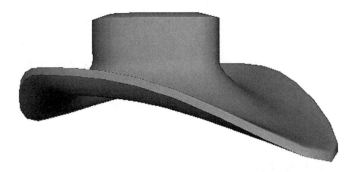

Figure 7-49 *The final model*

Saving the File

In this section, you need to save the wine glass model that you have created.

1. Choose **File > Save Scene** from the main menubar; the **Save As** dialog box is displayed.

   As the project folder is already set, by default the path *\Documents\Maya_Tutorials\c07_tut1\ scenes* is displayed in **Look In** text box of the dialog box.

2. Enter **c07_tut1** in the **File name** text box and then select **Maya Binary** from the **Files of type** drop-down list. Next, choose the **Save As** button.

You can view the final rendered image of the model by downloading the *c07_Maya_2012_render.zip* file from *http://www.cadcim.com*.

Tutorial 2

In this tutorial, you will create the model of a ship, as shown in Figure 7-50, using the combination of NURBS and polygonal modeling.   **(Expected time: 30 min)**

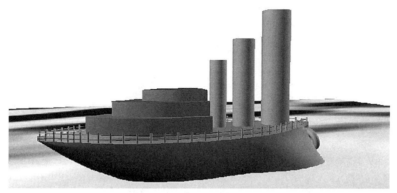

Figure 7-50 *Model of a ship*

The following steps are required to complete this tutorial:

a. Create a project folder.
b. Create the base of the ship.
c. Create railings.
d. Create deck.
e. Create chimney.
f. Save the file.

Creating the Project Folder

Before starting a new file, it is recommended that you set the project folder.

1. Create a project with the name *c07_tut2* in the folder *Maya_Tutorials*.

Creating the Base of the Ship

In this section, you need to create the base of the ship using the NURBS curves and the loft method.

1. Activate the Side viewport and choose **Create > EP Curve Tool** from the main menubar. Next, create a curve for the base of the ship in the Side viewport. Press and hold the d key and move the manipulators to set the pivot point at one end of the curve.

2. Choose **Edit > Duplicate Special > Option Box** from the main menubar; the **Duplicate Special Options** dialog box is displayed in the viewport. Enter required values in the dialog box, refer to Figure 7-51, and then choose the **Duplicate Special** button; duplicate curves are created in the viewport.

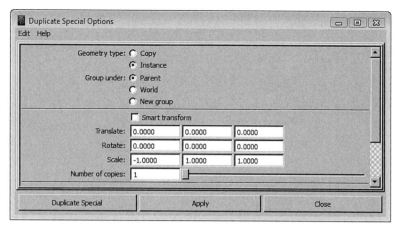

Figure 7-51 *The **Duplicate Special Options** dialog box*

3. Activate the Perspective viewport. Press and hold the SHIFT key and then select all the curves in the viewport one-by-one. Next, choose **Surfaces > Loft** from the main menubar; a surface is created defining half part of the ship base. Press 5 to change the view to shaded mode.

4. Select the loft surface, repeat the step 2, and then enter values in the dialog box, as shown in Figure 7-52. Next, choose the **Duplicate Special** button to make a duplicate copy of the surface such that the model looks like the complete base of the ship.

Note
Press 4 for wireframe mode, 5 for shaded mode, 6 for viewing texture, and 7 to view the light effect in the viewport.

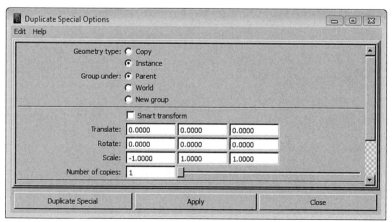

Figure 7-52 *Partial view of the **Duplicate Special Options** dialog box*

5. Select all curves and surfaces in the viewport. Press and hold the SHIFT key and click on the surface; all curves are selected. Next, choose **Display > Hide > Hide Selection** from the main menubar; the selected curves get hidden. Activate the Side viewport and select

the NURBS surface. Now, choose **Edit NURBS > Rebuild Surfaces > Option Box** from the main menubar; the **Rebuild Surface Options** dialog box is displayed. Set the values in this dialog box, refer to Figure 7-53, and then choose the **Rebuild** button to rebuild the surface.

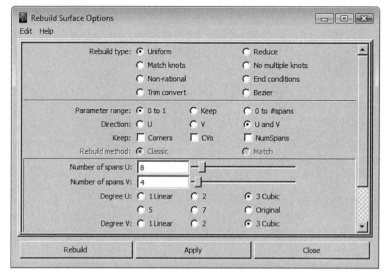

*Figure 7-53 The **Rebuild Surface Options** dialog box*

6. Press and hold the right mouse button over the model and choose **Control Vertex** from the marking menu. Next, press and hold the SHIFT key and select the vertices, as shown in Figure 7-54. Invoke the **Move Tool** from the toolbox and move the vertices downward to create the tail of the ship, as shown in Figure 7-55.

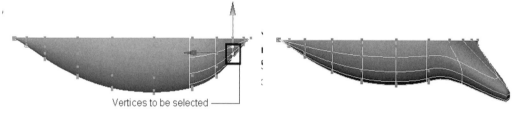

Figure 7-54 Selecting vertices   *Figure 7-55 Moving the vertices to create the tail of the ship*

8. Select one half of the ship base. Press and hold the right mouse button over the ship, choose **Isoparm** from the marking menu, and then select the topmost isoparm.

9. Press the SHIFT key and choose another half of the base ship and repeat step 8; two isoparms are selected, as shown in Figure 7-56. Next, choose **Surfaces > Loft** from the main menubar to create a surface between the selected isoparms.

10. Select the newly created surface and choose **Edit NURBS > Rebuild Surfaces > Option Box** from the main menubar; the **Rebuild Surfaces Options** dialog box is displayed. Enter

8 and **4** in the **Number of spans U** and **Number of spans V** edit boxes, respectively. Next, choose the **Rebuild** button.

11. Activate the Top viewport. Select the newly created surface, press and hold the right mouse button on the selected surface, and then choose **Isoparm** from the marking menu. Insert the two isoparms at the positions shown in Figure 7-57. Now, choose **Edit NURBS > Insert Isoparms** from the main menubar; two new isoparms are created.

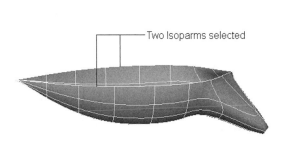

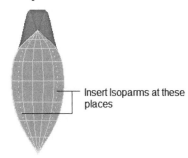

Figure 7-56 *The two isoparms selected* *Figure 7-57* *Inserting isoparms*

12. Press and hold the right mouse button over the new surface and choose **Hull** from the marking menu. Now, select all hulls, except those that lie on the border of the surface, as shown in Figure 7-58.

13. Activate the Perspective viewport. Invoke the **Move Tool** from the toolbox and move the hulls up along the Y axis so that they do not touch the base of the ship. Next, invoke the **Scale Tool** from the toolbox, select the red handle, and scale the hulls along the X axis, as shown in Figure 7-59.

Figure 7-58 *Selecting hulls* *Figure 7-59* *Scaling the hulls along the X axis*

Creating Railings

In this section, you need to create railings for the ship by using the NURBS cylinder. There are two ways to create railings: by creating cylinders and aligning them manually, or aligning the cylinders on a curve. In this section, you need to align the cylinders on a curve.

1. Activate the Top viewport. Choose **Create > EP Curve Tool** from the main menubar and create a curve, taking the boundary of the ship as reference, refer to Figure 7-60. Now, move this curve using the **Move Tool**.

2. Activate the Perspective viewport and choose **Create > NURBS Primitives > Cylinder** from the main menubar. Now, create a cylinder in the viewport. Next, delete the upper cap and the lower cap of the cylinder.

3. Choose **Display > UI Elements > Channel Box/Layer Editor** from the main menubar; the **Channel box** is displayed at the right of the viewport. Change the parameters of the cylinder in the **INPUTS** node of the **Channel box**, as given next.

    Radius: **0.1**   Sections: **10**   Height Ratio: **10**

4. Choose the **Animation** menuset from the status line and select the curve. Next, press and hold the SHIFT key and select the cylinder. Choose **Animate > Motion Paths > Attach to Motion Path** from the main menubar; the cylinder gets attached to the curve.

Figure 7-60 Creating the NURBS curve

5. Choose **Animate > Create Animation Snapshot > Option Box** from the main menubar; the **Animation Snapshot Options** dialog box is displayed in the viewport. Enter **30** in the **End Time** edit box, **2** in the **Increment** edit box, and then choose the **Snapshot** button; the cylinders are aligned on the curved surface, as shown in Figure 7-61.

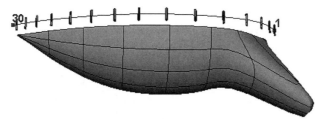

Figure 7-61 The cylinders aligned on the curve surface

Note
*The value in the **End Time** edit box may vary depending on the size of the NURBS surface created.*

6. Activate the Front viewport and choose **Create > NURBS Primitives > Circle** from the main menubar and create a circle in the viewport. Next, choose **Display > UI Elements > Channel Box/Layer Editor** from the main menubar; the **Channel box** is displayed. In the **Channel box**, adjust the radius of the circle to 0.1.

7. Choose the **Surfaces** menuset from the status line. Now, select the circle and then the curve from the viewport. Choose **Surfaces > Extrude** from the main menubar; the circle is extruded and the handrail is created.

8. Select the extruded surface. Choose **Display > UI Elements > Attribute Editor** from the main menubar; the **Attribute Editor** is displayed. Choose the **extrude1** tab and enter values in the **Attribute Editor**, as shown in Figure 7-62. Invoke the **Move Tool** from the toolbox and align the handrail over the cylinders.

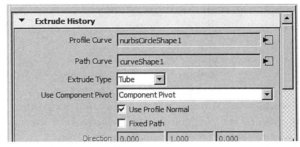

*Figure 7-62 Setting the parameters in the **extrude1** tab*

9. Activate the Perspective viewport. Select the curve and choose **Display > Hide > Hide Selection** from the main menubar to hide the curve. Make a duplicate copy of the railing and move it down, as shown in Figure 7-63. Next, select the complete railing and press CTRL + g to group them. Then, align the railings on the base of the ship.

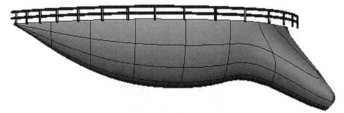

Figure 7-63 The railings aligned on half part of the ship

10. Select the railing group and choose **Edit > Duplicate Special** from the main menubar to make a duplicate of the railings to create another half part of the railing. Next, invoke the **Move Tool** from the main menubar and align the duplicate pair of the railings with the ship, as shown in Figure 7-64.

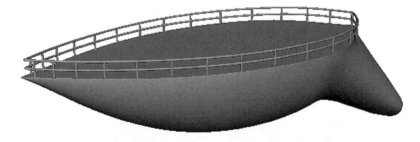

Figure 7-64 The final railings

Creating the Deck

In this section, you need to create the deck of the ship using the polygon modeling method.

1. Activate the Top viewport. Choose **Create > Polygon Primitives > Cube** from the main menubar to create a cube in the viewport. Choose **Display > UI Elements > Channel**

Box/Layer Editor from the main menubar; the **Channel box** is displayed. Modify the parameters of the cube in the channel box as given next:

Width: **10**   Height: **5**   Depth: **10**
Subdivisions Width: **2**   Subdivisions Height: **1**   Subdivision Depth: **4**

2. Press and hold the right mouse button on the cube; a marking menu is displayed. Choose **Vertex** from the marking menu. Next, invoke the **Move Tool** from the toolbox and adjust the vertex of the cube to form the shape as shown in Figure 7-65.

3. Select the cube and choose **Edit > Duplicate** from the main menubar to make the duplicate of the cube in the viewport. Similarly, create one more duplicate of the deck. Invoke the **Move Tool** and then the **Scale Tool** to align the duplicated decks on the ship, as shown in Figure 7-66.

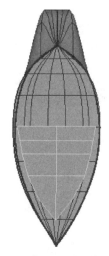

Figure 7-65 *The shape of the deck created*

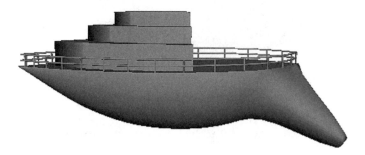

Figure 7-66 *The duplicate decks aligned together*

Creating the Chimney

In this section, you need to create the chimney for the ship using the polygon cylinder tool.

1. Activate the Top viewport. Choose **Create > Polygon Primitives > Cylinder** from the main menubar to create three cylinders in the viewport. The cylinders will act as chimneys for the ship. Choose **Display > UI Elements > Channel Box/Layer Editor**; the **Channel box** is displayed. Adjust the parameters in the channel box as given below:

Cylinder	Radius	Height
Cylinder1	2	20
Cylinder2	1.5	15
Cylinder3	1	10

Note

The radius and height of the cylinders may vary depending upon the size of the ship. Therefore, you need to set the respective values accordingly.

2. Activate the Perspective viewport and align the cylinders to create chimneys, as shown in Figure 7-67.

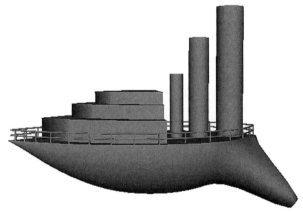

Figure 7-67 The chimneys created

Saving the File

In this section, you need to save the ship model that you have created.

1. Choose **File > Save Scene** from the main menubar; the **Save As** dialog box is displayed.

    As the project folder is already set, by default the path *\Documents\Maya_Tutorials\c07_tut2\ scenes* is displayed in **Look In** text box of the dialog box.

2. Enter **c07_tut2** in the **File name** text box and then select **Maya Binary** from the **Files of type** drop-down list. Next, choose the **Save As** button.

You can view the final rendered image of the model by downloading the file *c07_Maya_2012_ render.zip* from *http://www.cadcim.com*.

Self-Evaluation Test

Answer the following questions and then compare them to those given at the end of this chapter:

1. Which of the following tools is used to create a new segment at the intersection of two surfaces?

    (a) **Intersect Surfaces**   (b) **Untrim Surfaces**
    (c) **Attach Surfaces**   (d) None of these

2. Which of the following tools is used to paint a mesh to give it a smoother look?

    (a) **Pull**   (b) **Push**
    (c) **Smooth**   (d) **Relax**

3. The _____ tool is used to rebuild the U and V spans.

4. The _____ tool is used to untrim a trimmed area.

5. The _____ tool is used to reverse the U and V directions of a selected surface.

6. More the number of patches on an object, better you can operate on it using the _____ **Geometry Tool**.

7. The **NURBS to Subdiv** conversion tool is used to convert a NURBS mesh into a subdiv mesh. (T/F)

8. The process of converting an object from one mesh to another is known as mesh conversion. (T/F)

9. The **Offset Surfaces** tool is used to create a copy of a selected surface at a particular distance. (T/F)

10. The **Insert Isoparms** tool is used to insert an isoparm into an existing NURBS surface. (T/F)

Review Questions

Answer the following questions:

1. Which of the following operations is used to relax bumps over a surface?

    (a) **Push**   (b) **Pull**
    (c) **Relax**   (d) **Erase**

2. Which of the following tools is used to align the selected surface?

    (a) **Offset Surface**   (b) **Attach Surface**
    (c) **Align Surface**   (d) None of these

3. The _____ tool is used to extend a NURBS surface.

4. The _____ **knots** radio button is used to remove the extra knots formed while rebuilding a surface.

5. The _____ tool is used to create the copy of a selected surface.

6. The **Pinch** tool is used to pull selected vertices toward each other. (T/F)

7. The tessellation method is used to set the initial and secondary tessellation controls for an object. (T/F)

8. Tessellation is a method, which is used to convert a NURBS mesh into a set of polygons. (T/F)

9. The **Erase** operation is used to push the NURBS mesh inside a surface. (T/F)

10. The **Extend Surfaces** tool is used to rebuild a NURBS surface. (T/F)

Exercises

Exercise 1

Use various modeling techniques to build the model of a handbag, shown in Figure 7-68. You can view the final rendered image of this model by downloading the file *c07_maya_2012_render.zip* from *http://www.cadcim.com*. The path of file is as follows:

Textbooks > Animation and Visual Effects > Maya > Autodesk Maya 2012: A Comprehensive Guide
(Expected time: 45 min)

Figure 7-68 *The model of a handbag*

Exercise 2

Use various modeling techniques to create the model of a chair, as shown in Figure 7-69. You can view the final rendered image of this model by downloading the *c07_maya_2012_render.zip* file from *http://www.cadcim.com*. The path of the file is mentioned in Exercise 1.

(Expected time: 30 min)

Figure 7-69 *The model of a chair*

Answers to Self-Evaluation Test
1. a, **2.** c, **3. Rebuild Surface**, **4. Untrim Surface**, **5. Reverse Surface Direction**, **6. Sculpt**, **7.** T, **8.** F, **9.** T, **10.** T

Chapter 8

Lighting

Learning Objectives

After completing this chapter, you will be able to:
- *Understand standard lights*
- *Add the glow and halo effects to lights*
- *Apply physical sun and sky effect in a scene*
- *Work with the camera*

INTRODUCTION TO LIGHTS

Lights are objects that simulate real lights such as street lights, flash lights, house-hold lights or office lamp, and so on. When there is no light in a scene, the scene is rendered with default lighting. In addition to illuminating the scene, light can be used to project the images. In this chapter, you will learn about various lights that you can use in your scene to give it realistic lighting effects.

TYPES OF LIGHTS

There are six types of lights in Maya. To create a light, choose **Create > Lights** from the main menubar; a submenu will be displayed. Choose the required light from the submenu and click in the viewport; the light will be created in your scene on a grid. Different types of lights in Maya are discussed next.

1. Ambient Light
2. Directional Light
3. Point Light
4. Spot Light
5. Area Light
6. Volume Light

Ambient Light

Main menubar:	Create > Lights > Ambient Light

Ambient Light is a single point light that projects the rays uniformly in all directions and lights up the scene. To create an ambient light, choose **Create > Lights > Ambient Light** from the main menubar; Ambient Light will be created at the center of the viewport. To modify the parameters of a light, select the light in the viewport. Then, choose **Window > Attribute Editor** from the main menubar; the attribute editor displaying the properties of the ambient light will be displayed on the right of the viewport. Some attributes in Maya are common for all the lights. These attributes are discussed next.

Ambient Light Attributes

The Ambient Light Attributes control the general attributes related to a particular light. To access these attributes, select the light in the viewport and choose **Window > Attribute Editor** from the main menubar; the **Attribute Editor** will be displayed. Expand the **Ambient Light Attributes** area, if not already expanded; different options will be displayed in the attribute area, as shown in Figure 8-1. These options are discussed next.

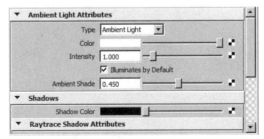

*Figure 8-1 The **Ambient Light Attributes** area*

Type

The **Type** option is used to change the type of light used in the viewport. To change a light type, select the required light type from the **Type** drop-down list; the current light will be replaced by the light selected from the drop-down list.

Color

The **Color** option is used to change the color of light. To do so, choose the white box on the right of the **Color** option; the **Color History** palette will be displayed, as shown in Figure 8-2. Set the color of the light from this palette and click anywhere outside this palette; the selected color will be applied to the light. You can also assign a map to the selected light. To do so, choose the checker button on the right of the **Color** attribute, refer to Figure 8-1; the **Create Render Node** window will be displayed. Choose the texture from the **Create Render Node** window and then choose the **Close** button; the texture will be assigned to the selected light. You need to render the scene to see the effect of light. To do so, invoke the **Render the current frame (Maya Software)** tool from the status line. Figure 8-3 shows an ambient light without applying the checker map and Figure 8-4 shows the ambient light with the checker map assigned to it.

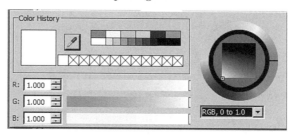

*Figure 8-2 The **Color History** palette*

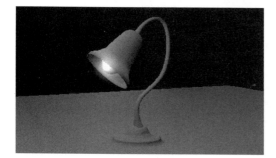

Figure 8-3 Ambient light without texture

Figure 8-4 Ambient light with the checker map assigned to it

Intensity

The **Intensity** option is used to set the brightness of light. To do so, enter the value in the **Intensity** option edit box or move the slider at its right to adjust the intensity. If there is 0 value in this edit box, no light will be simulated in the scene and the scene will appear completely dark on rendering. The **Illuminates by Default** check box is selected by default and is used to illuminate all objects in the viewport. When this check box is not selected, the light would only illuminate the objects to which it is linked. You will learn about the light linking later in the chapter.

Ambient Shade

The **Ambient Shade** option is used to spread light in a scene. To do so, enter a value in the **Ambient Shade** edit box or adjust the slider placed next to this edit box. The **Ambient Shade** value ranges from 0 to 1. If the ambient shade value is 0, the light will come from all directions and if the slider range value is 1, the light will come from a particular source. The default value in the **Ambient Shade** edit box is 0.45. Figure 8-5 shows the ambient light with the ambient shade value **0.25** and Figure 8-6 shows the ambient light with the ambient shade value **1**.

Figure 8-5 *Ambient light with the **Ambient Shade** value 0.25*

Figure 8-6 *Ambient light with the **Ambient Shade** value 1*

Shadows

The **Shadow Color** option in this area is used to define the color of the shadow produced by the light. The default shadow color is black. You can also map textures to the shadows.

Raytraced Shadow Attributes

These attributes are used to control the appearance of raytraced shadows produced by a light. Raytraced shadows produce soft and transparent shadows but they are computational intensive. These shadows will be visible in the render, only when raytrace is enabled in the **Global Render Settings**. To do so, choose **Windows > Rendering Editors** from the main menubar; the **Render settings window** will be displayed. Choose the **Maya Software** tab and in the **Raytracing Quality** area, select the **Raytracing** check box to enable raytracing.

Use Raytrace Shadows

Select the **Use RayTrace Shadows** check box to ensure that the raytrace shadows is displayed in the scene.

Shadow Radius

This attribute is used to control the softness of the shadow edges.

Shadow Rays

This attribute is used to control the graininess of the shadow edges. The higher the number of shadow rays, the softer will be the graininess of the shadow edges but it will also increase the render time.

Ray Depth Limit

This attribute is used to specify the number of times a light ray can be reflected and refracted to cast the shadows.

Directional Light

Main menubar:	Create > Lights > Directional Light

The directional light is used to simulate a very distant point light source. The light rays coming from the directional light are parallel to each other. To create a directional light, choose **Create > Lights > Directional Light** from the main menubar; a directional light will be created on the grid in the viewport, as shown in Figure 8-7. To modify the parameters of the light, select the light and choose **Window > Attribute Editor** from the main menubar; the **Attribute Editor** showing the attributes of the directional light will be displayed on the right of the viewport. Some of the attributes of the directional

Figure 8-7 *A directional light created*

light are same as those of the ambient light as discussed earlier. Rest of them are discussed next.

Depth Map Shadow Attribute

These attributes are used to control the depth map shadows produced by the lights. A depth map shadow is simply an image output. It gives good result and does not take more render time. A depth map contains the depth data rendered from a light's position in the scene.

Use Depth Map Shadows

This attribute is used to enable depth map shadow calculations.

Resolution

This attribute is used to set the resolution of the depth map shadows. When you increase the resolution, the render time of the depth map shadows also increases.

Filter Size

This attribute is used to control the softness of the shadow edges. Higher the value of the filter size, softer will be the shadow edges.

Bias

This attribute is used to offset the shadow map towards or away from the light.

Directional light can be used to view the area illuminated by that particular light. To do so, choose **Panels > Look Through Selected** from the **Panel menu**; you can now look through the selected light. Use ALT+MMB to pan the view; ALT+ RMB to zoom in and out of the view, and the ALT+ LMB to rotate in the viewport. To go back to the previous view, choose **Panels > Perspective > persp** from the **Panel menu**; the Perspective view will be activated.

Note
MMB stands for Middle Mouse Button, LMB for Left Mouse Button, and RMB for Right Mouse Button. These conventions will be followed throughout the textbook.

You can set the focus point of the selected light by using the light manipulators from the main menubar. To do so, choose **Display > Show > Light Manipulators** from the main menubar; the light manipulators will be displayed on the selected light. To hide it, choose **Display > Hide > Light Manipulators** from the main menubar. Similarly, you can add the light manipulators to all the lights in Maya.

Point Light

Main menubar:	Create > Lights > Point Light

A point light is a single source of light that projects light evenly in all directions. It is very much similar to the ambient light. To create a point light, choose **Create > Lights > Point Light** from the main menubar; a point light will be created at the center of the viewport, as shown in Figure 8-8. The attributes of the point light are similar to the attributes discussed under the ambient light section. Some of its other attributes are discussed next.

Figure 8-8　A point light created

Light Effects Attribute

The **Light Effects** attribute area in the **Attribute Editor** is used to add additional parameters to a selected light. To access this area, select the light in the viewport and choose **Window > Attribute Editor** from the main menubar; the **Attribute Editor** will be displayed. Expand the **Light Effects** area in the **Attribute Editor**, if it is not already expanded. The attributes in the **Light Effects** area of the **Attribute Editor** are shown in Figure 8-9 and are discussed next.

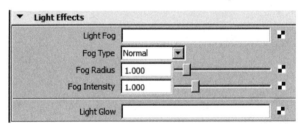

*Figure 8-9　The **Light Effects** area*

Light Fog

The **Light Fog** attribute is used to add the fog effect to a selected light. To do so, choose the checker button on the right of the **Light Fog** option in the **Attribute Editor** window, refer to Figure 8-9; the **Light Fog Attributes** area will be displayed. Adjust the light fog attributes in the **Light Fog Attributes** area of the **Attribute Editor**, refer to Figure 8-10. Adjust the **Color** and **Density** attributes as discussed earlier. The density of the fog will be high near the light and will gradually decrease as you move away from it.

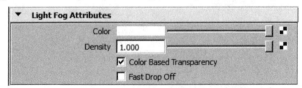

*Figure 8-10　The **Light Fog Attributes** area*

Fog Type

The **Fog Type** drop-down list is used to select the type of the fog. By default, **Normal** is selected in the **Fog Type** drop-down list. Choose **Linear** to diminish the fog from the centre of the edge, or choose **Exponential** to diminish the fog from the center of the light.

Fog Radius

The **Fog Radius** attribute is used to set the radius of the fog for the selected light. To do so, enter the radius value in the edit box or adjust the slider bar at its right.

Fog Intensity

The **Fog Intensity** attribute is used to increase or decrease the intensity of the fog. To do so, enter the required value in the edit box or adjust the slider bar at its right.

Light Glow

The **Light Glow** attribute is used to add glow to a selected light. Choose the checker box on the right of the **Light Glow** attribute; the opticalFX glow will be added to the selected light, as shown in Figure 8-11.

Figure 8-11 The light glow effect

Spot Light

Main menubar:	Create > Lights > Spot Light

The spot light is used to put focus on a particular object. This light is projected in the shape of a cone, as shown in Figure 8-12. It emits light from a specific point, which is radiated out in a conical shape. Figure 8-13 shows a flower pot with a spot light. The working of the spot light is very much similar to that of the directional light. To create a spot light, choose **Create > Lights > Spot Light** from the main menubar; the spot light will be created at the center of the viewport. Most of the attributes of the spot light are similar to those discussed under the ambient light section. Some of its other attributes are discussed next.

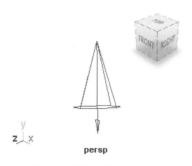

Figure 8-12   *The spot light*

Figure 8-13   *A flower pot illuminated by a spot light*

Spot Light Attributes

The **Spot Light Attributes** area in the **Attribute Editor** is used to adjust the attributes related to the spot light such as adjusting the cone angle, penumbra angle, and so on. To access these attributes, choose **Window > Attribute Editor** from the main menubar; the **Attribute Editor** window will be displayed. Expand the **Spot Light Attributes** tab, if not already expanded. The attributes in this area are discussed next.

Cone Angle

The **Cone Angle** attribute is used to set the focus area for the spot light. To do so, enter the value in the edit box or move the slider bar at its right. By default, the value is set to 40.00.

Penumbra Angle

The **Penumbra Angle** attribute is used to control the brightness of a spot light near edges. Higher the value of the **Penumbra Angle** attribute, lower will be the intensity at edges, as shown in Figure 8-14 and Figure 8-15.

Figure 8-14   *Spot Light with* **Penumbra Angle**: *0*

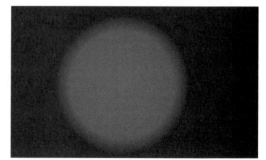

Figure 8-15   *Spot Light with* **Penumbra Angle**: *10*

Dropoff

The **Dropoff** attribute is used to control the intensity of the light from the center to the edge of the spot light beam area. Higher the value of the **Dropoff** attribute, lower will be the intensity of the spot light beam.

Light Effects

The **Light Effects** attribute area in the **Attribute Editor** is used to assign fog effects to light such as adding fog to a light. To access these attributes, choose **Window > Attribute Editor** from the main menubar; the **Attribute Editor** will be displayed. Expand the **Light Effects** area, if not already expanded. The attributes in this area are discussed next.

Light Fog

The **Light Fog** attribute is used to add fog effect to the selected light. To do so, select a light and then choose the checker button on the right of the **Light Fog** attribute; the light fog attributes will be added to the selected light in the **Attribute Editor**.

Fog Spread

The **Fog Spread** attribute is used to spread fog coming from a spot light. The more the **Fog Spread** value, the thicker will be the fog at the edges of the spot light, as shown in Figure 8-16 and Figure 8-17.

Figure 8-16 Spot Light with *Fog Spread: 1*   *Figure 8-17* Spot Light with *Fog Spread: 5*

Fog Intensity

The **Fog Intensity** attribute is used to adjust the intensity of the selected light. To do so, enter the value in the edit box or move the slider at the right of the **Fog Intensity** attribute.

If you want the light to be displayed in a certain shape, or as if it is coming from a half opened door, you can do so by adjusting its parameters. To do so, select the **Barn Doors** check box in the **Light Effects** area of the **Attribute Editor**; the attributes related to the barn doors will be activated. Enter the required values in the **Barn Doors** attributes area and render the scene to display the effect. The default values in all the input boxes are shown in Figure 8-18.

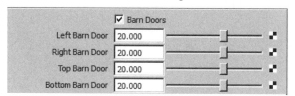

Figure 8-18 The *Barn Doors* attribute area

You can also set shadows for an object in viewport. To do so, expand the **Shadows** attribute tab in the **Attribute Editor**. Next, choose the **Use Depth Map Shadows** checker box from the

Depth Map Shadow Attributes area to make shadows active in the viewport. Render the scene to view the shadow effect, as shown in Figure 8-19.

Area Light

Main menubar:	Create > Lights > Area Light

The light effect created by an area light is similar to the one created by a point light. It emits light from a rectangular area. The larger the size of the light, more the scene will illuminate. To create an area light, choose **Create > Lights > Area Light** from the main menubar; an area light will be created at the center of the viewport, as shown in Figure 8-20. The area light can be used to create high quality still images. The scene with an area light will take more time for rendering as compared to other lights. The attributes of the area light are similar to those discussed under the ambient light section except Decay Rate and it is discussed next.

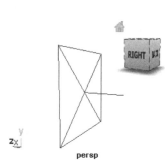

Figure 8-19 The shadow attribute applied to the spot light   *Figure 8-20* An area light

Decay Rate

This attribute is found only in Spot Light, Area Light, and Point Light. It is used to determine the rate at which the light decreases or fades away with distance. The options in **Decay Rate** are discussed next.

No Decay

If you use this option, the light will not fade away with distance. It will illuminate all the objects in the scene.

Linear

If you use this option, then on increasing the distance of the light, the intensity of light will decrease on a linear rate. This rate is slower than the real world light.

Quadratic

If you use this option, then as the distance from the light increases, the intensity of light will decrease with the square of the distance. This rate imitates the real world decay rate.

Cubic

If you use this option, then the instensity of light will decrease faster.

Volume Light

Main menubar:	Create > Lights > Volume Light

A volume light is used to add light only to the area that is enclosed within a volume light icon. To create a volume light, choose **Create > Lights > Volume Light** from the main menubar; a volume light will be created at the center of the viewport, as shown in Figure 8-21. Figure 8-22 shows the volume light effect. The attributes of the volume light are similar to those discussed in other lights.

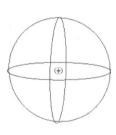

Figure 8-21 *The volume light*   *Figure 8-22* *The volume light effect*

GLOW AND HALO EFFECTS

The glow and halo effects add realistic effect to a scene. The glow and halo effects can be added to any light using the **Attribute Editor**. To do so, create a light in the viewport. Next, select the light and choose **Window > Attribute Editor** from the main menubar; the **Attribute Editor** displaying the attributes of the selected light will be displayed. Choose the checker button on the right of the **Color** attribute, as shown in Figure 8-23; the **Create Render Node** window will be displayed in the viewport. Choose the **Glow** attribute from the left of the **Create Render Node** window. Next, choose **Optical FX** from the right of the window; the **Optical FX Attributes** area will be displayed in the **Attribute Editor**, as shown in Figure 8-24. Various attributes in the **Optical FX Attributes** area are discussed next.

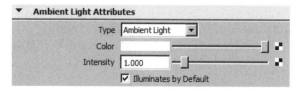

Figure 8-23 *The **Ambient Light Attributes** area*

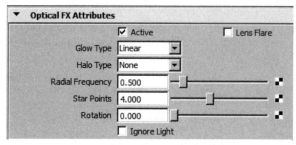

*Figure 8-24 The **Optical FX Attributes** area*

Active

The **Active** check box is used to switch the optical effects on or off. This check box is selected by default.

Lens Flare

The **Lens Flare** check box is used to add lens effect to a selected light. Lens flare is an unwanted light that is reflected within a lens or a camera. It results in the reduction of contrast and creation of bright streak patterns on an image. To apply the lens effect to a scene, select the **Lens Flare** check box from the **Optical FX Attributes** area; the lens effect will be created on the selected light. Figure 8-25 shows the light without lens flare and Figure 8-26 shows the light with lens flare.

Glow Type

The **Glow Type** drop-down list is used to apply various glow effects to a selected light. The options available in this drop-down list are: **Linear**, **Exponential**, **Ball**, **Lens Flare**, and **Rim Halo**. Figures through 8-27 through 8-31 show all these glow effects.

Radial Frequency

The **Radial Frequency** attribute is used to control the smoothness of the glow radial noise. To do so, enter the value in the **Radial Frequency** edit box or adjust the slider. The default range of slider is from 0 to 5, but manually you can enter a value to any extent in the edit box.

Halo Type

The **Halo Type** drop-down list is used to apply various halo effects to a selected light. Various halo type options available in this drop-down list are: **Linear**, **Exponential**, **Ball**, **Lens Flare**, and **Rim Halo**. Figures through 8-32 through 8-36 show various halo effects.

Star Points

The **Star Points** attribute is used to change the number of star points emitting from a light. Figures 8-37 and 8-38 show lights with different values in the **Star Points** edit box.

Figure 8-25 Light without lens flare

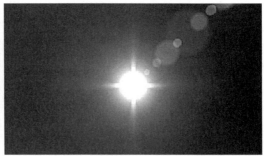

Figure 8-26 Light with lens flare

Figure 8-27 Glow **Linear** effect

Figure 8-28 Glow **Exponential** effect

Figure 8-29 Glow **Ball** effect

Figure 8-30 Glow **Lens Flare** effect

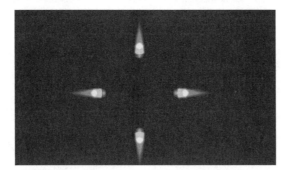

Figure 8-31 Glow **Rim Halo** effect

Figure 8-32 Halo *Linear effect*

Figure 8-33 Halo *Exponential effect*

Figure 8-34 Halo *Ball effect*

Figure 8-35 Halo *Lens Flare effect*

Figure 8-36 Halo *Rim Halo effect*

Figure 8-37 Light with *Star Points = 3*

Figure 8-38 Light with *Star Points = 15*

Rotation

The **Rotation** attribute is used to rotate the star effects from the center of the light. To do so, enter a value in the **Rotation** edit box or adjust the slider to its right. The value of slider ranges from 0 to 360, but you can also enter any other value as per your requirement in the edit box. Its default value is 0 degree. Below the **Optical FX Attributes** area, other attributes such as **Glow Attributes, Halo Attributes**, **Lens Flare**, and so on are available. You can modify these attributes using the **Attribute Editor** to get the desired effects.

PHYSICAL SUN AND SKY EFFECT

The **Physical Sun and Sky** feature is used to simulate natural daylight effect in a scene by using the mental ray renderer. To apply the Physical Sun and Sky effect to your scene, choose **Window > Settings/Preferences > Plug-in Manager** from the main menubar; the **Plug-in Manager** dialog box will be displayed, as shown in Figure 8-39. In this dialog box, select the **Loaded** check box on the right of the **Mayatomr.mll** plug-in type and choose the **Refresh** button. Next, choose the **Close** button; the physical sun and sky feature will be activated.

Next, choose the **Display Render Settings Window (Maya Software)** button from the status line; the **Render Settings** window will be displayed in the viewport. Select **mental ray** from the **Render Using** drop-down list; the mental ray renderer for rendering the scene will be activated. Choose the **Indirect Lighting** tab from this window; all attributes of indirect lighting will be displayed. Expand the **Environment** attribute area, as shown in Figure 8-40 and then choose the **Create** button on the right of the **Physical Sun and Sky** attribute; a directional light will be created in the viewport. The directional light displays the effect of physical sun and sky in the scene. Figure 8-41 shows the **Physical Sun and Sky** effect applied to a scene.

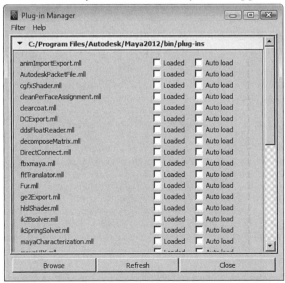

*Figure 8-39 The **Plug-in Manager** dialog box*

Figure 8-40 The **Environment** *area*

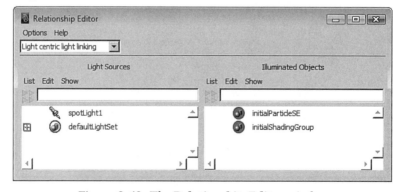

Figure 8-41 The physical sun and sky effect applied to a scene

LIGHT LINKING

Light linking is a phenomenon of linking light to specific objects in a scene. On linking light to an object, the light affects only the linked object in a scene. To do so, create a light in the scene and choose the **Rendering** module from the status line. Next, choose **Lighting/ Shading > Light Linking Editor > Light Centric** from the main menubar; the **Relationship Editor** window will be displayed in the viewport, as shown in Figure 8-42. Choose the light source that you want to link and then select the object from the **Illuminated Objects** area of the **Relationship Editor** window; the light source will illuminate only the linked object. Close the **Relationship Editor** window.

Figure 8-42 The **Relationship Editor** *window*

CAMERAS

In Autodesk Maya, **Cameras** are used to present a scene from different angles. These cameras play the role of still and video cameras of the real world. There are four types of cameras in Maya: **Camera**, **Camera and Aim**, **Camera Aim and Up**, and **Stereo Camera**. These camera types are discussed next.

Camera

Main menubar:	Create > Cameras > Camera

To create a camera, choose **Create > Cameras > Camera** from the main menubar; a camera will be created in the viewport, as shown in Figure 8-43. You can adjust this camera to focus on any object, as shown in Figure 8-44. You can set the properties of the **Camera** camera type in the **Attribute Editor**. To do so, select the camera and choose **Display > UI Elements > Attribute Editor** from the main menubar; the **Attribute Editor** will be displayed with camera attributes, as shown in Figure 8-45. These attributes are discussed next.

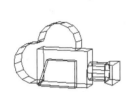

Figure 8-43 *A camera created*

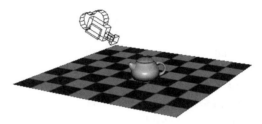

Figure 8-44 *The camera focusing on an object*

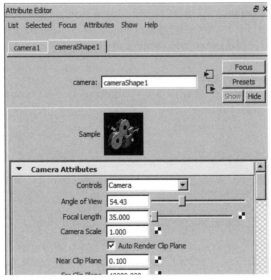

Figure 8-45 *Partial view of the camera attributes in the **Attribute Editor***

Controls

The **Controls** drop-down list is used to change the type of camera in the viewport. To do so, select the required camera from the drop-down list; the selected camera will be displayed in the viewport.

Angle of View

The **Angle of View** option is used to set the view angle of a camera. Choose **Panels > Perspective > camera1** from the panel menu to switch from current view to the camera view. Next, move the **Angle of View** slider or enter a value in the edit box to set the view angle. By changing the view angle, you can view the effect of the camera on the screen simultaneously.

Focal Length

The **Focal Length** option is used to zoom in and zoom out the camera. Choose **Panels > Perspective > camera1** from the **Panel menu** to switch the current view to the camera view. Next, move the **Focal Length** slider or enter a value in the edit box to set the focal length. Increasing the **Focal Length** value will allow you to zoom in the view, thereby enabling you to have an enlarged view of the objects, whereas decreasing this value will make the objects appear smaller.

Camera Scale

The **Camera Scale** option is used to scale the size of the camera that is indirectly proportional to the scene. For example, on increasing the size of the camera, the scene will zoom out and vice versa.

Auto Render Clip Plane

This option is turned on by default. It automatically sets near and far clipping planes in such a way that all the objects in the scene come within the camera view.

Near and Far Clipping Planes

The **Near and Far Clipping Planes** are defined as two separate clipping planes set at some distance from the camera.

Note
Only objects placed between the clipping planes will be rendered.

Camera and Aim

Main menubar:	Create > Cameras > Camera and Aim

This type of camera has a target and an aim handle. It stays in accordance to the level of horizon. To create a Camera and Aim camera, choose **Create > Cameras > Camera and Aim** from the main menubar; a camera with aim will be created in the viewport, as shown in Figure 8-46. Select the aim of the camera to focus it on an object, as shown in Figure 8-47. To modify the attributes of the **Camera and Aim** camera, select the camera in the viewport and choose **Window > Attribute Editor** from the main menubar; the **Attribute Editor** with the properties of the **Camera and Aim** camera will be displayed. The attributes of the **Camera and Aim** camera are the same as those discussed in the **Camera** section.

Figure 8-46 *A camera with aim created*

Figure 8-47 *The camera with aim focusing on an object*

Camera, Aim and Up

Main menubar: Create > Cameras > Camera, Aim and Up

This type of camera has two handles: a **Direction Aim** handle and a **Target Aim** handle. To create a **Camera, Aim and Up** camera, choose **Create > Cameras > Camera, Aim and Up** from the main menubar; a camera with the **Direction Aim** and **Target Aim** handles will be created in the viewport, as shown in Figure 8-48. Select the target aim of the camera to focus it on an object, as shown in Figure 8-49. You can select the direction aim of the camera to rotate it, that keeps the target fixed.

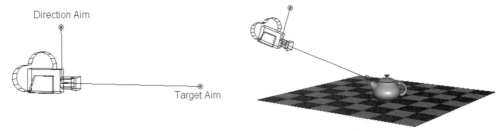

Figure 8-48 *A camera with the **Direction Aim** and **Target Aim** handles created*

Figure 8-49 *The camera with **Direction Aim** and **Target Aim** handles focusing on an object*

To modify the attributes of the **Camera, Aim and Up** camera, select the camera in the viewport and choose **Windows > Attribute Editor** from the main menubar; the **Attribute Editor** will be displayed. The attributes of **Camera, Aim and Up** are same as those discussed in the **Camera** type section.

Stereo Camera

Main menubar: Create > Cameras > Stereo Camera

This type of camera is used to create three-dimensional renders with illusion of a 3Ddepth of a scene. In this type of setting, Maya calculates all stereoscopic camera attributes to produce anaglyph/parallel kind of image. To create a stereo camera, choose **Create > Cameras > Stereo Camera** from the main menubar; a Stereo camera will be created in the viewport. To change the view to a stereo camera view, choose **Panels > Stereo > stereoCamera** from the **Panel menu**; the viewport will switch to a stereo camera view.

Multi-Stereo Rig

Main menubar:	Create > Cameras > Multi Stereo Rig

This tool is used to create multi-camera rig for stereo cameras. By default, it is done by three layered multi-layered camera rig.

TUTORIALS
Tutorial 1

In this tutorial, you will create the light scattering through a cylinder, as shown in Figure 8-50.   **(Expected time: 15 min)**

The following steps are required to complete this tutorial:

a. Create a project folder.
b. Create a cylinder.
c. Apply volume light to the cylinder.
d. Render the scene and then save it.

Figure 8-50 *The scattering light effect*

Creating the Project Folder
Before starting a new file, it is recommended that you set the project folder.

1. Create a project with the name *c08_tut1* in the folder *Maya_Tutorials*.

Creating a Cylinder
In this section, you need to create a cylinder through which the light will scatter in all directions.

1. Activate the Top viewport. Next, choose **Create > Polygon Primitives > Cylinder** from the main menubar and then create a cylinder in the viewport.

2. Choose **Display > UI Elements > Channel Box/Layer Editor** from the main menubar;

the **Channel box** is displayed. Enter the following values in the **INPUTS** area of the channel box to adjust the properties of the cylinder:

Radius: **2**   Height: **10**   Subdivisions Axis: **50**
Subdivisions Height: **25**   Subdivisions Caps: **0**

3. Press the numeric key 5 to switch to the shaded mode. Next, press and hold the right mouse button on the cylinder and then choose **Face** from the marking menu.

4. Activate the Perspective viewport, select the top and bottom faces of the cylinder and delete them. Similarly, delete the other faces of the cylinder randomly, as shown in Figure 8-51.

5. Choose **Create > Polygon Primitives > Plane** from the main menubar. Next, create a plane in the viewport. Now, choose the **Move Tool** from the toolbox and place the plane below the cylinder.

Figure 8-51 *Randomly deleted faces*

6. Select all faces of the cylinder as discussed earlier. Next, choose **Edit Mesh > Extrude** from the main menubar. Now, choose the **Scale** tool from the toolbox and then scale the selected faces to increase the thickness of the cylinder. Next, press F8 to switch to the object mode.

7. Select the cylinder and then choose **Mesh > Smooth** from the main menubar to make the cylinder smooth.

Applying the Volume Light to the Cylinder

In this section, you need to create a volume light in the center of the cylinder that will act as the source of light.

1. Choose **Create > Lights > Volume Light** from the main menubar to create a volume light. Next, choose **Display > UI Elements > Channel Box/Layer Editor** from the main menubar; the **Channel box** is displayed. Set the values in the **Scale X**, **Scale Y**, and **Scale Z** attributes to **15**.

2. Choose the **Move Tool** from the toolbox, select the volume light from the viewport, and then place it at the center of the cylinder.

3. Select the light and choose **Window > Attribute Editor** from the main menubar; the **Attribute Editor** is displayed with the properties of the volume light.

4. Choose the white color box on the right of the **Color** attribute; the **Color History** palette

is displayed. Set the color of the light to yellow. Click anywhere outside the palette; the color of the light changes to yellow. Enter **2.4** in the **Intensity** input box area.

5. Expand the **Light Effects** attribute tab in the **Attribute Editor**. Set the **Fog Intensity** to 4.0.

6. Choose the checker box on the right of the **Light Fog** attribute to apply the fog effect to the light.

7. Choose **VolumeLightShape1** tab in the **Attribute Editor**. Expand the **Shadows** attribute tab from the **Attribute Editor**. Next, select the **Use Depth Map Shadows** check box in the **Depth Map Shadow** attributes area to add shadow to your scene. Then, set the value in the **Resolution** edit box to **2000** for better resolution of shadows.

Rendering and Saving the Scene

In this section, you need to render the scene and then save it for the final output.

1. Choose **Render the Current Frame (Maya Software)** button from the status line to render the scene.

    The **Render View** window is displayed with the final output, as shown in Figure 8-52.

2. Choose **File > Save Scene** from the main menubar; the **Save As** dialog box is displayed.

    As the project folder is already set, by default the path *\Documents\Maya_Tutorials\c08_tut1\ scenes* is displayed in **Look In** text box of the dialog box.

3. Enter **c08_tut1** in the **File name** text box and then select **Maya Binary** from the **Files of type** drop-down list. Next, choose the **Save As** button.

You can view the final rendered image of the model by downloading the *c08_Maya_2012_render.zip* file from *http://www.cadcim.com*.

Figure 8-52 *The final output after rendering*

Tutorial 2

In this tutorial, you will create an underwater scene, as shown in Figure 8-53.

(Expected time: 30 min)

Figure 8-53 *An underwater scene*

The following steps are required to complete this tutorial:

a.   Set a project folder.
b.   Apply lights to the scene.
c.   Render and save the file.

Setting the Project Folder

Before starting a new file, it is recommended that you set the project folder.

1.   Set a project with the name *c08_tut2* in the folder *Maya_Tutorials*.

Applying Lights to the Scene

In this section, you need to apply lights to the scene.

1.   Choose **Create > Lights > Spot Light** from the main menubar; a spot light is created in the viewport.

2.   Activate the Front viewport; the light is placed in the viewport, as shown in Figure 8-54. Use the **Rotate** and **Move** tools to adjust the spot light, as shown in Figure 8-55.

3.   Choose **Display > Show > Light Manipulators** from the main menubar; the light manipulators are displayed, as shown in Figure 8-56. Select the manipulator ring 10, press and hold the left mouse button on it, and then move it downward till the number on the ring changes to 100; the fog area of the light is increased.

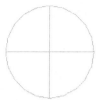

Figure 8-54 *Placement of spot light in the front viewport*

Figure 8-55 *Spot light after the adjustment in the front viewport*

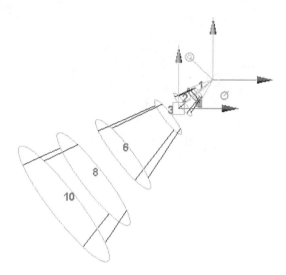

Figure 8-56 *The light manipulators*

4. Choose **Display > Hide > Light Manipulators** from the main menubar to hide the manipulators. Next, select the light and choose **Display > UI Elements > Channel Box/Layer Editor** from the main menubar; a **Channel box** is displayed. Enter **20** in the **Translate Y** edit box of the **Channel box** to position the spot light.

5. Select the spot light and choose **Window > Attribute Editor** from the main menubar; the **Attribute Editor** is displayed. Next, choose the checker button on the right of the **Color** attribute; the **Create Render Node** window is displayed. Choose the **File** button from the **Create Render Node** window; the **File Attributes** are displayed in the **Attribute Editor**.

6. Choose the open folder icon from the **Image Name** attribute in the **Attribute Editor**; the **Open** window is displayed. Locate the *texture_light.jpg* file in the **sourceimages** in project folder and assign it. Next, choose the **Open** button to open the selected file.

7. Select the spot light and set the **Cone Angle** to **60** in the **Attribute Editor**. Expand the **Light Effects** attribute tab in the **Attribute Editor**. Next, choose the checker button on the right of the **Light Fog** attribute to apply the fog effect to the spot light.

8. Select the spot light, and then set **Fog Spread** to **1.5** and **Fog Intensity** to **2** in the **Attribute Editor**.

9. Choose **Display > UI Elements > Channel Box/Layer Editor** from the main menubar; a channel box is displayed. Enter the following values in the **Channel box**:

    TranslateX: **1.034**   TranslateY: **51.527**   TranslateZ: **1.499**
    RotateX: **121.306**   RotateY: **73.369**   RotateZ: **-180**

10. Activate the Perspective viewport and choose **Render the current frame (Maya Software)** from the status line to view the fog effect, as shown in Figure 8-57.

Figure 8-57 Fog effect applied to the spot light

11. Choose **Create > Lights > Ambient Light** from the main menubar to create one more light in the scene. Set the parameters of the ambient light in the channel box as follows:

    TranslateX: **65**   TranslateY: **26**   TranslateZ: **152**

12. Choose the **Rendering** module from the status line. Next, choose **Lighting/Shading > Light Linking Editor > Light-Centric** from the main menubar; the **Relationship Editor** window is displayed.

13. Choose spot light from the **Light Sources** area and group1 from the **Illuminated Objects** area in the **Relationship Editor** window to link the light to the object.

14. Choose **Panels > Perspective > camera1** from the panel menu to switch from the Perspective view to the camera view. Adjust the camera, if required.

 Note
You can also adjust the camera, based on your requirement.

Rendering and Saving the Scene

In this section, you need to render the scene for the final output and then save the file.

1. Choose **Render the Current Frame (Maya Software)** button from the status line to render the scene.

    The **Render View** window is displayed with the final output, as shown in Figure 8-58.

2. Choose **File > Save Scene** from the main menubar; the **Save As** dialog box is displayed.

    As the project folder is already set, by default the path *\Documents\Maya_Tutorials\c08_tut2\ scenes* is displayed in **Look In** text box of the dialog box.

3. Enter **c08_tut2** in the **File name** text box and then select **Maya Binary** from the **Files of type** drop-down list. Next, choose the **Save As** button.

You can view the final rendered image of the model by downloading the *c08_Maya_2012_render.zip* file from *http://www.cadcim.com.*

Figure 8-58 *Final output after rendering*

Tutorial 3

In this tutorial, you will add lighting effects to a living room, as shown in Figure 8-59.

(Expected time: 15 min)

Figure 8-59 *The living room*

The following steps are required to complete this tutorial:

a. Set a project folder.
b. Apply lights to the scene.
c. Render and save the file.

Setting the Project Folder

Before starting a new file, it is recommended that you set the project folder.

1. Set a project with the name *c08_tut3* in the folder *Maya_Tutorial*.

Applying Lights to the Scene

In this section, you need to create point lights and then apply them to the scene.

1. Activate the Top viewport. Choose **Create > Lights > Point Light** from the main menubar; a point light is created.

2. Choose the **Move Tool** from the toolbox and move the point light to point 1 in Top viewport, as shown in Figure 8-60. Select the light and choose **Window > Attribute Editor** from the main menubar; the **Attribute Editor** is displayed. Set the parameters of the light in the **Attribute Editor** as follows:

Intensity : **0.3**   Decay rate : **Quadratic**

3. Similarly, create more point lights and adjust them to different points in the dining room, as shown in Figure 8-60. Now, enter values for these lights in the **Attribute Editor,** as shown in Table 8-1.

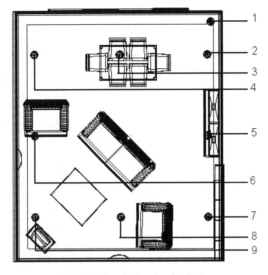

Figure 8-60 Point lights in the living room

Light No.	Intensity	Decay Rate
1	0.3	Quadratic
2	0.2	Quadratic
3	0.2	Quadratic
4	0.3	Quadratic
5	0.2	Quadratic
6	0.3	Quadratic
7	0.3	Quadratic
8	0.3	Quadratic
9	0.2	Quadratic

Table 8-1 Point lights with their intensity and decay rate values

4. Activate the Side viewport. Select all lights in the viewport. Next, choose the **Move Tool** and move all the lights up in the Y axis, toward the ceiling of the room, as shown in Figure 8-61.

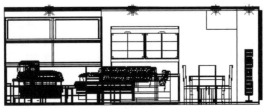

Figure 8-61 The lights moved toward the ceiling

5. Activate the Top viewport and then create a point light in the viewport, as shown in Figure 8-62. This light acts as a fill light for the scene. Select the light and choose **Display > UI Elements > Channel Box/ Layer Editor** from the main menubar; a **Channel box** is displayed. In the **Channel box**, set the **Translate Y** value to **2.8**.

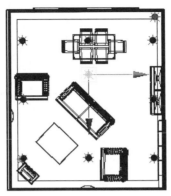

Figure 8-62 Point light created

6. Select the light and choose **Edit > Duplicate** from the main menubar; a duplicate of the selected light is created in the viewport overlapping on the selected light. Place the duplicate light near the point light 8, refer to Figure 8-62. Next, choose **Window > Attribute Editor** from the main menubar; the **Attribute Editor** is displayed. Enter the following values for the point light in the **Attribute Editor**:

   Intensity : **0.8**   Decay Rate : **No decay**

7. Choose **Panels > Perspective> Persp1** from the **Panel menu** to set the current view to the camera view (**persp1** is the name of the camera used in the scene). Render the scene to preview the lighting of the scene, as shown in Figure 8-63.

 Note
You can try various options to get different effects of lights in the scene.

Figure 8-63 The preview

8. There are certain areas in the scene that are still not lit up. To light them up, apply a light through the camera angle and create point lights, as shown in Figure 8-64.

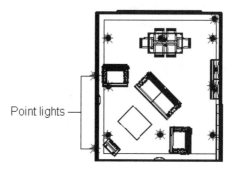

Figure 8-64 Point lights created

9. Choose **Window > Attribute Editor** from the main menubar; the attributes of the selected light are displayed. Set **Intensity** to **0.7** and **Decay Rate** to **quadratic** for the selected light in the **Attribute Editor**.

Rendering and Saving the File

In this section, you need to render the scene to get the final output and then save the file.

1. Choose **Render the Current Frame (Maya Software)** button from the status line to render the scene.

    The **Render View** window is displayed with the final output, as shown in Figure 8-65.

2. Choose **File > Save Scene** from the main menubar; the **Save As** dialog box is displayed.

    As the project folder is already set, by default the path *\Documents\Maya_Tutorials\c08_tut3\scenes* is displayed in **Look In** text box of the dialog box.

3. Enter **c08_tut3** in the **File name** text box and then select **Maya Binary** from the **Files of type** drop-down list. Next, choose the **Save As** button.

You can view the final rendered image of the model by downloading the *c08_Maya_2012_render.zip* file from *http://www.cadcim.com*.

Figure 8-65 *The final scene after rendering*

Self-Evaluation Test

Answer the following questions and then compare them to those given at the end of this chapter:

1. Which of the following lights is mostly used as a background light?

    (a) Ambient Light   (b) Point Light
    (c) Directional Light   (d) Area Light

2. Which of the following lights is particularly used to focus on an object?

    (a) Spot Light   (b) Ambient Light
    (c) Area Light   (d) None of these

3. A _____ emits light from a specific point and radiates it out in a conical shape.

4. A Point Light works similar to an _____.

5. The _____ is a phenomenon of linking light to particular objects in a scene.

6. The _____ light is used to add light to the area enclosed within the volume light icon.

7. The _____ **Frequency** attribute helps you control the smoothness of the glow radial noise.

8. The **Physical Sun and Sky** option works only with the mental ray. (T/F)

9. The **Focal Length** option is used to zoom in and out of the camera. (T/F)

10. The **Angle of View** option is used to set the view angle of the camera. (T/F)

Review Questions

Answer the following questions:

1. How many types of cameras are there in Maya?

    (a) Two   (b) Five
    (c) Four   (d) One

2. Which of the following lights is used to create high quality still images?

    (a) Volume Light   (b) Area Light
    (c) Point Light   (d) Directional Light

3. The _____ attribute is used to spread fog coming from the spot light.

4. The _____ is a phenomenon of linking light to specific objects.

5. The _____ **Angle** attribute is used to set the focus area of the spot light.

6. The _____ **Flare** is used to add the lens flare effect to a selected light.

7. An _____ light is a single point light that projects rays uniformly in all directions.

8. The **Cone Angle** attribute is used to control the brightness of spot light near edges. (T/F)

9. The glow types in the halo type pull down menu are: **Linear, Exponential, Ball, Lens Flare**, and **Rim Halo**. (T/F)

10. Increasing **Focal Length** allows you to zoom in a view and enlarges objects in the view and vice versa. (T/F)

Exercises

Exercise 1

Open the model shown in Figure 8-66 and apply textures to it. You can view the final rendered image of this model by downloading the *c08_maya_2012_render.zip* file from *http://www.cadcim.com*. The path of file is as follows:

Textbooks > Animation and Visual Effects > Maya > Autodesk Maya 2012: A Comprehensive Guide

Apply the physical sun and sky effect to the textured model to get the output shown in Figure 8-67.   (**Expected time: 15 min**)

Figure 8-66 *The textured model of Chapter 5*

Figure 8-67 The physical sun and sky effect applied to the model

Exercise 2

Open the model shown in Figure 8-68 and apply textures to it. You can view the final rendered image of this model by downloading the *c08_maya_2012_render.zip* file from *http://www.cadcim.com*. The path of file follows is mentioned in Exercise 1.

By default, the textured model will be visible in the viewport, as shown in Figure 8-68. Apply lights to the textured model to get the output shown in Figure 8-69.

(Expected time: 30 min)

Figure 8-68 *The textured model of an interior*

Figure 8-69 *The model after applying lights*

Answers to Self-Evaluation Test
1. a, **2.** a, **3.** Spot light, **4.** Ambient light, **5.** Light linking, **6.** Volume, **7. Radial**, **8.** T, **9.** T, **10.** T

Chapter 9

Animation-I

Learning Objectives

After completing this chapter, you will be able to:

• *Understand the basic concepts of animation*
• *Understand different types of animation*
• *Use the Graph Editor for editing curves*
• *Use Animation Layers*

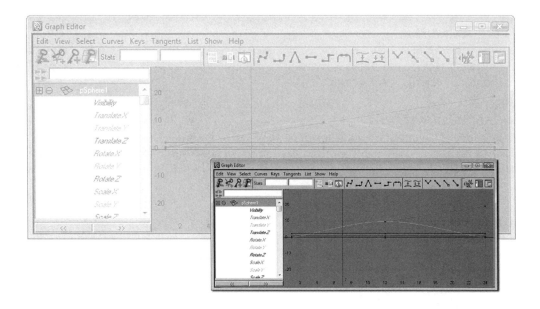

INTRODUCTION TO ANIMATION

Animation is a process of adding life to a model. In this chapter, you will learn to animate 3D models using various types of animations such as character animation, path animation, nonlinear animation, technical animation, and other types of motion that you see in the real world.

To animate a 3D object, you need to define different positions, rotations, and scaling of the object at different frames in the time slider. These frames are known as keyframes. The keys between the keyframes contain information of the actions performed in an animation. When an animation is played, the frames are displayed one after another in quick succession and thus create optical illusion of motion. In this chapter, you will also learn about the playback control buttons available at the bottom of the viewport and various other additional tools used in animation.

Animation Types

In Maya, there are various types of animations. Some of them are discussed below.

1.   Keyframe Animation
2.   Effects Animation
3.   Nonlinear Animation
4.   Path Animation
5.   Motion Capture Animation
6.   Technical Animation

Keyframe Animation

The Keyframe Animation is used to transform objects by setting the keyframes manually on the time slider. It is the most commonly used animation type, as it is highly flexible and helps to create complex animations easily.

Effects Animation

The Effects Animation is also known as the Dynamic Animation. It is used in simulating the natural forces by using Maya's internal programming. Animation of fluids, particles, and hair/fur are some examples of Effects Animation.

Nonlinear Animation

The Nonlinear Animation is an advanced method of animation. It is used to blend, duplicate, and split animation clips to achieve different motion effects. Nonlinear animation is controlled by using Trax Editor. For example, you can loop the walk cycle of your character by using Graph Editor.

Path Animation

The Path animation is used to animate an object's translation and rotation attributes on the basis of the NURBS curve. This type of animation is used to animate an object along a path such as moving a car on the road or moving a train on rail.

Motion Capture Animation

Motion Capture is a recording of human body movement for immediate or delayed analysis and playback. It is used to animate a character by using the motion capturing devices. A motion capture device helps in real time monitoring and recording of data.

Technical Animation

Technical Animation is used to animate an object by linking the translation and rotation attributes of one object with another object. The linking is done by setting driven keys in such a way that the attributes of one object are governed by the attributes of the another object. For example, if you want to animate a locomotive engine, you need to link various parts of the engine for animating it. You can do so by using the technical animation.

EDITABLE MOTION TRAILS

The **Editable Motion Trails** tool is used to take a sneak peek of the animation of current object in the viewport itself. To understand the working of the tool, choose **Animate > Create Editable Motion Trail > Option Box** from the main menubar; the **Motion Trail Options** dialog box will be displayed, as shown in Figure 9-1. It is also used to modify the keys in the viewport only.

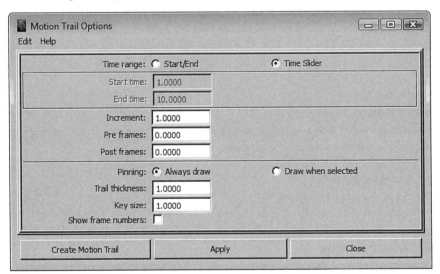

*Figure 9-1 The **Motion Trail Options** dialog box*

Playback Controls

The Playback Controls is, as shown in Figure 9-2, are used to control the animation in a scene by starting or stopping the animation clip. These buttons are located on the time slider and range slider at the bottom of the viewport. The time slider and range slider have been discussed in Chapter 1. The animation playback control buttons in Maya are discussed next.

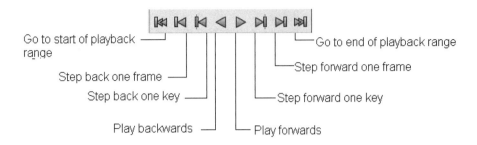

Figure 9-2 *The playback controls*

Play forwards

The **Play forwards** button is used to play or start the animation in the forward direction. When you choose this button, it turns into the **Stop playback** button.

Play backwards

The **Play backwards** button is used to play or start the anmation in backward direction. When you choose the **Play backwards** button, it turns into the **Stop playback** button.

Stop playback

The **Stop playback** button is used to stop an animation clip. You can stop an animation at any frame in the time segment to view the effect at that particular frame. Alternatively, you can press the ESC key to stop the animation.

Step forward one key

The **Step forward one key** button is used to jump from one key to the next one in   the forward direction in the active time segment.

Step backward one key

The **Step backward one key** button is used to jump from one key to the next one in the backward direction in the active time segment.

Step back one frame

The **Step back one frame** button is used to step one frame at a time in the backward direction. You can view the current frame on the time slider when it moves from one frame to another. The keyboard shortcut for this button is ALT + ,(comma).

Step forward one frame

The **Step forward one frame** button is used to step one frame at a time in the forward direction in the active time segment. The keyboard shortcut for this button is ALT+.(dot).

Go to end of playback range

 The **Go to end of playback range** button is used to go to the last frame of the active time segment.

Go to beginning of playback range

 The **Go to beginning of playback range** button is used to go to the first frame of the active time segment.

Animation preferences

The **Animation preferences** button is used to set the attributes of an animation. To do so, choose the **Animation preferences** button located below the **Go to end of playback range** button in the **Playback Control** area; the **Preferences** dialog box will be displayed in the viewport, as shown in Figure 9-3. Alternatively, you can choose **Windows > Setting Preferences > Preferences** from the main menubar to display the **Preferences** dialog box. Next, choose **Time Slider** from the **Categories** list in the **Preferences** dialog box; the **Time Slider: Animation Time Slider**, and **Playback Preferences** area will be displayed to the right of the **Categories** list in the **Preferences** window. Adjust the playback controls in the **Preferences** dialog box as per your requirement. The attributes in this dialog box are discussed next.

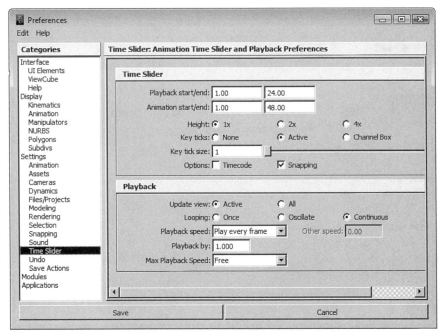

Figure 9-3 *The **Preferences** dialog box*

Time Slider

Time slider is used to specify the time range, play back start/end, and so on. and end of the The various controls in **Time Slider** are discussed below.

Playback start/end

The **Playback start/end** attribute is used to determine the playback start and end of in terms of frames. The default playback start time and end time are 1.00 and 24.00, respectively.

Animation start/end

The **Animation start/end** attribute is used to determine the starting and ending time of animation. The default animation start time and end time are 1.00 and 48.00, respectively.

Height

The **Height** attribute is used to specify the vertical space taken by the **Time Slider** in the interface.

Key ticks

The **Key ticks** attribute is used to specify the appearance of the line markers on the **Time Slider**. By default, it is set to Active mode.

Key tick size

The **Key tick size** attribute is used to specify the thickness of the key.

Options

This option is used to choose between **Timecode** or **Snapping**. **Timecode** is used to display current time in video standard timecode. **Snapping** is used to snap the animation to nearest integer. By default, the **Snapping option** is selected.

Playback

This area is used to playback the scene in real time.

Update view

The **Update view** attribute is used to play the animation clip in the active view only. By default, it is set to **Active** mode. On selecting the **All** button, it will enable the animation clip to be played in all the views.

Looping

The **Looping** attribute is used to specify the way the playback will start/end. By default, it is set to Continuous mode.

Playback speed

The **Playback speed** attribute is used to specify the speed of the playback. By default, it is set to Play every frame.

Playback by

The **Playback by** attribute is used to play the animation clip at every frame. For example if it set to 10.00; the animation will be played on every 10th frame.

Max Playback Speed

The **Max Playback Speed** attribute is used to clamp the playback speed of the current animation. By default, it is set to Free mode.

COMMONLY USED TERMS IN ANIMATION

In Maya, certain terms are commonly used while animating an object. These terms are discussed next.

Frame Rate

The **Frame rate** is termed as the number of frames or imges displayed per second in a sequence. It is abbreviated as fps (frames per second). It is the total number of frames played per second in an animation.

Range

The term **Range** is used to define the total length of an animation. The range of an animation is calculated in frames. For calculating the range of an animation, multiply the frame rate with the total time of animation. For example, if you have a frame rate of 24 fps and the total time of the animation is 5 secs, then the range of the animation will be: 24 X 5 = 120 frames

Setting Keys

Setting Keys is defined as a process of specifying the translation and rotational values of an object on a particular frame. These keys can be deleted, and duplicated. To set the key for an object in the viewport, select the object for which you want to set the key and choose a frame in the timeline on which you want to set the key. Then, select the **Animation** module from the module drop-down list in the status line. Next, choose **Animate > Set Key** from the main menubar; the key will be set at the selected frame in the timeline. Alternatively, choose **Display > UI Elements > Channel Box/Layer Editor** from the main menubar; the **Channel box** will be displayed. Press and hold the right mouse button on any translate axes; a flyout will be displayed. Choose **Key Selected** from the flyout to set the key for the selected translate axis. On setting the keys, the default background color of the attributes in the **Channel box** changes to peach color, indicating that the keys are set for the selected attributes.

CREATING DIFFERENT TYPES OF ANIMATIONS

You have already learned briefly about different types of animation at the beginning of this chapter. Now, you will learn to animate objects using some of these animation types.

Path Animation

As discussed earlier, the **Path Animation** method is used to animate an object along a path. To do so, activate the Top viewport, choose **Create > EP Curve Tool** from the main menubar, and then create a curve, as shown in Figure 9-4. Next, choose **Create > NURBS Primitives >**

Sphere from the main menubar and create a sphere in the viewport, as shown in Figure 9-4. Now, press and hold the SHIFT key to select the sphere first and then the curve. Next, select the **Animation** module from the menu set drop-down list in the status line. Next, choose **Animate > Motion Paths > Attach to Motion Path** from the main menubar; the sphere will be attached to the curve. Choose the **Play forwards** button from the animation control; the sphere will start moving along the path. You can also use a closed path to animate an object.

Sometimes, when you choose the **Play forwards** button from the animation playback controls, the sphere may not sail smoothly on the curve. To overcome this problem, select the sphere from the viewport and choose **Animate > Motion Paths > Flow Path Object** from the main menubar; a lattice will be created for the object throughout the curve. The lattice provides smoothness to the motion of the sphere. To detach the sphere from the curve, select it and choose **Display > UI Elements > Channel Box/Layer Editor** from the main menubar; the **Channel box** will be displayed. Next, press and hold the SHIFT key and select the **TranslateX**, **TranslateY**, **TranslateZ**, **RotateX**, **RotateY**, and **RotateZ** axis options from the **Channel box**. Now, press and hold

Figure 9-4 The NURBS curve and the sphere

the right mouse button over the selected attributes; a flyout will be displayed. Choose **Break Connections** from the flyout; the sphere will be detached from the curve. Similarly, you can detach the curve from the sphere.

Tip. *To animate multiple objects on a single path curve, select the objects that you want to animate and then choose the path curve; all objects will be attached to the path through their pivot points. You can change the pivot points to help the objects move separately.*

Note
If the object gets distorted on applying the **Flow Path Object** *option, choose* **Window > Outliner** *from the main menubar and select the* **FFD1 lattice** *and* **FFD1Base** *lattices from the* **Outliner** *window. Then, scale the two selected lattices such that the object fits well into the lattice structure.*

Keyframe Animation

The **Keyframe Animation** method is the standard method used for animating an object. It is used to animate an object by creating smooth transitions between different keyframes. This is done by setting the keys for object at two extreme positions. Maya then interpolates the value for the keyed attributes with the change in the timeline between the two set keys.

You can set the key for animating an object by pressing **S** on the keyboard. Alternatively, select the frame at which you want to set the key and choose **Animate > Set Key** from the main menubar; a key will be set at the selected frame. You can also use the **Auto Keyframe** method to set the keys for creating an animation. To understand the method of animating an object by setting the keys in the timeline in a better way, follow the steps given next.

1. Activate the Perspective viewport and choose **Create > Polygon Primitives > Cube** from the main menubar; you will be prompted to create a polygon cube in the viewport. Create a polygon cube in the viewport.

2. Choose the **Animation preferences** button located below the animation playback controls; the **Preferences** dialog box will be displayed with the **Animation Time Slider and Playback Preferences** attributes, as shown in Figure 9-5. Set the required parameters in this dialog box and choose the **Save** button.

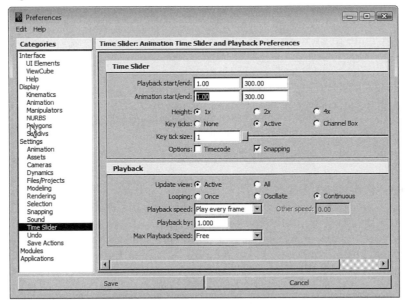

Figure 9-5 *The Animation Time Slider and Playback Preferences attributes*

3. Select the polygon cube from the viewport and choose **Modify > Freeze Transformations** from the main menubar. Move, Rotate and Scale attributes of the cube will be set to **0**.

4. Set the current time indicator to **frame 1** (you can move the gray vertical bar on the timeline to set the keyframe). Next, choose **Animate > Set Key** from the main menubar; the key will be set on **frame 1**.

5. Set the value in the current time indicator to frame **300**. Next, set the **TranslateX** value in the channel box to **15** and choose **Animate > Set Key** from the main menubar; the key will be set for the selected frame. Now, choose the **Play forwards** button from the playback controls to preview the animation.

6. Move the current time indicator to frame **150**. Next, set the **TranslateZ** value to **5**. Now, choose **Animate > Set Key** from the main menubar to set the key. Then, choose the **Play forwards** button from the playback controls to preview the animation; the cube will move on the curve path.

If you want the cube to rotate while animating, select the cube and set the current time indicator to frame **0** on the timeline. Now, press SHIFT+e to set the keys for rotation. Next, choose **Display > UI Elements > Channel Box/Layer Editor** from main menubar; the **Channel box/layer editor** will be displayed. Next, set the current time indicator to frame **24** and set the **RotateY** attribute to **300** in the channel box. Again, press SHIFT+e to set the keys for rotation. Finally, choose the **Play forwards** button from the animation playback controls to preview the animation; the cube will rotate on its own axis. To translate the position of the cube in the viewport, move the current time indicator to **frame 1** in the timeline. Now, press SHIFT+w to set the keys for translation. Next, move the current time indicator to frame **24**. Now, set the **TranslateX** attribute to **20** in the **Channel Box** to move the cube along the X axis. Press SHIFT+w to set the translate key and choose the **Play forwards** button from the animation playback controls to preview the animation; the cube will translate and rotate simultaneously. You can also set the keys for animation by enabling the **Auto keyframe toggle** button in the timeline. It is a toggle button which turns red when it is on, refer to Figure 9-6.

Off   On

*Figure 9-6 The **Auto Keyframe Toggle** button*

Nonlinear Animation

The Nonlinear Animation is used to animate an object that is independent of time. These clips can be used repeatedly to add motion to your scene which in turn saves a lot of time for creating the animation. To apply nonlinear animation to an object, you need to use the **Trax Editor** window. To display the **Trax Editor** window, choose **Window > Animation Editor > Trax Editor** from the main menubar. Figure 9-7 shows the **Trax Editor** window.

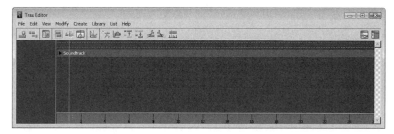

*Figure 9-7 The **Trax Editor** window*

ANIMATION MENUS

The animation menus contain tools that are used to edit animations in Maya. These menus are discussed next.

Edit Menu

The **Edit** Menu is mainly used to edit the animation keys set on the timeline. To do so, select the **Animation** module from the menu set drop-down list in the status line. Next, select a key on the timeline and choose **Edit > Keys** from the main menubar; a flyout will be displayed. The options in this flyout are discussed next.

Cut Keys

The **Cut Keys** option is used to cut keys from the timeline and then store them in the clipboard of Maya.

Copy Keys

The **Copy Keys** option is used to copy keys from the timeline and then store them in the clipboard of Maya.

Paste Keys

The **Paste Keys** option is used to paste keys from the clipboard into the place where the current time indicator is located.

Delete Keys

The **Delete Keys** option is used to delete the keys selected from the timeline.

Delete FBIK Keys

The **Delete FBIK Keys** option is used to delete all the selected FBIK keys and body part keys from the timeline.

Scale Keys

The **Scale Keys** option is used to scale the selected keys in the timeline.

Snap Keys

The **Snap Keys** option is used to snap the selected keys in the timeline.

Bake Simulation

The **Bake Simulation** option is used to bake the current simulation. To bake a simulation, choose **Edit > Keys > Bake Simulation** from the main menubar; the keys that were not visible by default in the timeline will become visible. You can select a particular key from the timeline and edit it.

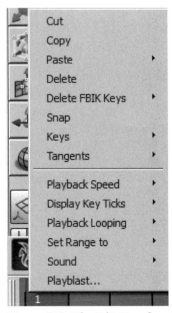

Alternatively, you can perform the same process by pressing and holding the right mouse button on any key in the active time segment and then choosing the required option from the flyout displayed, as shown in Figure 9-8.

The Animate Menu

The **Animate** menu is used to make changes in the timeline to modify an animation. To do so, select the **Animation** module from the menu set drop-down list in the status line. Next, select a key from the timeline and choose **Animate** from the main menubar; a flyout will be displayed with different options. These options are discussed next.

Figure 9-8 *The Edit Keys flyout*

Set Key

The **Set Key** option is used to set the key for the object in the viewport. To set a key on the timeline, choose **Animate > Set Key** from the main menubar; a red-colored key will be created indicating that a key is set in the timeline for the selected object.

Set Breakdown

Choose **Animate > Set Breakdown** from the main menubar to maintain proportional time relationship between the adjacent keys. On doing so, the color of the selected key will change to green in the timeline.

Hold Current Keys

Choose **Animate > Hold Current Keys** from the main menubar to hold all keys of the selected object in the viewport at current time.

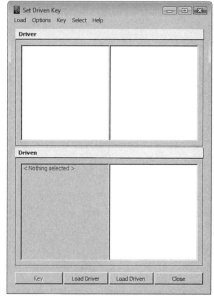

Figure 9-9 *The **Set Driven Key** dialog box*

Set Driven Key

The **Set Driven Key** option is used to link different objects together such that the attributes of one object control the attributes of another object. In this case, one object acts as a driver and the other object acts as a driven, and all attributes of the driven are controlled by the driver. To set the driver and driven object, choose **Animate > Set Driven > Set** from the main menubar; the **Set Driven Key** dialog box will be displayed, as shown in Figure 9-9. Now, select the object that you want to set as the driver key from the viewport and choose the **Load Driver** button from the **Set Driven Key** dialog box; the selected object will act as the driver key and its attributes will be displayed on the right in the **Set Driven Key** dialog box. Next, select another object from the viewport and choose the **Load Driven** button from the **Set Driven Key** dialog box; the selected object will act as the driven key. The **Set Driven Key** dialog box is discussed in detail in the next chapter.

Set Transform Keys

The **Set Transform Keys** option is used to set the transform keys for rotating, translating, or scaling an object. To perform these actions, choose **Animate > Set Transform Keys** from the main menubar; a cascading menu will be displayed. Choose the required option from the cascading menu; the Transform key will be set for the corresponding option. For example, if you want to set the keys for rotation, choose **Animate > Set Transform Keys > Rotate** from the main menubar; the keys will be set only for rotation. Similarly, you can set the keys for translating and scaling an object.

Create Clip

The **Create Clip** option is used to create a clip for the animation created in the viewport. To do so, choose **Animate > Create Clip** from the main menubar; a new clip for the animation scene will be created.

Create Pose

The **Create Pose** option is used to create a snapshot of an object's current position while the object is being animated. To do so, choose **Animate > Create Pose** from the main menubar; a pose of the selected object will be created. Poses are similar to clips in which only a single frame is captured at a time. This option is mainly used in character animation to compare various positions of a character while it is being animated.

Ghost Selected

Ghosting is a technique in which an animator rapidly flips through drawings to evaluate the timing of the action he is working on. To activate it, choose **Animate > Ghost Selected > Option Box** from the main menubar; the **Ghost Options** dialog box will be displayed, as shown in Figure 9-10. Now, when you animate an object, the object will be trailed by the shadow of the corresponding ghost object. This will help you calculate the time taken for animation. You can set the parameters for ghosting as per your requirement in the **Ghost Options** dialog box.

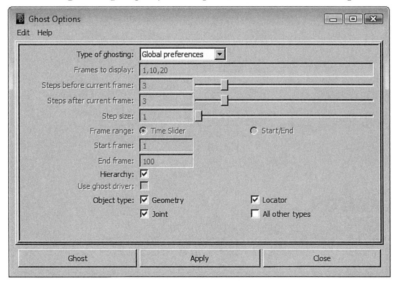

*Figure 9-10 The **Ghost Options** dialog box*

Unghost Selected

The **Unghost Selected** option is used to undo the changes made by the **Ghost Selected** option. To do so, choose **Animate > Unghost Selected** from the main menubar; the selected object will be unghosted.

Unghost All

The **Unghost All** option is used to unghost the objects in the viewport that were ghosted previously. To do so, choose **Animate > Unghost All** from the main menubar; all objects that were ghosted previously will be unghosted.

The Window Menu

The **Window** menu consists of different windows that are used to modify the animations as per your requirement. One of the windows is discussed next.

Playblast

By default, the **Playblast** window is used to preview the current animation from the current time range in the time slider. To invoke the **Playblast** window, choose **Window > Playblast** from the main menubar; the **Playblast** window will be displayed. The **Playblast** window reduces the resolution of the animation to one-fourth of the original resolution. You can also set the properties of the **Playblast** window. To do so, choose **Window > Playblast > Option Box** from the main menubar; the **Playblast Options** window will be displayed, as shown in Figure 9-11. You can set different properties in this window.

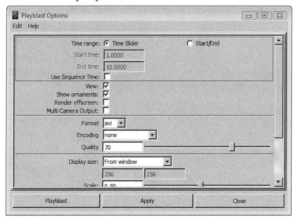

Figure 9-11 The **Playblast Options** *window*

GRAPH EDITOR

Menu:	Window > Animation Editors > Graph Editor

The **Graph Editor** window is used to edit animation curves, refer to Figure 9-12. This window provides you with graphical representation of the animated object in the viewport. The graphs help you to change or set the values of keys in this window as per your requirement. In other words, this window stores all information about animation and provides you the direct access to fine-tune the animation.

Each animation in Maya generates a value vs time graph. In this graph, the horizontal axis represents the time and the vertical axis represents the value. In the **Graph Editor** window, the keyframes are represented by points on curves. You can move these points freely to fine-tune the animation. To move a point on the curve, select a key, press and hold the middle mouse button, and then drag the point in the timeline to adjust the animation as per your requirement. You can also snap the keys to the grids in the editor window using the snap icons from the **Graph Editor** toolbar.

Note
*To navigate in the **Graph Editor** window, you can use the same shortcuts that are used to navigate in the viewport.*

All tools of the **Graph Editor** window are displayed in the **Graph Editor** toolbar, as shown in Figures 9-13 and 9-14. Note that all tools are contained in a single toolbar, but for clear visualization, it is given in two parts. The tools and the options in the **Graph Editor** toolbar are discussed next.

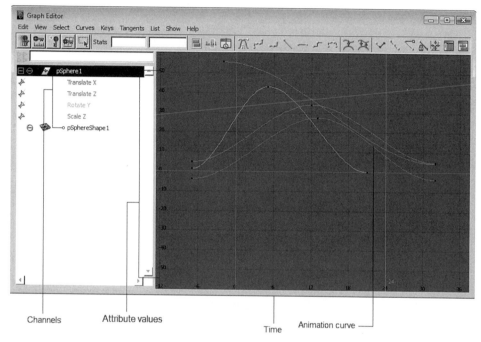

*Figure 9-12 The **Graph Editor** window*

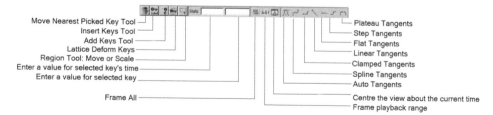

*Figure 9-13 The **Graph Editor** toolbar (part-I)*

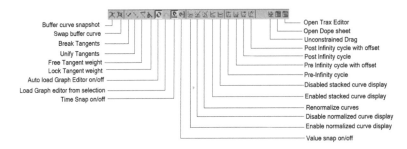

*Figure 9-14 The **Graph Editor** toolbar (part-II)*

Move Nearest Picked Key Tool

The **Move Nearest Picked Key Tool** button works on a single key at a time. It is different from the **Move** tool as it moves individual keys. Select a key from the timeline and then choose the **Move Nearest Picked Key Tool** button from the toolbar. Now, press the middle mouse button in the **Graph Editor** to move the selected key for making changes in the animation.

Insert Keys Tool

The **Insert Keys Tool** button is used to add a new key to an animation curve. To do so, select the curve on which you want to add a new key and then choose the **Insert Keys Tool** button from the **Graph Editor** toolbar. Now, click the middle mouse button on the selected curve; a new key will be created without changing the shape of the original animation curve.

Add Keys Tool

The **Add Keys Tool** button is used to add a new key to the selected animation curve in the **Graph Editor** window. To do so, select the curve on which you want to add a new key and then choose the **Add Keys Tool** button from the **Graph Editor** toolbar. Next, click anywhere in the **Graph Editor** window using the middle mouse button to add a new key to the curve.

Lattice Deform Keys Tool

The **Lattice Deform Keys Tool** button is used to draw a lattice around a group of keys in the **Graph Editor** window so that the selected keys can be transformed uniformly. To transform the keys using this tool, choose the **Lattice Deform Keys Tool** button from the **Graph Editor** toolbar. Next, press and hold the left mouse button and then select the keys in the **Graph Editor** window; a lattice will be formed around the selected keys. Now, you can deform the lattice to transform the selected keys. This tool provides a high level of control over animation.

Region Tool: Scale or Move keys

The **Region Tool: Scale or Move keys** tool is used to move or scale the selected keys in the **Graph Editor** window. To do so, choose the **Region Tool: Scale or Move keys** button from the **Graph Editor** toolbar. Next, select the key on the curve and then move the key in any direction by using the middle mouse button.

Frame All

The **Frame All** button is used to frame all keys in the **Graph Editor** window. To do so, choose the **Frame All** button from the **Graph Editor** toolbar; all keys in the **Graph Editor** window will zoom in to fit in the **Graph Editor** window.

Frame playback range

The **Frame playback range** button is used to frame all keys present in the current playback range in the **Graph Editor** window. To do so, choose the **Frame playback range** button from the **Graph Editor** toolbar; the keys present in the current playback range are displayed in the **Graph Editor** window. Alternatively, press F to frame keys in the **Graph Editor** window.

Center the view about the current time

The **Center the view about the current time** button is used to adjust the view of the **Graph Editor** window with the current time slider in the timeline. The red line in the **Graph Editor** window indicates the current time of animation in the timeline. If you play the animation, the red line will also move simultaneously, refer to Figure 9-15.

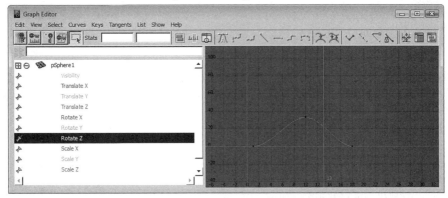

Figure 9-15 *Adjusting the view of the* **Graph Editor**

Spline

The **Spline** tool is used to adjust the tangents on a curve so that it becomes smoother. To do so, select an animation key on the animation curve in the **Graph Editor** window and then choose the **Spline** tool from the **Graph Editor** toolbar. Alternatively, choose **Tangents > Spline** from the **Graph Editor** menubar, as shown in Figure 9-16.

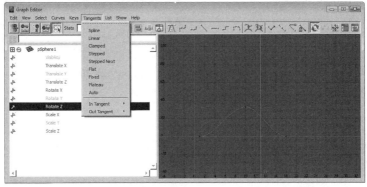

Figure 9-16 *The* **Tangents** *menu in the* **Graph Editor**

Linear

The **Linear** tool is used to create a straight animation curve by joining two keys on the selected curve. Figures 9-17 and 9-18 show the animation curve before and after using the **Linear** tool.

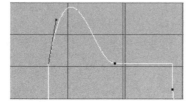

Figure 9-17 *The animation curve before using the* **Linear** *tool*

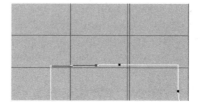

Figure 9-18 *The animation curve after using the* **Linear** *tool*

Note
The process of using or accessing the remaining tangent tools is similar to that discussed under the **Spline** *tangent tool area.*

Clamped

The **Clamped** tangent tool has the characteristics of both the **Spline** and the **Linear** tangent tools and it works similar to these tools.

Flat

The **Flat** tangent tool is used to set the tangent of the selected curves horizontally. When you throw a ball up in the air, the ball stays at the topmost point for a moment before it comes down. To represent such an animation, you can use the **Flat** tangent tool. Figures 9-19 and 9-20 show the animation curve before and after using the **Flat** tangent tool.

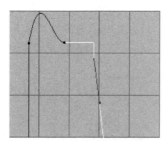

Figure 9-19 *The animation curve before using the* **Flat** *tangent tool*

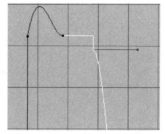

Figure 9-20 *The animation curve after using the* **Flat** *tangent tool*

Stepped

The **Stepped** tangent tool is used to set a flat curve in the shape of steps, refer to Figures 9-21 and 9-22. You can get the effect of blinking light using this tool.

Stepped Next

The **Stepped Next** tangent tool is used by FBIK animation keys. This type of tangent tool is used to key the models with FBIK effectors while modifying it.

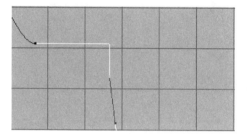

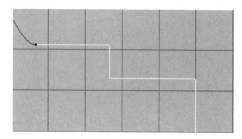

Figure 9-21 *The animation curve before using the **Step** tangent tool*

Figure 9-22 *The animation curve after using the **Step** tangent tool*

Plateau

The **Plateau** tangent tool works similar to the **Spline** and **Clamped** tangents tools. It is used to set the animation curves in such a way that they do not go beyond the position of their respective keyframes, refer to Figures 9-23 and 9-24.

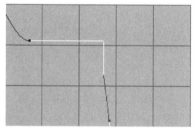

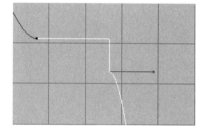

Figure 9-23 *The animation curve before using the **Plateau** tangent tool*

Figure 9-24 *The animation curve after using the **Plateau** tangent tool*

Auto

The **Auto** tangent tool is used to make the selected curve smooth by automatically adjusting the keys on the curve. By default, this tangent type is turned off.

Buffer Curve Snapshot

The **Buffer Curve Snapshot** tool is used to take a snapshot of the selected curve. To do so, select the curve whose snapshot you want to take. Next, invoke the **Buffer Curve Snapshot** tool from the **Graph Editor** toolbar; the buffer curve snapshot will be taken for the selected curve. To view the buffer curve snapshots, choose **View > Show Buffer Curves** from the **Graph Editor** menubar, as shown in Figure 9-25.

Tip. *Tangents can be edited using the marking menus by pressing SHIFT +CTRL and the middle mouse button.*

*Figure 9-25 Choosing the **Show Buffer Curves** option from the **Graph Editor** menubar*

Swap Buffer Curves

The **Swap Buffer Curves** option is used to swap between the original curve and the edited curve. You can use the **Buffer Curve Snapshot** tool and the **Swap Buffer Curves** tool to compare the changes made in the animation curve. The changes in the animation curve will be indicated by a grey line.

Break

The **Break** tool is used to break the tangents joined to a key such that both handles of the broken tangent work separately to fine-tune the animation. Note that the broken tangent will be displayed in blue color.

Unify

The **Unify** tool is used to retain tangents at their original location. This tool works in such a way that if you manipulate changes in one tangent, the other tangent of the key will be affected equally. If you break two tangents, which are joined to a key, using the **Break** tool and then apply the **Unify** tool on them, the two tangents will start acting as a single tangent.

Free Tangent Weight

The **Free Tangent Weight** tool is used to change the angle and weight of the selected key. You can apply this tool only to a weighted curve.

Lock Tangent Weight

The **Lock Tangent Weight** tool is used to lock the weight of a tangent. You can visually identify the weight of locked and unlocked tangents. By default, an unlocked tangent is displayed in green color in the **Graph Editor** window. On invoking the **Lock Tangent Weight** tool, both the tangents will be displayed in same color. You can apply this tool only for a weighted curve.

Auto Load Graph Editor on/off

The **Auto Load Graph Editor on/off** button is activated by default. If this button is activated, then the objects selected in outliner will change automatically whenever the curves are selected.

Load Graph Editor From Selection

The **Load Graph Editor From Selection** tool can be chosen only if the **Auto load Graph Editor on/off** is deactivated. If you choose this button, then the objects selected in the outliner will not be linked with the curves selected in **Graph Editor** window.

Time Snap on/off

The **Time Snap on/off** tool is used to move the keys in the graph view to their nearest integer time unit value by applying force on them. By default, this tool is turned on.

Value Snap on/off

The **Value Snap on/off** tool is used to move the keys in the graph view to their nearest integer value by applying force on them.

Enable normalized curve display

The **Enable normalized curve display** tool in the **Graph Editor** toolbar is used to fit the key values of the selected animation curves within the range of normalization. The normalization range is between -1 and 1.

Disable normalized curve display

The **Disable normalized curve display** tool in the **Graph Editor** toolbar is used to denormalize the curve in the graph view.

Renormalize curve

The **Renormalize curve** in the **Graph Editor** toolbar is used to quickly normalize the selected curve to fit the key values of the selected animation curves within the range of normalization. The normalization range is between -1 and 1.

Enable stacked curve display

The **Enable stacked curve display** tool is used to display the curves in a stacked way on their axis without overlapping the curves on each other, as shown in Figure 9-26.

Disable stacked curve display

The **Disable stacked curve display** tool is used to disable the stacked way of curves to the default way of displaying curves.

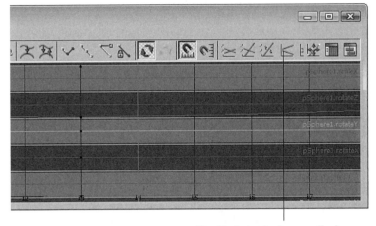

Enabled stacked curve display

*Figure 9-26 The **Enable Stacked Display Curve** tool in the **Graph Editor** window*

Pre-Infinity Cycle

The **Pre-Infinity Cycle** tool is used to copy a selected animation curve and then repeat the animation infinitely in the graph view before the selected curve. The copied animation curve will be displayed as a dotted line, as shown in Figure 9-27.

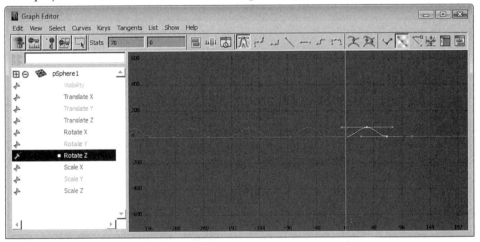

*Figure 9-27 The pre-infinity cycle graph in the **Graph Editor** window*

Pre-Infinity Cycle with Offset

The **Pre-Infinity Cycle with Offset** tool is also used to repeat the selected animation curve infinitely through the graph view. This tool differs from the **Pre-Infinity Cycle** tool as it adds the first key value of the original curve to the last key value of the cycled curve.

Post-Infinity Cycle

The **Post-Infinity Cycle** tool is used to copy an animation curve and then join it after the same curve infinite number of times. Therefore, unlike the **Pre-Infinity Cycle** tool, this tool copies the animation curve and repeats it after the curve. The copied animation curve will be displayed in the form of a dotted line.

Post-Infinity Cycle with Offset

The **Post-Infinity Cycle with Offset** tool works similar to the **Pre-Infinity Cycle with Offset** tool, except that on using this tool, the last key value of the original curve is added to the first key value of the cycled curve.

Isolate Curve

The **Isolate Curve** tool is used to isolate a selected curve in the graph view area. To do so, select the curve and then choose **Curves > Isolate Curve** from the **Graph Editor** menubar; the selected curve will be displayed in the graph view area.

Open the Dope Sheet

The **Open the Dope Sheet** tool is used to open the **Dope Sheet** window and then load the animation keys of the current object into the **dope shee**t area, as shown in Figure 9-28. The dope sheet is used to display the time horizontally in blocks. To open a dope sheet, choose **Window > Animation Editors > Dope Sheet** from the main menubar; the dope sheet will open. Alternatively, you can open the dope sheet from the **Graph Editor** window.

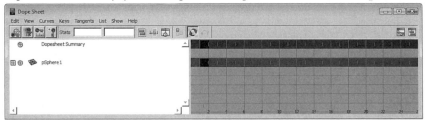

*Figure 9-28 The **Dope Sheet** window*

Open the Trax Editor

The **Open the Trax Editor** tool is used to open the **Trax Editor** window and then load the animation clips of the current object into it. Figure 9-29 shows the **Trax Editor** window. To open this window, choose **Window > Animation Editors > Trax Editor** from the main menubar; the **Trax Editor** window will be displayed. In this window, you can position, scale, cycle, and blend the animation sequences as per your need.

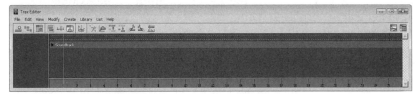

*Figure 9-29 The **Trax Editor** window*

ANIMATION LAYERS

Animation layers are used to add or blend two animations together. In other words, these layers help you organize a keyframe animation without overlapping the original animation. You can control these animations using the animation layer editor. To open the animation layer J3, choose **Display > UI Elements > Channel Box/Layer Editor** from the main menubar; the **Channel box** will be displayed on the right of the viewport. Choose the **Show the Layer Editor** button from the **Channel box**; the options for the **layer editor** will be displayed. To activate the **Animation Layer Editor**, select the **Anim** tab from the layer editor; the attributes for the animation will be displayed in the **layer editor**, as shown in Figure 9-30. To set the **Animation Layer Editor** as a floating window, choose **Show > Floating Window** from the **layer editor** menubar; the **Animation Layer Editor** floating window will be displayed, as shown in Figure 9-30. You can create a number of animation layers using this editor.

Figure 9-30 The Animation Layer Editor

Creating an Animation Layer

To create an animation layer, choose **Display > UI Elements > Channel Box/Layer Editor** from the main menubar; the **Channel box** will be displayed. Choose the **Show the Layer Editor** button from the layer editor area; the layer editor will become active, refer to Figure 9-30. Select the **Anim** radio button from the layer editor; the **Animation Layer Editor** will get activated. Now, choose the **Layers** menu from the **Animation Layer Editor** menubar; a flyout will be displayed. Choose **Create Empty Layer** from the flyout, as shown in Figure 9-31; a new layer will be created. Alternatively, choose the **Create Empty Layer** button available on the right of the layer editor to create a new layer, refer to Figure 9-32. The **Animation Layer Editor** contains various buttons that help you control animations. These buttons are discussed next.

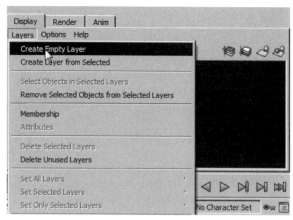

Figure 9-31 The **Animation Layer Editor** *floating window*

Figure 9-32 *A new layer created in the* **Animation Layer Editor**

Zero Key Layer

 The **Zero Key Layer** button is used to set the start and end time for the animation in a particular layer. It defines a point of time at which the layer's animation has no offset from the original animation. For example, if you keyframe an animation of 100 frames and want to modify the animation between the frames 40 and 60, then you can choose this button to set the zero key at frames 40 and 60 to define the range of animation for editing. Now, any change made between these frames will not affect the original animation.

Zero Weight and Key Layer

 The **Zero Weight and Key Layer** button is used to set the key with zero weight in the **Animation Layer Editor**. Setting weight of a layer means determining the amount of animation that will be played in the final animation.

Set Weight to 1.0 and Key Layer

 The **Set Weight to 1.0 and Key Layer** button is used to set the key with the layer weight 1 in the **Animation Layer Editor**.

Move selection up in list

The **Move Selection Up in List** button is used to move the selected layer one step up from the original position in the **Animation Layer Editor**.

Move selection down in list

 The **Move Selection Down in List** button is used to move the selected layer one step down from the original position in the **Animation Layer Editor**.

Create Empty Layer

 The **Create Empty Layer** button is used to create an empty layer in the layer pane of the **Animation Layer Editor**.

Create Layer from Selected

 The **Create Layer from Selected** button is used to create a layer in the layer pane of the **Animation Layer Editor** such that the new layer contains all attributes of the selected object.

The **Animation Layer** pane in the **Animation Layer Editor** window is discussed next.

Animation Layer Pane

The **Animation Layer Pane** hierarchy of animation layers that has been created is displayed in the **Animation Layer Pane**, refer to Figure 9-30. By default, the animation layers in this pane are arranged from bottom to top, as shown in Figure 9-33. Whenever you create a new layer, it gets added on the top of the **Animation Layer Pane**. You can change the arrangement of these layers by choosing **Options > Reverse Layer Stack** from the animation layer editor menubar. On doing so, the layers will be arranged from top to bottom, as shown in Figure 9-34. Also, all newly created layers will be added at the bottom of the layer stack.

Figure 9-33 *Layer arrangement from bottom to top*

Figure 9-34 *Layer arrangement from top to bottom*

Apart from the layers created, there is one more layer in the animation layer pane called **Base Animation** layer. This layer is created by default, refer to Figure 9-30. It is not an animation layer, but it represents the animation that is not assigned to other layers in the animation layer editor. The **Animation Layer pane** has three major components, which affect animation layers in the hierarchy. These components are discussed next.

Animation Layer Buttons

The animation layer buttons are displayed in front of each animation layer in the animation layer editor. These buttons are discussed next.

Lock Layer

 The **Lock Layer** button is used to lock an animation layer. A locked animation layer cannot be keyframed further, unless it is unlocked. Also, only the frames that were keyframed before locking the animation layer, will be played in the final animation. When you choose the **Lock Layer** button, the color of the set keys changes from red to grey in the timeslider.

Solo Layer

The **Solo Layer** button is used to make the selected layer solo. Making a layer solo means it would be the only layer that will be played in the final animation.

Mute Layer

The **Mute Layer** button is used to make the selected layer mute. Making an animation layer mute means the animation of that particular layer will not be evaluated in the final output.

Ghost/Color Layer

The **Ghost/Color Layer** button is used to preview the position of an object on each added layer while it is being animated. You can turn the **Ghosting On** or **Off** by choosing this button. Note that the ghost option cannot be applied to objects in the top most layer of the hierarchy.

To display ghosts for the selected objects, choose **Options > Auto Ghost Selected Objects** from the animation layer editor menubar. Select the objects that you want to ghost from the viewport and then choose the **Ghost/Color Layer** button; the effect of ghosting will be displayed on the selected objects. To display the effect of ghosting on all objects in the **Animation Layer Editor**, choose **Options > Auto ghosts objects in layer** from the **Animation Layer Editor** menubar.

By default, the color of this button is dark red. To change the color of the **Ghost/Color Layer** button, right-click on this button; the **Color Index Settings** dialog box will be displayed, as shown in Figure 9-35. Change the color of the ghost button by dragging the slider on the right of the **Select Color** option in the **Color Index Settings** dialog box.

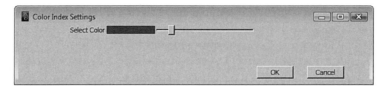

Figure 9-35 The **Color Index Settings** *dialog box*

Active Keying Feedback

The **Active Keying Feedback** is the visual feedback of layers in the **Animation Layer pane**. The visual feedback is indicated by the colored indicators located on the right of each keyed layer in the animation layer pane. Depending upon the active keying feedback, a layer can further be classified into three animation layer states: **Active**, **Affected**, and **Selected**. The **Active** animation layer represents the layer that receives keys. The **Affected** animation layer represents the layer that receives the attributes of the object selected in the viewport, but it will not be selected. The **Selected** animation layer represents the layer that is highlighted in the layer editor. The active keying feedback indicators are discussed next.

Green

A layer with the **Green** indicator represents the layer containing attributes of the selected object. The indicated layer will be in active animation state and therefore, can receive keys.

Green with dot

A layer with the **Green with dot** indicator represents the layer containing the attributes of the selected object and that it can receive keyframes.

Red

A layer with the **Red** indicator represents the layer containing attributes of the selected object in the viewport, but it is not selected.

Red with dot

A layer with the **Red with dot** indicator represents the layer that has a child layer collapsed under the parent layer and is not active. The layer with this indicator cannot be keyframed.

Weight slider

The **Weight Slider** is located at the bottom of the **Animation Layer Editor**. This slider is used to control the amount of animation to be played on the selected layer. It is similar to setting transparency between two layers.

By default, the value of the **Weight slider** is **1**, which indicates that the animation of the selected layer will be played completely. Set the **Weight slider** value to **0** to mute the animation of the selected layer.

Adding and Removing Attributes in Animation Layers

In Maya, you can add and remove attributes of an object in the **Animation Layer Editor**. The methods of adding and removing attributes are discussed next.

Adding Attributes in Animation Layers

When you create a new layer in the **Animation Layer Editor**, by default some general attributes are added to that layer. You can also add specific attributes to a layer as per your requirement. To do so, choose **Layers > Add Selected Objects > Option Box** from the **Animation Layer Editor** menubar; the **Add Objects To Animation Layers Options** dialog box will be displayed, as shown in Figure 9-36. Before setting the options in this dialog box, first select the object from the viewport and then set its parameters as per your requirement.

You can also add attributes to a layer using the **Channel Box**. To do so, first select the layer to which you want to add attributes and then select the object from the viewport, whose attributes you want to add to that layer. Now, from the **Channel box**, select the attributes you want to add to the layer in the animation layer editor. Now, press and hold the right mouse button over the selected attribute in the **Channel box**; a flyout will be displayed. Choose **Add To Selected Layers** from the flyout; the selected attribute will be added to the animation layer. Also, the color of the selected attribute will be changed in the **Channel Box**, indicating that it is now linked with the layer.

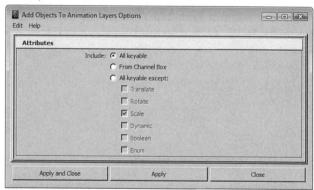

*Figure 9-36 The **Add Objects To Animation Layers Options** dialog box*

Removing Attributes from Animation Layers

You can also remove the attributes of particular objects from the animation layer editor. To do so, select the object whose attributes you want to remove. Next, select the layer from which you want to remove the attributes of the selected object and also, select the attribute that you want to remove from the channel box. Next, press and hold the right mouse button over the attribute in the channel box that you want to remove; a flyout will be displayed. Choose **Remove From Selected Layers** from the flyout to remove the selected attribute. The color of the selected attribute will be changed, indicating that it is no longer linked with the layer.

Animation Layer Modes

Animation Layer modes are used to evaluate the final animation. There are two main modes for evaluating the animation layers: **Additive** and **Override**. These modes are discussed next.

Additive Mode

In the **Additive** mode, an animation layer adds its animation to the layer that is higher in the hierarchy in the animation layer editor. For example, if the **TranslateY** value for a cube in **AnimLayer1** is **5** and the value for the same attribute in **AnimLayer2** is **10**, the resulting **TranslateY** value will be the sum of the **TranslateY** values of both the layers; it means the resultant value will be 15.

By default, attributes are added only to the layers in the **Additive** mode. To set a layer to the Additive Mode (if it is not present in that mode), choose **Layers > Layer Mode > Additive** from the Animation Layer Editor menubar; the selected layer will be switched to the **Additive** mode.

Override Mode

In the **Override** mode, an animation layer overrides the animation of another layer, if both the layers have similar attributes. For example, if both **AnimLayer1** and **AnimLayer2** are in the **Override** mode and the **TranslateY** value for a cube is **10** in **AnimLayer1** and **15** in **AnimLayer2**, the resulting value of **TranslateY** for the cube will be **15** because **AnimLayer2** is higher in the hierarchy. In the **Override** mode, an animation layer is always displayed in bold face, as shown in Figure 9-37. If you change the order of the overridden layers, the final animation will also be affected accordingly.

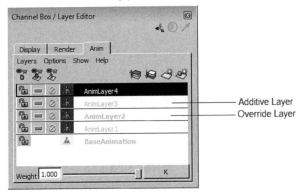

Figure 9-37 Overridden layer displayed in bold

Creating the Parent-Child Relationship in the Animation Layer Editor

The **Animation Layer Hierarchy** is used to parent and unparent an animation layer. To create a parent-child relationship between layers, select a layer from the **Animation Layer Editor** and drag-drop it over another layer using the middle mouse button. The layer on which another layer is dropped will now act as the parent layer of the dropped layer. Also, an up arrow will be displayed in the parent layer, as shown in Figure 9-38. Similarly, you can create any number of parent-child relationships in the **Animation Layer Editor**.

Figure 9-38 *Layers showing the parent-child relationship*

You can also unparent a layer in the animation layer editor. To do so, select the child layer that you want to unparent and drag-drop it over any layer that is higher in the hierarchy; the selected layer will be unparented.

TUTORIALS

Tutorial 1

In this tutorial, you will create an animated logo, as shown in Figure 9-39, using profile curves. **(Expected time: 30 min)**

The following steps are required to complete this tutorial:

a. Create a project folder.
b. Create the text for the logo.
c. Create the profile curve for animating the text.
d. Fine-tune the animation.
e. Save the animation.

Figure 9-39 *An animated logo*

Creating the Project Folder

Before starting a new file, it is recommended that you create the project folder.

1. Create a project with the name *c09_tut1* in the folder *Maya_Tutorials*.

Creating the Text for the Logo

In this section, you need to create the text for the logo.

1. Choose **Create > Text > Option Box** from the main menubar; the **Text Curves Options** dialog box is displayed. Select the **Bevel** radio button, if it is not selected by default, from the **Type** attributes area and set the parameters in the dialog box, as shown in Figure 9-40.

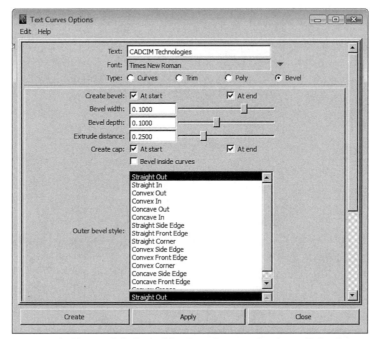

Figure 9-40 *Partial view of the **Text Curves Options** dialog box*

2. Choose the **Create** button from the **Text Curves Options** dialog box; a 3D text is created in the wireframe mode in the perspective viewport.

3. Activate the Front viewport and choose **Shading > Flat Shade All** from the **Panel menu** to convert the text into the shaded mode. Figure 9-41 shows a 3D text created in the viewport.

Creating the Profile Curve for Animating the Text

In this section, you need to create a profile curve to animate the text on the curve.

1. Choose **Create > EP Curve Tool** from the main menubar and create a profile curve in the viewport; a profile curve is created, as shown in Figure 9-42.

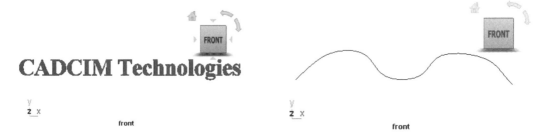

Figure 9-41 *The 3D text created in the viewport*

Figure 9-42 *The profile curve created*

2. Set the start time to **1** and the end time to **100** in the timeline.

3. Activate the Perspective viewport. Select the text created, press and hold the SHIFT key, and then select the profile curve. Activate the **Animation** module from the status line. Next, choose **Animate > Motion Paths > Attach to Motion Path > Option Box** from the main menubar; the **Attach to Motion Path Options** dialog box is displayed. Set the required parameters in this dialog box, as shown in Figure 9-43.

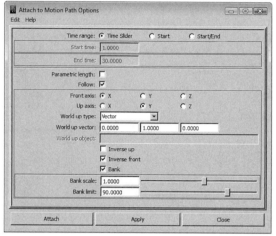

Figure 9-43 *The **Attach to Motion Path Options** dialog box*

4. After specifying all the parameters, choose the **Attach** button from this dialog box; the 3D text is attached to the profile curve at its pivot point. Next, choose the **Play forwards** button from **Playback controls** to preview the animation. Figure 9-44 shows a 3D text attached to the profile curve.

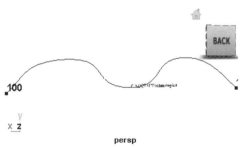

Figure 9-44 *The 3D text attached to the profile curve*

Fine-tuning the Animation

In this section, you need to fine-tune the animation so that the 3D text flows smoothly on the profile path.

1. Select the 3D text surface and then choose **Animate > Motion Paths > Flow Path Object > Option Box** from the main menubar; the **Flow Path Object Options** dialog box will be displayed.

2. Set the parameters in the **Flow Path Object Options** dialog box, as shown in Figure 9-45, and then choose the **Flow** button; the 3D text surface will get distorted.

3. Choose **Window > Outliner** from the main menubar; the **Outliner** window is displayed, as shown in Figure 9-46.

4. Select the **ffd1Lattice** and **ffd1Base** options from the **Outliner** window; the respective lattices are selected in the viewport.

5. Activate the Perspective viewport. Invoke the **Scale Tool** from the toolbox and scale the two selected lattices outward such that the 3D text surface is enclosed entirely inside the lattice structure, as shown in Figure 9-47.

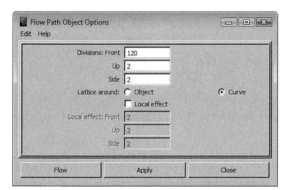

Figure 9-45 *The Flow Path Object Options dialog box*

Figure 9-46 *The Outliner window*

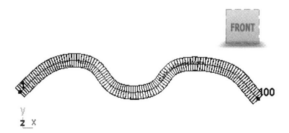

Figure 9-47 *The enlarged lattice area*

6. Set the frames in the timeline from **1** to **80**. Choose the **Play forwards** button from the playback controls area to preview the animation. If the 3D text surface gets distorted again, scale the lattices once again. Figure 9-48 displays the final output.

Saving the Animation

In this section, you need to save the animation.

1. Choose **File > Save Scene** from the main menubar; the **Save As** dialog box is displayed.

   As the project folder is already set, by default the path *\Documents\Maya_Tutorials\c09_tut1\ scenes* is displayed in **Look In** text box of the dialog box.

2. Enter **c09_tut1** in the **File name** text box and then select **Maya Binary** from the **Files of type** drop-down list. Next, choose the **Save As** button.

You can view the final rendered image of the model by downloading the file *c09_Maya_2012_ render.zip* from *http://www.cadcim.com*.

Tip. *You can add color and glow to a 3D text surface by using the **Attribute Editor**. To do so, select the 3D text from the viewport, press and hold the right mouse button over it, and then choose **Assign Favorite Material > Lambert** from the flyout; the **Attribute Editor** will be displayed. Expand the **Special Effects** attribute tab from the **Attribute Editor**. Next, move the slider placed on the right of the **Glow Intensity** option to set the intensity for the 3D text. Choose **Render the current frame (Maya Software)** from the status bar to render the scene. Figure 9-48 shows the rendered image of a 3D text logo after adding the glowing effect to it.*

Figure 9-48 The glowing animated logo

Tutorial 2

In this tutorial, you will create the model of a wall clock and then animate its second hand using the **Graph Editor**. **(Expected time: 30 min)**

The following steps are required to complete this tutorial:

a. Create a project folder.
b. Create the model of a wall clock.
c. Set the animation keys and refine them.
d. Save the file.

Creating the Project Folder

Before starting a new file, it is recommended that you create the project folder.

1. Set a project with the name *c09_tut2* in the folder *Maya_Tutorials* as discussed in Tutorial 1 of Chapter 3.

Creating the Model of a Clock

In this section, you need to create the basic model of a clock using the NURBS and polygonal modeling methods.

1. Activate the Top viewport. Choose **Create > NURBS Primitives > Circle** from the main menubar and create a circle of radius **5** units in the viewport.

2. Activate the Front viewport and create another circle with radius **0.5** units, as discussed in step 1.

3. Select the smaller circle, press SHIFT, and then select the bigger circle. Next, choose **Surfaces > Extrude** from the **Surfaces** module in the main menubar; the circles are extruded.

4. Select the extruded surface created in the viewport and choose **Window > Attribute Editor** from the main menubar; the **Attribute Editor** is displayed. Choose the **extrude1** tab from the **Attribute Editor** and select the **Component Pivot** option from the **Use Component Pivot** drop-down list to set the extrusion along the pivot center of the object. Next, select the **Fixed Path** check box from the **Attribute Editor** so that the extrusion can take place along the specified path.

Figure 9-49 The adjusted wall clock model

5. Activate the Perspective viewport. Choose **Window > Outliner** from the main menubar; the **Outliner** window is displayed. Choose **nurbsCircle1** from the **Outliner** window. Next, choose **Surfaces > Planar** from the main menubar; a circular NURBS surface is created. Now, arrange this surface using the **Move Tool**, as shown in Figure 9-49.

6. Choose **Create > Text > Option Box** from the main menubar; the **Text Curves Options** dialog box is displayed. In the dialog box, select the **Bevel** radio button and enter **3** in the **Text** text box. Next, choose the **Create** button; a 3D text is created in the viewport.

7. Select the 3D text, display the **Channel box**, and enter the following values in the **Channel box**:

RotateX : **-90**   ScaleX : **0.4**   ScaleY : **0.4**
ScaleZ : **0.4**

8. Similarly, create the numbers **9, 6**, and **12** as text. Next, arrange the text in the Top and Perspective viewports to set the text at appropriate place in the model, as shown in Figure 9-50.

9. Choose **Create > Polygon Primitives > Cylinder** from the main menubar and create a cylinder in the Top viewport. Next, open the **Channel box** and set the following parameters for the cylinder:

   Radius: **0.3**   Height: **1**
   Caps divisions: **0**

   Next, fix the cylinder to the center of the clock model.

Figure 9-50 The text arranged on the clock model

10. Choose **Create > Polygon Primitives > Cube** from the main menubar and create a cube in the Top viewport. Next, adjust the vertices of the cube to create the second hand and then align it with the cylinder, as shown in Figure 9-51.

11. Press INSERT and set the pivot point of the second hand to the center of the cylinder.

Setting and Refining Animation Keys Using the Graph Editor

In this section, you need to animate the second hand using the **Graph Editor**.

Figure 9-51 The second hand of the clock

1. Select the second hand from the viewport. Next, choose **Modify > Freeze Transformations** from the main menubar to set move, rotate, and scale attribute values to **0**.

2. Set the **Time slider** from **1** to **1500**. Next, select the **second hand** and press **S** to set the key on frame **1**. Now, move the time slider to frame **24**. Display the **Channel box** and set the **RotateY** value to **-6**. Again, press S to set the key at frame **24**.

3. Choose **Window > Animation Editors > Graph Editor** from the main menubar; the **Graph Editor** window is displayed. Select **RotateY** from the left panel in the **Graph Editor** window; the **RotateY** attribute of the animation curve is displayed. Now, select the **RotateY** animation curve.

4. Choose **View > Infinity** from the **Graph Editor** menubar so that the graph in the **Graph Editor** continues till the end and you need not set the keys repeatedly. Choose **Curves > Post Infinity > Cycle with Offset** from the main menubar and play the animation. The movement of the second hand will become smooth.

5.   To make the movement of the second hand realistic, select the animation curve from the **Graph Editor**. Next, choose **Tangents > Stepped** from the **Graph Editor** menubar to add steps in the animation curve in the **Graph Editor**.

6.   Preview the animation; the movement of the second hand is not smooth now as it is jerky.

7.   To give the animation a realistic effect, choose the **Animation Preferences** button from the right of the **Auto KeyframeToggle** key; the **Preferences** dialog box is displayed. Change **Playback Speed** to **Real Time [24 fps]** in the **Playback** area at the bottom of the viewport. Next, choose the **Save** button to save the animation.

8.   Preview the animation to see the real world effect of the second hand in the wall clock.

Note
Using the steps given in this tutorial, you can create a complete clock with the minute and the hour hands. If needed, you can apply texture to the clock to give it a realistic effect.

Saving the File
In this section, you need to save the file for further reference.

1.   Choose **File > Save Scene** from the main menubar; the **Save As** dialog box is displayed.

As the project folder is already set, by default the path *\Documents\Maya_Tutorials\c09_tut2\ scenes* is displayed in **Look In** text box of the dialog box.

2.   Enter **c09_tut2** in the **File name** text box and then select **Maya Binary** from the **Files of type** drop-down list. Next, choose the **Save As** button.

You can view the final rendered image of the model by downloading the file *c09_Maya_2012_render.zip* from *http://www.cadcim.com*.

Self-Evaluation Test

Answer the following questions and then compare them to those given at the end of this chapter:

1.   In which of the following animation types, can you transform objects by setting keyframes?

(a) Keyframe   (b) Nonlinear
(c) Technical   (d) Effects

2. Which of the following windows is used to edit animation curves?

   (a) **Graph Editor**   (b) **Dope Sheet**
   (c) **Trax Editor**   (d) None of these

3. The _____ option is used to paste keys from the virtual memory to the place where the current time indicator is located.

4. The _____ animation is used to import the motion-captured data to apply a realistic animation to the character.

5. The _____ button is used to make the selected layer solo.

6. The _____ tool is used to adjust both angles of a tangent to the same angle.

7. The technical animation type is used to set the driven keys to animate an object by linking the attributes of one object to those of another object. (T/F)

8. The **Buffer Curve Snapshot** tool is used to take a snapshot of the selected curve. (T/F)

9. The **Unify Tangent** tool is used to retain the original position of tangents. (T/F)

10. The **Post-Infinity Cycle** tool is used to copy an animation curve and repeat it infinitely through the graph view. (T/F)

Review Questions

Answer the following questions:

1. Which of the following options is used to define the total length of an animation?

   (a) **Range**   (b) **Frame Rate**
   (c) Keyframe Animation   (d) None of these

2. The _____ method is used to animate an object on a particular path.

3. The _____ tool is used to copy an animation curve and then join it after the same curve infinite number of times.

4. The _____ tool is used to lock the tangent weight.

5. You can animate an object over a surface by using the _____ option.

6. The _____ of **Playback range** button is used to move to the last frame of the active time segment.

7. The **Plateau** tangent tool is similar to the **Spline** and **Clamped** tangent tools. (T/F)

8. The **Pre-infinity cycle with Offset** tool is not similar to the **Post-infinity cycle with Offset** tool. (T/F)

9. The playback control buttons are used to control the animation in the viewport. (T/F)

10. The **Swap Buffer Curve** tool is used to swap between the original and the edited curves. (T/F)

Exercise

Exercise 1

Open the model shown in Figure 9-52 by using the **Graph Editor** and then animate the light of the bulb. You can view the final rendered image of this model by downloading the file *c09_maya_2012_render.zip* from *http://www.cadcim.com*. The path of file is as follows:

Textbooks > Animation and Visual Effects > Maya > Autodesk Maya 2012: A Comprehensive Guide
(Expected time: 15 min)

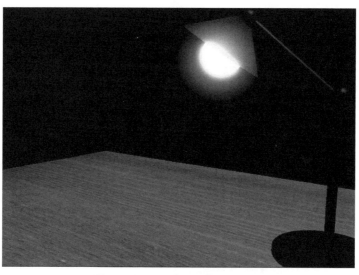

Figure 9-52 *The Bulb animation*

Answers to Self-Evaluation Test
1. a, **2.** a, **3. Paste Keys**, **4.** motion capture, **5. Solo Layer**, **6. Spline**, **7.** T, **8.** T, **9.** T, **10.** T

Chapter 10

Animation-II

Learning Objectives

After completing this chapter, you will be able to:

• *Understand different types of joints*
• *Understand the parent and child relationship in animation*
• *Use different deformers for animating an object*
• *Use different types of constraints in animation*
• *Use the set driven keys to link objects*

INTRODUCTION

A skeleton is a group of hierarchical structures that helps in providing motion to an object. In Maya, the skeleton is formed by combining joints and bones and provides support to an object in the same way as the human skeleton does to human body. In this process, the skeleton is joined to the corresponding object by the skinning method. This method is discussed in detail later in this chapter. In the following section, you will learn about bones and joints.

Bones and Joints

In Maya, bones and joints are grouped together to form a complete skeleton. In other words, bones and joints act as the building block for creating a skeleton. They are visible only in the viewport and cannot be rendered. Each joint may have one or more bones attached to it, as shown in Figure 10-1. To create a bone structure, choose **Skeleton > Joint Tool** from the main menubar.

By default, the size of bones and joints is set to 1. To change the size of bones and joints, choose **Display > Animation > Joint Size** from the main menubar; the **Joint Display Scale** dialog box will be displayed, as shown in Figure 10-2.

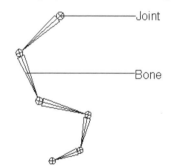

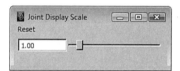

Figure 10-1 *The bones and joints*   *Figure 10-2* *The **Joint***
                                               ***Display Scale** dialog box*

In this dialog box, enter the required value for the joint size in the text box and press ENTER. Alternatively, move the slider on the right of the edit box to adjust the size of joints and bones. You can also set the joint size by using the **Preferences** dialog box. To do so, choose **Window > Setting/Preferences > Preferences** from the main menubar; the **Preferences** dialog box will be displayed. In this dialog box, select **Kinematics** from the **Categories** list; various attributes in the **Kinematics: Kinematic Display Preferences** area will be displayed on the right of the **Categories** list, as shown in Figure 10-3. Now, enter a value in the **Joint size** edit box or move the slider on the right of the edit box to adjust the joint size in the **Inverse Kinematics** area of the **Preferences** dialog box.

Creating a Bone Structure

To create a bone structure in a scene, choose the **Animation** module from the menuset in the status line and activate the Front, Side, or Top viewport. Next, choose **Skeleton > Joint Tool** from the main menubar and then click in the viewport; the bone structure will be created in the viewport. Press ENTER to exit the **Joint Tool**.

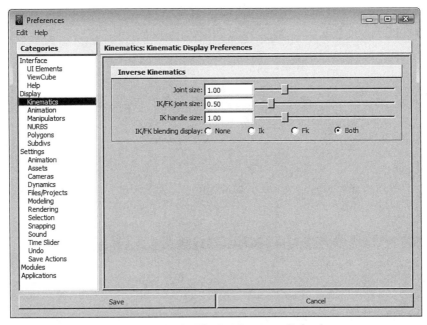

*Figure 10-3 The **Preferences** dialog box*

To animate an object, you should first set the local axes of all joints. To display the local axes of a joint, select a joint from the joint system created in the viewport. Next, choose **Display > Transform Display > Local Rotation Axes** from the main menubar; the local axes will be displayed on a single joint, as shown in Figure 10-4. Similarly, to select the local axes of all joints in a skeleton, select the topmost joint in the skeleton hierarchy and choose **Edit > Select Hierarchy** from the main menubar. Next, choose **Display > Transform Display > Local Rotation Axes** from the main menubar; the local axes will be displayed on all joints, as shown in Figure 10-5.

Figure 10-4 The local axes displayed on a single joint

Figure 10-5 The local axes displayed on the entire hierarchy

Types of Joints

In Maya, there are three types of joints that determine the movement of the bones attached to them. These joints are discussed next.

Ball Joint

The ball joint provides free movement to a joint in the skeleton. This type of joint can rotate about all three of its local axes freely. The human shoulder is an example of the ball joint.

Universal Joint

The universal joint provides motion to bones only in two directions. This means the joint can move freely along two axes only. The human wrist is an example of the universal joint.

Hinge Joint

The hinge joint provides rotation to bones in one direction only. The human knee is an example of the hinge joint.

PARENT-CHILD RELATIONSHIP IN ANIMATION

The parent-child relationship is the most important relationship in animation. The parent object passes its transformations down the hierarchy chain to its children, and each child object inherits all properties of its parent. Note that a parent object can have more than one child object, but not vice versa.

To understand the parent-child relationship, create two NURBS spheres in the viewport such that one sphere is larger than the other, as shown in Figure 10-6. Select the smaller sphere, press and hold the SHIFT key, and then select the larger sphere. Now, choose **Edit > Parent** from the main menubar; the larger sphere will become the parent of the smaller sphere. Note that the object that you select later will act as parent of the object that you selected earlier. Invoke the **Move Tool** from the

Figure 10-6 Spheres created

toolbox and move the parent object; the child object will move along with the parent object.

KINEMATICS

Kinematics is the science of motion. In the case of skeletons used in Maya, kinematics specifies the motion of bones. **Kinematics** is of two types: Forward and Inverse.

In **Forward Kinematics** (FK), the child objects are animated based on the transformations of the parent object. It is a one-way process, in which, if a parent object moves, the child objects will also move. However, if a child object is moved, the corresponding parent object will not move. In other words, you can use the topmost object in the hierarchy to animate the entire chain. Note that when you create a hierarchy, the **Forward Kinematics** is set by default.

The **Inverse Kinematics** (IK) is just the opposite of the **Forward Kinematics**. In **Inverse Kinematics**, you can use the object at the bottom of hierarchy to animate the entire chain. In this kinematics, if you move a child object, the objects that are higher in the hierarchy will also move.

DEFORMERS

The deformers are the tools that are used to change the geometry of an object. Moving or scaling the vertex, face or edges is known as deforming. You can deform any object in Maya by defining the control points of deformers. Various deformers in Maya are discussed next.

Blend Shape Deformer

Main menubar:	Create Deformers > Blend Shape

The **Blend Shape** deformer is used to change the shape of an object into another object by morphing. Morphing is an animation technique which is used to combine the motion of two or more objects by matching their vertices in a sequential form to produce the final animation. The original object that is used in this process is known as the base object, and the object into which the base object gets blended is known as the target object.

To deform a shape, first create a base object. Next, create a copy of the base object and modify its shape, as shown in Figure 10-7. Now, select the target object, press and hold the SHIFT key, and then select the base object; both the base object and the target object will be selected. Next, select the **Animation** module from the menu set drop-down list in the status line and choose **Create Deformers > Blend Shape** from the main menubar; the blending will be done on the base object. Now, to view the blending of the object in the viewport, you need to set the parameters in the **Attribute Editor**. To do so, select the base object and choose **Windows > Attribute Editor** from the main menubar; the **Attribute Editor** will be displayed. Choose the **blendShape1** attribute tab from the **Attribute Editor**. In the **Weight** attribute area in this tab, adjust the slider to view the blending of the object in the viewport.

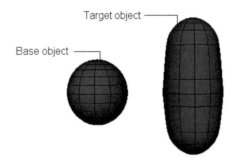

Figure 10-7 *The base and target objects for blending*

Note
*You can apply the **Blend Shape** deformer on mesh objects only if they have equal number of vertices. The **Blend Shape** deformer is mainly used for creating facial expressions.*

Lattice Deformer

Main menubar:	Create Deformers > Lattice

The **Lattice** deformer is used to modify an object using lattices. To modify an object using lattices, create the object in the viewport. Next, select the object and choose **Create Deformers > Lattice** from the main menubar; lattice will be created around the selected object, as shown in Figure 10-8. To control the influence of lattice on the mesh, select the lattice in the viewport and choose **Display > UI Elements > Channel Box / Layer Editor** from the main menubar; a **Channel box** will be displayed with different properties. To set the local influence of lattices, enter the required value in the **ffd1** area of the **OUTPUTS** node, as shown in Figure 10-9. To set the number of lattice segments, set the required values in the **S**, **T**, and **U Division** edit boxes of the **SHAPES** node in the **Channel Box**.

OUTPUTS	
ffd1	
Envelope	1
Local Influence S	2
Local Influence T	2
Local Influence U	2

Figure 10-8 Lattice created around the selected object   *Figure 10-9 Setting the local influences*

After setting the required parameters of the lattice, you can deform the object. To do so, select the lattice, press and hold the right mouse button anywhere in the viewport and choose **Lattice Point** from the marking menu; the lattice points will be displayed around the selected object. Now, select these lattice points to deform the object as per your requirement. A very good example of lattice deformer is sack animation. To create a sack animation, first create a sack model and then select it. Next, choose **Create Deformers > Lattice** from the main menubar; a lattice will be created around the sack model. Select the lattice and press and hold the right mouse button anywhere in the viewport and choose **Lattice Point** from the marking menu. Now, you can create different shapes for the sack model using these points. Next, set the keys as discussed in Chapter 9.

Wrap Deformer

Main menubar:	Create Deformers > Wrap

The **Wrap** deformer is used to deform an object using NURBS surfaces, NURBS curves, or polygonal surfaces (meshes). To apply the **Wrap** deformer to an object, create a polygonal plane and then a polygonal cone in the viewport. The polygonal cone should be placed such that it intersects with the polygonal plane at some point. Next, invoke the **Move Tool** from the toolbox and select the polygonal plane. Next, press and hold the SHIFT key and select the polygonal cone. Now, choose **Create Deformers > Wrap** from the main menubar to apply the **Wrap** deformer.

Cluster Deformer

Main menubar:	Create Deformers > Cluster

The **Cluster** deformer is used to modify a particular area of the mesh. To do so, select a group of vertices from the object that you want to deform. Next, choose **Create Deformers > Cluster** from the main menubar; a C symbol will be displayed in the viewport. Select the C symbol and move it using the **Move Tool**; the vertices linked to the symbol will move along with it. Figures 10-10 and 10-11 show an object before and after applying the **Cluster** deformer.

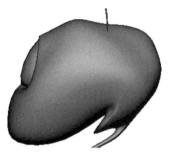 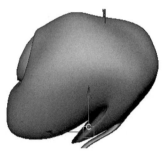

Figure 10-10 *The object before applying the **Cluster** deformer*

Figure 10-11 *The object after applying the **Cluster** deformer*

Soft Modification Deformer

Main menubar:	Create Deformers > Soft Modification

The **Soft Modification** deformer helps you deform high density surface meshes without adjusting the vertices manually. The falloff attributes of this deformer are adjustable. To use this deformer, create a high density plane in the viewport and choose **Create Deformers > Soft Modification** from the main menubar. Alternatively, invoke the **Soft Modification** tool from the toolbox; a colored falloff attributes area will be created at the center of the plane, as shown in Figure 10-12. The colored area defines the deformer on the surface. Darker the color, greater will be the influence of deformation, and vice-versa. By default, the amount of deformation is greatest at the center and it gradually decreases toward the end. Move the manipulators in this area to deform the plane as per your requirement.

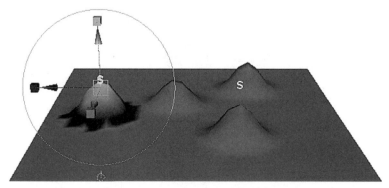

Figure 10-12 *A plane after applying the **Soft Modification** deformer*

Nonlinear Deformers

Main menubar: Create Deformers > Nonlinear

In Maya, there are different types of nonlinear deformers. These are discussed next.

Bend Deformer

The **Bend** deformer is used to bend an object along a circular arc, as shown in Figures 10-13 and 10-14. To bend an object, select the object from the viewport. Next, choose **Create Deformers > Nonlinear > Bend** from the main menubar; the **Bend** deformer will be applied to the selected object. Again, select the object in the viewport and choose **Window > Attribute Editor** from the main menubar; the **Attribute Editor** will be displayed, as shown in Figure 10-15. Choose the **bend1** tab from the **Attribute Editor** and adjust the attributes in the **Nonlinear Deformer Attributes** area to bend the object, refer to Figure 10-15.

Note

You should avoid changing the number of CVs, vertices, or other lattice points after applying a deformer on an object. Any change in the object will lead to a change in the functioning of that particular deformer.

Figure 10-13 The object before applying the **Bend** *deformer*

Figure 10-14 The object after applying the **Bend** *deformer*

Flare Deformer

The **Flare** deformer is used to taper an object along the X, Y, and Z axes. To taper an object using this deformer, create a NURBS cylinder in the viewport. Next, choose **Create Deformers > Nonlinear > Flare** from the main menubar; the **Flare** deformer will be applied to the object, refer to Figures 10-16 and 10-17. Again, select the cylinder in the viewport and choose **Window > Attribute Editor** from the main menubar; the **Attribute Editor** will be displayed, as shown in Figure 10-18. Choose the **flare1** tab from the **Attribute Editor** and set the values for various attributes in the **Nonlinear Deformer Attributes** area to deform the object, refer to Figure 10-18.

Sine Deformer

The **Sine** deformer is used to deform an object in the shape of a sine wave. Figures 10-19 and 10-20 show a cylinder before and after applying the **Sine** deformer, respectively. To apply this deformer, create an object in the viewport and then choose **Create Deformers > Nonlinear > Sine** from the main menubar; the **Sine** deformer will be applied to the object. Now, select the object again and choose **Window > Attribute Editor** from the main menubar; the **Attribute Editor** will be displayed, as shown in Figure 10-21. Choose the **sine1** tab from the **Attribute Editor** and set the values of various attributes in the **Nonlinear Deformer Attributes** area to deform the object.

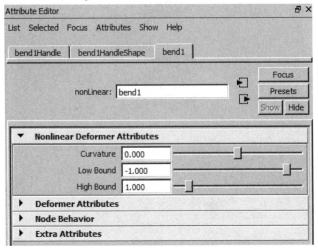

Figure 10-15 The **Bend** deformer attributes area in the *Attribute Editor*

Figure 10-16 The cylinder before applying the **Flare** deformer

Figure 10-17 The cylinder after applying the **Flare** deformer

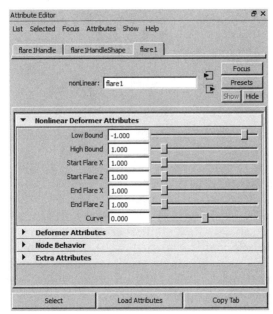

Figure 10-18 Partial view of the **Flare** deformer attributes in the *Attribute Editor*

Figure 10-19 *The cylinder before applying the **Sine** deformer*

Figure 10-20 *The cylinder after applying the **Sine** deformer*

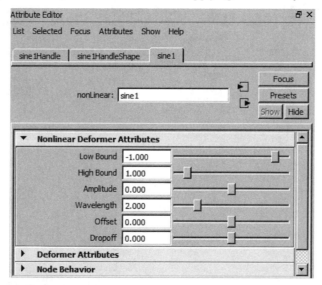

Figure 10-21 *Partial view of the **Sine** deformer attributes in the **Attribute Editor***

Squash Deformer

The **Squash** deformer is used to squash and stretch an object along a specific axis, as shown in Figures 10-22 and 10-23. To squash or stretch an object, select the object in the viewport and choose **Create Deformers > Nonlinear > Squash** from the main menubar; the **Squash** deformer will be applied to the selected object. Again, select the deformer in the viewport and choose **Window > Attribute Editor** from the main menubar; the **Attribute Editor** will be displayed, as shown in Figure 10-24. Choose the **squash1** tab from the **Attribute Editor** and set the values of attributes in the **Nonlinear Deformer Attributes** area to deform the object.

Figure 10-22 *An object before applying the* **Squash** *deformer*

Figure 10-23 *An object after applying the* **Squash** *deformer*

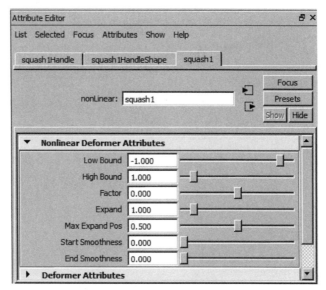

Figure 10-24 *Partial view of the* **Squash** *deformer attributes in the* **Attribute Editor**

Twist Deformer

The **Twist** deformer is used to twist an object along a specific axis. Figures 10-25 and 10-26 show a cylinder before and after applying the **Twist** deformer. To apply this deformer, create an object in the viewport and choose **Create Deformers > Nonlinear > Twist** from the main menubar; the **Twist** deformer will be applied to the object. Now, select the object again from the viewport and choose **Window > Attribute Editor** from the main menubar; the **Attribute Editor** will be displayed. Choose the **twist1** tab from the **Attribute Editor** and set the values of various attributes in the **Nonlinear Deformer Attributes** area to deform the object, as shown in Figure 10-27.

Figure 10-25 *The cylinder before applying the* **Twist** *deformer*

Figure 10-26 *The cylinder after applying the* **Twist** *deformer*

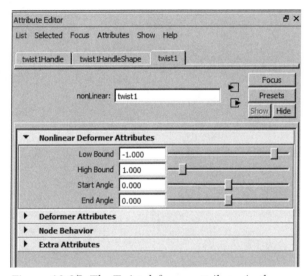

Figure 10-27 *The* **Twist** *deformer attributes in the* **Attribute Editor**

Wave Deformer

The **Wave** deformer is used to propagate waves on an object in the X and Z directions. Figures 10-28 and 10-29 show a plane before and after applying the **Wave** deformer. To apply the **Wave** deformer, create an object in the viewport and then increase the number of segments on it from the **Channel box**. Next, choose **Create Deformers > Nonlinear > Wave** from the main menubar; the **Wave** deformer will be applied to the selected object. Select the object again and choose **Window > Attribute Editor** from the main menubar; the **Attribute Editor** will be displayed. Next, choose the **wave1** tab from the **Attribute Editor** to deform the selected object as desired. The attributes of the **Wave** deformer are similar to those of the **Sine** deformer and are shown in Figure 10-30.

Figure 10-28 *The plane before applying the* **Wave** *deformer*

Figure 10-29 *The plane after applying the* **Wave** *deformer*

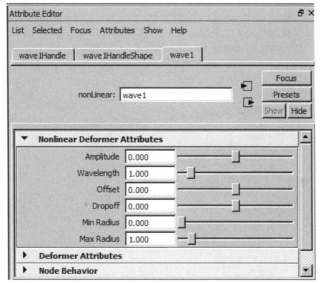

Figure 10-30 *The* **Wave** *deformer attributes in the Attribute Editor*

Sculpt Deformer

Main menubar: Create Deformers > Sculpt Deformer

The **Sculpt Deformer** is used to create a rounded deformation on an object. To apply the **Sculpt Deformer**, select an object or the vertices of an object where you need deformation. Now, choose **Create Deformers > Sculpt Deformer** from the main menubar; a spherical influence object called sculpt sphere will be created around the selected object or vertices. Now, move this sculpt sphere to deform the object. Note that the object will be sculpted better if there are more number of segments on the object.

Jiggle Deformer

Main menubar: Create Deformers > Jiggle Deformer

The **Jiggle Deformer** is used to shake an object or its parts while animating. This deformer is applied to a complete object or to its CV's, lattice points, and vertices. For example, you can use this deformer to show the affect of shaking the stomach of a fat man or a wrestler while he is walking.

Wire Tool

Main menubar:	Create Deformers > Wire Tool

The **Wire Tool** is used to change the shape of an object by setting one or more of its NURBS curves. This tool is mainly used for setting lips or eyebrow deformations. To understand the working of the **Wire Tool**, choose **Create > Polygon Primitives > Plane** from the main menubar; a plane will be created. Next, choose **Create > EP Curve Tool** from the main menubar and create a curve on the plane created in the viewport. Next, invoke the **Move Tool** from the toolbox, and click anywhere in the viewport to deselect the selection, if any. Now, select the **Animation** module from the menuset in the status line and choose **Create Deformers > Wire Tool** from the main menubar. Then, select the shapes from the viewport that are required to be deformed and press ENTER. Now, select a wire curve and press ENTER; the **Wire Tool** will change the shape of the object. Clear the selection, if any, and press ENTER again to set the **Wire Tool** on the objects in the viewport.

Wrinkle Tool

Main menubar:	Create Deformers > Wrinkle Tool

The **Wrinkle Tool** is used to create a detailed wrinkle effect on an object. The **Wrinkle** deformer works in collaboration with the **Wire** and **Cluster** deformers. The **Wrinkle Tool** is preferably used on NURBS surfaces. To understand the working of this tool, choose **Create > NURBS Primitives > Sphere** from the main menubar and create a sphere in the viewport. Next, select the **Animation** module from the menuset in the status line. Next, choose **Create Deformers > Wrinkle Tool** from the main menubar; a UV region will be highlighted on the selected surface. The UV surface lets you set the wire cluster to deform the object. Use the middle mouse button to shape the UV region and press ENTER; a 'C' icon is created on the object. The 'C' icon is the cluster deformer handle that is used to deform the object. Invoke the **Move Tool** to move vertices and deform the object as per your requirement.

Point On Curve

Main menubar:	Create Deformers > Point On Curve

The **Point On Curve** tool is used to deform points on the NURBS curve. To understand the working of this tool, choose **Create > EP curve tool** from the main menubar and create a curve on the viewport. Next, right-click on a point on the curve and then choose **Curve Point** from the marking menu displayed. Next, select the **Animation** module from the menuset in the status line and then choose **Create Deformers > Point On Curve** from the main menubar; a star-shaped point is created on the curve. Next, invoke the **Move Tool** from the toolbox, and move the point in any direction in the viewport. As a result, the curve will also move along with it.

APPLYING CONSTRAINTS

Constraints are used to restrict the motion of an object to a particular mode by specifying their limits. Different types of constraints in Maya are discussed next.

Point Constraint

Main menubar: Constrain > Point

The **Point** constraint is used to restrict the movement of an object such that the constrained object follows the movement of another object. To apply this constraint, create two cubes of different sizes in the viewport. Now select one cube, and press and hold the SHIFT key to select another cube. Next, choose **Constrain > Point** from the main menubar to coordinate the motion of one cube with another cube. The object selected first controls the movement of the object selected later. On applying the **Point** constraint, the objects may overlap when they are moved. To avoid this situation, choose **Constrain > Point > Option Box** from the main menubar; the **Point Constraint Options** dialog box will be displayed, as shown in Figure 10-31. The **Offset** attribute in this dialog box is used to set the distance between the two selected objects. Enter the required values in the **Offset** edit boxes and choose the **Add** button from the dialog box; the **Point** constraint will be applied to the selected object.

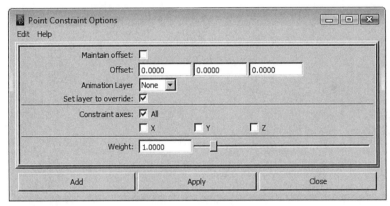

*Figure 10-31 The **Point Constraint Options** dialog box*

Note that the working of constraints is opposite to that of the parent-child relationship. In a parent-child relationship, the object selected later acts as the parent, but in case of constraints, the object selected first acts as the parent of the object selected later.

Aim Constraint

Main menubar: Constrain > Aim

The **Aim** constraint is used to aim one object at another object. To create one object aiming at another object, create two objects in the viewport. Next, select one object, press and hold the SHIFT key and then select another object. Choose **Constrain > Aim** from the main menubar to apply the **Aim** constraint to the selected object; the object selected first will act as the aim for the object selected later. You can also set the object to aim in a particular direction. To do so, choose **Constrain > Aim > Option Box** from the main menubar; the **Aim Constraint Options** dialog box will be displayed, as shown in Figure 10-32. Set the required axis in the **Constraint axes** area and choose the **Add** button; the object will be set to aim in a particular direction.

Orient Constraint

Main menubar: Constrain > Orient

The **Orient** constraint is used to match the orientation of one object with the other such that the objects are aligned together. To do so, create two objects in the viewport. Select one object, press and hold the SHIFT key and then select another object. Choose **Constrain > Orient** from the main menubar to apply this constraint to the objects. Now, invoke the **Rotate** tool from the toolbox, select the object created first and then rotate it; the other object will also rotate with it. To set the constraint axes, choose **Constrain > Orient > Option Box** from the main menubar; the **Orient Constraint Options** dialog box will be displayed, as shown in Figure 10-33. In this dialog box, set the required constraint axis in the **Constraint axes** area and choose the **Add** button.

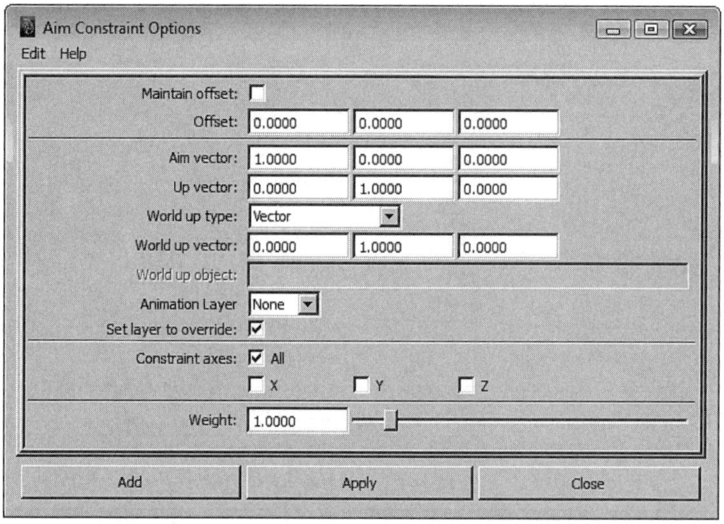

Figure 10-32 The **Aim Constraint Options** *dialog box*

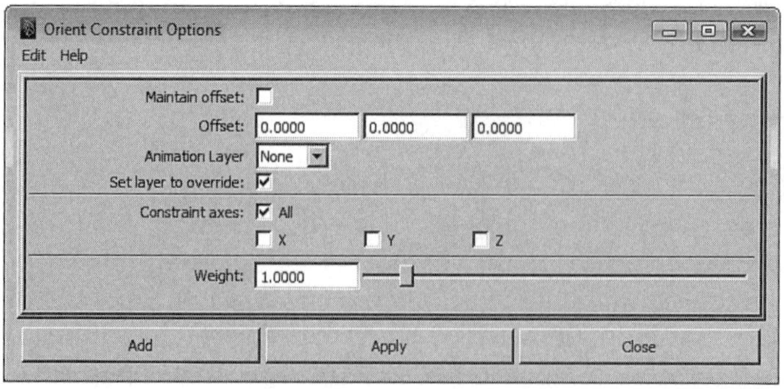

Figure 10-33 The **Orient Constraint Options** *dialog box*

Scale Constraint

Main menubar:	Constrain > Scale

The **Scale** constraint is used to match the orientation of one object with the other object such that the scaling of one object matches with the other object. To apply this constraint, create two objects in the viewport. Select one object, press and hold the SHIFT key, and then select the other object. Next, choose **Constrain > Scale** from the main menubar to apply the **Scale** constraint. Now, invoke the **Scale** tool from the toolbox and select the object that you created first and scale it; the other object will also be scaled with it.

Parent Constraint

Main menubar:	Constrain > Parent

The **Parent** constraint is used to relate the orientation of one object with the other object such that both of them follow the parent-child relationship. To apply this constraint, create two objects in the viewport. Select one object, press and hold the SHIFT key, and then select the other object. Next, choose **Constrain > Parent** from the main menubar to apply the **Parent** constraint to the selected objects. Change the position of the parent object; the objects follow the parent-child relationship. The **Parent** constraint is different from the **Point** and **Orient** constraints. When an object is rotated using the **Point** or **Orient** constraints, the constrained object rotates about its local axis. Whereas in case of the **Parent** constraint, the constrained object rotates with respect to the world axis.

Geometry Constraint

Main menubar:	Constrain > Geometry

The **Geometry** constraint is used to restrict one object to the geometry of another object. To apply this constraint, choose **Create > Polygon Primitives > Plane** from the main menubar and create a plane in the viewport. Similarly, choose **Create > Polygon Primitives > Sphere** from the main menubar and create a sphere in the viewport. Select the plane from the viewport, press and hold the SHIFT key, and then select the sphere. Now, choose **Constrain > Geometry** from the main menubar; the movement of the sphere will be restricted to the geometry of the plane. Invoke the **Move Tool** from the toolbox and move the sphere; the sphere will not move beyond the geometry of the plane.

Normal Constraint

Main menubar:	Constrain > Normal

The **Normal** constraint is used to orient the selected objects together in such a way that they align with the normal vectors of the mesh object. To apply this constraint, create two objects in the viewport. Next, select the objects created, and choose **Constrain > Normal** from the main menubar to align one object to the normal vector of another object. On applying the **Normal** constraint, the constrained object will move along the normal vector of another object. For example, if you want to show a person sweating, instead of animating the sweat drops manually, apply the **Normal** constraint to it; the sweat drops will move while the drop is still attached to the skin.

Tangent Constraint

Main menubar:	Constrain > Tangent

The **Tangent** constraint is used to keep an object aligned and oriented toward a curve. To apply this constraint, create an object and a curve in the viewport. Next, select both entities and choose **Constrain > Tangent** from the main menubar to constrain the object on the curve in such a way that the object moves along the curve. For example, you can use the **Tangent** constraint to animate a locomotive such that it moves on the track.

Pole Vector Constraint

Main menubar:	Constrain > Pole Vector

The **Pole Vector** constraint is used to constrain one object with the other object such that the end of one pole vector moves with the movement of another object. Select both entities from the viewport and choose **Constrain > Pole Vector** from the main menubar; the constrained object will move with the movement of another object with which it is constrained. The **Pole Vector** constraint is mainly used for setting up joints in a character setup.

Point On Poly

Main menubar:	Constrain > Point On Poly

The **Point On Poly** constraint is used to constrain an object with the mesh or another object such that the object remains stuck to the mesh or another object even if the mesh is deformed or moved from one place to another. To apply this constraint, create two objects in the viewport. Next, select the objects created and choose **Constrain > Point On Poly** from the main menubar. This constraint can be used to create objects such as a handle on the door, which remains stuck to the door even if the door is deformed.

ADDING CONSTRAINTS TO ANIMATION LAYERS

With the advancement in Autodesk Maya 2012, you can now add various constraints to animation layers. To do so, follow the steps given below:

1. Choose **Display > UI Elements > Channel Box/ Layer Editor** from the main menubar; the **Channel box/layer editor** will be displayed. Next, activate the animation layer editor from the **Channel box** by choosing the **Anim** tab.

2. Create a new animation layer in the **Animation Layer Editor** and rename it as **constraint**.

3. Select the target objects followed by the object on which you want to apply constraints from the viewport and choose **Contrain > Orient > Option Box** from the main menubar; the **Orient Constraint Options** dialog box is displayed.

4. From the **Animation Layer** drop-down list in the **Orient Constraint Options** dialog box, choose the layer to which you want to add constraint and then choose the **Add** button; the constraint will be added to the selected layer.

MOCAP EXAMPLES

Autodesk Maya 2012 now comes with additional inbuilt Mocap (Motion Capture examples). You can find the examples of Mocap in the **Visor** window. To access these motion capture examples, choose **Window > General Editors > Visor** from the main menubar; the **Visor** window will be displayed. Next, choose the **Mocap Examples** tab from the **Visor** window; the list of all the motion capture examples will be displayed, such as cartwheel.ma, dance1.ma, and so on. To preview a motion capture animation, press and hold the middle mouse button over a motion capture example and drag it to the viewport; a character will be displayed in the viewport.

HUMAN IK CHARACTER SET UP TOOLS

Autodesk Maya 2012 comes up with two **New Human IK Character set up** tools. These tools are added along with the existing **Skeleton Generator** tool. The human IK character set up tools are: **Character Control** and **Characterization Tool**. To access these tools, choose **Window > Animation Editors > Human IK** from the main menubar. These tools are discussed next.

Character Control

To invoke the **Character Controls** tool, choose **Window > Animation Editors > Human IK > Character Controls** from the main menubar; a **Character Controls** window will be displayed, giving a visible interface of **IK** and **FK** of the current rig, as shown in Figure 10-34. It is mainly used to animate a character using a control rig.

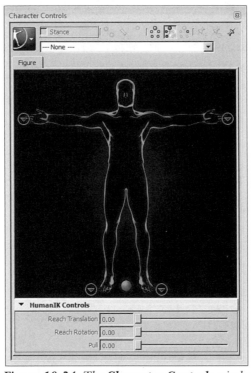

Figure 10-34 The **Character Controls** window

Characterization Tool

Characterization tool is used to define and map the structure of human IK characters. To invoke the **Characterization Tool**, choose **Window > Animation Editors > Human IK > Characterization Tool** from the main menubar; the **Characterization Tool** window will be displayed, as shown in Figure 10-35.

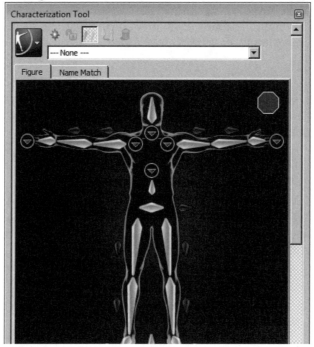

Figure 10-35 *Partial view of the Characterization Tool window*

SKINNING AN OBJECT

Skinning is a process that is used to bind the object to the bones or to skeleton. The following steps will help you understand the process of skinning:

1. Choose **Create > Polygon Primitives > Cylinder** from the main menubar and create a cylinder in the viewport.

2. Select the cylinder created in the viewport and choose **Display > UI Elements > Channel Box/ Layer Editor** from the main menubar; the **Channel box** will be displayed. Next, set the value of **Subdivisions Height** to **5** in the channel box.

3. Select the **Animation** module from the status line. Next, select the cylinder from the viewport again and choose **Modify > Freeze Transformations** from the main menubar to reset the orientation of the cylinder to zero.

4. Activate the Front viewport. Next, choose **Skeleton > Joint Tool** from the main menubar and then create the bone structure, as shown in Figure 10-36.

5. Select the cylinder from the viewport, press and hold the SHIFT key, and then select the lowest bone from the bone structure. Note that the lowest bone is the parent bone of other bones. Now, choose **Skin > Bind Skin > Smooth Bind** from the main menubar; the color of the bones changes in the viewport, indicating that the bones are bound with the objects.

 Note
*It is recommended that you always specify the names of joints so that it becomes easy to work on hierarchy at later stages. To specify the name of a joint, select it and open the **Attribute Editor**. At the top of the **Attribute Editor**, the name of the corresponding joint will be displayed in the **Joint** edit box. Change the name as per the hierarchy setup.*

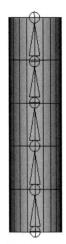

Figure 10-36 The bone structure created

Paint Skin Weights Tool

You can add or delete the influence of bone on different parts of an object. To do so, select the skinned object from the viewport and choose **Skin > Edit Smooth Skin > Paint Skin Weights Tool > Option Box** from the main menubar; the **Paint Skin Weights Tool** property window will be displayed, as shown in Figure 10-37. Expand the **Influence** attribute area, as shown in Figure 10-38, and then select the bone whose influence you want to put on other parts of the object from the **Transform** area; the influence will be added. Additionally, the area on which the bone has the influence will be displayed in white and the remaining part of the object will be displayed in black. The other most commonly used options in the **Paint Skin Weights Tool** property window are discussed next.

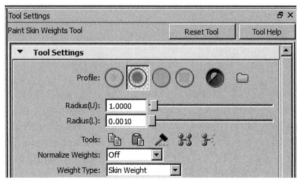

Figure 10-37 Partial view of the **Tool Settings** (**Paint Skin Weights**) **Tool** property window

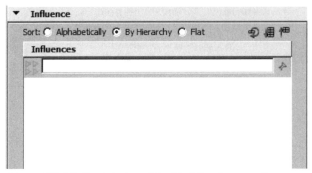

*Figure 10-38 Partial view of the **Tool Settings** attribute area*

Tool Settings

The **Tool Settings** area is used to set the size and type of the paint weight brush. To do so, expand the **Tool Settings** attribute area, refer to Figure 10-36, and then specify values in the **Radius(U)** and **Radius(L)** edit boxes to set the size of the paint weight brush. You can also specify these values by pressing and holding the B key and then dragging the mouse by pressing the left mouse button. If you have deformed the basic shape of an object after skinning, choose **Skin > Go to Bind Pose** from the main menubar; the object gets back to the bind position.

Bind Pose

Main menubar:	Skin > Go to bind pose

The **Bind Pose** is defined as a pose in which the skeleton gets bound to the mesh object before any deformations begin. Maya creates a default bind pose node for every skeleton. This bind pose node stores the transformation attributes of joints. To invoke this tool choose **Skin > Bind Pose** from the main menubar.

INTRODUCING THE MAYA MUSCLE DEFORMER

Maya muscle deformer is a skin deformer which helps you create quick and easy rigs. Before you start working with the Maya muscle deformer, you need to activate it. To do so, choose **Window > Settings/Preferences > Plug-in Manager** from the main menubar; the **Plug-in Manager** window will be displayed. Select the **Loaded** check box in front of the **MayaMuscle. mll** option and choose the **Refresh** button from the window. The tools related to the Maya muscle deformer will be added to the **Muscle** menu as well as in the **Muscle** shelf in the shelf bar. The muscles in Maya are formed by the combination of various muscle objects. These muscle objects are discussed next.

Muscle Objects

The components that together make up a bone are known as muscle objects. These components are discussed next.

Capsules

The capsules are similar to the joints in Maya and are used to convert polygon or NURBS objects into muscle objects so that they can be connected with the skin easily. To create a capsule,

choose **Muscle > Muscles/Bones > Make Capsule**
from the main menubar; a basic capsule object will be
created, as shown in Figure 10-39. You can also create a
capsule with an end locator (the end locator defines the
end of a capsule). To do so, choose **Muscle > Muscles/
Bones > Make Capsule with End Locator** from the
main menubar; a capsule object will be created with an
end locator, as shown in Figure 10-40. Select the locator
and move it to change the size of the capsule, as shown
in Figure 10-41. After resizing, you can also select the
end locator and spin the capsule on its axis. To add the
locator after creating a capsule, select the capsule from
the viewport and choose **Muscle > Muscles/Bones >
Add End Locator to Capsule** from the main menubar;
the locator will be added to the capsule.

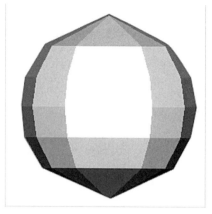

Figure 10-39 A basic capsule object

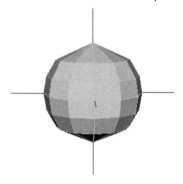

Figure 10-40 The capsule with an end locator

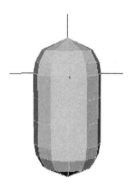

*Figure 10-41 The size of the capsule changes
with the movement of locator*

Polygon Bones

A polygon bone is created by converting a polygon mesh
into a bone. To do so, select a polygon mesh from the
viewport and choose **Muscle > Muscles/Bones > Convert
Surface to Muscle/Bone** from the main menubar; the
selected polygon mesh will be converted into a bone. Also,
the **Muscle Object** shape node will be added to the selected
object. Next, select any object from the viewport and choose
Display > UI Elements > Channel Box/Layer Editor
from the main menubar; a **Channel box** will be displayed.
In the **SHAPES** node of the **Channel Box**, a new **Muscle
Object shape** node will be created. Figure 10-42 shows the
general attributes of a muscle object shape.

SHAPES	
pSphereShape1	
cMuscleObject_pSphere1Shape1	
Sticky Strength	1
Sliding Strength	1
Fat	0.1
Reverse Normals	off
Relative	on
Lock Sticky Wt	off
Lock Sliding Wt	off
Affect Sticky	on
Affect Sliding	on
Draw	off
Shaded	shaded
Highlight	1
Highlight Shaded	1

*Figure 10-42 The **Muscle
Object Shape** attributes*

Types of Muscles

In Maya, there are two types of muscles, Muscles and Simple Muscles. These muscle types differ from each other in their respective deforming abilities. The Muscles muscle type is a parametric style NURBS shape that has its own deforming ability, whereas the Simple Muscles type uses the NURBS model with a spline deformer to deform the object.

Muscle Creator

The **Muscle Creator** dialog box helps you create muscles in a viewport. To invoke this dialog box, choose **Muscle > Muscles / Bones > Muscle Creator** from the main menubar; the **Muscle Creator** dialog box will be displayed, as shown in Figure 10-43. Some of important attributes in this dialog box are discussed next.

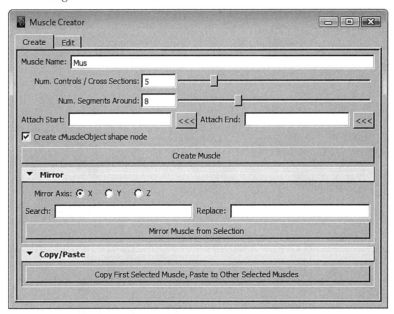

*Figure 10-43 The **Muscle Creator** dialog box*

Create Tab

The **Create** tab is used to define the attributes of the muscle to be created in the viewport. Various options in this tab are discussed next.

Muscle Name

The **Muscle Name** text box is used to assign a name to the new muscle. Enter a name according to the placement of the muscles in this text box.

Num. Controls / Cross Sections

The **Num. Controls / Cross Sections** edit box is used to define the total number of control objects for the muscles and total number of modeling cross-sections existing to create the shape of the muscle.

Num. Segments Around

The **Num. Segments Around** edit box is used to define the number of segments in the muscles.

Attach Start

The **Attach Start** option is used to add an object as the start object of the muscles such that it defines one end of a muscle.

Attach End

The **Attach End** option is used to add an object as the end object of the muscles such that it defines one end of a muscle.

Create cMuscleObject shape node

Select the **Create cMuscleObject shape node** check box to create the **MuscleObject shape** node.

Create Muscle

The **Create Muscle** button is used to create a NURBS muscle as per the attributes set in the dialog box.

Mirror Area

The options in this area are discussed next.

> **Mirror Axis**: The **Mirror Axis** option is used to set mirror the axis of the muscle. You can set the mirror axis by selecting a radio button from this area.

> **Search/Replace**: The **Search/Replace** input box is used to change the name of the muscles after mirroring. This option helps in preventing duplication of muscle with the same name.

> **Mirror Muscle from Selection**: The **Mirror Muscle from Selection** button is used to create a mirror of the specified muscle as per the attributes set in the dialog box.

Copy/Paste Area

The option in this area is discussed next.

> **Copy First Selected Muscle, Paste to Other Selected Muscles**: This button is used to copy the attributes of one muscle and paste them on the selected muscle. To do so, select a muscle from the viewport and then choose this button; the attributes of the muscle get copied. Next, select the muscle on which you want to paste these attributes and again choose this button; the attributes gets pasted on the new muscle and its name gets interchanged with the previous muscle.

USING THE SET DRIVEN KEY

The **Set Driven Key** is used to link the attribute of one object to another object. When you set the driven key, you need to specify a driver value and a driven attribute value. In such a case, the value of the driven attribute is locked to the corresponding value of the driver attribute. Therefore, a change in the driver attribute will change the value of the driven attribute as well. To set a driven key, choose **Animate > Set Driven Key > Set** from the main menubar; the **Set Driven Key** dialog box will be displayed, as shown in Figure 10-44. Select the object that you want to set as the driver from the viewport and then choose the **Load Driver** button; the name of the object with its attributes will be displayed in the **Driver** area of the **Set Driven Key** dialog box.

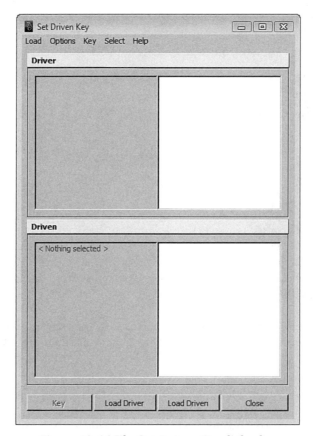

*Figure 10-44 The **Set Driven Key** dialog box*

Similarly, you can display the attributes of the driven objects in the **Set Driven Key** dialog box. You can also set the attributes of the driver and driven objects by invoking the **Channel box**. To do so, select the name of an object from the **Driver** area of the **Set Driven Key** dialog box. Next, select the attribute that you want to set for the selected object. Now, choose **Display > UI Elements > Channel Box/ Layer Editor** from the main menubar; the **Channel box** will be displayed. Set the required value for the selected attribute in the **Channel box** and choose the **Key** button from the **Set Driven Key** dialog box to set the key. You can also add a new attribute in the **Channel box**. To do so, select the object to which you want to add a new attribute in the viewport and then choose **Modify > Add Attribute** from the main menubar; the **Add Attribute** dialog box will be displayed, as shown in Figure 10-45.

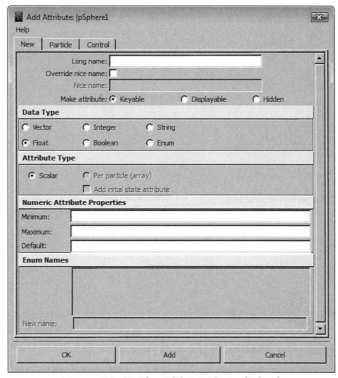

*Figure 10-45 The **Add Attribute** dialog box*

Various options in the **Add Attribute** dialog box are discussed next.

Long name

The **Long name** option is used to specify a name for an attribute, which makes it easier to recognize the functions added to that particular attribute later.

Make attribute

The **Make attribute** option is used to assign different display options to an attribute. Select the **Keyable** radio button to make the attribute keyable for animation. This option lets you animate an object by setting the keys for that attribute. Select the **Displayable** radio button to make the attribute display in the **Channel box** and select the **Hidden** radio button to create the attribute such that it is not visible in the viewport.

Data Type Area

The **Data Type** area is used to set the data types of various attributes. The data type of a programming element refers to the type of data it can hold and store. Different data types in this area are discussed next.

Vector

The **Vector** data type radio button is used to create a vector attribute consisting of three floating point values.

Float

The **Float** data type radio button is used to create a floating point attribute. This radio button is selected by default.

Integer

The **Integer** data type radio button is used to create an integer attribute.

Boolean

The **Boolean** data type radio button is used to create an attribute that has an 'on' or 'off' value.

String

The **String** data type is an ordered sequence of symbols. The **String** data type radio button is used to create a string attribute that accepts alphanumeric characters as data entries.

Enum

The **Enum** data type radio button is used to create a drop-down attribute.

Numeric Attribute Properties Area

The **Numeric Attribute Properties** area is used to set the minimum and maximum values that can be entered for a particular attribute in the **Channel box**. The **Default** edit box displays the default value for an attribute. In the **Channel box**, you can also hide and lock a particular attribute so that the other attributes are not affected when you animate an object. To do so, select the attribute from the **Channel box** that you want to hide and lock. Next, press and hold the right mouse button over the attribute and choose the **Lock and Hide Selected** option from the marking menu; the selected attribute will be locked and hidden. There are many attributes in Maya that are not displayed in the **Channel box** by default. To display those attributes, choose **Window > General Editor > Channel Control** from the main menubar; the **Channel Control** dialog box will be displayed, as shown in Figure 10-46. The **Keyable** list box displays the list of attributes that are displayed in the **Channel box** and the **Nonkeyable Hidden** list box lists the attributes that are not displayed and are hidden in the **Channel box**. To make the hidden attributes visible, select the attributes from the **Nonkeyable Hidden** list box and choose the **Move>>** button; the selected attributes will move to the **Keyable** list box.

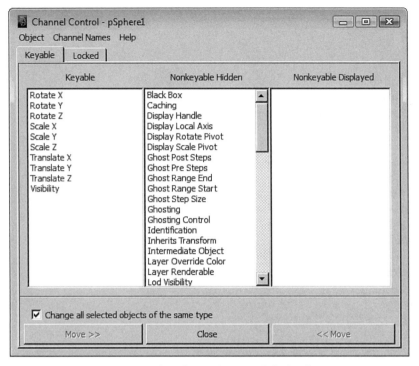

Figure 10-46 The ***Channel Control*** *dialog box*

TUTORIALS

Tutorial 1

In this tutorial, you will create the bone structure of a human leg, as shown in Figure 10-47 using the **Joint Tool**.   **(Expected time: 15 min)**

The following steps are required to complete this tutorial:

a.   Create a project folder.
b.   Create the bone structure of a leg.
c.   Apply IKs to the bone structure.
d.   Create the reverse foot setup.
e.   Create a pole vector to control knee joint.
f.   Save the file.

Creating the Project Folder

Before starting a new file, it is recommended that you create the project folder.

1.   Create the project with the name *c10_tut1* in the folder *Maya_Tutorials*.

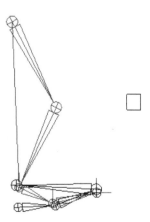

Figure 10-47 The bone structure of a human leg

Creating the Bone Structure of a Leg

In this section, you need to create the bone structure of a human leg.

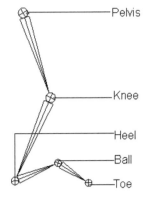

1. Activate the Side viewport. Select the **Animation** module from the menuset drop-down list in the status line. Next, choose **Skeleton > Joint Tool** from the main menubar and then create the bone structure in the viewport, as shown in Figure 10-48. (It is recommended to start the structure from the pelvis joint).

2. Select the pelvis joint from the bone structure, refer Figure 10-48, and choose **Display > UI Elements > Channel Box/Layer Editor** from the main menubar; a channel box is displayed. Click on the default joint name and rename it to **left_pelvisjoint**. Similarly, name other joints as given below:

Figure 10-48 The bone structure

Joints	Names
Pelvis	left_pelvisjoint
Knee	left_kneejoint
Heel	left_heeljoint
Ball	left_balljoint
Toe	left_toejoint

 Note

Naming the joints of a character is very important because it helps you while animating and skinning the character. Use the word 'left' to name the left body joints and 'right' to name the right body joints.

Applying IKs to the Bone Structure

In this section, you need to apply IKs to the bone structure.

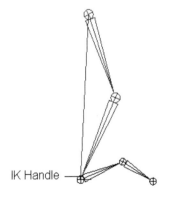

1. Choose **Skeleton > IK Handle Tool > Option Box** from the main menubar; the **IK Handle Tool** property window is displayed on the left of the viewport. Select **ikRPsolver** from the **Current solver** drop-down list, if not already selected, to set the solver type.

2. Select the **left_pelvisjoint** joint and then the **left_heeljoint** joint from the viewport or the **Outliner** window; an IK handle is created between these two joints, as shown in Figure 10-49.

Figure 10-49 An IK Handle created between joints

3. Similarly, create other IK handles between the left_heeljoint and left_balljoint joints, and also between the **left_balljoint** and **left_toejoint joints**, as shown in Figure 10-50.

Creating the Reverse Foot Setup

In this section, you need to create the reverse foot setup that will provide control to the movements of leg. You can use either a NURBS object or a polygonal mesh, or joints to create the reverse foot setup. Here, you need to use joints.

1. Activate the Side viewport and choose **Skeleton > Joint Tool** from the main menubar; the **Joint Tool** is activated. Next, use this tool to create the reverse foot setup, as shown in Figure 10-51.

Figure 10-50 *The IK Handles*

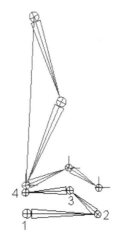

Figure 10-51 *The reverse foot setup*

2. Invoke the **Move Tool**. Next, select the IK handle of the **left_heeljoint**, press SHIFT and then select the joint 4, refer to Figure 10-51. Now, press p from the keyboard to make the joint 4 of the reverse foot as parent of the IK handle.

3. Similarly, make the joint 2 as the parent of the **left_toejoint** IK handle and the joint 3 as the parent of the **left_balljoint** IK handle. Now, hold the IK handles and move the foot based on your requirement.

Tip. *To adjust the joints of a bone structure, press and hold the d key and invoke the Move Tool. Once the tool is invoked, you can move the joints to adjust the bone structure. You can also resize the bone structure by choosing **Display > Animation > Joint Size** from the main menubar. On doing so, the **Joint Display Scale** window will be displayed. Next, you can adjust the joint size as per your requirement.*

Creating the Pole Vector

In this section, you need to create the pole vector to control the movement of the knee joint.

1. Create a polygon cube in the active viewport. Invoke the **Move Tool** from the toolbox and align it near the knee.

2. Select the polygon cube, press SHIFT, and then select the **left_heeljoint** IK handle. Next, choose **Constrain > Pole Vector** from main menubar; the polygon cube pole vector of the knee is created.

3. Activate the Perspective viewport and invoke the **Move Tool** to check the movement of the foot by using the IKs and the pole vector.

Saving the File

In this section, you need to save the file.

1. Choose **File > Save Scene** from the main menubar; the **Save As** dialog box is displayed.

   As the project folder is already set, by default the path *\Documents\Maya_Tutorials\c10_tut1\ scenes* is displayed in **Look In** text box of the dialog box.

2. Enter **c10_tut1** in the **File name** text box and then select **Maya Binary** from the **Files of type** drop-down list. Next, choose the **Save As** button.

You can view the final rendered image of the model by downloading the file *c10_Maya_2012_ render.zip* from *http://www.cadcim.com*.

Tutorial 2

In this tutorial, you will set the animation of a seesaw model shown in Figure 10-52 by using the **Set Driven Key**.   **(Expected time: 15 min)**

Figure 10-52 A seesaw model

The following steps are required to complete this tutorial:

a. Set a project folder.
b. Download the file.
c. Create a driver.
d. Set the driven key.
e. Animate the seesaw model.
f. Save the file.

Setting the Project Folder

Before starting a new file, it is recommended that you set the project folder.

1. Set the project with the name *c10_tut2* in the folder *Maya_Tutorials*.

Downloading and Opening the Files

1. Download the *c10_Maya_2012_tut.zip* file from *http://www.cadcim.com*. The path of the file is as follows:

    Textbooks > Animation and Visual Effects > Maya > Autodesk Maya 2012: A Comprehensive Guide

    Extract the contents of the zipped file and save them in the *\Documents* folder.

2. Choose **Scene** from the **File** menu; the **Open File** dialog box is displayed. In this dialog box, browse to the *c10_Maya_2012_tut2* folder and select *c10_tut2_start.mb* file from it. Next, choose the **Open** button.

3. Choose **Save As** from the main menubar; the **Save As** dialog box is displayed. Browse to the scenes folder at the location *\Documents\Maya\c10_tut2*. Save the file with the name *c10tut2.mb* in this folder.

Creating a Driver

In this section, you need to create a driver for the seesaw model.

1. Activate the Perspective viewport. Next, choose **Create > Polygon Primitives > Sphere** from the main menubar and create a sphere anywhere in the viewport.

2. Choose **Display > UI Elements > Channel Box / Layer Editor** from the main menubar; the **Channel box** is displayed. Enter **15** in the **Translate Y** edit box of the **Channel box**. Rename the sphere to **driver_ball** in the **Channel box**.

3. Choose **Window > Outliner** from the main menubar; the **Outliner** window is displayed. Now, choose **main_frame** from the **Outliner** window. Press and hold the CTRL key and then select **driver_ball**. Next, choose **Modify > Freeze Transformations** from the main menubar to set the orientation of the X, Y, and Z axes to zero. Close the **Outliner** window and then deselect **main_frame** and **driver_ball** in the viewport.

Setting the Driven Key

In this section, you need to set the driven key for the seesaw model.

1. Choose the **Animation** module from the status line. Next, choose **Animate > Set Driven Key > Set** from the main menubar; the **Set Driven Key** dialog box is displayed, as shown in Figure 10-53. Select **driver_ball** from the viewport and then choose the **Load Driver** button from the **Set Driven Key** dialog box to set the driver.

2. Similarly, select **main_frame** from the viewport and choose the **Load Driven** button from the **Set Driven Key** dialog box to load the **Driven** attributes, refer to Figure 10-53.

3. Select **driver_ball** from the **Set Driven Key** dialog box. Next, select the **TranslateX** attribute of **driver_ball** in the **Set Driven Key** dialog box under the **Driver** area. Next, select the **main_frame** and **RotateZ** attributes from the **Set Driven Key** window under the **Driven** area. Next, choose the **Key** button to set the positions.

4. Again, select **driver_ball** from the **Set Driven Key** dialog box. Next, select the **TranslateX** attribute of **driver_ball** in this dialog box. Enter **5** in the **TranslateX** attribute in the **Channel box**. Select **main_frame** from the **Set Driven Key** dialog box and select the **RotateZ** attribute of **main_frame**. Enter **-5** in the **RotateZ** attribute in the **Channel box**. Now, choose the **Key** button to set the key attributes as specified.

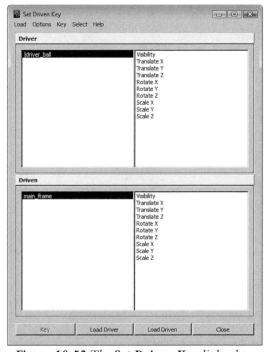

Figure 10-53 The Set Driven Key dialog box

5. Select **driver_ball** from the **Set Driven Key** dialog box and then select the **TranslateX** attribute of **driver_ball**. Then, enter **-5** in the **TranslateX** attribute of the **Channel box**.

Select **main_frame** in the **Set Driven Key** dialog box, and select the **RotateZ** attribute of **main_frame** to rotate the object in the Z axis. Enter **15** in the **RotateZ** attribute in the channel box. Choose the **Key** button in the **Set Driven Key** dialog box to create a connection between **driver_ball** and **main_frame**.

6. Move **driver_ball** in the viewport; the seesaw starts swinging with the movement of the **driver_ball**.

7. Select **driver_ball** and choose **Window > Attribute Editor** from the main menubar; the **Attribute Editor** is displayed. Choose the **driver_ball** tab from the **Attribute Editor** and then expand the **Limit Information** attribute to limit the translation, rotation, and scaling of the object. Set limits in the **Translate** area to limit the movement of **driver_ball** in the viewport, as shown in Figure 10-54.

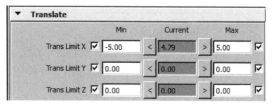

*Figure 10-54 The **Translate** area in the **Attribute Editor***

Animating the Seesaw Model

In this section, you need to animate the driver ball. The seesaw will swing with the movement of **driver**.

1. Close all open windows in the viewport. Next, choose the **Animation preferences** button on the right of the animation playback buttons; the **Preferences** dialog box is displayed. Set **Playback speed** to **Real-time (24fps)** and then set **Animation start/end** from **1** to **48** frames.

2. Select **driver_ball** and move the time slider to the first frame in the timeline. Enter **-5** in the **TranslateX** edit box and then choose **Animate > Set Key** from the main menubar; the key is set to the first frame.

3. Move the slider to the 24th frame. Next, select **driver_ball** and enter **5** in the **TranslateX** edit box. Choose **Animate > Set Key** from the main menubar; the **TranslateX** value for **driver_ball** is set to the 24th frame.

4. Move the current time indicator to the 48th frame. Next, select **driver_ball** and enter **-5** in the **TranslateX** edit box of the **Channel box**. Choose **Animate > Set Key** from the main menubar; the **TranslateX** value for **driver_ball** is set to **-5** on frame **48**.

5. Next, choose the **Play forwards** button from the playback control area to preview the animation; the seesaw starts swinging with the movement of driver_ball.

Saving the File

In this section, you need to save the file.

1. Choose **File > Save Scene** from the main menubar; the **Save As** dialog box is displayed.

    As the project folder is already set, by default the path *\Documents\Maya_Tutorials\c10_tut2\ scenes* is displayed in **Look In** text box of the dialog box.

2. Enter **c10_tut2** in the **File name** text box and then select **Maya Binary** from the **Files of type** drop-down list. Next, choose the **Save As** button.

You can view the final rendered image of the model by downloading the file *c10_Maya_2012_ render.zip* from *http://www.cadcim.com*.

Tutorial 3

In this tutorial, you will create the model of palm trees, as shown in Figure 10-55, using the **Bend** deformer.   **(Expected time: 30 min)**

Figure 10-55 Palm trees

The following steps are required to complete this tutorial:

a. Create a project folder.
b. Create the trunk of the palm tree.
c. Create leaves.

d.   Apply the **Bend** deformer.
e.   Save the file.

Creating the Project Folder
Before starting a new file, it is recommended that you create the project folder.

1.   Create the project with the name *c10_tut3* in the folder *Maya_Tutorials*.

Creating the Trunk
In this section, you need to create the trunk of the palm tree using the **Loft** surface method.

1.   Open a new file in Maya. Choose **Create > NURBS Primitives > Circle** from the main menubar. Create seven circles of different radii and arrange them in the Perspective viewport, as shown in Figure 10-56.

2.   Select the lowermost circle in the viewport, press and hold the SHIFT key, and then select all circles above it in a sequence. Next, choose the **Surfaces** module from the status line.

3.   Choose **Surfaces > Loft** from the main menubar; a trunk is created along the selected circles, as shown in Figure 10-57.

4.   Select the trunk in the viewport and choose **Modify > Convert > NURBS to Polygons > Option Box** from the main menubar; the **Convert NURBS to Polygons Options** dialog box is displayed. Set the required values in this dialog box, as shown in Figure 10-58, and choose the **Tessellate** button; the NURBS trunk changes to polygons.

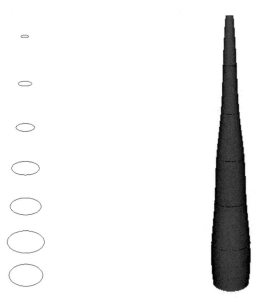

Figure 10-56 *Arrangement of NURBS circles*

Figure 10-57 *The trunk*

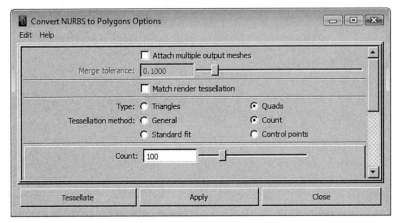

Figure 10-58 The **Convert NURBS to Polygons Options** *dialog box*

5. Select the NURBS trunk and curves from the viewport and delete them (note that the surface and curves will not be used in this tutorial). Next, select the polygon trunk and press and hold the right mouse button over it; a marking menu is displayed. Choose **Vertex** from the marking menu; the vertex component is activated on the polygonal object. Select the topmost vertices of the trunk and select the **Polygons** module from the menuset drop-down list in the status line. Next, choose **Edit Mesh > Merge To Center** from the main menubar; the selected vertices are merged to the center.

Creating Leaves

In this section, you need to create the leaves of the palm tree by using polygon primitives.

1. Activate the Top viewport and choose **Create > Polygon Primitives > Cone > Option Box** from the main menubar; the **Polygon Cone Tool** property window is displayed. Enter the following values in the property window:

Radius: **0.2**   Height: **40**   Axis: **X**

Click in the viewport to create the petiole of a leaf. Next, invoke the **Rotate** tool from the toolbox and align the petiole with the trunk, as shown in Figure 10-59.

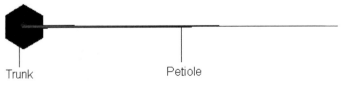

Trunk   Petiole

Figure 10-59 Aligning petiole with the trunk

2. Choose **Create > Polygon Primitives > Plane > Option Box** from the main menubar; the **Polygon Plane Tool** property window is displayed. Enter the following values for plane in the property window:

Width: **1**   Height: **6**   Height Divisions: **6**

Click in the Top viewport to create a plane, as shown in Figure 10-60.

3. Press and hold the right mouse button over the plane and then choose **Vertex** from the marking menu; the vertex component is activated on the plane. Adjust the vertices to get the desired shape of the leaf, as shown in Figure 10-61.

Figure 10-60 The plane for creating a leaf   *Figure 10-61* The final shape of the leaf

4. Press and hold the D key on the keyboard and set the pivot point of the leaf, as shown in Figure 10-62. Next, adjust the leaf with the petiole, as shown in Figure 10-63.

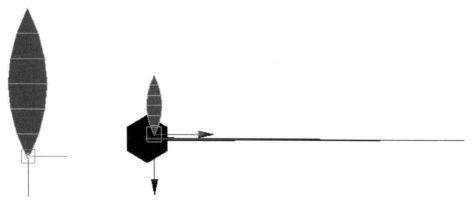

Figure 10-62 Adjusting the pivot point of the leaf   *Figure 10-63* A leaf aligned with the petiole

5. Select the leaf created in the viewport and press CTRL+D; a duplicate leaf is created. Move the duplicate leaf to the right of the original leaf. Next, press SHIFT+D to create multiple copies of the leaf. Create leaves on both sides of the petiole and arrange them, as shown in Figure 10-64.

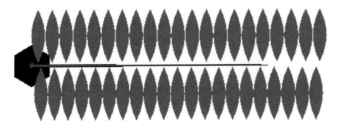

Figure 10-64 Duplicate leaves aligned with the petiole

Note
While aligning leaves in the top viewport, you must align them in other viewports as well.

6. Press and hold the SHIFT key and select all leaves and petioles from the viewport. Next, press CTRL+G to group them.

7. Invoke the **Scale Tool** from the toolbox and scale the leaves individually to get the effect shown in Figure 10-65. Now, choose **Modify > Center Pivot** from the main menubar; the pivot point is set to the center of the leaf.

Figure 10-65 Leaves after scaling

Applying the Bend Deformer

In this section, you need to apply the **Bend** deformer to leaves to give them a realistic effect.

1. Activate the Perspective viewport. Select any leaf from the bunch of leaves and press the up arrow key on the keyboard select to the complete group.

2. Choose the **Animation** module from the status line and then choose **Create Deformers > Nonlinear > Bend** from the main menubar; the bend deformer is applied to leaves.

3. Choose **Display > UI Elements > Channel Box/Layer Editor** from the main menubar; a **Channel box** is displayed. Set the following values in the **Channel box** for the **Bend** deformer:

RotateZ : **90**   RotateX : **90**

4. Expand the **bend1** attribute area from the **INPUTS** node of the **Channel box** and set the value of **Curvature** to **-2.58** to get the bend effect, as shown in Figure 10-66.

5. Choose **Create Deformers > Nonlinear > Bend** from the main menubar; another bend deformer is applied to leaves.

6. Enter the following value in the **Channel box** to further modify the shape of leaves:

RotateZ : **90**

7. Expand the **bend2** attribute area and set the **Curvature** value to **-0.93** to get the bend effect, as shown in Figure 10-67.

*Figure 10-66 Leaves after applying the **Bend** deformer*

Figure 10-67 *Leaves after applying the second* ***Bend*** *deformer*

8. Select all leaves and choose **Edit > Delete All by Type > History** from the main menubar
    to delete history to avoid unwanted result.

9. Invoke the **Move Tool** and then the **Rotate Tool** from the toolbox to align the leaves with
    the trunk.

10. Create several copies of leaves and align them with the trunk to get the final output, as
    shown in Figure 10-68.

Figure 10-68 *The final output of the palm tree model*

Saving the File

In this section, you need to save the file.

1. Choose **File > Save Scene** from the main menubar; the **Save As** dialog box is displayed.

   As the project folder is already set, by default the path *Documents**Maya_Tutorials**c10_tut3*\\ *scenes* is displayed in **Look In** text box of the dialog box.

2. Enter **c10_tut3** in the **File name** text box and then select **Maya Binary** from the **Files of type** drop-down list. Next, choose the **Save As** button.

You can view the final rendered image of the model by downloading the *c10_Maya_2012_render. zip* file from *http://www.cadcim.com*.

Self-Evaluation Test

Answer the following questions and then compare them to those given at the end of this chapter:

1. Which of the following joints provides free movement to a skeleton?

   (a) **Hinge joint**   (b) **Universal joint**
   (c) **Ball joint**   (d) None of these

2. Which of the following deformers is used to deform an object by using lattices?

   (a) **Cluster**   (b) **Blend shape**
   (c) **Lattice**   (d) **Flare**

3. _____ are a group of hierarchical structures that provide motion to an object.

4. _____ an object helps you bind corresponding objects to bones.

5. The _____ deformer is used to deform a particular area of a polygonal mesh.

6. The _____ option is used to impose specific limits to objects.

7. The **Pole Vector** constraint is used to move the end of a pole vector based on the movement of the other object it is constrained with. (T/F)

8. The **Flare** deformer is used to taper an object in the X and Y axes. (T/F)

9. A Muscle is a parametric type of NURBS shape that can be deformed, whereas a Simple Muscle type uses the NURBS model with a sine deformer to deform the object. (T/F)

10. The **Jiggle** deformer is used to shake a part of an object while it is being animated. (T/F)

Review Questions

Answer the following questions:

1. Which of the following deformers is used to morph an object?

   (a) **Cluster**   (b) **Blend shape**
   (c) **Lattice**   (d) **Flare**

2. Which of the following data types is used to create a vector attribute that has three floating point values?

   (a) **Vector**   (b) **Float**
   (c) **Enum**   (d) **Integer**

3. The _____ deformer helps you deform high density surface meshes without adjusting vertices manually.

4. The _____ deformer is used to create a rounded deformation on an object.

5. The _____ constraint is used to match the orientation of one object with the other such that the objects are aligned together.

6. The _____ tools are used to alter a portion of the geometric shape.

7. You should avoid changing the number of CVs, vertices, or other lattice points after applying a deformer to an object. (T/F)

8. In inverse kinematics, you can use an object at the bottom of the hierarchy to animate the entire chain. (T/F)

9. A constraint is used to restrict the motion of a body to a particular mode while it is animated. (T/F)

10. You can apply the **Blend Shape** deformer only to the objects that have equal number of vertices. (T/F)

Exercises

Exercise 1

Use the **Set Driven Key** attribute to set keys for the doors of a toy car and then animate them by setting the attributes in the channel box. You can view the final animation of this model by downloading the *c10_maya_2012_render.zip* file from *http://www.cadcim.com*. The path of file is as follows:

Textbooks > Animation and Visual Effects > Maya > Autodesk Maya 2012: A Comprehensive Guide
(Expected time: 30 min)

Exercise 2

Create the scene of a pencil stand with a pencil in it. Next, apply texture to the scene, as shown in Figure 10-69. Apply the **Lattice** deformer to the pencil. Next, use the keyframe animation technique to make the pencil jump out of the pencil stand, as shown in Figure 10-70. You can view the final animation of this model by downloading the *c10_maya_2012_render.zip* file from *http://www.cadcim.com*. The path of file is mentioned in Exercise 1. **(Expected time: 45 min)**

***Figure 10-69** The pencil stand with a pencil*

Figure 10-70 The pencil jumping out of the pencil stand

Answers to Self-Evaluation Test
1. c, **2.** c, **3.** Skeleton, **4.** Skinning, **5. Cluster**, **6. Constraint**, **7.** T, **8.** T, **9.** F, **10.** T

Chapter *11*

Paint Effects

Learning Objectives

After completing this chapter, you will be able to:

- *Use the Visor window*
- *Render the paint effect strokes*
- *Use shadow effects*
- *Modify the paint effect brush settings*

INTRODUCTION TO PAINT EFFECTS

In Autodesk Maya, you can create realistic natural objects such as trees, plants, rain, and so on by using paint effects. The paint effect lets you paint a scene by using mouse or pressure sensitive tablet. Different brushes are used to create different paint strokes for giving effects such as rain, thunder, storm, and so on. You can also animate these paint effects to create natural motion. All these paint effects and brushes are available in the **Visor** window of Maya, and are discussed next.

Working with the Visor Window

Main menubar:	Window > General Editors > Visor

The **Visor** window comprises of preloaded animation clips, default brushes, shader libraries or texture libraries, and so on. To display the **Visor** window, as shown in Figure 11-1, choose **Window > General Editors > Visor** from the main menubar. There are different tabs in the **Visor** window such as **Paint Effects**, **Toon Examples**, **Ocean Examples**, and so on. When you choose a particular tab, the corresponding folders will be displayed on the left of the **Visor** window. When you choose a folder from the left of the window, various paint strokes in that folder will be displayed on the right. The major functions of this window are discussed next.

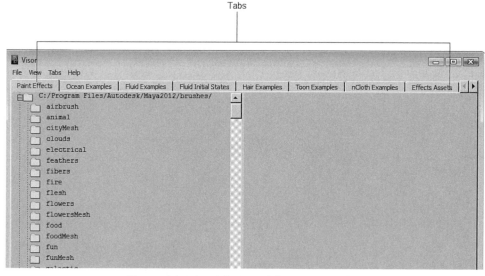

Figure 11-1 Partial view of the Visor window

Creating New Tabs

You can also create a new tab in the **Visor** window. To do so, choose **Tabs > Create New Tab** from the **Visor** menubar; the **Create New Tab** dialog box will be displayed, as shown in Figure 11-2. Enter a name for the new tab in the **New tab name** edit box. There are three options in the **Tab type** drop-down list: **Scene**, **Disk**, and **Paint Effects**. The **Scene** option is used to display a collection of nodes in the current scene, the **Disk** option is used to display files on the disk, and the **Paint Effects** option is used to display the paint effect files. The options in the **Show nodes which are** drop-down list are used to display only particular nodes in the new tab. After setting all parameters, choose the **Create** button; a new tab will be created in the **Visor** window.

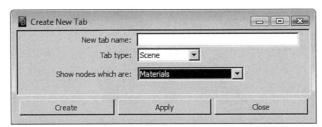

*Figure 11-2 The **Create New Tab** dialog box*

Deleting and Renaming Tabs

You can also delete a tab from the **Visor** window. To do so, choose the tab that you want to delete and then choose **Tabs > Remove Tab** from the **Visor** menubar; the **Confirm Remove Current Tab** message box will be displayed, prompting you to delete the corresponding tab, as shown in Figure 11-3. To delete the tab, choose the **Yes** button from this message box. You can also rename a tab in the **Visor** window. To do so, choose the tab that you want to rename and then choose **Tabs > Rename Tab** from the **Visor** menubar; the **Rename Tab** dialog box will be displayed, as shown in Figure 11-4. Enter a new name in the **New tab name** edit box and then choose the **Rename** button; the new name will be applied to the selected tab.

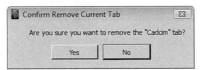

*Figure 11-3 The **Confirm Remove Current Tab** message box*

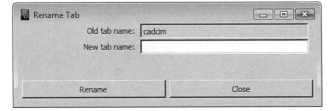

*Figure 11-4 The **Rename Tab** dialog box*

Creating Objects

You can create a realistic object such as tree mesh using the **Visor** window. To do so, choose the **Paint Effects** tab in the **Visor** window; various folders will be displayed on the left of the window. Choose the **treesMesh** folder; different options will be displayed on the right of the **Visor** window. Now, choose the **oakAutumn.mel** paint stroke from the displayed options. Activate the Top viewport; the cursor will change to a pencil. Press and hold the left mouse button and drag the cursor to create tree mesh. Next, activate the Perspective viewport and render the view to get the output shown in Figure 11-5.

You can also edit the paint stroke created in the viewport. To do so, select the paint stroke created in the viewport and choose **Display > UI Elements > Channel Box/Layer Editor** from the main menubar; a **Channel Box** will be displayed and the name of the selected paint stroke will be displayed in the **INPUTS** node in this channel box. Click on the paint stroke name to expand its attributes. You can now modify the selected paint stroke as per your requirement using the attributes in the **Channel Box**.

Figure 11-5 *The rendered scene*

You can also see the rendered effect of the paint stroke in the viewport without rendering the scene. To do so, choose **Window > Paint Effects** from the main menubar; the **Paint Effects** window will be displayed, as shown in Figure 11-6. Alternatively, press the numeric key **8**; the active viewport will change to the paint effects view.

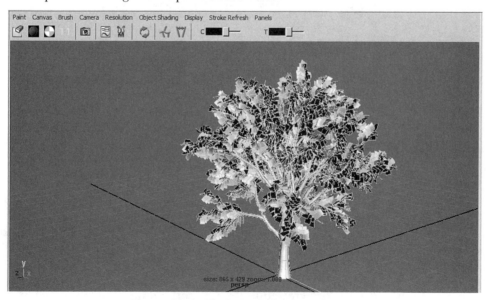

Figure 11-6 *The **Paint Effects** window*

The **Paint Effects** window has its own toolbar, as shown in Figure 11-7. You can use this toolbar to create different effects by using the paint strokes. To choose a paint stroke brush, choose the **Get brush** tool from the toolbar, refer to Figure 11-7; the **Visor** window will be displayed. Choose the paint brush stroke from the **Visor** window and then paint the stroke in the **Paint Effects** window. You can also edit the attributes of the selected paint brush stroke by using this window. To do so, select the paint stroke from the **Visor** window and choose the **Edit template brush** tool from the toolbar; the **Paint Effects Brush Settings** dialog box will be displayed, as shown in Figure 11-8. Alternatively, press CTRL+B to invoke the **Paint Effects Brush Settings** dialog box. Some of the basic attributes of this dialog box are discussed next.

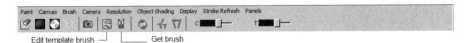

*Figure 11-7 The toolbar of the **Paint Effects** window*

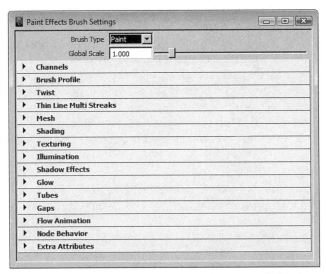

*Figure 11-8 The **Paint Effects Brush Settings** dialog box*

Brush Type
The **Brush Type** drop-down list is used to set different brush styles. There are six options in this drop-down list: **Paint**, **Smear**, **Blur**, **Erase**, **ThinLine**, and **Mesh**. The **Paint** option is used to paint normally and is selected by default. The **Smear** option gives a smearing effect to the brush. The **Blur** option is used to give a blurred paint effect in the viewport. Select the **ThinLine** option to render the paint effects quicker than the other brush types. The **Mesh** option is used to create accurate conical geometry with textures that correctly map on the surface.

Global Scale
The **Global Scale** edit box is used to set the size of the brush. To do so, enter a value in the edit box. Alternatively, drag the slider on the right of the edit box to set the global scale value. By default, the value in the **Global Scale** edit box is 1. Figures 11-9 and 11-10 show an object created using different values of the global scale.

Figure 11-9 *Object with the **Global***
***Scale** value = 1*

Figure 11-10 *Object with the **Global***
***Scale** value = 2*

Channels

The **Channels** attribute is used to make changes in the rendered image by specifying its depth, color, and alpha. Choose the arrow on the left of the **Channels** attribute to expand it; the **Depth**, **Modify Depth**, **Modify Color**, and **Modify Alpha** check boxes will be displayed. The **Depth** check box is used to add a realistic effect to the scene on rendering. The **Modify Depth** check box is not activated by default. To activate it, select the **Depth** check box and then modify the depth as per your requirement. The **Modify Color** check box is used to paint the color channel. The **Modify Alpha** check box is used to paint the alpha mask in the scene. Select this check box if you want to composite your own paint effect scene.

Brush Profile

The **Brush Profile** attribute is used to set the brush settings. On expanding this attribute, various options will be displayed, as shown in Figure 11-11. These options are discussed next.

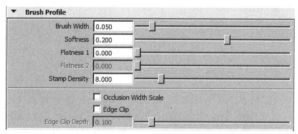

Figure 11-11 *The **Brush Profile** attribute area*

Brush Width

The **Brush Width** option is used to define the width of the brush. The brush width is defined by the outline of the paint effect generated. Enter a value in the edit box or move the slider on its right to set the value of the brush width.

Softness

The **Softness** option is used to define the softness on the edges of the stroke path. Higher the softness value, more blurred will be the edges. Refer to Figures 11-12 and 11-13 for variations in the **Softness** value.

Figure 11-12 Paint stroke with **Softness** = 0   *Figure 11-13* Paint stroke with **Softness** = 1

Flatness1

The **Flatness1** option is used to flatten paint stroke. This attribute is used mainly for the paint strokes that are formed of tubes. You can enter the flatness value in the **Flatness1** edit box or drag the slider on its right to adjust the flatness. Activate the side viewport to display the variations in the flatness of the paint stroke. Figures 11-14 and 11-15 show the paint strokes created by using different values of flatness. Similarly, the **Flatness2** option defines the flatness of the paint stroke at the base and the tip.

Figure 11-14 Paint stroke with **Flatness1** = 0   *Figure 11-15* Paint stroke with **Flatness1** = 0.5

Stamp Density

The **Stamp Density** option is used to adjust the density of the paint stroke. Higher the stamp density, more will be the visibility of the paint stroke.

Twist

The **Twist** attribute is used to twist a paint stroke on its own axis. On expanding the **Twist** attribute, some options will be displayed, as shown in Figure 11-16. These options are discussed next.

Figure 11-16 The **Twist** attribute area

Forward Twist

Select the **Forward Twist** check box to reverse the direction of the twist on the paint stroke.

Twist

You can enter the value for the twist attribute in the **Twist** edit box. Alternatively, you can move the slider on its right to adjust the **Twist** attribute. More the twist value, better will be the visibility of twist effect on the paint stroke.

Twist Rate

The **Twist Rate** edit box is used to specify the rate of twist of a paint stroke. Figure 11-17 shows a tube before applying the **Twist Rate** option and Figure 11-18 shows a tube after applying the **Twist Rate** option.

Figure 11-17 *Tube before applying the **Twist Rate** option*

Figure 11-18 *Tube after applying the **Twist Rate** option*

Mesh

The **Mesh** attribute is used to set the mesh for paint strokes. On expanding this attribute, the **Mesh** attribute area will be displayed, as shown in Figure 11-19. Enter a value in **Tube Sections** edit box to set the number of segments in the tube. Similarly, enter a value in the **Sub Segments** edit box to set the number of cross-sections per segment of the paint stroke. Select the **Single Sided** check box to cull away the facing triangles of the paint strokes. Select the **Per Pixel Lighting** check box to light up each pixel opposite to the vertices in the paint strokes. Select the **End Caps** check box to add end caps geometry to the paint strokes. Select the **Hard Edges** check box to make edges of the brush stroke look hard on rendering.

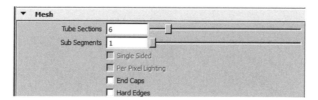

Figure 11-19 *The **Mesh** attributes area*

Thorns on Mesh

The **Thorns on Mesh** attribute is used to add thorns on a mesh object. This attribute is inactive by default. To activate it, choose the **Mesh** brush type from the **Paint Effects Brush Settings** dialog box and then expand the **Thorns on Mesh** attributes area. Next, choose the **Branch Thorns** check box to activate the remaining attributes, as shown in Figure 11-20. Note that the thorns are not visible in the viewport. They are visible only at the time of rendering, as shown in Figures 11-21 and 11-22. You can modify the values of density, elevation, length, base width, tip width, specular, and so on for thorns in the respective edit boxes of this area to get the desired result.

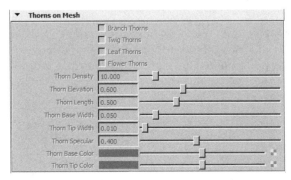

*Figure 11-20 The **Thorns on Mesh** attributes area*

Shading

The **Shading** attribute is used to define the shading brush attributes. On expanding this attribute, the **Shading** attributes area will be displayed, as shown in Figure 11-23. Set the **Color1** attribute to set the shadow color of the paint stroke. The **Incandescence1** attribute defines the brightness of the shadow and the **Transparency 1** attribute defines the transparency level of the paint stroke shadow. You can modify these values as per your requirement.

*Figure 11-21 Paint stroke before using the **Thorns on Mesh** attribute*

*Figure 11-22 Paint stroke after using the **Thorns on Mesh** attribute*

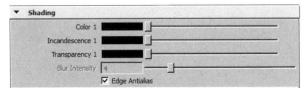

*Figure 11-23 The **Shading** attributes area*

Illumination

The **Illumination** attribute is used to set the amount of self-lighting to be applied to the paint strokes in the viewport. Expand the **Illumination** attributes area, as shown in Figure 11-24. Next, select the **Illuminated** check box to illuminate the strokes in the scene and apply real lights. Similarly, select the **Real Lights** check box to determine the position of shading and specular lights on the paint strokes. Figure 11-25 shows an object before using the **Illumination** attribute and Figure 11-26 shows the same object after using the **Illumination** attribute.

Shadow Effects

The **Shadow Effects** attribute is used to apply the shadow effect to the brush strokes on rendering. Expand the **Shadow Effects** attributes area, as shown in Figure 11-27, and then adjust the attributes as per your requirement to assign the shadow effect to brush strokes. Some of the options in the **Shadow Effects** attribute area are explained next.

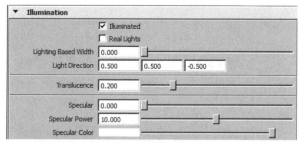

*Figure 11-24 The **Illumination** attribute area*

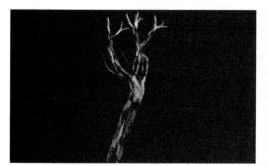

Figure 11-25 Paint stroke before using the
***Illumination** attribute*

Figure 11-26 Paint stroke after using the
***Illumination** attribute*

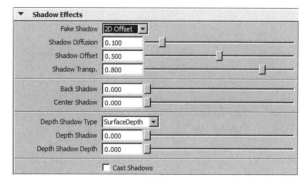

*Figure 11-27 The **Shadow Effects** attribute area*

Shadow Diffusion

The **Shadow Diffusion** option is used to control the softness of shadow in a scene. Higher the value of the attribute, more will be the softness of the fake shadow on rendering, refer to Figures 11-28 and 11-29.

*Figure 11-28 Paint stroke with the **Shadow Diffusion** value = 0*

*Figure 11-29 Paint stroke with the **Shadow Diffusion** value = 1*

Shadow Offset

The **Shadow Offset** option is used to control the distance between the shadow and the casting stroke. This option is inactive by default. To activate this option, select **2D Offset** from the **Fake Shadow** drop-down list in the **Shadow Effects** area. Then, set the offset distance in the **Shadow Offset** edit box or move the slider on its right as per your requirement. Figures 11-30 and 11-31 show an object with different shadow offset values.

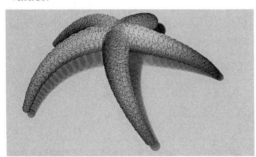

*Figure 11-30 Paint stroke with the **Shadow Offset** value = 0.5*

*Figure 11-31 Paint stroke with the **Shadow Offset** value = 1*

Shadow Transp

The **Shadow Transp** option is used to specify the value of transparency of the shadow of the paint stroke. Higher the transparency value, lighter will be the shadow effect and vice versa. Figures 11-32 and 11-33 show an object with different values of the **Shadow Transp** attribute.

Note
*You can adjust the attributes of the building paint stroke to get different results. Try using different **cityMesh** paint strokes from the **Visor** window to create different types of buildings.*

Figure 11-32 *Paint stroke with the* **Shadow** **Transp** *value = 0*

Figure 11-33 *Paint stroke with the* **Shadow** **Transp** *value = 0.8*

Glow

The **Glow** attribute is used to add glow effect to paint strokes. For example, you can create the effect of fire in a scene by using the **Glow** attribute. To do so, expand the **Glow** attributes area, as shown in Figure 11-34. The **Glow** option in this area is used to add brightness to the standard glow. If the value in the **Glow** edit box is 0, then no glow will be produced. In other words, higher the value in this edit box, more will be the glow effect, as shown in Figures 11-35 and 11-36. Enter a value in the **Glow Spread** edit box to define the area of the halo effect created around the glow. Similarly, enter a value in the **Shader Glow** edit box to define the brightness of the shader glow.

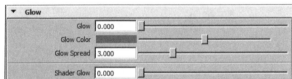

Figure 11-34 *The* **Glow** *attribute area*

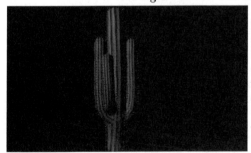

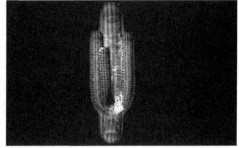

Figure 11-35 *Paint stroke with the Glow value = 0*

Figure 11-36 *Paint stroke with the Glow value = 0.5*

TUTORIALS

Tutorial 1

In this tutorial, you will create a street scene, as shown in Figure 11-37, by using the paint effects in Maya.   **(Expected time: 20 min)**

Figure 11-37 *A street scene*

The following steps are required to complete this tutorial:

a.   Set a project folder.
b.   Download the texture file.
c.   Create a road for the street scene.
d.   Create buildings.
e.   Create clouds.
f.   Create lights.
g.   Render and save the scene.

Setting the Project Folder

Before starting a new file, it is recommended that you set the project folder.

1.   Set a project with the name *c11_tut1* in the folder *Maya_Tutorials*.

Downloading the Texture File

1.   Download the *c11_maya_2012_tut.zip* file from *http://www.cadcim.com*. The path of the file is as follows:

   Textbooks > Animation and Visual Effects > Maya> Autodesk Maya 2012: A Comprehensive Guide

2.   Extract *roadtexture.jpg* to *sourceimages* folder at the location *\Documents\Maya_Tutorials\ c11_tut1*.

Creating a Road for the Street Scene

In this section, you need to create a base for the street scene using polygon primitives.

1. Activate the Top viewport and choose **Create > Polygon Primitives > Plane** from the main menubar. Press and hold the left mouse button and drag the cursor to create a plane for the road.

polyPlane1	
Width	40
Height	170
Subdivisions Width	1
Subdivisions Height	4
Create UVs	Normalize...

2. Next, choose **Display > UI Elements > Channel Box/ Layer Editor** from the main menubar; the **Inputs** node is displayed in the **ChannelBox/LayerEditor** window. Select the displayed name of the polyplane and set the parameters of the plane, as shown in Figure 11-38.

Figure 11-38 The INPUTS node of plane

3. Choose **Window > Rendering Editors > Hypershade** from the main menubar; the **Hypershade** window is displayed. Choose **Lambert** from the **Create** area of this window; the **lambert2** shader is created in the **Work Area** of the **Hypershade** window.

4. Press and hold the CTRL key and double-click on the **lambert2** shader; the **Rename node** dialog box is displayed. Enter **road** in the dialog box and choose the **OK** button; the shader is renamed to **road**.

5. Select the plane in the viewport, press and hold the right mouse button over the **road** shader, and choose **Assign Existing Material** from the marking menu; the **road** shader is applied to the plane.

6. Double-click on the **road** shader in the **Hypershade** window; the **Attribute Editor** is displayed. Choose the checker button on the right of the **Color** attribute in the **Common Material Attributes** area of the **Attribute Editor**, as shown in 11-39; the **Create Render Node** window is displayed. Choose the **File** button from the **Create Render Node** window; the **File Attributes** area is displayed in the **Attribute Editor**, as shown in Figure 11-40.

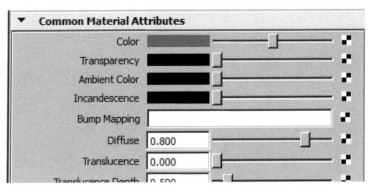

Figure 11-39 The Common Material Attributes area

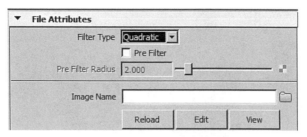

*Figure 11-40 The **File Attributes** area*

7. Choose the **Open** button on the right of the **Image Name** attribute from the **File Attributes** area in the **Attribute Editor**, refer to Figure 11-40; the **Open** dialog box is displayed. Next, select the *roadtexture.jpg* and then choose the **Open** button.

8. Make sure the **Polygons** option is selected in the menuset drop-down list in the status line. Next, to align the texture on the plane, select the plane and choose **Edit UVs > Unitize** from the main menubar. Next, press **6** to view the texture applied on the road, as shown in Figure 11-41.

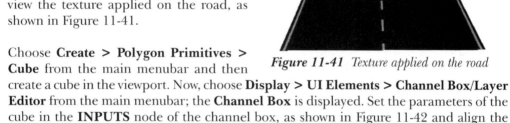

Figure 11-41 Texture applied on the road

9. Choose **Create > Polygon Primitives > Cube** from the main menubar and then create a cube in the viewport. Now, choose **Display > UI Elements > Channel Box/Layer Editor** from the main menubar; the **Channel Box** is displayed. Set the parameters of the cube in the **INPUTS** node of the channel box, as shown in Figure 11-42 and align the cube with the road. Next, duplicate the cube and move it to the other side to get base for the street scene, as shown in Figure 11-43.

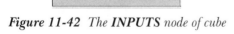

polyCube1	
Width	30
Height	0.8
Depth	170
Subdivisions Width	1
Subdivisions Height	1
Subdivisions Depth	1
Create UVs	Normalize

*Figure 11-42 The **INPUTS** node of cube*

Figure 11-43 The base of the street

Creating Buildings

In this section, you need to create buildings by using the paint strokes in Maya.

1. Choose **Window > General Editors > Visor** from the main menubar, the **Visor** window is displayed. Choose the **Paint Effects** tab, if not already chosen, and then select the **cityMesh** folder from the left of the **Visor** window; the corresponding paint strokes are displayed on the right, as shown in Figure 11-44. Choose the **chicagoTower.mel** paint stroke from the **Visor** window.

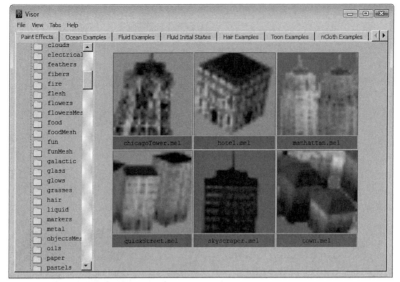

*Figure 11-44 Choosing the **cityMesh** paint stroke from the **Visor** window*

2.   Press CTRL+B; the **Paint Effects Brush Settings** dialog box is displayed, as shown in
     Figure 11-45. Enter **6** in the **Global Scale** edit box of this dialog box to set the brush
     stroke.

3.   Activate the Top viewport, and then press and drag the mouse in it; buildings are created, as
     shown in Figure 11-46. Next, choose **Window > Attribute Editor** from the main menubar;
     the building **Attribute Editor** window is displayed. Choose the **chicagoTower1** attribute tab
     from the **Attribute Editor** and expand the **Tubes** property area. Now, expand the **Creation**
     tab in this area and set values for various parameters in it, as shown in Figure 11-47.

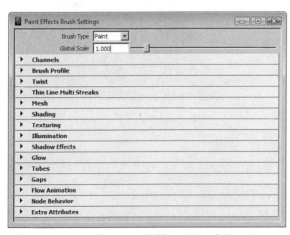

*Figure 11-45 The **Paint Effects Brush Settings**
dialog box*

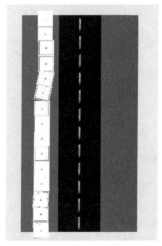

*Figure 11-46 Buildings
created*

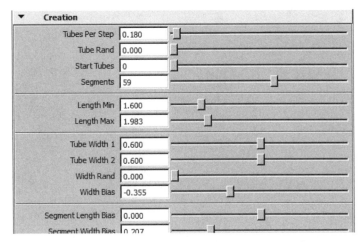

*Figure 11-47 The attributes in the **Creation** tab*

4. Select all building paint strokes from the viewport. Choose **Edit > Duplicate Special > Option Box** from main menubar to make a duplicate of the buildings created earlier; the **Duplicate Special Options** dialog box is displayed, as shown in Figure 11-48. In this dialog box, set the parameters and then choose the **Duplicate Special** button; a duplicate of the building paint stroke is created on the opposite side of the plane, as shown in Figure 11-49. Also, you need to align the duplicated paint strokes.

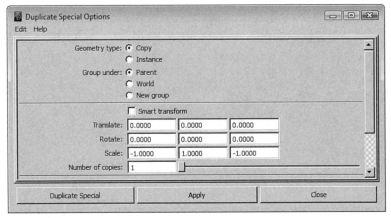

*Figure 11-48 The **Duplicate Special Options** dialog box*

Note
*You can adjust the attributes of the building paint stroke to get different results. Try using different **cityMesh** paint strokes from the **Visor** window to create different types of buildings.*

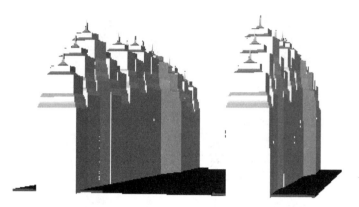

Figure 11-49 *Building paint stroke created on the opposite side of the plane*

Creating Clouds

In this section, you need to create clouds in the scene by using the paint strokes in Maya.

1. Activate the Perspective viewport and choose **Window > Outliner** from the main menubar; the **Outliner** window is displayed. Double-click on the **persp** camera in the **Outliner** window; the **Attribute Editor** with various attributes of the **persp** camera is displayed.

2. Ensure that the **perspShape** tab is chosen in the **Attribute Editor** and then expand the **Environment** area from the **Attribute Editor**, as shown in Figure 11-50. Next, double-click on the **Background Color** box in this tab; the **Color History** palette is displayed. Enter the **RGB** values in the **Color History** palette, as shown in Figure 11-51, and click anywhere in the **Attribute Editor**.

Figure 11-50 *Attributes in the **Environment** area*

3. Activate the Top viewport and choose **Window > General Editors > Visor** from the main menubar; the **Visor** window is displayed. In the **Paint Effects** tab of this window, select the **cumulusPurple.mel** cloud type from the **clouds** folder. Next, press and hold the b key on the keyboard and then drag the cursor with the left mouse button. Now, paint the cloud in the top viewport, as shown in Figure 11-52.

4. Choose **Display > UI Elements > Channel Box/Layer Editor** from the main menubar; the **Channel Box** is displayed. Set the **RotateX** attribute to **-50** in the channel box and then align the clouds paint stroke to the back of the building.

5. Choose the **Render the Current frame (Maya Software)** button from the status line to render the scene.

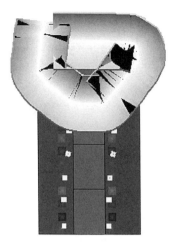

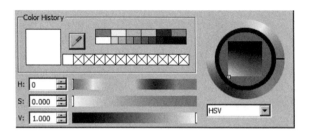

*Figure 11-51 The **Color History** palette*

Figure 11-52 Clouds painted in the top viewport

Creating Lights

In this section, you need to create lights to illuminate the scene.

1. Choose **Create > Lights > Ambient Light** from the main menubar; the ambient light is created. Select the ambient light and choose **Display > UI Elements > Channel Box/ Layer Editor** from the main menubar; the **Channel Box** is displayed. Set the parameters of the light in the channel box, as shown in Figure 11-53.

2. Similarly, create another ambient light and set its parameters in the channel box, as shown in Figure 11-54.

ambientLight1	
Translate X	0
Translate Y	52
Translate Z	77
Rotate X	0
Rotate Y	0
Rotate Z	0
Scale X	1
Scale Y	1
Scale Z	1
Visibility	on

ambientLight2	
Translate X	-27.939
Translate Y	49.625
Translate Z	-76.784
Rotate X	0
Rotate Y	0
Rotate Z	0
Scale X	1
Scale Y	1
Scale Z	1
Visibility	on

*Figure 11-53 The **ambientLight1** attributes in the transform node*

*Figure 11-54 The **ambientLight2** attributes in the transform node*

Rendering and Saving the Scene

In this section, you need to create a camera, set the view to render, and then save the scene.

1. Choose **Create > Cameras > Camera and Aim** from the main menubar; the camera is created with an aim in the viewport. Now, open the channel box, choose the camera, and then enter values for the camera in the transform node of the channel box, as shown in Figure 11-55.

2. Similarly, enter values for setting the aim of the camera, as shown in Figure 11-56.

camera1	
Translate X	0
Translate Y	2.554
Translate Z	78.914
Rotate X	7.34
Rotate Y	0
Rotate Z	0
Scale X	1
Scale Y	1
Scale Z	1
Visibility	on

Figure 11-55 *The camera1 attributes in the transform node*

camera1_aim ...	
Translate X	0
Translate Y	7.661
Translate Z	39.267
Rotate X	0
Rotate Y	0
Rotate Z	0
Scale X	1
Scale Y	1
Scale Z	1
Visibility	on

Figure 11-56 *The camera1_aim attributes in the transform node*

3. Choose the **Single Perspective View** button from the toolbox. Then, choose **Panels > Perspective > camera1** from the **Panel menu**; the camera1 view is activated in the viewport.

4. Choose **File > Save Scene** from the main menubar; the **Save As** dialog box is displayed.

    As the project folder is already set, by default the path *\Documents\Maya_Tutorials\c11_tut1\ scenes* is displayed in **Look In** text box of the dialog box. Enter **c11_tut1** in the **File name** text box and then select **Maya Binary** from the **Files of type** drop-down list. Next, choose the **Save As** button.

You can view the final rendered image of the model by downloading the *c11_Maya_2012_render.zip* file from *http://www.cadcim.com*.

Figure 11-57 *The final output after rendering*

Tutorial 2

In this tutorial, you will create a desert scene, as shown in Figure 11-58, by using the paint strokes in Maya. **(Expected time: 30 min)**

Figure 11-58 *A desert scene*

The following steps are required to complete this tutorial:

a. Set a project folder.
b. Download the texture file.
c. Create a base for the desert scene.
d. Create tree and cactus on the plane.
e. Create camels and background scene.
f. Render and save the scene.

Setting the Project Folder

Before starting a new file, it is recommended that you set the project folder.

1. Set the project with the name *c11_tut2* in the folder *Maya_Tutorials*.

Downloading the Texture File

1. Download the *c11_maya_2012_tut.zip* file from *http://www.cadcim.com*. The path of the file is as follows:

   Textbooks > Animation and Visual Effects > Maya> Autodesk Maya 2012: A Comprehensive Guide

2. Extract *sandbase.jpg* to *sourceimages* folder at the location *\Documents\Maya_Tutorials\ c11_tut2*.

Creating a Base for the Desert Scene

In this section, you need to create a base for the desert scene.

1. Activate the Top viewport and choose **Create > Polygon Primitives > Plane** from the main menubar. Now, create a plane in the top viewport. Select the plane created and then choose **Display > UI Elements > Channel Box/Layer Editor** from the main menubar; the **Channel Box** is displayed. Set the parameters of the plane in the **Channel Box**, as shown in Figure 11-59.

2. Activate the Perspective viewport and choose **Mesh > Sculpt Geometry Tool > Option Box** from the main menubar; the **Sculpt Geometry Tool** property window is displayed.

3. Choose the **Pull** sculpt parameter from the **Sculpt Geometry Tool** property window and sculpt the plane, as shown in Figure 11-60.

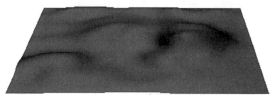

polyPlane1	
Width	38.882
Height	21.965
Subdivisions Width	30
Subdivisions Height	30
Create UVs	Normalize...

Figure 11-59 *Setting the parameters*   *Figure 11-60* *The sculpted plane*
of the plane in the channel box

4. Now, select the plane from the viewport. Press and hold the right mouse button over the plane and choose **Assign Favorite Material > Lambert** from the marking menu, as shown in Figure 11-61; the lambert shader is applied to the plane and the **Attribute Editor** showing the attributes of the lambert shader is displayed.

5. Choose the **Open** button on the right of the **Image Name** attribute from the **File Attributes** area in the **Attribute Editor**; the **Open** dialog box is displayed. Next, select the *sandbase.jpg* and then check the **Open** button.

6. Select the base plane and choose **Create UVs > Planar Mapping** from the main menubar to apply the texture, as shown in Figure 11-62.

Creating a Tree and a Cactus Plant on the Plane

In this section, you need to create a tree and a cactus plant on the plane by using the paint strokes in Maya.

1. Activate the Top viewport and choose **Window > General Editors > Visor** from the main menubar; the **Visor** window is displayed. Choose the **treeBare.mel** paint stroke from the **trees** paint strokes folder, as shown in Figure 11-63. You can also increase the paint stroke size as per your requirement.

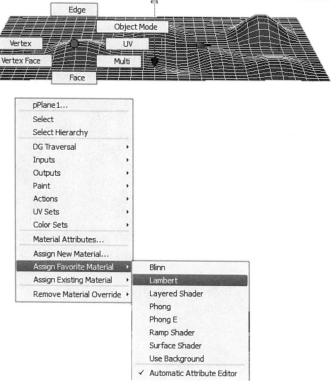

Figure 11-61 *Choosing the **Lambert** option from the marking menu*

Figure 11-62 *Texture applied on the plane*

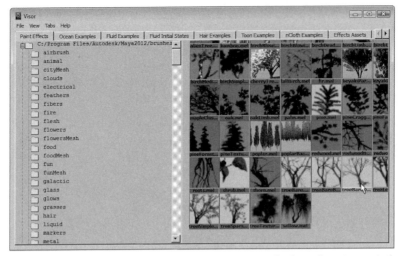

*Figure 11-63 Choosing the **treeBare.mel** paint stroke from the **Visor** window*

2. Activate the Perspective viewport and paint the tree. Next, adjust the tree in the viewport to get the output, as shown in Figure 11-64.

*Figure 11-64 Tree created using the **treeBare.mel** paint stroke*

3. Similarly, choose **cactus.mel** from the **fun** paint strokes folder, as shown in Figure 11-65. Next, activate the Top viewport, paint the **cactus** plant at different positions on the plane, and then scale them to different sizes.

4. Activate the Perspective viewport, if not already activated, the scene is displayed, as shown in Figure 11-66.

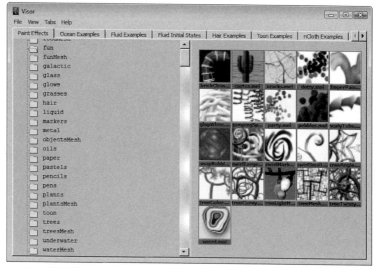

Figure 11-65 *Choosing the* **cactus.mel** *paint stroke from the* **Visor** *window*

Figure 11-66 *Cactus plants created using the* **cactus.mel** *paint stroke*

Note
The size of the cactus plant should be proportional to the size of the tree.

Creating Camels and the Background Scene

In this section, you need to create two planes and assign the alpha map of the camels to the plane.

1. Activate the Side viewport. Choose **Create > Polygon Primitives > Plane** from the main menubar and then create a polygon plane in the side viewport.

2. Choose **Display > UI Elements > Channel Box/ Layer Editor** from the main menubar; the **Channel Box** is displayed. Set the parameters of the plane in the **INPUTS** node, as shown in Figure 11-67.

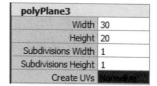

polyPlane3	
Width	30
Height	20
Subdivisions Width	1
Subdivisions Height	1
Create UVs	Normalize...

Figure 11-67 *The INPUTS node of the plane*

3. Activate the Perspective viewport. Select the plane, press and hold the right mouse button over it, and then choose **Assign Favorite Material > Lambert** from the marking menu; the lambert shader is applied to the plane and the **Attribute Editor** is displayed on the right of the viewport.

4. Choose the **Open** button on the right of the **Image Name** attribute from the **File Attributes** area in the **Attribute Editor**; the **Open** dialog box is displayed. Next, select the *camel.png* and then choose the **Open** button.

5. Activate the Perspective viewport and adjust the plane in the scene, as shown in Figure 11-68.

Figure 11-68 The plane adjusted in the scene

6. Now, select the plane and choose **Edit > Duplicate** from the main menubar to duplicate the plane. Use the **Move** and **Scale** tools from the toolbox to adjust the two planes, as shown in Figure 11-69.

Figure 11-69 The complete scene

7. Choose **Window > Outliner** from the main menubar; the **Outliner** window is displayed. Next, double-click on the **persp** camera; the **persp** camera attributes are displayed in the **Attribute Editor**.

8. Expand the **Environment** attribute area in the **Attribute Editor**. Next, choose the **Open** button on the right of the **Image Plane** attribute, as shown in Figure 11-70; the **Image Plane Attributes** are displayed on the right of the viewport in the **Attribute Editor**.

*Figure 11-70 The **Environment** attributes area*

9. Choose the **Open** button on the right of the **Image Name** attribute from the **File Attributes** area in the **Attribute Editor**; the **Open** dialog box is displayed. Next, select the *sky.jpg* and then choose the **Open** button.

Figure 11-71 The image plane attributes

Rendering and Saving the Scene

In this section, you need to render the scene to get the final output.

1. Activate the Perspective viewport and adjust the scene.

2. Choose the **Render the current frame (Maya Software)** button from the status line to render the scene and get the final output, as shown in Figure 11-72.

3. Choose **File > Save Scene** from the main menubar; the **Save As** dialog box is displayed.

    As the project folder is already set, by default the path *Documents**Maya_Tutorials**c11_tut2*\ *scenes* is displayed in the **Look In** text box of the dialog box.

2. Enter *c11_tut2* in the **File name** text box and then select **Maya Binary** from the **Files of type** drop-down list. Next, choose the **Save As** button.

You can view the final rendered image of the model by downloading the *c11_Maya_2012_render.zip* file from *http://www.cadcim.com*.

Figure 11-72 *The final rendered scene*

Self-Evaluation Test

Answer the following questions and then compare them to those given at the end of this chapter:

1. Which of the following attributes is used to adjust the density of a paint stroke?

    (a) **Stamp Density**   (b) **Flatness**
    (c) **Twist**   (d) **Brush Density**

2. Which of the following attributes is used to control the distance between the shadow and the casting stroke?

    (a) **Shadow Offset**   (b) **Shadow Diffusion**
    (c) **Shadow Transparency**   (d) None of these

3. The _____ attribute is used to define the softness on the edges of the stroke path.

4. The _____ window comprises preloaded animation clips, brushes, shader libraries, or texture libraries.

5. The _____ attribute is used to set the profile for the brush preset.

6. The _____ attribute is used to twist paint strokes about their own axes.

7. The **Glow** attribute is used to add shadow to paint strokes. (T/F)

8. The **Global Scale** edit box is used to set the size of the brush. (T/F)

9. The **Twist** attribute is used to set the profile for the brush preset. (T/F)

10. The **Thorns on Mesh** attribute is used to give a glow effect to a mesh object. (T/F)

Review Questions

Answer the following questions:

1. Which of the following attributes is used to control the softness of shadow?

   (a) **Shadow Diffusion**   (b) **Shadow Offset**
   (c) **Shadow Transparency**   (d) None of these

2. Which of the following brush types is used to render paint effects quicker than the remaining brush types?

   (a) **Smear**   (b) **Blur**
   (c) **ThinLine**   (d) **Mesh**

3. The _____ brush type is used to create an accurate conical geometry with the textures that correctly map on the surface.

4. The _____ attribute is used to twist a paint stroke from one end, while keeping the other end fixed.

5. You can create realistic objects such as tree mesh, water effect, and so on by using the _____ window.

6. The _____ attribute is used to illuminate brush stroke.

7. The **Flatness2** option is used to define the flatness of a paint stroke at the base and the tip. (T/F)

8. The **Brush Profile** attribute is used to set the size of a brush. (T/F)

Exercises

Exercise 1

Use paint strokes to create an underwater scene around the ant model, as shown in Figure 11-73. You can view the final rendered image of this model by downloading the *c11_maya_2012_render.zip* file from *http://www.cadcim.com*. The path of file is as follows:

Textbooks > Animation and Visual Effects > Maya > Autodesk Maya 2012: A Comprehensive Guide
(Expected time: 30 min)

Figure 11-73 The underwater scene

Exercise 2

Create a model of hut shown in Figure 11-74. Next, apply texture to it and create a tree on its left side by using the Visor window, as shown in Figure 11-74. You can view the final rendered image of this model by downloading the *c11_maya_2012_render.zip* file from *http://www.cadcim. com*. The path of file is mentioned in Exercise 1.   **(Expected time: 30 min)**

Figure 11-74 *The tree created on the left side of model*

Exercise 3

Create the model of a flower pot shown in Figure 11-75. Next, apply texture to it and use the **Visor** window to create flowers in the flower pot. Render the scene to get the final output, as shown in Figure 11-76. You can view the final rendered image of this model by downloading the *c11_maya_2012_render.zip* file from *http://www.cadcim.com*. The path of file is mentioned in Exercise 1.   **(Expected time: 30 min)**

Figure 11-75   *The flower pot*   *Figure 11-76*   *The rendered flower pot*

Answers to Self-Evaluation Test
1. a, **2.** a, **3. Softness**, **4. Visor**, **5. Brush Profile**, **6. Twist**, **7.** F, **8.** T, **9.** T, **10.** F

Chapter 12

Rendering

Learning Objectives

After completing this chapter, you will be able to:

- *Use the render layer editor*
- *Understand the basic concepts of rendering*
- *Add motion blur to animation*
- *Add caustics to a scene*
- *Understand the basic concepts of Final Gather and Global Illumination*
- *Add Physical Sun and Sky effect to a scene*
- *Use the mental ray rendering in Maya*

INTRODUCTION TO RENDERING

Rendering is the process of generating a 2-dimensional image of a 3-dimensional scene. It is considered as the final stage in 3D computer graphics. The rendering process helps in visualizing the lighting effects, materials applied, background, and other settings that you set for the scene. In the latest version of Maya, you can create render layers and render individual or multiple layers using the render layer editor. This editor is discussed next.

RENDER LAYER EDITOR

The **Render Layer Editor** helps you to render individual or multiple layers. To invoke the **Render Layer Editor**, choose **Display > UI Elements > Channel Box/ Layer Editor** from the main menubar; the **Channel box** will be displayed on the right of the viewport. Next, select the **Render** tab on the top of the **layer editor**; the **Render Layer Editor** will be displayed in the **channel box/layer editor**, as shown in Figure 12-1. The tools in the render layer editor are similar to those discussed in the **Animation Layer Editor** in Chapter 9.

Figure 12-1 *The render layer editor*

TYPES OF RENDERING

In Maya, different types of rendering are used to view the final output of the scene such as **software rendering**, **hardware rendering**, **vector rendering**, and **mental ray rendering**. All these types of rendering are discussed next.

Software Rendering

The software renderer is the default renderer in Maya. It is an advanced, multi-threaded renderer that produces high quality images. This type of rendering supports most of the entities in Maya such as all geometries, particles, fluid effects, and paint effects.

The software renderer has an advance feature called **IPR**. **IPR** stands for Interactive Photorealistic Rendering. The **IPR** rendering helps you to make interactive adjustments of the final rendered scene in the viewport. The **IPR** rendering creates a special image file that not only stores the pixel information of an image, but also the data of the surface normals, materials, and objects associated with each of these pixels. This information is updated regularly as you make changes to the shades of the scene.

Hardware Rendering

Hardware rendering is a process used to render particles to create fast and simple rendering. For using hardware rendering in Maya, you should have a graphic card with good memory fitted in the system. A graphic card helps you calculate the color, light, and other aspects of an object in a scene.

If you are rendering a scene for the first time by using the hardware rendering technique, it may take more time to render the scene. It is so because in this rendering technique, the scene is first converted into data structure, which is later on well calculated by the graphic division of the CPU. The hardware renderer uses the same tessellation settings as are used in the software renderer. Various hardware render settings are discussed next.

Hardware Render Settings

The hardware render settings helps you adjust the settings of a scene such that you get the best results on rendering. To adjust the settings, choose **Window > Rendering Editors > Render Settings** from the main menubar; the **Render Settings** window will be displayed in the viewport, as shown in Figure 12-2. Select **Maya Hardware** from the **Render Using** drop-down list in this window to set the hardware renderer for rendering the scene. Next, choose the **Maya Hardware** tab from the **Render Settings** window; the hardware render settings will be displayed. Also, the **Quality** and **Render Options** attribute areas are displayed under the **Maya Hardware** tab.

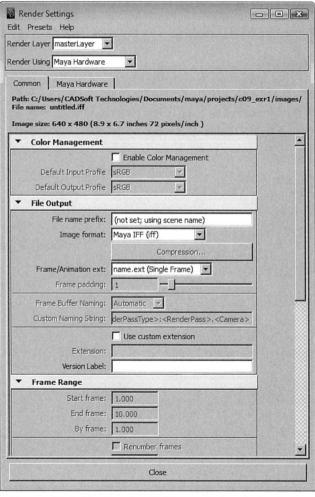

Figure 12-2 The **Render Settings** *window for hardware rendering*

The options in the **Quality** attribute area are discussed next.

Presets

The **Presets** drop-down list is used to set the quality and effect of the scene to be rendered. On changing the **Preset** attributes, the settings in the rest of the attributes also change accordingly. These settings also affect the time taken for rendering a scene. Higher the quality set for the **Presets** option, better will be the render quality, but it will take more time in rendering. Select the **High quality lighting** check box from the **Presets** area to set a high quality hardware render lighting.

Number Of Samples

The **Number Of Samples** option is used to determine the number of light samples created per pixel on rendering. This attribute results in the anti-aliasing of a scene. More the number of samples created per pixel, better will be the anti-aliasing of the scene. But, it will take more time to render the scene.

Frame buffer format

The **Frame buffer format** drop-down list is used to set the video memory for holding the pixels from which the video display is refreshed. You can select the required frame buffer format from this drop-down list. Select the **Transparent shadow maps** check box from this area, if you want to use transparent shadow maps in your scene.

Transparency sorting

The **Transparency sorting** drop-down list is used to detect and draw transparent objects. There are two options in this drop-down list. Select the **Per object** option to sort the farthest point of the object in the scene to closest point with reference to the camera. Select the **Per polygon** option from the drop-down list to sort the farthest point of the object's polygon to closest in distance from the camera. The **Per polygon** option is used for better transparency sorting than the **Per object** option. Therefore, in case of the **Per polygon** option, the scene takes longer time to render as compared to the **Per object** option.

Color resolution

The **Color resolution** option is used to bake the shading network to a 2D image. To set the color resolution, you can move the slider located at the right of this option or enter a value in the **Color resolution** input box. The default value of the **Color resolution** is 256.

Bump resolution

The **Bump resolution** option is used to apply the bump effect on an object by baking the shading network to a 2D image. The baked 2D image will have a high resolution. To set the resolution, move the slider located at the right of this option or enter a value in the **Bump resolution** input box. The default value of the **Bump resolution** is 512.

Texture compression

The **Texture compression** drop-down list is used to reduce the memory usage by 75% at the time of rendering. The options in this drop-down list use an algorithm that helps in controlling the memory usage.

The options in the **Render Options** attribute area are discussed next.

Culling

The **Culling** drop-down list is used to render an object in the viewport, depending on the direction of the object with respect to the camera. Select the **Per Object** option from this drop-down list to use the settings of the objects that are available in the rendering section of the **Attribute Editor**. Select the **All Double Sided** option from the drop-down list to render both sides of polygons in the scene. Select the **All Single Sided** option to render the polygons whose normals are facing toward the camera.

Percent of image size

The **Percent of image size** option is used to specify the percentage of image size that the object will occupy on rendering. To set the value of this option, either enter a value in the **Percent of image size** input box or move the slider located on the right of this option. This input box is activated by default. To deactivate it, clear the **Small object culling threshold** check box located above the **Percent of image size** option in the **Render Settings** window.

Maximum cache size (MB)

The **Maximum cache size (MB)** option is used to set the cache memory in the video card memory upto 512 MB. The default value of this option is 64. Clear the **Hardware geometry cache** check box to make the **Maximum cache size** option inactive.

Motion blur

Select the **Motion blur** check box to add the motion blur to an animating object.

Motion blur by frame

The **Motion blur by frame** option is used to evaluate an object in different positions in the timeline by blending its position in different frames, as shown in Figure 12-3. The blurriness of an image is measured by calculating approximate blur of the object at different frames. Also, the software adjusts the time range in accordance with the camera's shutter angle attribute in the **Attribute Editor**.

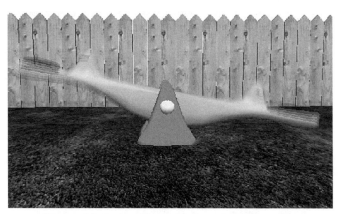

Figure 12-3 *An object with the motion blur effect*

Number of exposures

The **Number of exposures** option is used to specify the number of samples required for creating a smooth motion blur on an animated object.

Vector Rendering

In Maya, the vector rendering is used to create unrealistic images such as cartoons, tonal art, wireframe, and so on. Such rendered images can be saved in various formats such as *.swf*, *.ai*, *.tiff*, and *EPS*.

One of the vector rendered images is shown in Figure 12-4. In this figure, you will notice that the image is more stylized and has more color effects on it as compared to the images created by using other rendering types.

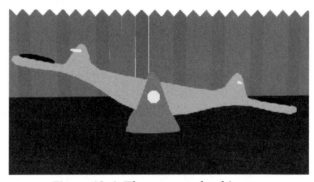

Figure 12-4 *The vector rendered image*

To understand the process of creating effects using the vector rendering better, compare Figure 12-5 with Figure 12-6. In these figures, you will notice that Figure 12-5 displays a more real life character than the one shown in Figure 12-6. This is because the character in Figure 12-6 displays the tonal art effect, and such effect is mainly used for creating logos and diagrams.

Figure 12-5 *A software rendered image*   ***Figure 12-6*** *A vector rendered image*

The vector renderer is based on the concept of the **RAViX Technology**. **RAViX** stands for Rapid Visibility Extension. This technology converts a 3D model into a 2D vector-based imagery by detecting the lines and vertices that make up a 3D model and then converts them into shaded polygons for recreating the 3D image in a 2D vector format (specifically Adobe Flash SWF and EPS formats). RAViX provides per polygon shading capabilities that are superior to other rendering technologies. Also, the file size created by using this technology is smaller than the other technologies. In Maya, the vector rendering does not support any light, except the point light. If there is no light in a scene, the vector renderer creates a default light at the camera position on rendering.

The Maya vector renderer cannot render some features such as bump maps, displacement maps, Maya fluid effects, image planes, Maya fur, multiple UVs, Maya Paint Effects, particles, post-render effects, and textures. To render an object with any of these features using the Maya vector renderer, first you need to convert the object into a polygon and then render the object as per your requirement. To convert an object into a polygon, select the object from the viewport and then choose **Modify > Convert** from the main menubar; a flyout comprising of all tessellation methods will be displayed. Choose the required option from the flyout; the object will be converted into a polygon.

Vector Render Settings

The vector render settings help you adjust the settings of a scene to get unreal rendering outputs. To modify the vector render settings, choose **Window > Rendering Editors > Render Settings** from the main menubar; the **Render Settings** window will be displayed. In this window, select **Maya Vector** from the **Render Using** drop-down list. Next, choose the **Maya Vector** tab from the **Render Settings** window; the vector render settings will be displayed, as shown in Figure 12-7.

*Figure 12-7 The **Render Settings** window for vector rendering*

If the **Maya Vector** option is not displayed by default in the **Render Using** drop-down list, choose **Window > Setting/Preferences > Plug-in Manager** from the main menubar; the **Plug-in Manager** dialog box will be displayed, as shown in Figure 12-8. Select the **VectorRender.mll** check box from the **Plug-in Manager** dialog box. Next, choose the **Refresh** button and then the **Close** button; the **Maya Vector** option will be displayed in the drop-down list. Some of the properties in the **Render Settings** window of the vector render are discussed next.

Image Format Options (maya) Area

By default, there is no option in the **Image Format Options** area. To activate these formats, choose the **Common** tab from the **Render Settings** window. Next, select **Macromedia SWF** or **SVG (svg)** from the **Image format** drop-down list in the **Render Settings** window. Again, choose the **Maya Vector** tab from the **Render Settings** window; the **Image format Options (swf)** area will be displayed in the **Maya Vector** tab of the **Render Settings** window, as shown in Figure 12-9.

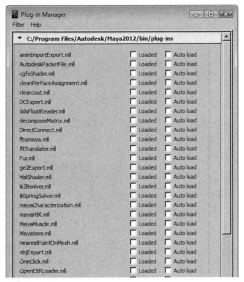

*Figure 12-8 Partial view of the **Plug-in Manager** dialog box*

*Figure 12-9 The **Image Format Options (swf)** area*

Frame rate

The **Frame rate** edit box is used to specify the number of frames for the output animation that will be created on rendering in *.swf* format. The default **Frame rate** value is 12.

Flash version

The **Flash version** drop-down list is used to specify the version of the rendered flash player file. The *.swf* file can be imported from any flash version. Select the **Open in browser** check box from the **Image format Options (swf)** area to enable the animation to display in the browser after the rendering is completed. Select the **Combine fills and edges** check box to make the outlines and fills of the rendered output as a single object. Selecting this check box also helps you reduce the file size of the rendered output.

Appearance Options Area

The **Appearance Options** area consists of attributes that control the complexity of the final vector image. These attributes are discussed next.

Curve Tolerance

The **Curve tolerance** edit box is used to set the outline of the rendered object. You can specify the curve tolerance value either by entering a value between 0 and 15 in the **Curve tolerance** input box or by moving the slider bar located on the right of the input box. The default value of this attribute is 7.5. If you enter 0 in the input box, a series of straight line segments, one for each polygon cube, will be created when you render the final vector image. This results in producing large sized files. But if you enter the value **15** in this input box, then a series of distorted outlines will be created, thus resulting in smaller sized files.

The **Secondary curve fitting** check box is used to control the conversion of line segments into curves. Select this check box to produce better render results and smaller file size.

Detail level preset

This drop-down list is used to add detail to the final rendered image. Higher the detail value selected from this drop-down list, more will be the accuracy of the rendered image and more will be the value in the **Detail level** attribute. By default, **Automatic** is selected in this drop-down list. As a result, the renderer automatically calculates the appropriate level of detail for a scene. Figures 12-10 and 12-11 display two rendered images with low and high values selected in the **Detail level Preset** drop-down list respectively.

Figure 12-10 *Image with low value selected in the **Detail level preset***   *Figure 12-11* *Image with high value selected in the **Detail level preset***

Fill Options Area

The **Fill Options** area is used to set the type of fill color for the scene being rendered. Different fill options are discussed next.

Fill objects

You can select the **Fill objects** check box to increase the file size of the rendered output. When you select this check box, the **Fill Style** attribute in the **Fill Options** area gets activated.

Single color

The **Single color** attribute is used to render an object such that it gives a cartoon-like effect, as shown in Figure 12-12. On applying the **Single color** attribute, the object will appear flat and there will be no effect of light in the scene.

Two color

The **Two color** attribute is used to give a shaded appearance to an object on rendering, as shown in Figure 12-13. The **Two color** attribute uses two solid colors to render the scene. In this case, the final rendered image will have the shades of only these two solid colors.

*Figure 12-12 Image created using the **Single color** fill style*

*Figure 12-13 Image created using the **Two color** fill style*

Four color

The **Four color** attribute is similar to the **Two color** attribute except that it uses four solid colors to render the scene, as shown in Figure 12-14.

Full color

The **Full color** attribute is used to produce realistic render effects, as shown in Figure 12-15. However, this attribute makes the file size heavier than other fill color attributes.

*Figure 12-14 Image created on applying the **Four color** fill style*

*Figure 12-15 Image created on applying the **Full color** fill style*

Average color

The **Average color** attribute is used to shade each face and surface of an image with one solid color, as shown in Figure 12-16.

*Figure 12-16 Image created on applying the **Average color** fill style*

Area gradient

The **Area gradient** attribute is enabled only when the *.swf* or *.svg* file format is selected as the output format. This attribute adds a radial gradient to each face of the object, depending on the surface material, color, and lighting used in the scene.

Mesh Gradient

The **Mesh gradient** attribute is enabled only when the *.swf* or *.svg* file format is selected as the output format. This attribute is used to add a linear gradient on each polygon along the surface of the object, depending on the color of the material and lighting used in the scene.

Edge Options Area

The **Edge Options** attribute area is used to define the edges of an object on rendering. Various options in this area are discussed next.

Include Edges

Select the **Include edges** check box to render the surface edges of an object as outlines. Figures 12-17 and 12-18 show the images created before and after selecting the **Include edges** check box, respectively.

*Figure 12-17 Image before selecting the **Include edges** option*

*Figure 12-18 Image after selecting the **Include edges** option*

Edge weight preset

The **Edge weight preset** drop-down list is used to set the thickness of edges on rendering. To set the thickness of edges, select the required thickness from this drop-down list. Hairline is the default option selected in this drop-down list.

Edge weight

The **Edge weight** option is used to add weight/thickness to edges. To do so, enter the required value in the **Edge weight** input box or move the slider on the right of this option. The default value in the input box is 0. Figures 12-19 and 12-20 show the difference between the images when different edge weights are selected. If you change the value of an edge weight, the corresponding edge weight preset value will also change automatically.

Figure 12-19 Image with the **Edge weight** *value = 3*

Figure 12-20 Image with the **Edge weight** *value = 10*

Edge style

The **Edge style** drop-down list is used to render only the edges or silhouettes of a surface. To do so, select any edge style type, for example the **Outlines** edge style from this drop-down list; only the outlines of the selected object will be rendered, as shown in Figure 12-21. If you select the **Mesh** option from this drop-down list, all polygon edges of the selected object will be rendered, as shown in Figure 12-22.

Figure 12-21 Image displayed on selecting the **Outlines** *edge style option*

Figure 12-22 Image displayed on selecting the **Mesh** *edge style option*

Edge color

The **Edge color** option is used to add color to the rendered edges of the object in the viewport. To add color to the rendered edges, choose the color box beside this option; the **Color Chooser** window will be displayed. Select a color from this dialog box to set the color and then choose the **Close** button.

Hidden edges

The **Hidden edges** check box is used to show all hidden edges of an object when it is rendered, refer to Figure 12-23. However, it is recommended to avoid using this option because on choosing this option, all hidden edges are displayed, and you do not get an appropriate view of the rendered image.

Note

*Using the **Hidden edges** option increases the file size. This happens due to increase in the formation of vector images on rendering.*

Edge detail

The **Edge detail** check box is used to add detail to the final rendered output and helps to give the rendered image a 3D look. To activate this check box, first you need to select the **Outline** option from the **Edge Style** drop-down list. On selecting the **Edge detail** check box, the Min edge angle attribute gets activated. This attribute is used to define the **minimum angle** between the two adjacent polygons so that the common edges between them are rendered as a single outline. The **Edge detail** check box helps in giving the rendered image a 3D look, as shown in Figure 12-24.

*Figure 12-23   Image after turning on the **Hidden edges** option*

*Figure 12-24   Image on selecting the **Edge detail** check box*

Render optimizations Area

The **Render optimizations** attribute area is used to reduce the file size of the vector rendered images. The option in this area is discussed next.

Render optimization

The **Render optimization** drop-down list has three options: **Safe**, **Good**, and **Aggressive**. Select the **Safe** option to delete the outlines that are visible only on zooming in to the scene. Select the **Good** option to remove the sub-pixel geometry, especially in the region of high detail. This is done to reduce the file size. Select the **Aggressive** option to reduce the file size to around 30% of the original file size.

mental ray Rendering

The mental ray is the most production-proved renderer used in the industry. It generates images of outstanding quality, unsurpassed realism as well as gives scalable performance. The mental ray has certain important attributes such as caustics, global illumination, final gathering, and HDRI that provide a realistic look to a scene. These attributes are discussed later in the chapter.

mental ray Shaders

The mental ray shaders in Maya support all shaders, textures, and lights. Also, mental ray has its own shader library. To set the mental ray shaders, first you need to set the default renderer to mental ray. To set the renderer type to the mental ray, choose **Window > Setting / Preferences > Plug-in Manager** from the main menubar; the **Plug-in Manager** dialog box will be displayed, as shown in Figure 12-25. Select the **Loaded** and **Auto Load** check boxes next to the **Mayatomr.mll** plug-in. Next, choose the **Refresh** button and close the dialog box.

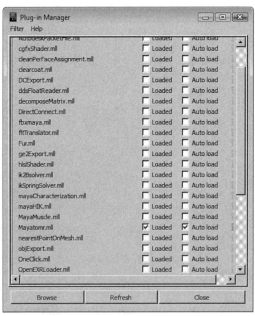

*Figure 12-25 Partial view of the **Plug-in Manager** dialog box*

Now, choose the **Render Settings** button from the status line; the **Render Settings** window will be displayed. In this window, select **mental ray** from the **Render Using** drop-down list and then choose the **Close** button; the mental ray renderer will be set to render the scene. To display various Maya shaders, choose **Window > Rendering Editors > Hypershade** from the main menubar; the **Hypershade** window will be displayed, as shown in Figure 12-26. The mental ray shaders are available on the left of the **Hypershade** window. You can also load or upload these libraries by choosing **Window > Rendering Editors > mental ray > Shader Manager** from the main menubar. On doing so, the **mental ray Shader Manager** dialog box will be displayed, as shown in Figure 12-27. Figure 12-28 shows the mental ray shaders in the **Create Render Node** window. The **Create Render Node** window has already been discussed in the earlier chapters.

The **Render Settings** window for mental ray is divided into six different tabs. The attributes in the **Common** tab of this window are the same as those in other types of renderers discussed earlier. The important attributes in the rest of the tabs are discussed next.

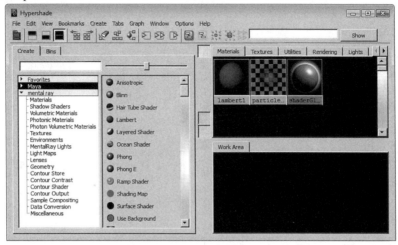

*Figure 12-26 Displaying the **mental ray** shaders in the **Hypershade** window*

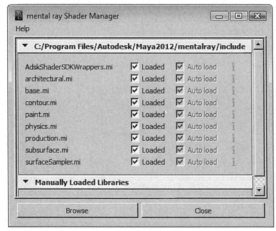

*Figure 12-27 The **mental ray Shader Manager** dialog box*

Raytrace

Raytracing is an algorithm used to create photorealistic scenes, resulting in a high computation time. To activate the raytrace attribute and apply it to a scene, choose **Window > Rendering Editors > Render Settings** from the main menubar; the **Render Settings** window will be displayed. Select **mental ray** from the **Render Using** drop-down list; the **mental ray** attributes will be displayed in the **Render Settings** window. Next, choose the **Quality** tab from the **Render Settings** window and then expand the **Raytracing** attributes area; the raytrace parameters will be displayed, as shown in Figure 12-29. Various options in this area are discussed next.

Raytracing

The **Raytracing** check box is selected by default and is used to calculate the path of particles when they pass through a surface.

Reflections

The **Reflections** option is used to set the maximum number of times a ray can reflect from a surface. Enter the required value in the **Reflections** input box or move the slider to specify the value of this option. The default value of this option is 1.

Refractions

The **Refractions** option is used to set the maximum number of times a ray can refract through a non-opaque object. Enter a value in the **Refractions input box** or move the slider located on the right of this option to set the value of this option. The default value of this option is 1.

Max Trace Depth

The **Max Trace Depth** option is used to set the total number of ray penetrations that will occur, regardless of how many times refraction or reflection has occurred in the scene.

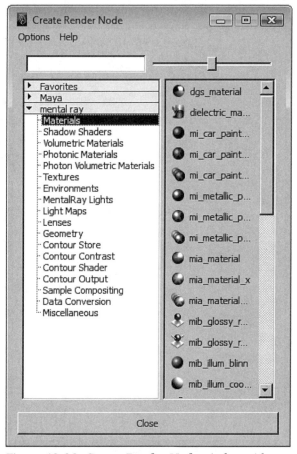

Figure 12-28 Create Render Node window with mental ray attributes

Shadows

The **Shadows** option is used to define the total number of times a ray can penetrate through a transparent or refracting object.

Reflection Blur Limit

The **Reflection Blur Limit** option is used to determine the blurriness of reflection. Higher the reflection blur limit value, more will be the blurriness of the reflection.

Refraction Blur Limit

The **Refraction Blur Limit** option is used to define the blurriness of the refraction in a scene. Higher the refraction blur limit value, more will be the blurriness of the refraction.

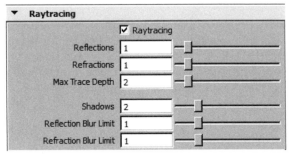

*Figure 12-29 The **Raytracing** attribute area*

Motion Blur

The **Motion Blur** attribute is used to add realistic effect to a scene. Even in the real world, when you look at a moving object, the object appears to be blurring in the direction of motion. To apply this attribute to your scene, choose **Window > Rendering Editors > Render Settings** from the main menubar; the **Render Settings** window will be displayed. In this window, select **mental ray** from the **Render Using** drop-down list; the mental ray attributes will be displayed in the **Render Settings** window. Choose the **Quality** tab from the **Render Settings** window and expand the **Motion Blur** attributes area; the motion blur parameters will be displayed, as shown in Figure 12-30. Various options in this area are discussed next.

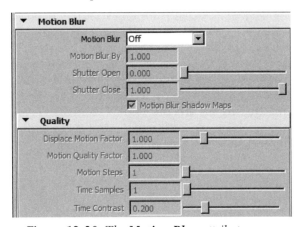

*Figure 12-30 The **Motion Blur** attributes area*

Motion Blur

The **Motion Blur** drop-down list is used to set the motion blur for animation in the viewport. Select the **Off** option from this drop-down list to turn off the effect of motion blur in the scene. Select the **No Deformation** option from this drop-down list to apply the motion blur only to the open and close points of the camera shutter in animation. Select the **Full** option to get the effect of real world motion blur in the scene, when the scene is rendered. The scene takes more time to render when the **Full** option is selected, as compared to the other options.

Motion Blur By

The **Motion Blur By** option is used to increase the motion blur effect of a scene on rendering. Higher is the motion blur value specified in this input box, more will be the time taken to render the scene, and also the scene would be less realistic. To set the value for this option, either enter the required value in the input box or move the slider on the right of this option. The default value of this option is 1.

Shutter Open

The **Shutter Open** option is used to specify the time at which the camera shutter has to be opened and accordingly the motion blur will be calculated.

Shutter Close

The **Shutter Close** option is also used to define the time at which the camera shutter has to be closed and accordingly the motion blur will be calculated.

Motion Blur Shadow Maps

The **Motion Blur Shadow Maps** check box is used to define whether the shadow map will be calculated in the motion blur rendering or not. Clear the check box to render the scene quickly.

Caustics

Caustics are the refraction patterns formed by highly transparent objects such as a glass filled with fluid, as shown in Figure 12-31. They are light patterns formed by focusing the light on a particular object. Each light in Maya supports the mental ray renderer. To enable caustics, open the **Render Settings** window by choosing the **Display Render Settings window** button on the right in the status line. Next, set the **mental ray** renderer type from the **Render Settings** window. Choose the **Quality** tab from the **Render Settings** window and select the **Preview Caustics** option from the **Quality Presets** drop-down list; this will set the default settings for applying the caustics in your scene. Next, choose the **Indirect Lighting** tab from the **Render Settings** window and then expand the **Caustics** attribute area. The options in the **Caustics** attribute area are discussed next.

Caustics

The **Caustics** check box is used to activate the parameters related to setting caustics in the **Render Settings** window.

Accuracy

The **Accuracy** option is used to set the total number of photons required to set the brightness in a scene. Higher the frequency of photons, more will be the smoothness of the caustics applied to the scene.

Scale

The **Scale** option is used to control the effect of indirect illumination on a scene. Choose the white color box on the right of the **Scale** attribute to vary the effect of indirect illumination on the caustics applied to the scene.

Figure 12-31 *The caustics effect on a glass*

Radius

The **Radius** option is used to set the distance up to which the caustics will be applied.

Merge Distance

The **Merge Distance** option is used to merge the photons that come in the specified world space distance.

Caustic Filter Type

The **Caustic Filter Type** drop-down list is used to increase the photon weight by specifying the shape of the caustics created on rendering.

Caustic Filter Kernel

The **Caustic Filter Kernel** option is used to smoothen the caustics created while rendering the scene. Higher the value specified for this option, smoother will be the caustics created.

Global Illumination

Global illumination is the physical simulation of all lights in a scene. It adds more realistic effect of lights into your scene. The global illumination uses indirect illumination in a scene.

To apply global illumination to your scene, choose **Window > Rendering Editors > Render Settings** from the main menubar; the **Render Settings** window will be displayed. In this window, select **mental ray** from the **Render Using** drop-down list; the mental ray attributes will be displayed in the **Render Settings** window. Now, choose the **Indirect Lighting** tab from the **Render Settings** window and then expand the **Global Illumination** attributes area in this tab; the global illumination parameters will be displayed, as shown in Figure 12-32. Various options in this area are discussed next.

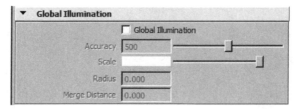

*Figure 12-32 The **Global Illumination** attribute area*

Global Illumination

The **Global Illumination** check box is used to add the global illumination effect to a scene. This check box is not selected by default.

Note

The global illumination effect is calculated only for the photon emitting lights. Therefore, before applying global illumination, you need to enable the photon emission to get the desired result.

Accuracy

The **Accuracy** option is used to set the number of photons in a scene. The total number of photons in a scene determines the intensity of global illumination in the final output. Higher is the number of photons in a scene, more time it will take to render and more will be the smoothness in the scene.

Scale

The **Scale** option is used to control the effect of indirect illumination on a scene. Select the white color box on the right of the **Scale** attribute to vary the effect of indirect illumination on the caustics applied to the scene.

Radius

The **Radius** option is used to set the distance up to which the global illumination will have its effect on the photons in the scene.

Merge Distance

The **Merge Distance** option is used to merge the photons created in the specified world space distance.

Color Bleed

Color Bleed is an important process in which the light reflected from one object diffusely projects color on its nearby object or surface. In this process, only the diffuse colors are partially reflected, while the rest of the colors are absorbed. The Color Bleed depends on the following three terms:

1. Reflection
2. Refraction
3. Absorption

These terms are discussed next.

Reflection is the change in the direction of incident light at an interface between two different media so that the light returns into the medium from which it is originated. The reflection of light depends on the type of surface from which the light will reflect. If the surface is smooth, the light rays will bounce back at an angle equal to the angle of the incoming light rays. However, if the surface is rough, the light rays will bounce at many angles.

Refraction is the change in the direction of light when it passes from one medium to another.

Absorption is the process in which the incident radiated energy is retained by the medium, on which it is incident, without reflection or transmission. As a result, the object appears dark or opaque.

Final Gather

The **Final Gather** is a rendering option that is used to yield extremely realistic shading effects. You can use this option with global illumination to obtain fine details on rendering. To apply this option, first rays are cast from a light source to a scene. Next, a series of rays is diverted at random angles to calculate the light energy transmitting from the surrounding objects. This light energy is stored in photon maps. The photon maps are used to add the bouncing light effect. This process basically turns every object into a light source. As a result, each object in the scene influences the color of its surroundings, as shown in Figure 12-33.

To render a scene using the final gather option, choose **Window > Rendering Editors > Render Settings** from the main menubar; the **Render Settings** window will be displayed. In this window, select **mental ray** from the **Render Using** drop-down list; the mental ray attributes will be displayed in the **Render Settings** window. Choose the **Indirect Lighting** tab from the **Render Settings** window and then expand the **Final Gathering** attributes area in it; the parameters related to this option will be displayed, as shown in Figure 12-34. Various options in this area are discussed next.

Figure 12-33 *The final gather effect in a scene*

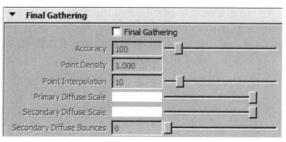

Figure 12-34 The ***Final Gathering*** *attribute area*

Final Gathering

The **Final Gathering** check box is used to turn the final gathering option on/off in the scene.

Accuracy

The **Accuracy** option is used to define the number of rays emitted from the sampled rays. Higher is the value of this option, better will be the render quality. The default value of this option is 100.

Point Density

The **Point Density** option is used to define the total number of final gather points to be calculated on rendering. When you increase the value of point density, the rendering time also increases.

Point Interpolation

The **Point Interpolation** option is used to define the total number of final gather points required for interpolation.

Primary Diffuse Scale

The **Primary Diffuse Scale** option is used to control the intensity of final gather. To set the intensity, you need to choose the color box on the right of this option and then select the required color.

Secondary Diffuse Scale

The **Secondary Diffuse Scale** option is used to control the secondary bouncing of the final gather in the scene.

Secondary Diffuse Bounces

The **Secondary Diffuse Bounces** option is used to set multiple diffuse bounces for the final gather effect such that it adds more light and color bleed effect to the final render.

High Dynamic Range Image (HDRI)

The **High Dynamic Range Image (HDRI)** is a set of techniques that accurately represents a wide range of intensity levels found in real scenes ranging from direct sunlight to shadows.

High dynamic range images are a series of photos that are taken at different exposure levels and then combined into a high range image format. The advantage of using the HDRI maps is that they provide a greater dynamic range of lights and colors in a scene.

Physical Sun and Sky

The mental ray **Physical Sun and Sky** option is used to produce the accurate renders of daylight scenes, as shown in Figure 12-35. It uses the **mia_physicalsun** and **mia_physicalsky** shaders. To add the physical sun and sky effect to a scene, select the **Rendering** module from the status line. Next, choose **Window > Rendering Editors > Render Settings** from the main menubar; the **Render Settings** window will be displayed. In this window, select **mental ray** from the **Render Using** drop-down list to set the render type to **mental ray**. Next, choose the **Indirect Lighting** tab and expand the **Environment** attribute area, as shown in Figure 12-36; the **Physical Sun and Sky** attribute will be displayed. Next, choose the **Create** button on the right of the **Physical Sun and Sky** attribute; a directional light will be created in the viewport.

Figure 12-35 *The image with the physical sun and sky effect*

Figure 12-36 *The **Environment** attribute area*

TUTORIAL

Tutorial 1

In this tutorial, you will render a glass with the help of mental ray attributes to get the final
output, as shown in Figure 12-37.   (Expected time: 30 min)

The following steps are required to complete this tutorial:

a.   Set a project.
b.   Download and open the files.
c.   Assign textures to objects.
d.   Set the light in the scene.
e.   Set the mental ray rendering attributes.
f.   Render the scene.
g.   Save the file.

Figure 12-37 *The image of a glass rendered with the help of mental ray attributes*

Setting the Project Folder

Before starting a new file, it is recommended that you set the project folder.

1.   Set the project with the name *c12_tut1* in the folder *Maya_Tutorials*.

Downloading and Opening the Files

1.   Download the *c12_Maya_2012_tut.zip* file from *http://www.cadcim.com*. The path of the file
     is as follows:

Textbooks > Animation and Visual Effects > 3ds Max > Autodesk 3ds Max 2012: A Comprehensive Guide

Extract the contents of the zipped file and save them in the *\Documents* folder.

2. Choose **Scene** from the **File** menu; the **Open File** dialog box is displayed. In this dialog box, browse to the *\Documents\ c12_Maya_2012_tut1* folder and select *c12_tut1_start.mb* file in it. Choose the **Open** button.

3. Now, choose **Save As** from the main menubar; the **Save As** dialog box is displayed. Browse to the *\Documents\Maya\c12_tut1\scenes* folder. Save the file with the name *c12tut1.mb* in this folder.

Assigning Textures to Objects

In this section, you need to assign textures to the objects created in the viewport.

1. Choose **Window > Rendering Editors > Hypershade** from the main menubar; the **Hypershade** window is displayed. Choose the **Lambert** shader from the **Create** area; a **lambert** shader is created in the **Work Area**. Next, change the name of the lambert shader to **box**. Now, select the box in the viewport and press and hold the right mouse button on the **box** shader in the **Hypershade** window; a marking menu is displayed. Choose **Assign Material to Selection** from the marking menu; the selected shader is applied on the **box** in the viewport.

2. Double-click on the **box** shader; the **Attribute Editor** is displayed on the right in the viewport. Set the color of the **Color** attribute to white by moving the slider to the right.

3. Choose the **Phong** shader from **Create** area in the **Hypershade** window; a **Phong** shader is created in the **Work Area**. Rename the phong shader to **glass**. Select the glass from the viewport and press and hold the right mouse button on the **glass** shader in the **Hypershade** window; a marking menu is displayed. Choose **Assign Material to Selection** from the marking menu; the **glass** shader is applied to the glass.

4. Double-click on the **glass** shader in the **Hypershade** window; the **Attribute Editor** is displayed. Set the **Color** attribute to black to change the color of the glass. Next, choose the **Transparency** color box from the **Attribute Editor**; the **Color History** palette is displayed. Specify the **HSV** values in the palette as given below:

H: **202**   S: **0.0**   V: **0.9**

Set the **Diffuse** attribute value to **0.1** in the **Attribute Editor**.

5. Expand the **Specular Shading** attribute tab in the **Attribute Editor** to set the reflection properties of the glass. Set the value in **Cosine Power** to **100** and the value in **Specular Color** to **white**. Similarly, set the **Reflectivity** value to **0.2**.

6. Expand the **Raytrace Options** attribute tab in the **Attribute Editor** and select the

Refractions check box to switch on the refraction for rendering. Next, set the value of **Refractive Index** to **1.520** and **Refraction Limit** to **10**. Choose **Render the current frame (Maya Software)** from the status line to render the scene. Figure 12-38 shows the rendered image of the glass.

7. Choose **Window > Rendering Editors > Hypershade** from the main menubar; the **Hypershade** window is displayed. Choose the **Phong** shader from the **Create** area and rename this shader to **water**.

8. Choose **Display > UI Elements > Channel Box / Layer Editor** from the main menubar; a **Channel box** is displayed. Hide the **glass** layer, as shown in Figure 12-39, by choosing the V mark in the layer editor; only the water mesh is displayed in the viewport, as shown in Figure 12-40.

Figure 12-38 The rendered image of the glass

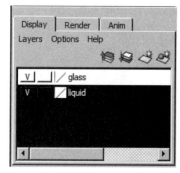

*Figure 12-39 Hiding the **glass** layer*

9. Select the water mesh in the viewport. Next, select the **water** shader from the **Hypershade** window and then press and hold the right mouse button over it; a marking menu is displayed. Choose the **Assign Material to Selection** option from the marking menu; the **water** shader is applied to the water mesh.

10. Double-click on the **water** shader in the **Hypershade** window; the **Attribute Editor** is displayed with various attributes of the **water** shader. Set the color in the **Color** attribute to **black**. Next, choose the

Figure 12-40 The water mesh

Transparency color box; the **Color History** palette is displayed. Set the **HSV** values in the **Color History** palette as follows:

H: **202**   S: **0.5**   V: **0.4**

Set the **Diffuse** value to **0.8** to adjust the brightness level of the glass.

11. Expand the **Specular Shading** attribute area in the **Attribute Editor** to set the reflectivity level of the glass. In this attribute area, set the value in the **Cosine Power** edit box to **120** and **Specular Color** to **white**. Also, set the **Reflectivity** value to **0.2** and **Reflected Color** to **white**.

12. Expand the **Raytrace Options** attribute area in the **Attribute Editor** and select the **Refractions** check box. Next, set **Refractive Index** to **1.360** and **Refraction Limit** to **6**.

13. Choose **Display > UI Elements > Channel Box / Layer Editor** from the main menubar; the **channel box / layer editor** is displayed. Make the glass layer visible in the layer editor as discussed in the earlier steps. Choose the **Render the current frame (Maya Software)** button from the status line to render the scene. Figure 12-41 shows the rendered glass after applying the raytrace attributes to it.

Figure 12-41 The rendered glass after applying the raytrace attributes

14. Open the **Hypershade** window and choose the **Lambert** shader from the **Create** area; a new **lambert** shader is created. Rename the **lambert** shader to straw. Select the straw from the viewport and then select the **straw** shader from the **Hypershade** window. Next, press and hold the right mouse button on the **straw** shader; a marking menu is displayed. Choose **Assign Material to Selection** from the marking menu to apply the shader to the straw in the viewport.

15. Double-click on the **straw** shader in the **Hypershade** window; the **Attribute Editor** displays the properties of the **straw** shader. Next, choose the **color** box from the **Color** attribute in the **Attribute Editor**; the **Color History** palette is displayed. Enter the following **HSV** values in the **Color History** palette:

H: **55**   S: **0.2**   V: **0.9**

Setting Light in the Scene
In this section, you need to add a spot light to the scene.

1.   Choose **Create > Lights > Spot Light** from the main menubar; a spot light is created in the viewport. Next, choose **Display > UI Elements > Channel Box / Layer Editor** from

the main menubar; a **Channel box** is displayed. To align the light in the viewport, set the values of the spot light in the **Channel box** as follows:

TranslateX: **5**   TranslateY: **21**   TranslateZ: **8**
RotateX: **-60**   RotateY: **35**   RotateZ: **-5**

2. Choose **Window > Attribute Editor** from the main menubar and then set the **Intensity** value to **800** and the **Decay Rate** value to **Quadratic**. Set the values for the remaining options as follows:

Cone Angle: **120**   Penumbra Angle: **1**   Dropoff: **5**

3. Expand the **mental ray** tab of the **Attribute Editor** to activate the **mental ray** in the viewport. Next, select the **Emit Photons** check box in the **Caustics and Global Illumination** attribute area; the light starts emitting photons in the scene. Set the values of **Photon Intensity** to **25000** and **Caustic Photons** to **20000**.

Setting the mental Ray Rendering Attributes

In this section, you need to set the **mental ray** rendering attributes for rendering the scene because the normal scanline rendering will give the output, as shown in Figure 12-42. By setting the **mental ray** rendering attributes, you will create photons and caustics in the scene.

1. Choose **Window > Setting Preferences > Plug-in Manager** from the main menubar; the Plug-in Manager dialog box is displayed. Select the **Loaded and Autoload** check boxes from the **Mayatomr.mll plug-in** to activate the mental ray renderer. Choose the **Refresh** button and then the **Close** button from the **Plug-in Manager** dialog box; the **mental ray** renderer gets activated in the **Render Settings** window.

2. Choose **Window > Rendering Editors > Render Settings** from the main menubar; the **Render Settings** window is displayed. Select **mental ray** from the **Render Using** drop-down list to set the mental ray renderer as the current renderer. Next, choose the **Indirect Lighting** tab and then expand the **Caustics** attributes area in the window. In the **Caustics** attribute area, select the **Caustics** check box; the caustics are activated in the scene.

Figure 12-42 *Image created by using the normal scanline rendering*

3. Now, choose the **Quality** tab from the **Render Settings** window and expand the **Raytracing** attribute area in the **Render Settings** window. Next, set the values as follows:

Reflections: **2**   Refractions: **6**   Max Trace Depth: **8**
Shadows: **2**

4. Set the view in the viewport from where you want to render the glass. Choose **Render the current frame (mental ray)** from the status line to render the scene, as shown in Figure 12-43.

Note
*You can change the values of different parameters in the **Render Settings** window to get various rendering effects.*

Saving the File
In this section, you need to save the file.

1. Choose **File > Save Scene** from the main menubar; the **Save As** dialog box is displayed.

Figure 12-43 The final rendered image of the glass

As the project folder is already set, by default the path *\Documents\Maya_Tutorials\c12_tut1\ scenes* is displayed in **Look In** text box of the dialog box.

2. Enter **c12_tut1** in the **File name** text box and then select **Maya Binary** from the **Files of type** drop-down list. Next, choose the **Save As** button.

You can view the final rendered image of the model by downloading the *c12_Maya_2012_render.zip* file from *http://www.cadcim.com*.

Self-Evaluation Test

Answer the following questions and then compare them to those given at the end of this chapter:

1. Which of the following is a refraction pattern formed due to light reflecting on highly transparent objects?

   (a) **Global Illumination**   (b) **Caustics**
   (c) **Final Gather**   (d) **Raytrace**

2. Which of the following options is used to produce the accurate renderings of daylight scenes?

   (a) **Physical sun and sky**   (b) **Daylight**
   (c) **Volume light**   (d) None of these

3. The_____ renderer generates images with outstanding quality and unsurpassed realism as well as gives scalable performance.

4. In Maya, the _____ algorithm is used to calculate the movement of light rays.

5. _____ is a series of photons taken at different exposure levels and then combined into a high range image format.

6. The _____ check box is used to emit photons from a selected object or light.

7. In Maya, the mental ray rendering does not support spot lights. (T/F)

8. The **Mayatomr.mll** plug-in is used to activate the mental ray rendering. (T/F)

9. In Maya, the vector renderer cannot render bump maps, displacement maps, and Maya fluid effects. (T/F)

10. The **Caustic Filter Kernel** option is used to make the caustics smooth on rendering. (T/F)

Review Questions

Answer the following questions:

1. Which of the following rendering options yields extremely realistic shading effects?

    (a) **Caustics**   (b) **Final gather**
    (c) **Global illumination**   (d) **Raytracing**

2. Which of the following techniques has a greater dynamic range of values between the light and dark areas than any other normal digital imaging techniques?

    (a) **Global illumination**   (b) **Final gather**
    (c) **Caustics**   (d) **HDRI**

3. The _____ and _____ define the final gather rays sampling region.

4. The **Physical Sun and Sky** attribute uses the _____ and _____ shaders.

5. The _____ is a process in which the incident-radiated energy is retained completely by an object.

6. You need to understand _____, _____, and _____ to learn the concept of **Color Bleeding**.

7. The **Reflection** option is used to set the maximum number of times a ray can refract through a non-opaque object. (T/F)

8. Reflection is a change in the direction of light at the interface between two dissimilar media such that the light returns to the medium from where it originated. (T/F)

9. The **Curve tolerance** edit box is used to set the outline of a rendered object. (T/F)

10. Refraction is a phenomenon in which light deviates while passing from one medium to another medium. (T/F)

Exercises

Exercise 1

Create a scene, as shown in Figure 12-44. Apply textures to the scene and then render it using the mental ray renderer to get the output shown in Figure 12-45. You can view the final rendered image of this scene by downloading the file *c12_maya_2012_render.zip* from *http://www.cadcim.com*. The path of file is as follows:

Textbooks > Animation and Visual Effects > Maya > Autodesk Maya 2012: A Comprehensive Guide

(Expected time: 45 min)

Figure 12-44 *Scene before rendering*

Figure 12-45 *Scene after rendering*

Exercise 2

Open the model file that you had created in Exercise 5 of Chapter 3. Next, apply texture to it and create a tree on its left using the **Visor** window, as shown in Figure 12-46. Next, add lights and render the scene using the mental ray renderer to get the output, as shown in Figure 12-47. You can view the final rendered scene by downloading the file *c12_maya_2012_render_zip* from *http://www.cadcim.com*. The path of file is mentioned in Exercise 1.

(Expected time: 45 min)

Figure 12-46 *The tree created on the left of the model*

Figure 12-47 *The rendered scene*

Answers to Self-Evaluation Test
1. b, **2.** a, **3. mental ray**, **4. Raytrace**, **5.** HDRI, **6. Emit Photons**, **7.** F, **8.** T, **9.** T, **10.** T

Chapter 13

Particle System

Learning Objectives

After completing this chapter, you will be able to:

- *Create particles*
- *Create emitters*
- *Adjust the render attributes of particles*
- *Collide particles*
- *Use the hardware buffer rendering*
- *Use different types of fields and pre-defined effects*

INTRODUCTION TO PARTICLES

The particle system in Maya is used to create sci-fi visual effects in a scene. In this chapter, you will learn how to create different effects using particles. Apart from that, you will learn about the concept of **Goal** which is used to control the flow of particles, and create predefined particle effects in Maya. Moreover, you will also learn about the tools used with particle systems.

Creating Particles

Particles are points in 3D space and can be grouped together to create different effects. To create particles in 3D space, first select the **Dynamics** menu set from the menuset drop-down list in the status line. Next, choose **Particles > Particle Tool** from the main menubar and click in the viewport; a particle will be created in 3D space. By default, Maya creates one particle on a single click. You can change the settings of the options used in the particle creation method to create more particles per click. To do so, choose **Particles > Particle Tool > Option Box** from the main menubar; the **Particle Tool** settings window with the attributes of the particle will be displayed on the right of the viewport, as shown in Figure 13-1. Various options in this window are discussed next.

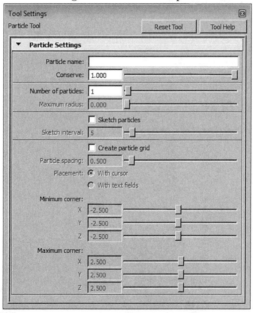

*Figure 13-1 The **Particle Tool** settings window*

Particle name

Enter a name for the particle in the **Particle name** input box. Naming a particle helps you identify that particle in the **Outliner** window. By default, the name **particle1** is assigned to the particle created.

Conserve

The **Conserve** attribute is used to influence the motion of particles.

Number of particles

The **Number of particles** attribute is used to specify the number of particles to be created in the viewport with a single click. The default value of this attribute is 1. If you specify a value greater than 1, the **Maximum radius** attribute will get highlighted. The **Maximum radius** attribute is used to specify a spherical region in which the specified number of particles will be randomly distributed. After creating the desired number of particles in the viewport, press the ENTER key; the complete particle system will be created.

 Note
If you want to undo the last action performed in the viewport, press the BACKSPACE key. This process can only function till you have not pressed the ENTER key.

Sketch particles

The **Sketch particles** attribute is used to sketch a continuous stream of particles. It works similar to the pencil tool used in other 2D software applications. To create a stream of particles, select the **Sketch particles** check box, press and hold the left mouse button in the viewport and drag the mouse to create the particle stream. Press ENTER to create the complete particle system in the viewport. On selecting the **Sketch particles** check box, the **Sketch interval** edit box will be highlighted. This edit box is used to specify the spacing between the particles while sketching a continuous stream of particles. Higher the value specified in this edit box, more will be the distance between the particles. Note that the **Sketch particles** attribute will work only when the value set in the **Sketch interval** option is 1.

Create particle grid

The **Create particle grid** check box is used to create a 2D grid of particles in the workspace. To create a grid of particles, select this check box and click once in the viewport. This location will be considered as the first point of the grid particles. Next, click at a location that is diagonal to the first point and press ENTER; the grid of particles will be created. On selecting this check box, the **Particle spacing** and **Placement** options will be enabled. The **Particle spacing** edit box is used to specify the spacing between particles in the particle grid. Next, in the **placement** option. You can select the **With cursor** radio button to set the particle grid by using the cursor or select the **With text fields** radio button to set the grid coordinates manually.

Creating Emitters

Emitters are the objects that emit particles continuously from a source. Emitters can be used to create various effects such as fireworks, smoke, fire, and so on. To create an emitter, choose **Particles > Create Emitter** from the main menubar; the emitter will be created in the viewport, as shown in Figure 13-2.

Figure 13-2 The emitter

You can modify the attributes of an emitter depending on your need. To do so, choose **Particles > Create Emitter > Option Box** from the main menubar; the **Emitter Options (Create)** dialog box will be displayed, as shown in Figure 13-3. Various attributes in this dialog box are discussed next.

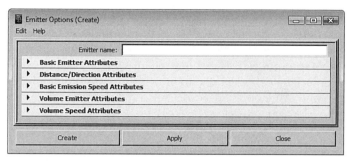

*Figure 13-3 The **Emitter Options (Create)** dialog box*

Emitter name

The options in this area are used to specify the name of the emitter. Naming an emitter lets you identify the emitter in the outliner. To name an emitter, enter a name in the input box. By default, emitter1 is displayed as the name of the emitter created.

Basic Emitter Attributes

This area of the dialog box is used to set the basic attributes of an emitter, as shown in Figure 13-4. All attributes in the **Basic Emitter Attributes** area are discussed next.

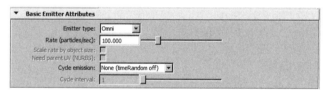

*Figure 13-4 The **Basic Emitter Attributes** area*

Emitter type

The **Emitter type** drop-down list is used to select an emitter type. Select the **Omni** emitter type from the drop-down list to emit particles in all directions. Select the **Directional** emitter type if you want the particles to be emitted only in one direction. Select the **Volume** emitter type to emit particles from a closed volume.

Rate (particles/sec)

The **Rate (particles/sec)** attribute is used to set the average rate at which the particles will be emitted per second from an emitter. To set the value for this attribute, enter a value in the edit box or adjust the slider bar. The default value of this attribute is 100.

Scale rate by object size

Select the **Scale rate by object size** check box if you want the particles to be emitted as per the size of the object. By default, this check box is inactive. To make it active, select the **Volume** emitter type from the **Emitter type** drop-down list. Larger the size of the object, more will be the particles emitted.

Cycle emission

The **Cycle emission** drop-down list is used to restart the emission of particles. Select the **Frame (timeRandom on)** option from this drop-down list; the **Cycle interval** input box below this drop-down list will get activated. Enter a value in this input box to specify the number of frames after which the emission of the particles will restart.

Distance/Direction Attributes

The **Distance/Direction Attributes** area is used to specify the distance and the direction for particle emission, as shown in Figure 13-5. The attributes under this area are discussed next.

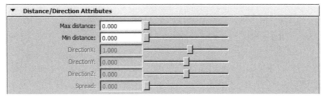

Figure 13-5 The **Distance/Direction Attributes** area

Max distance

The **Max distance** attribute is used to set the maximum distance of particles from the emitter.

Min distance

The **Min distance** attribute is used to set the minimum distance of particles from the emitter. Note that the minimum distance value should always be smaller than the maximum distance value.

The **Min distance** and **Max distance** attributes will be enabled only when the **Omni** and **Directional** emitter types are selected.

Direction

The **DirectionX** attribute is used to set the direction of emission of particles along the X direction. Similarly, you can set the direction of emission of particles along the Y and Z axes by entering values in the **DirectionY** and **DirectionZ** edit boxes, respectively. Note that these attributes will become active only when the **Directional** emitter type is selected.

Spread

The **Spread** attribute is used to set the spread angle for the particles. This attribute is inactive by default. To activate it, select the **Directional** emitter type from the attribute editor.

Basic Emission Speed Attributes

The **Basic Emission Speed Attributes** area is used to set the speed attributes of the particles emitted from the emitter, as shown in Figure 13-6. The attributes in this area are discussed next.

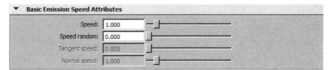

*Figure 13-6 The **Basic Emission Speed Attributes** area*

Speed

The **Speed** attribute is used to set the speed of the emitted particles. Enter **1** to set the default speed; **0.5** to reduce the speed to half; and **2** to double the speed.

Speed random

The **Speed random** attribute is used to add randomness to the emission speed.

Tangent speed

The **Tangent speed** attribute is used to set the magnitude of the tangent component of the emitted particles.

Normal speed

The **Normal speed** attribute is used to set the magnitude of the normal component of the emitted particles.

Render Attributes

The **Render Attributes** area is used to set the shape of the particles in the viewport. Various types of particles are points, sphere, cloud, and so on. By default, **Points** is selected in the **Particle Render Type** drop-down list. To change the particle render type, choose the particles created in the viewport. Next, open the **Attribute Editor** and choose the **particleShape1** tab in it. Next, expand the **Render Attributes** area in the attribute editor, as shown in Figure 13-7.

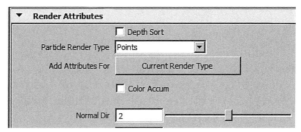

*Figure 13-7 The **Render Attributes** area*

Select the required option from the **Particle Render Type** drop-down list to change the shape of particles in the viewport. Next, choose the **Current Render Type** button located next to the **Add Attributes For** option; the attributes of the selected particle type will be displayed. Now, set the attributes as per your requirement.

Creating Goals

A goal is used to set the movement of particles toward a particular direction. You can create the trailing effect of particles by using goals. To create a goal, select the particles that you want to be affected by the goal. Next, press and hold the SHIFT key and then select the object that you want to make as goal. Now, choose **Particles > Goal** from the main menubar to set the goal for the selected objects. Play the animation to create the movement of the selected particles moving toward the goal. You can also set multiple goals for a particle system. To do so, repeat the steps discussed in the previous paragraph with other particles. You can set the weight value on a goal object to specify the particle attracting power. To do so, choose **Particles > Goal > Option Box** from the main menubar; the **Goal Options** dialog box will be displayed, as shown in Figure 13-8. You can set the **Goal weight** value between 0 and 1. The default value in the **Goal Weight** edit box is 0.5. You can also make a camera act as a goal object. To do so, follow the steps discussed earlier.

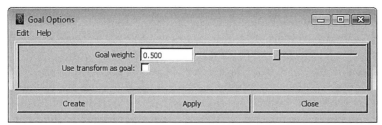

*Figure 13-8 The **Goal Options** dialog box*

Colliding Particles

In Maya, you can collide particles with the specified surface. To do so, select the particles, press SHIFT, and then select the object to which you want the particles to collide. Now, choose **Particles > Make Collide** from the main menubar to make the particles collide with the selected object. Play the animation to see the collision effect. You can also make changes in the collision effect. To do so, choose **Particles > Make Collide > Option Box** from the main menubar; the **Collision Options** dialog box will be displayed, as shown in Figure 13-9. The attributes of the **Collision Options** dialog box are discussed next.

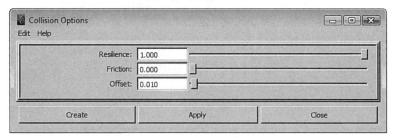

*Figure 13-9 The **Collision Options** dialog box*

Resilience

The **Resilience** attribute is used to set the value upto which the particles will bounce when they collide with a surface. To set this parameter, enter a value in the **Resilience** edit box or adjust the slider bar on its right. Enter **0** for zero bounce and **1** for maximum bounce. The default value of this attribute is 1.

Friction

The **Friction** attribute is used to set the velocity of colliding particles. To set the value of this attribute, enter a value in the **Friction** edit box or adjust the slider bar on its right. If you want the particles to remain unaffected, enter **0**. The default value of this attribute is 0.

Rendering Particles

The rendering of particles depends on the particle type selected in the viewport. In Maya, there are two types of particles: **Hardware** and **Software**. The Hardware rendered particles can have various render types such as **Multipoint**, **Multistreak**, **Numeric**, **Points**, **Spheres**, **Sprites**, or **Streak**. Similarly, the Software rendered particles can have various render types such as **Blobby Surface**, **Cloud**, or **Tube**. The hardware rendering takes less time to render as compared to software rendering, but the render output of software rendering is better as compared to the Hardware renderer. However, you can render the hardware supported particles. To do so, choose **Window > Rendering Editors > Hardware Render Buffer** from the main menubar, the **Hardware Render Buffer** window will be displayed, as shown in Figure 13-10. You can also render **Points**, **MultiPoint**, **Spheres**, **Sprites**, **Streak**, and **MultiStreak** particle types using the **mental ray** renderer.

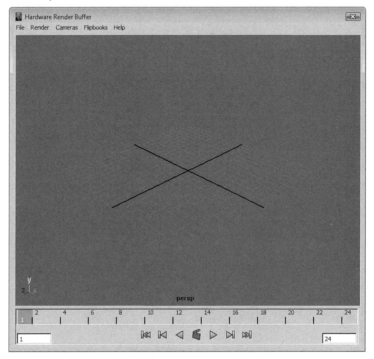

Figure 13-10 The **Hardware Render Buffer** *window*

Note

*The **Hardware renderer** will work only when there is a graphic card in your system. In other words, you cannot produce any effect without a graphic card.*

Animating Particles Using Fields

Fields are the physical properties that simulate the motion of natural forces. In Maya, there are a number of physical fields that can be used to animate the motion of particles, or soft or rigid bodies. To access the fields in Maya, select the **Dynamics** menuset option from the menuset drop-down list in the status line. Various types of fields available in this drop-down list are discussed next.

Air

Menubar:	Fields > Air

The **Air** field is used to simulate the effect of moving air. This field can be applied to objects such that the particles start moving with the movement of the selected object. To set this field, create a grid of particles in the viewport, and select it. Next, choose **Fields > Air > Option Box** from the main menubar; the **Air Options** dialog box will be displayed. Choose the **Wake** button from the dialog box .The **Wake** button is used to set the **Air** field attributes to default settings so that the air seems to be pulled along by a moving object. Then, choose the **Create** button. Now, create a poly sphere in the viewport and align it with the particles. Next, animate the poly sphere across the particle grid from one end to the other. Choose **Windows > Outliner** from the main menubar; the **Outliner** window will be displayed. Select the **airField1** option from the **Outliner** window, press and hold the SHIFT key, and then select the polysphere. Next, choose **Fields > Use Selected as Source of Field** from the main menubar to link particles to the polysphere. Preview the animation; the particles will move along the movement of the sphere. You can also make changes in the **Air** field. To do so, choose **Fields > Air > Option Box** from the main menubar; the **Air Options** dialog box will be displayed, as shown in Figure 13-11. You can change the settings in this dialog box as per your requirement.

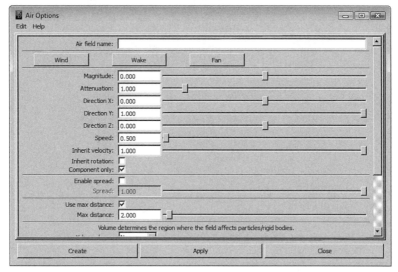

*Figure 13-11 The **Air Options** dialog box*

Drag

Menubar:	Fields > Drag

The **Drag** field is used to apply an opposite force on an object that is animated with dynamic motion. For example, you can add this field to the water fountain to control the rise of water. You can also make changes in the attributes of the **Drag** field. To do so, choose **Fields > Drag > Option Box** from the main menubar; the **Drag Options** dialog box will be displayed, as shown in Figure 13-12. Make necessary changes in the dialog box.

Gravity

Menubar:	Fields > Gravity

The **Gravity** field is used to simulate earth's gravitational force on to a particle system such that the particles start accelerating in a particular direction. To apply this field, create an emitter in the viewport and choose **Window > Outliner** from the main menubar. Next, select the particles emitted from the emitter. Now, choose **Fields > Gravity** from the main menubar and preview the animation; the particles will accelerate in the specified direction. You can also set attributes of the gravitational force. To do so, choose **Fields > Gravity > Option Box** from the main menubar; the **Gravity Options** dialog box will be displayed, as shown in Figure 13-13. Make necessary changes in the dialog box and choose the **Create** button.

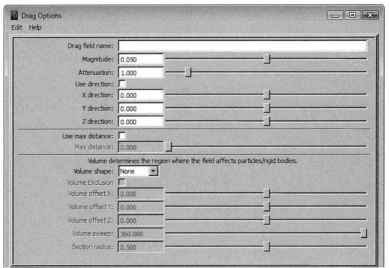

*Figure 13-12 The **Drag Options** dialog box*

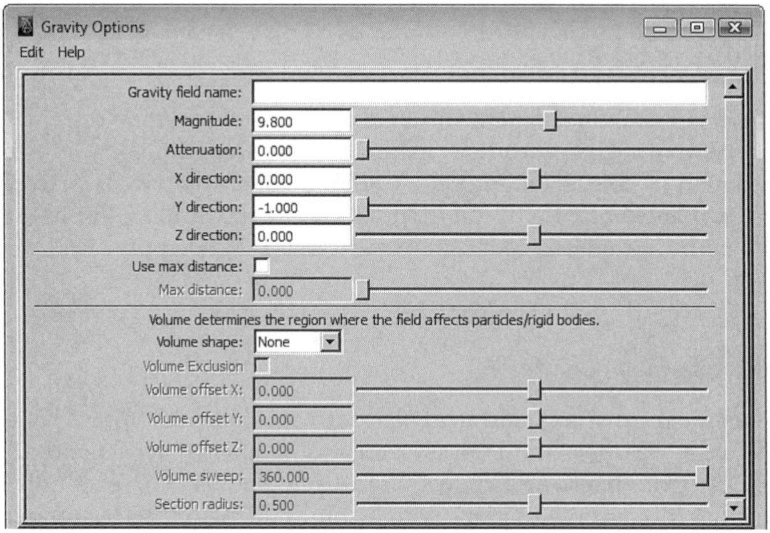

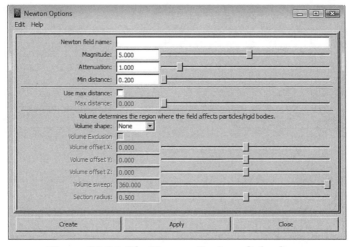

Figure 13-13 *The Gravity Options dialog box*

Newton

Menubar: Fields > Newton

The **Newton** field is used to pull a particle toward it. This field works according to Sir Issac Newton's theory of universal gravitation, which states that every point mass attracts every other point mass by a force pointing along the line intersecting both points. This force is proportional to the product of the point masses and inversely proportional to the square of the distance between the point masses. The force between the objects decreases with the increase in the distance between the objects.

To change the default settings of the **Newton** field, choose **Fields > Newton > Option Box** from the main menubar; the **Newton Options** dialog box will be displayed, as shown in Figure 13-14. Set the required attributes in this dialog box as per your requirement.

Figure 13-14 *The Newton Options dialog box*

Radial

Menubar:	Fields > Radial

The **Radial** field works like a magnet. This field can be used to attract or repel any object or particle in the viewport. The procedure of applying the **Radial** field is similar to the fields discussed earlier. To set the attributes of the **Radial** field, choose **Fields > Radial > Option Box** from the main menubar; the **Radial Options** dialog box will be displayed, as shown in Figure 13-15. Set the attributes as per requirement in this dialog box.

Turbulence

Menubar:	Fields > Turbulence

The **Turbulence** field is used to add irregularity to an object. To apply this field, create a NURBS plane in the viewport and then increase the number of height and width segments of the plane. Select the plane and choose **Soft/Rigid Bodies > Create Soft Bodies** from the main menubar to convert the plane into a soft body. Again, select the plane from the viewport and choose **Fields > Turbulence** from the main menubar; the **Turbulence** field will be applied on the plane. Now, play the animation to see the turbulence effect in the viewport. Figure 13-16 shows the plane before applying the **Turbulence** field and Figure 13-17 shows the plane after applying the **Turbulence** field. You can also make changes in the turbulence field. To do so, choose **Fields > Turbulence > Option Box** from the main menubar; the **Turbulence Options** dialog box will be displayed, as shown in Figure 13-18. Make necessary changes in the dialog box.

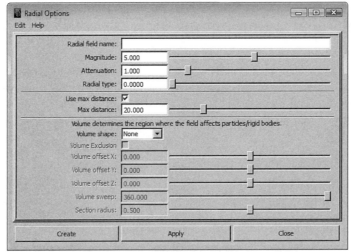

Figure 13-15 *The **Radial Options** dialog box*

Tip. *Soft body dynamics is a part of physics that reacts to dynamic fields, and not to collisions. A soft body is a polygonal or NURBS object that lets you create unyielding shapes in Maya. In Maya, when two objects collide with each other, they pass through each other, but the soft bodies collide together to create unyielding shapes.*

Uniform

Menubar: Fields > Uniform

The **Uniform** field is used to move particles in a uniform direction. To apply this field, create
a grid of particles in the viewport. Now, select the particles and choose **Fields > Uniform**
from the main menubar; a uniform field is applied to the selected particles. Preview the
animation to see the particles moving in one direction. You can make changes in the **Uniform**
field attributes. To do so, choose **Fields > Uniform > Option Box** from the main menubar;
the **Uniform Options** dialog box will be displayed, as shown in Figure 13-19. Set the required
attributes in this dialog box.

Figure 13-16 *A plane before applying
the **Turbulence** field*

Figure 13-17 *A plane after applying
the **Turbulence** field*

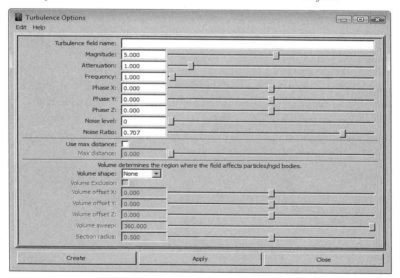

Figure 13-18 *The **Turbulence Options** dialog box*

*Figure 13-19 The **Uniform Options** dialog box*

Vortex

Menubar:	Fields > Vortex

The **Vortex** field is used to pull particles or objects in a circular or spiral path. For example, you can apply this field to create a tornado effect or a universe scene showing several galaxies. To apply this field, create a grid of particles in the viewport. Now, select particles and choose **Fields > Vortex** from the main menubar; the field will be applied to the particles. Now, play the animation to view the effect of the **Vortex** field effect. You can also modify the attributes of this field. To do so, choose **Fields > Vortex > Option Box** from the main menubar; the **Vortex Options** dialog box will be displayed, as shown in Figure 13-20. Now, you can set values in this dialog box based on your requirement.

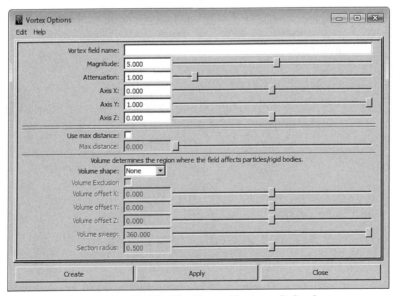

*Figure 13-20 The **Vortex Options** dialog box*

Volume Axis

Menubar: Fields > Volume Axis

The **Volume Axis** field is used to move particles uniformly in all directions, but in a specified volume. The procedure for applying this field is similar to procedures discussed earlier. Like other fields, you can change the attributes of this field as well. To do so, choose **Fields > Volume Axis > Option Box** from the main menu bar; the **Volume Axis Options** dialog box will be displayed, as shown in Figure 13-21. In this dialog box, you can set the values for different attributes as per your requirement.

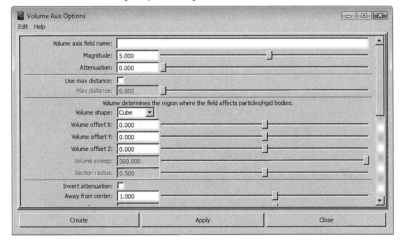

Figure 13-21 *The **Volume Axis Options** dialog box*

CREATING EFFECTS

In Maya, there are some in-built scripts that can be used to create different types of complex effects and animations in a scene. These effects are discussed next.

Creating the Fire Effect

Menubar: Effects > Create Fire

The **Create Fire** effect is used to create a realistic fire effect in a scene. To emit fire from an object, first convert the object into a polygon and then choose **Effects > Create Fire** from the main menubar. If you want to emit fire from a number of surfaces or objects, select all objects and choose **Mesh > Combine** from the main menubar; the objects will be combined. Now, select the combined objects and choose **Effects > Create Fire** from the main menubar. Next, play the animation. The emitted particles will appear as circles in the viewport, as shown in Figure 13-22. Render the scene to get the final output, as shown in Figure 13-23.

Figure 13-22 *The fire emitter emitting particles using the* **Cloud** *render type*

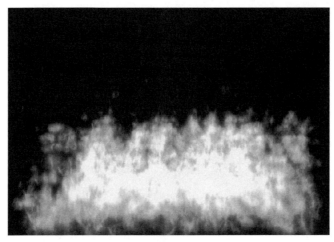

Figure 13-23 *The rendered fire effect*

Creating the Smoke Effect

Menubar: Effects > Create Smoke

The **Create Smoke** effect is used to create smoke in a scene. You can use this effect to emit smoke from an object or a group of objects. To emit smoke from a group of objects, you need to first combine the objects together and then apply the **Smoke** effect on the combined object. To apply the smoke effect, select the object from the viewport and choose **Effects > Create Smoke > Option Box** from the main menubar; the **Create Smoke Effect Options** dialog box will be displayed, as shown in Figure 13-24. Assign a name in the **Sprite image name** edit box and then choose the **Create** button. Next, preview the animation; the smoke will appear to be coming from the object you had selected in the viewport, as shown in Figure 13-25.

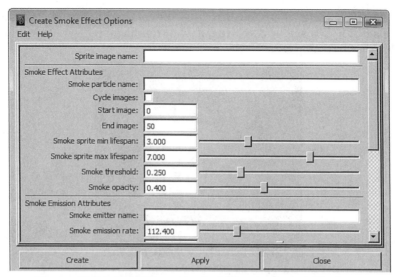

*Figure 13-24 The **Create Smoke Effect Options** dialog box*

Figure 13-25 The smoke emitting from an object

Note

*The **Smoke** effect can only be rendered using the Maya hardware renderer.*

Creating the Fireworks Effect

Menubar: Effects > Create Fireworks

The **Create Fireworks** effect is used to create firework effect in a scene. The fireworks thus created, can be rendered using the Maya software renderer. To create this effect in a scene, choose **Effects > Create Fireworks** from the main menubar; an emitter will be created in the viewport. Play the animation to see the fireworks effect. Render the fireworks effect to get the final result. Figure 13-26 shows the firework effect. The particle streaks in fireworks have pre-applied gravity field. You can set different fireworks attributes by choosing

Effects > Create Fireworks > Option Box from the main menubar; the **Create Fireworks Effect Options** dialog box will be displayed, as shown in Figure 13-27. Now, you can set the required values in this dialog box.

Figure 13-26 The fireworks effect

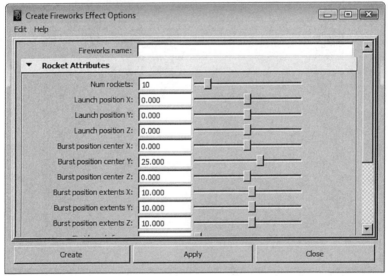

*Figure 13-27 The **Create Fireworks Effect Options** dialog box*

Creating the Lightning Effect

Menubar: Effects > Create Lightning

The **Create Lightning** effect is used to create lightning between two objects. To create the lightning effect, select two objects in the viewport. Next, choose **Effects > Create Lightning** from the main menubar; the lightning bolt will be created between the two objects. The lightning bolt is made up of soft body curves with extruded surfaces. Now, play the animation to view the lightning bolt. Now, render the scene; the lightning effect will appear, as shown in Figure 13-28. You can change the attributes of the lightning effect such as color, glow intensity, glow spread, and much more using the **Create Lightning Effect Options** dialog box. To invoke this dialog box, choose **Effects > Create Lightning > Option Box** from the main menubar; the **Create Lightning Effect Options** dialog box will be displayed, as shown in Figure 13-29. Now, you can change the attribute values in this dialog box.

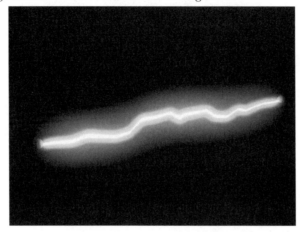

Figure 13-28 The lightning effect

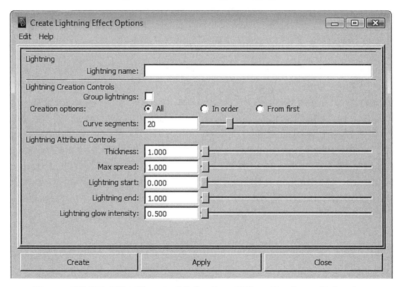

*Figure 13-29 The **Create Lightning Effect Options** dialog box*

Creating the Shatter Effect

Menubar: Effects > Create Shatter

The **Create Shatter** effect is used to break an object or a surface into pieces. In Maya, there are three different types of shatters: surface, solid, and crack. Before applying a shatter, you need to specify the shatter type that you want to apply to an object. To do so, choose **Effects > Create Shatter > Option Box** from the main menubar; the **Create Shatter Effect Options** dialog box will be displayed, as shown in Figure 13-30. You can set the attribute values in this dialog box to create the desired shatter effect.

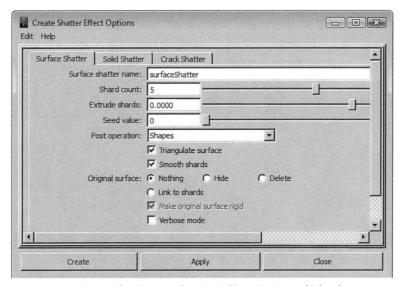

Figure 13-30 The *Create Shatter Effect Options* dialog box

Creating the Curve Flow Effect

Menubar: Effects > Create Curve Flow

The **Create Curve Flow** effect is used to make particles flow along a curve. When you apply this effect, a number of emitters are created along the curve. These emitters control the movement of particles. For example, this effect can be used to create a scene of water flowing from a valley or a waterfall. To create an effect using this option, create a NURBS curve in the viewport, defining the flow of particles. Next, select the curve and choose **Effects > Create Curve Flow** from the main menubar. Now, play the animation to view the effect; a number of flow locators will be created on the curve, as shown in Figure 13-31. Also, the particles will start flowing from the emitter such that they appear to be moving from one end to the other. The flow locators on the curve define the path for the movement of particles. You can also scale the flow locators using the **Scale** tool as per your requirement.

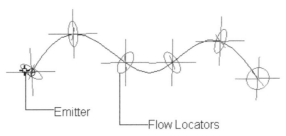

Figure 13-31 The *curve flow*

Creating the Surface Flow Effect

Menubar:	Effects > Create Surface Flow

The **Create Surface Flow** effect is used to create particles over a NURBS surface. The flow of particles changes automatically with the change in the NURBS surface. To apply this effect, first create a NURBS surface in the viewport. Next, choose **Effects > Create Surface Flow** from the main menubar; the effect will be applied on the surface. Now, you can play the animation to view the effect.

TUTORIALS

Tutorial 1

In this tutorial, you will use particles to create the effect of water coming out of a pipe, as shown in Figure 13-32. **(Expected time: 30 min)**

Figure 13-32 Water coming out of a pipe

The following steps are required to complete this tutorial:

a. Set a project folder.
b. Download and open the file.
c. Create an emitter.
d. Set emitter attributes.
e. Create the material for water.
f. Render the scene.
g. Save the scene.

Setting the Project Folder

Before starting a new file, it is recommended that you set the project folder.

1. Set a project with the name *c13_tut1* in the folder *Maya_Tutorials*.

Downloading and Opening the Files

1. Download the *c13_Maya_2012_tut.zip* file from *http://www.cadcim.com*. The path of the file is as follows:

    Textbooks > Animation and Visual Effects > Maya > Autodesk Maya 2012: A Comprehensive Guide

    Extract the contents of the zipped file and save them in the *\Documents* folder.

2. Choose **Scene** from the **File** menu; the **Open File** dialog box is displayed. In this dialog box, browse to the location *c13_Maya_2012_tut* folder and select *c13_tut1_start.mb* file from it. Choose the **Open** button.

3. Choose **Save As** from the main menubar; the **Save As** dialog box is displayed. Browse to the scenes folder at the location *\Documents\Maya\c13_tut1*. Save the file with the name *c13tut1.mb* in this folder.

Creating the Emitter

In this section, you will create an emitter that will emit particles in your scene.

1. Activate the Perspective viewport, if it is not already activated. Now, select the **Dynamics** menuset from the menuset drop-down list in the status line. Choose **Particles > Create Emitter > Option Box** from the main menubar; the **Emitter Options (Create)** dialog box is displayed.

2. Enter **water_flow** in the **Emitter name** input box and select **Volume** from the **Emitter type** drop-down list in the **Basic Emitter Attributes** area.

3. Next, expand the **Volume Emitter Attributes** area and select the **Cylinder** option from the **Volume Shape** drop-down list. Also, expand the **Volume Speed Attributes** area and set the following values in it:

    Away from axis: **0**   Along axis: **10**

    Now, choose the **Create** button from the **Emitter Options (Create)** dialog box; an emitter of the specified attributes is created in the viewport, as shown in Figure 13-33.

 Note
*The **Along Axis** attribute is used to define the speed of particles. More the value of speed, the better will be the movement of particles.*

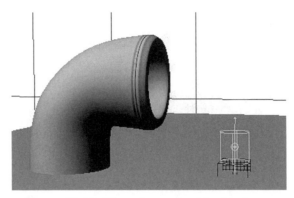

Figure 13-33 *The emitter created in the viewport*

4. Use the **Scale Tool**, **Move Tool**, and **Rotate Tool** in the toolbox to align the emitter with the opening of the pipe, as shown in Figure 13-34.

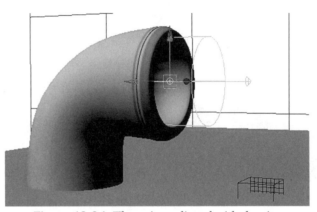

Figure 13-34 *The emitter aligned with the pipe*

Setting Emitter Attributes

In this section, you will set the attributes of the emitter created in the previous step.

1. Select the emitter from the viewport and choose **Display > UI Elements > Attribute Editor** from the main menubar; the **Attribute Editor** is displayed.

2. Choose the **water_flow** attribute tab from the **Attribute Editor**. Next, expand the **Basic Emitter Attributes** attribute area and set the **Rate (Particles/Sec)** attribute value to **8000**. Remember that **Rate (Particles/Sec)** attribute value is used to set the rate at which the emitter emits particles in the viewport. Next, preview the animation; the particles appear to be emitted from the emitter, as shown in Figure 13-35.

3. Next, choose the **particleShape1** attribute tab from the attribute editor; the attributes related to this tab are displayed. Expand the **Lifespan Attributes** (see also **per-particle** tab) attribute area and select the **Constant** option from the **Lifespan Mode** drop-down list to make the lifespan of the particles constant. Set the value of the **Lifespan** option to 2.

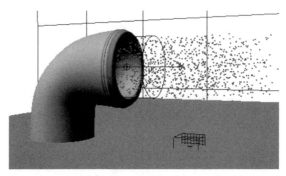

Figure 13-35 Particles being emitted

4. Next, scroll down the **Attribute Editor** and expand the **Render Attributes** attribute area. In this area, select the **Blobby Surface(s/w)** option from the **Particle Render Type** drop-down list; the shape of particles in the viewport changes to blobmesh, as shown in Figure 13-36.

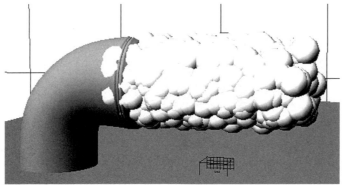

Figure 13-36 The emitter type set to blobmesh

5. Choose the **Current Render Type** button from the **Render Attributes** attribute area in the attribute editor; the attributes of the emitter type are displayed, as shown in Figure 13-37.

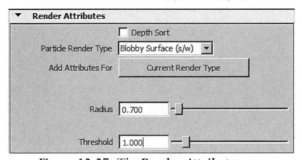

*Figure 13-37 The **Render Attributes** area*

6.　Now, enter the following values in the **Render Attributes** area:

Radius: **0.7**　　　　　　　　　Threshold: **1**

Note that the radius value helps in decreasing the size of the blob mesh particles, whereas the threshold value determines how realistic would be effect on the water. Figure 13-38 shows the particles after modifying the values.

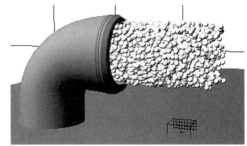

Figure 13-38 *The particles after modifying the radius and threshold values*

7.　Set the timeline to frame **200** and preview the animation; the particles appear to be crossing the front wall. To avoid it, select the particles coming out from the emitter, press and hold the SHIFT key, and select the wall. Now, choose **Particles > Make Collide** from the main menubar to make the particles collide with the plane. Then, preview the animation; the particles do not cross the wall now.

8.　Select the particles from the viewport and choose **Window > Display UI Elements > Channel Box** from the main menubar; the **Channel box** is displayed. Expand the **geoConnector1** attribute area in the **Channel box** and set the following values in it:

Resilience: **0.7**　　　　　　　　Friction Value: **0.7**

9.　Now, select the particles from the viewport and choose **Fields > Gravity** from the main menubar; the **Gravity** field is applied to the particles, resulting in the real-world movement of water, as shown in Figure 13-39.

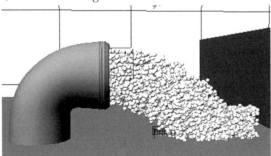

Figure 13-39 *The **Gravity** field applied to the particles*

Creating the Material for Water

In this section, you will create the material for water in the viewport.

1. Choose **Window > Rendering Editors > Hypershade** from the main menubar; the **Hypershade** window is displayed.

2. Choose the **Blinn** shader from the **Create Maya Nodes** area in the **Hypershade** window; the **blinn1** material is created in the **work area** (upper tab). Rename the **blinn1** shader to **water**, as discussed in Chapter 5.

3. Next, create the **Sampler Info** utility node and then the **Blend Colors** utility node in the **Create Maya Nodes** area; three nodes are created in the work area (lower tab), as shown in Figure 13-40.

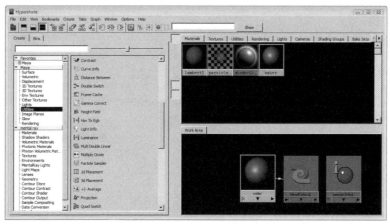

*Figure 13-40 Three nodes created in the **Hypershade** window*

4. Press and hold the middle mouse button over the **samplerInfo1** node, and then drag and drop it over the **blendColors1** node; a flyout is displayed. Choose the **Other** option from the flyout; the **Connection Editor** window is displayed, as shown in Figure 13-41.

5. Select the **facingRatio** option from the **Outputs** area and then the **blender** option from the **Inputs** area of the **Connection Editor** window. Next, close the **Connection Editor** window; the required connection is created between the two attributes.

6. Press and hold the middle mouse button over the **blendColors** node in the **work area** of the **Hypershade** window, and then drag and drop it over the **water** shader; a flyout is displayed. Choose the **Transparency** option from the flyout; the color of the **blendColors** node is linked to the transparency attribute of the **water** shader.

7. Double-click on the **blendColors** node to display its attributes in the **Attribute Editor**. Set the **Color1** attribute to light grey (RGB: 0,0,0.89) and the **Color2** attribute to dark grey (RGB: 0,0,0.341).

8. Now, double-click on the **water** shader; its attributes are displayed in the **Attribute Editor.** Set the **Ambient Color** attribute to bluish green.

9. Expand the **Specular Shading** attribute area and assign the **Brownian** 3D texture map to the **Specular Color** attribute, as discussed in the earlier chapters. On doing so, a realistic effect is added to the flow of water.

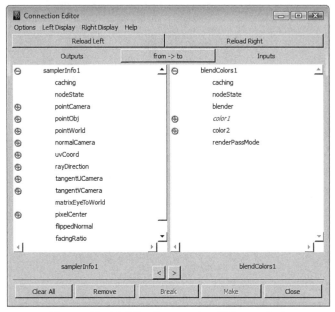

*Figure 13-41 The **Connection Editor** window*

10. Select the particles in the viewport and activate the **Hypershade** window. Next, press and hold the right mouse button over the **water** shader; a marking menu is displayed, as shown in Figure 13-42. Choose the **Assign Material To Selection** option from the marking menu; the **water** shader is applied to particles.

Rendering the Scene
In this section, you will render the scene to view the final output of water.

1. Select the **Rendering** menuset from the menuset drop-down list in the status line. Choose **Window > Rendering Editors > Render Settings** from the main menubar; the **Render Settings** window is displayed in the viewport.

2. Select the **mental ray** option from the **Render Using** drop-down list in the **Render Settings** window; the Maya renderer is set to **mental ray**.

3. Choose **Render > Render Current Frame** from the main menubar to render the scene on the current frame.

Note
*The current scene will take time in rendering depending upon the configuration of the system.
If a system does not have a graphic card, the **Render view** window will not show any output
on rendering.*

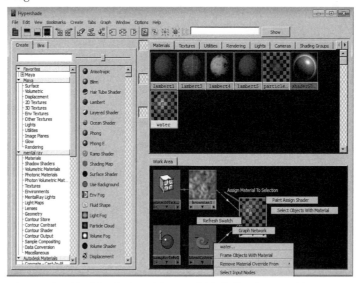

*Figure 13-42 The **Assign Material To Selection** marking menu*

You can also render the complete animation to show the water movement. To do so, follow
the steps given below:

1. Choose **Window > Rendering Editors > Render Settings** from the main menubar; the
    Render Settings window is displayed. Select the **Maya Software** option from the **Render
    Using** drop-down list to set the Maya renderer.

2. Next, choose the **Common** tab from the **Render Settings** window. Now, select **AVI(avi)**
    from the **Image format** drop-down list to set the format of the final render. In the **Frame
    Range** attribute area, set **End frame** to **144** and close the window.

3. Now, choose **Render > Batch Render** from the main menubar to render the animation.
    The render file is saved in the **c13_tut1/images** folder.

 Note
*Do not disturb the system until the rendering is over, as it may take time to render, depending upon
the configuration of the system.*

Saving the File

In this section you will save the file.

1. Choose **File > Save Scene** from the main menubar; the **Save As** dialog box is displayed.

    As the project folder is already set, by default the path *\Documents\Maya_Tutorials\c13_tut1\ scenes* is displayed in **Look In** text box of the dialog box.

2. Enter **c13_tut1** in the **File name** text box and then select **Maya Binary** from the **Files of type** drop-down list. Next, choose the **Save As** button.

You can view the final rendered image of this model by downloading the *c13_maya_2012_render.zip* file from *http://www.cadcim.com*.

Tutorial 2

In this tutorial, you will use particles to create the milkyway effect, as shown in Figure 13-43.

(Expected time: 30 min)

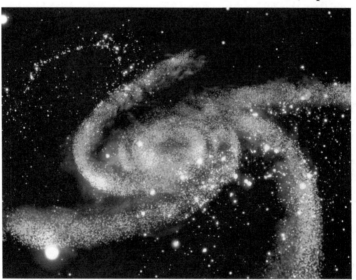

Figure 13-43 The milkyway

The following steps are required to complete this tutorial:

a. Create a project folder.
b. Create particles and apply field on them.
c. Set particle attributes.
d. Save the scene.

Creating the Project Folder

Before starting a new file, it is recommended that you create the project folder.

1. Create the project with the name *c13_tut2* in the folder *Maya_Tutorials*.

Creating Particles and Applying Field on Them

In this section, you will create particles in the viewport and apply field on them.

1. Select the **Dynamics** menuset from the menuset drop-down list in the status line and choose **Particles > Particle Tool > Option Box** from the main menubar; the **Particle Tool** property window is displayed. Set the following parameters in the **Particle Tool** property window:

    Particle name: **Galaxy**   Number of particles: **500**   Conserve: **0.9**
    Maximum radius: **2**   Sketch Particles: **On**

2. Activate the Top viewport and turn on the **Snap to grid** tool from the status line. Alternatively, press and hold the **X** key and drag the cursor in the viewport to create particles such that they form the shape shown in Figure 13-44. Next, press ENTER.

3. Select the particles in the viewport and choose **Fields > Vortex** from the main menubar; the **Vortex** field is applied to particles in the viewport.

4. Choose **Window > Setting/Preferences > Preferences** from the main menubar; the **Preferences** dialog box is displayed. In this dialog box, choose **Time Slider** from the **Categories** area; the **Time Slider: Animation Time Slider** and **Playback Preferences** attributes are displayed on the right of the dialog box.

5. Set the following attribute in the **Preferences** dialog box:

    Playback start/end: **1** to **1000**

    Then, choose the **Save** button.

6. Preview the animation till the shape of the particles in the viewport changes to the shape shown in Figure 13-45. Pause the animation at that particular frame.

7. Select the particles and choose **Solvers > Initial State > Set for Selected** from the main menubar; the shape of the particles at the paused frame is set to the starting frame. Now, go to the frame 1 and check the shape of particles. If the shape of the particles resembles Figure 13-44, you need to repeat Step 8 to get the shape shown in Figure 13-45.

8. Activate the Perspective viewport and select particles from it. Choose **Display > UI Elements > Channel Box/ LayerEditor** from the main menubar; the **Channel box** is displayed. In the **Channel box**, set the RotateX value to **15**; the particles start rotating about the X axis, as shown in Figure 13-46.

Figure 13-44 *Particles created in the Top viewport*

Figure 13-45 *The shape of the particles when activated*

Figure 13-46 *The changed position of particles*

Setting Particle Attributes

In this section, you will set the attributes of the particles in the viewport.

1. Select the particles in the viewport and choose **Display > UI Elements > Attribute Editor** from the main menubar; the attribute editor is displayed.

2. Choose the **galaxyshape** attribute tab from the attribute editor; the attributes related to the shape of particles are displayed.

3. Next, scroll down to the **Render Attributes** area in the attribute editor and set **Particle Render Type** to **Tube[s/w]**; the shape of particles changes. Next, choose the **Current Render Type** button from the Attribute Editor; the **Tube[s/w]** render type particles are displayed in the viewport.

4. Set the following **Tube[s/w]** render type attributes in the **Render Attributes** area:

    Radius 0: **0.1**   Radius 1: **0.1**   Tail Size: **0.1**

    Figure 13-47 displays the shape of the particles in the viewport after setting the values in the **Render Attributes** area.

Figure 13-47 *The particle shape changed to the **Tube(s/w)t** render type*

5. Choose the **particleCloud1** attribute tab from the attribute editor and expand the **Common Material Attributes** area in the **Attribute Editor**. Choose the checker button on the right of the **Color** attribute, as shown in Figure 13-48; the **Create Render Node** window is displayed.

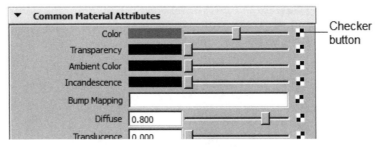

*Figure 13-48 The **Common Material Attributes** area*

6. Choose the **Solid Fractal** attribute from the **3D Textures** area of the **Create Render Node** window and choose the **Close** button; the **Solid Fractal** attributes are displayed in the attribute editor, as shown in Figure 13-49.

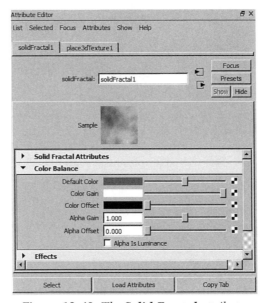

*Figure 13-49 The **Solid Fractal** attributes*

7. Set the **HSV** values for the following attributes in the **Color Balance** area:

Default Color: **22, 0, 0.25**   Color Gain: **65, 1, 1**
Color Offset: **32, 1, 1**

 Note
You can apply different colors to get different galaxy effects on rendering.

8. Invoke the **Render the Current Frame (Maya Software)** tool from the status line to render the scene; the **Render View** window is displayed, as shown in Figure 13-50.

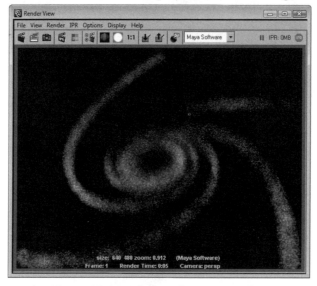

Figure 13-50 The **Render View** window

9. Select the particles in the viewport; the particle attributes are displayed in the **Attribute Editor**. Set the following attribute values in the attribute editor:

Glow Intensity: **0.8**   Density: **5.0**

Note
*The **Glow Intensity** attribute is used to add glow to particles and the **Density** attribute is used to make the particle area more dense. You can change the value of these attributes as per your requirement.*

10. Invoke the **Render the Current Frame (Maya Software)** tool from the status line to render the scene; the glow intensity and the density is applied to the particles in the **Render View window**, as shown in Figure 13-51.

11. Select the particles in the viewport and press CTRL+D to make their duplicates. Rotate the duplicated particles about the Y-axis.

12. Choose **Window > Rendering Editors > Hypershade** from the main menubar; the **Hypershade** window is displayed. Expand the **Volumetric** area in the **Create Maya Nodes** area and choose **Particle Cloud** from the **Hypershade** window; the **particleCloud2** node is created in the **Work Area** (Upper tab) of the **Hypershade** window.

13. Select the duplicated particle galaxy from the viewport and then press and hold the right mouse button over the **particleCloud2** node in the **Hypershade** window; a marking menu is displayed. Select the **Assign Material To Selection** option from the marking menu; the **particleCloud2** is applied on the selected particles.

Figure 13-51 *The glow intensity and the density applied*
to the particles in the **Render View** *window*

14. Double-click on the **particleCloud2** node; the **Attribute Editor** window is displayed. Choose
    the **particleCloud2** attribute tab from the **Attribute Editor** and expand the **Common
    Material Attributes** area.

15. In the **Common Material Attributes** area, choose the checker button on the right of the
    Color attributes; the **Create Render Node** window is displayed.

16. Repeat the step 6 and set the **HSV** values for the following attributes:

    Default Color: **60, 0, 0.5**   Color Gain: **23, 1, 0.8**
    Color Offset: **23, 1, 0**

17. Select the duplicated particles in the viewport; the particle attributes are displayed in the
    attribute editor. Set the following attributes in the **Attribute Editor**:

    Glow Intensity: **1.5**   Density: **2.0**

18. Invoke the **Render the Current Frame (Maya Software)** tool from the status line to render
    the scene; the **Render View** window is displayed, as shown in Figure 13-52.

Saving the Scene

In this section, you will save the scene for further reference.

1. Choose **File > Save Scene** from the main menubar; the **Save As** dialog box is displayed.

   As the project folder is already set, by default the path *\Documents\Maya_Tutorials\c13_tut2\ scenes* is displayed in the **Look In** text box of the dialog box.

2. Enter **c13_tut2** in the **File name** text box and then select **Maya Binary** from the **Files of type** drop-down list. Next, choose the **Save As** button.

You can view the final rendered image of this model by downloading the *c13_maya_2012_render.zip* file from *http://www.cadcim.com*.

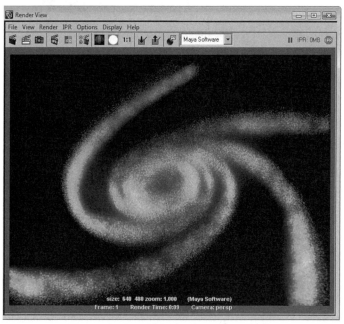

Figure 13-52 The **Render View** window

Tip. *You can also enhance the quality of your scene by applying some paint strokes to the scene. To do so, open the **Visor** window and expand the **galactic** paint stroke. Next, apply different paint strokes to get the final result on rendering. The final rendered image of milkyway is shown in Figure 13-53.*

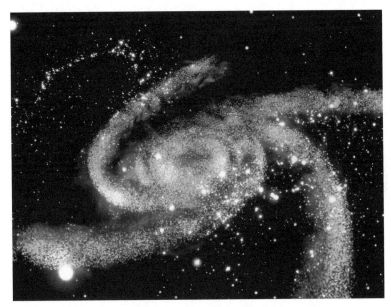

Figure 13-53 *The milkyway*

Self-Evaluation Test

Answer the following questions and then compare them to those given at the end of this chapter:

1. Which of the following attributes is used to sketch a continuous stream of particles?

   (a) **Sketch Particles**   (b) **Number of Particles**
   (c) **Grid Particles**   (d) None of these

2. Which of the following forces is used to exert opposite force on the object that is animated with dynamic motion?

   (a) **Gravity**   (b) **Turbulence**
   (c) **Vortex**   (d) **Drag**

3. _____ are physical properties that simulate the motion of natural forces.

4. The particle streaks in fireworks have a pre-applied _____ field applied to them.

5. The _____ effect is used to break an object or a surface into n number of pieces.

6. The **Create Surface Flow** effect is used to create particles over a _____ surface.

7. The **Uniform** field is used to move an particle in a uniform direction. (T/F)

8. The **Volume Axis** field creates a field to push particles within a volume axis. (T/F)

9. The **Turbulence** field is used to add an irregularity to an object. (T/F)

10. The **Gravity** field is used to simulate the effect of moving air. (T/F)

Review Questions

Answer the following questions:

1. Which of the following laws states that every point mass attracts every other point mass by a force pointing along the line intersecting both points?

    (a) **Newton's law**   (b) **Kirchoff's law**
    (c) **Gravitational law**   (d) None of these

2. Which of the following fields is used to simulate earth's gravitational force on to the particle system?

    (a) **Gravity**   (b) **Turbulence**
    (c) **Newton**   (d) **Air**

3. The _____ field is used to move particles uniformly in all directions, but within a specified volume.

4. The _____ effect is used to create lightning between two objects.

5. The smoke effect can only be rendered using the Maya _____ renderer.

6. The lightning effect is used to create on a single object. (T/F)

7. The **Radial** field is used to add irregularity to an object. (T/F)

8. A goal is used to set the movement of particles toward a particular direction. (T/F)

9. The **Normal Speed** attribute is used to set the magnitude of the normal component of the emitted particles. (T/F)

10. The **Vortex** field is used to push particles or objects in a circular or spiral path. (T/F)

Exercises

Exercise 1

Create the fireworks effect over a city, as shown in Figure 13-54, using the pre-effects given in the **Visor** window. You can view the final rendered image of this model by downloading the *c13_maya_2012_render.zip* file from *http://www.cadcim.com*. The path of file is as follows:

Textbooks > Animation and Visual Effects > Maya > Autodesk Maya 2012: A Comprehensive Guide
(Expected time: 30 min)

Figure 13-54 The fireworks effect

Exercise 2

Create the model of mountains and use the particle system to make the water flow through the mountains, as shown in Figure 13-55. Next, apply textures to the mountains and water to get the rendered output, as shown in Figure 13-56. You can view the final rendered image of this model by downloading the *c13_maya_2012_render.zip* file from *http://www.cadcim.com*. The path of file is mentioned in Exercise 1. **(Expected time: 45 min)**

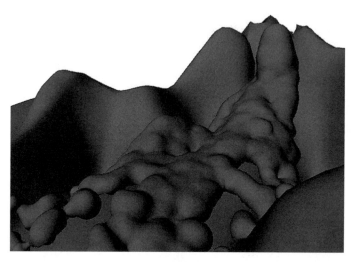

Figure 13-55 *Model for Exercise 2*

Figure 13-56 *The scene after rendering*

Exercise 3

Animate the hot air balloons using air field, as shown in Figure 13-57. You can view the final rendered image of this model by downloading the *c13_maya_2012_render.zip* file from *http:// www.cadcim.com*. The path of file is mentioned in Exercise 1.   **(Expected time: 15 min)**

Figure 13-57 The Final Scene

Exercise 4

Create the scene of a warehouse, as shown in Figure 13-58. Next, apply texture to the scene and then use the curve emitter on the rope to get the rendered output, as shown in Figure 13-59. You can view the final rendered image of this model by downloading the *c13_maya_2012_render.zip* file from *http://www.cadcim.com*. The path of file is mentioned in Exercise 1.

(Expected time: 30 min)

Figure 13-58   *The scene of a warehouse*

Figure 13-59   *The scene after rendering*

Answers to Self-Evaluation Test
1. a, **2.** d, **3.** Fields, **4.** Gravity, **5. Create Shatter**, **6. NURBS**, **7.** F, **8.** T, **9.** T, **10.** F

Chapter 14

Introduction to nParticles

INTRODUCTION

In Maya, the particle system is used to produce a wide variety of visual effects. nParticle system is a dynamic system and it was introduced in Maya 2009. nParticles are used to simulate a variety of effects such as liquids, smoke, clouds, spray, and dust. In this chapter, you will learn to create nParticle objects and simulate them. You will also learn about the concept of goal, which is used to control the flow of particles and create predefined effects in Maya.

nParticles are points in 3d space and they can be grouped together to create different effects. These points can be displayed in different styles such as dots, balls, cloud, thick cloud, and water. An nParticle object can collide and interact with another nParticle objects. The nParticle system allows you to create effects which are otherwise impossible to create with standard keyframe animation. The nParticles and their attributes are discussed next.

Creating nParticles

Main menubar: nParticle > Create nParticle > nParticle Tool

To create nParticles in 3d space, select **nDynamics** from the module drop-down list in the status line, as shown in Figure 14-1. Next, choose **nParticles > Create nParticles > nParticle Tool > Option Box** from the main menubar, as shown in Figure 14-2; the **Particle tool** window will be displayed. Most of the options in this window have already been discussed in Chapter 13. You can use these options to create nParticles in the viewport. After specifying all options in the nParticle tool window, press ENTER to complete the particle creation process.

*Figure 14-1 The **nDynamics** option selected from the module drop-down list in the status line*

*Figure 14-2 Choosing **nParticle Tool** from the main menubar*

nPARTICLE ATTRIBUTE EDITOR

The nParticle **Attribute Editor** has three tabs: **nParticle1**, **nParticleshape1**, and **nucleus1**. These tabs display various attributes of the selected nParticle object, as shown in Figure 14-3, and these tabs are discussed next.

nParticleShape1 Tab

The options in this tab are used to specify the attributes of the nParticle objects, refer to Figure 14-3. These options are discussed next.

Enable

By default, the **Enable** check box is selected. As a result, the nParticle object will be considered a part of the simulation system.

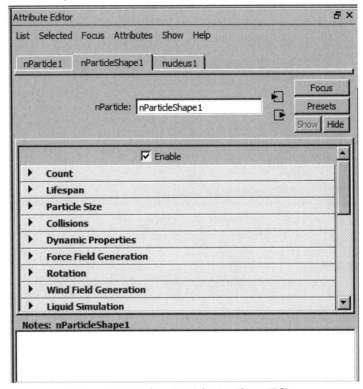

Figure 14-3 *The nParticle* ***Attribute Editor***

Count Area

This area has two options, **Count** and **Total Event Count**. Both of them are read-only attributes. The **Count** edit box is used to specify the total number of nParticles available for simulation. The **Total Event Count** edit box is used to specify the total number of collisions made on an nParticle object. The default value of **Total Event Count** attribute is 0.

Lifespan Area

The **Lifespan** area is shown in Figure 14-4 and is used to specify the life of the selected nParticle objects in the viewport. It determines at what point or age the nParticle object will come to an end. The options in this area are discussed next.

Lifespan mode

The **Lifespan mode** drop-down list is used to specify the time an the nParticle object will remain alive. By default, the **Live Forever** option is selected in this drop-down list. This option ensures that the nParticles will live forever unless they are killed by collision events or emission volume exit. If you select the **Constant** option from this drop-down list, nParticles will have a constant lifespan and will die at specified time. Selecting this option also activates the lifespan edit box. You can enter the value for the nParticles in this edit box. If you select **Random range** from this drop-down list, nParticle objects will die in a random manner. When you select this option, the **Lifespan Random** edit box in the **Lifespan** area will become active. You can assign a value in this edit box to ensure that some nparticles die randomly. The **lifespanPP** option is used in combination with expressions that are programmed into nParticle using the Maya Embedded Language (MEL).

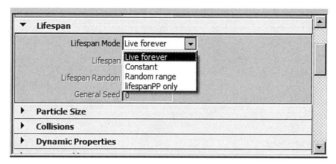

*Figure 14-4 Options in the **Lifespan** mode drop-down list of the **Lifespan** area*

Particle Size Area

This area is used to specify the size of an nParticle. The options in this area are discussed next.

Radius

This attribute is used to specify the radius of an nParticle in the viewport.

Radius Scale Area

The **Radius Scale** area is used to specify the per-nparticle radius scale values. The attributes in the **Radius Scale** area can be specified using the ramps, as shown in Figure 14-5. These ramps are found throughout Maya. The options in this area are explained next.

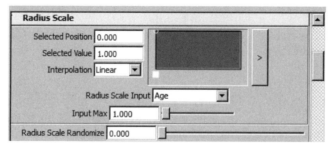

*Figure 14-5 The **Radius Scale** area in the nParticle **Attribute Editor***

Selected Position: The **Selected Position** edit box is used to specify the position of the value selected on the ramp.

Selected Value: The **Selected Value** edit box is used to specify the attribute value of the ramp at the selected position.

Interpolation: The **Linear option** is selected by default in this drop-down list. It is the most basic type of interpolation. The other types of interpolation are: **None**, **Smooth**, and **Spline**. The **None** option is used between points in a flat curve. The **Smooth** option is used to interpolate attribute values along a bell curve. The **Spline** option is used to interpolate attribute along a spline curve.

Radius Scale Input

The options in the **Radius Scale Input** drop-down list determine which attribute will be used to map the **Radius Scale** ramp values. The default value in this drop-down list is Age. The options in this list are, **Off**, **Age**, **Normalized Age**, **Speed**, **Acceleration**, **Particle ID**, and **Randomization ID**. These options are discussed next.

Off: On selecting the **Off** option, the per nParticle radius attributes will be deleted.

Age: On selecting the **Age** option, the per nParticle radius will be determined by its age, which will be dependant on the values set in the nParticle's **Lifespan** mode.

Normalized Age: On selecting the **Normalized Age** option, the nParticle radius will be determined by the normalized age of an nParticle. To use this option, the nParticle object should have the **Constant** or **Random range lifespan** mode.

Speed: On selecting the **Speed** option, the per nParticle's values will be calculated by the speed of an nParticle object.

Acceleration: On selecting the **Acceleration** option, the per nParticle values will be determined by its acceleration.

Particle ID: On selecting this option, the value of per nParticle object is determined by nParticle object ID.

Randomized ID: On selecting this option, per nParticle's radius is determined by randomized nParticle ID.

Input Max

This attribute is used to specify the maximum value for the range used by the ramp.

Radius Scale Randomize

This attibute is used to set a random multiplier for per-particle attribute value.

Collisions Area

This area is used to specify various collisions parameters when nParticles self-collide or collide with other nparticle objects, refer to Figure 14-6. Various options in this area are discussed next.

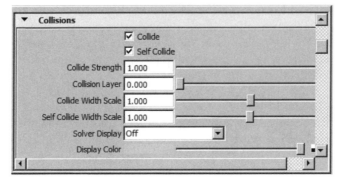

Figure 14-6 *Partial view of the* **Collisions** *area*

Collide

By default, the **Collide** check box is selected. As a result, the current nParticle objects collide with passive objects, nCloth objects, and other nParticle objects that share the same nucleus solver and vice versa.

Self Collide

If you select the **Self Collide** check box, then the nParticle objects will be allowed to collide with each other.

Collide Strength

The **Collide Strength** attribute is used to specify the amount of force generated by nParticle objects on collision with each other or with other nParticle objects that share the same nucleus solver. By default, the **Collide Strength** value is 1. As a result, nParticle objects fully collide with each other as well as with other nParticle objects. If you specify 0 in this edit box, the nParticle collision will not occur.

Collision Layer

This attribute is used to align an nParticle object to a specific collision layer.

Collide Width Scale

This attribute is used to specify the scale values for collisions between the current nParticle object and other nucleus objects. The greater the value of this attribute, farther will be the nParticle objects from each other. The default value of this attribute is 1.

Self Collide Width Scale

This attribute is used to determine a self collision scale value for current nParticle objects. It allows you to scale the thickness of collision that occurs between particles. The greater the value, the smoother will be the simulation.

Solver Display

The options in the **Solver Display** drop-down list are used to specify information about **Maya Nucleus solver** that is displayed in the viewport for current nParticle objects. The option in this drop-down list are discussed next.

Off: This option is selected by default. As a result, no information of **Maya Nucleus solver** is displayed on the scene.

Collision Thickness: On selecting **Collision Thickness**, the information of collision volumes for current nParticle objects will be displayed in the viewport.

Self Collision Thickness: On selecting **Self Collision Thickness**, it will display the information of self-collision volumes for current nParticle objects in the viewport.

Display Color

This attribute is used to specify the color of collision volumes of the nParticle object selected in the viewport.

Note
*The display color will be visible in the viewport only when you select the **Collision Thickness** or **Self Collision Thickness** option from the **Solver Display** drop-down list. Also, you need to make sure that the Display mode is set to **Shading > Smooth Shade Selected Item**s or **Shading > Flat Shaded Selected Items**.*

Bounce

The **Bounce** attribute is used to specify the way in which the nParticle will bounce off the surface on self collision or with other nParticle objects. This is dependant on the type of the surface on which nParticle bounces off. The default value of this attribute is 0.0.

Friction

This attribute is used to determine the friction of the nParticle objects. It specifies the reaction of nParticle on self collision or its collision with other nParticle objects. The default value of this attribute is 0.100.

Stickiness

The **Stickiness** attribute is used to define the adhering of nParticle objects on self-collision or its collision with other nParticle objects. The default value of this attribute is 0 which implies that the nParticles will not stick to each other.

Max Self Collide Iterations

The default value of this attribute is 4. It is used to display the number of iterations that occur at every step of collision. Increasing the value of this attribute will increase the calculation and slow down the simulation.

Collision Ramps Area

Collision ramps area is used to set collide strength, bounce, friction, and stickiness on nParticle objects.

Collide Strength Scale Area

The attributes in this area are used to determine the strength of the collision except the collide strength scale input resulting from self collisions or with other nParticle objects. All the options in this area have already been discussed. The **Collide Strength Scale Input** option is explained next.

Collide Strength Scale Input: This attribute is used to calculate the **Collide Strength Scale** ramp values. The options in this drop-down list are same as those discussed in the **Radius Scale Input** drop-down list. By default, this attribute is set to OFF.

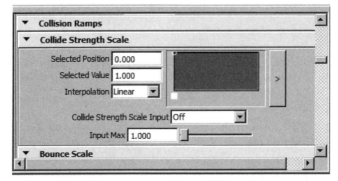

*Figure 14-7 Partial view of the **Collision Ramps** area*

Bounce Scale Area

The **Bounce scale** attribute is used to control the per-particle bounce scale. Most of the options in this area have been discussed earlier. The **Bounce Scale Input** and **Bounce Randomize** options are discussed next, refer to Figure 14-8.

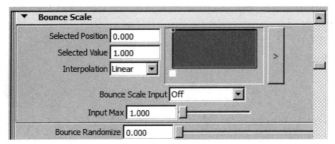

*Figure 14-8 The **Bounce Scale** area*

Bounce Scale Input: This drop-down list is used to determine per-particle bounce scale value. Various options in this list have already been discussed earlier in the **Radius Scale Input** area section. By default, the Off option is selected in the **Bounce Scale Input** drop-down list.

Bounce Randomize: You can set the random multiplier in this edit box. The default value of this attribute is 0.

Friction Scale Area

This area is used to determine the per nParticle friction scale values. The options in this area are, **Selected Position**, **Selected Value**, **Interpolation**, **Friction Scale Input**, **Input Max**, and **Friction Randomize**, as shown in Figure 14-9. Some of these attributes are discussed next.

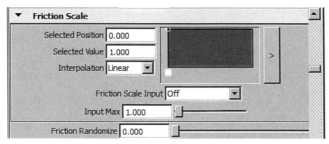

Figure 14-9 *The Friction Scale area*

Friction Scale Input: The options in this drop-down list are used to determine per-particle friction scale values. The options in this drop-down list are, **Off**, **Age**, **Normalized Age**, **Speed**, **Acceleration**, **Particle ID**, **Randomization ID**, and **Radius**. By default, the Off option is selected in this drop-down list.

Friction Randomize: You can set the random multiplier in this edit box. The default value is 0.

Stickiness Scale Area

This area is used to specify the adhering of nParticle objects on self-collision on collision with other nParticle objects together. It contains attributes such as **Selected Position**, **Selected Value**, **Interpolation**, **Stickiness Scale Input**, **Input Max**, and **Stickiness Randomize**, as shown in the Figure 14-10. The options in this list are same as those discussed in the **Radius Scale Input** area.

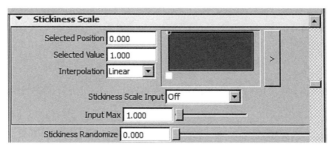

Figure 14-10 *The Stickiness Scale area*

Stickiness Scale Input: This attribute is used to determine per nParticle object stickiness scale values. You can select the **Off**, **Age**, **Normalized Age**, **Speed**, **Acceleration**, **Particle ID**, **Randomization ID**, or **Radius** option from this drop-down list. By default, this attribute editor is set to Off.

Dynamic Properties Area

The **Dynamic Properties** area displays various options related to nParticle dynamics, as shown in Figure14-11. The attributes in this area are discussed next.

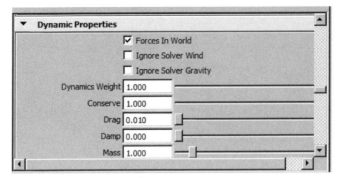

*Figure 14-11 The **Dynamic Properties** area*

Forces In World

This check box is selected by default. It is used to specify that nParticles affected by field will always fall in downward direction in world space, regardless of local axis orientation.

Ignore Solver Wind

If you select this check box, the solver will be disabled for the current nParticle object.

Ignore Solver Gravity

If you select this check box, the **Solver Gravity** will be disabled for the current nParticle object.

Local Force

This attribute is used to apply local force similar to **Gravity** on nParticle object without affecting the other nucleus objects.

Local Wind

This attribute is used to apply local force similar to **Nucleus Wind** on nParticle object without affecting the other nucleus objects.

Dynamics Weight

The **Dynamics Weight** attribute is used to control the effects of fields, collisions, springs, and goals connected to nParticle object. A value of 1 generates full effect.

Conserve

The **Conserve** attribute is used to control the velocity of nParticles retained from frame to frame. The default value of this attribute is 1, which implies that 100% of the selected particle's velocity is retained.

Drag

This attribute is used to specify the amount of drag added on to the selected nParticle object. The default value is 0.10.

Damp

This attribute is used to display the amount of damping on the selected nParticle. The default value is 0.

Mass

This attribute is used to specify the weight or density of the selected nParticle object. As a result, the behavior of particle object on self-collision or with other nParticle objects will be affected. The default value of this attribute is 1.

Mass Scale Area

This area is used to specify the mass scale values, as shown in Figure 14-12. The **Mass Scale Input** and **Mass Scale Randomize** options are discussed next.

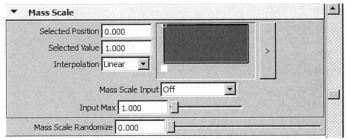

*Figure 14-12 The **Mass Scale** area*

Mass Scale Input: This attribute is used to determine mass scale of per-nparticle objects. You can select the **Off**, **Age**, **Normalized Age**, **Speed**, **Acceleration**, **Particle ID**, **Randomization ID**, or **Radius** option from this drop-down list. By default, the Off option is selected in this list.

Mass Scale Randomize: You can set the random multiplier for the per-nParticle value in this drop-down list.

Force Field Generation Area

This area is used to generate force that helps produce positive fields (push) or negative fields (pull) of the selected nParticles from the current nParticle objects that share the same nucleus solver. Various options in this area are shown in Figure 14-13 and are discussed next.

*Figure 14-13 The **Force Field Generation** area*

Point Force Field

This attribute is used to control the orientation of the point force field. This drop-down has the following options: **Off**, **Thickness Relative**, and **Worldspace**. By default, it is set to Off. If you select the **Thickness** or **Worldspace** option from this list, then the **Point Field Magnitude**, **Self Attract**, and **Point Field Distance** options in this area will be activated. These options are discussed next.

Point Field Magnitude: The **Point Field Magnitude** attribute is used to specify the strength of the **Point Force Field**. The default value of this attribute is 1. This attribute determines whether the selected nParticles generate positive or negative fields.

Self Attract: This attribute is used to specify the self-attracting strength between the individual particles of an nParticle object. It has both positive (push) and negative (pull) values. The default value of this attribute is 0.

Point Field Distance: The default value of this attribute is 2. This attribute is used to control the distance beyond which the **Point Field Distance** and **Point Force Field** will not affect any other particle objects.

Point Field Scale Area
The attributes in this area will be inactive by default, as shown in Figure 14-14. These options will be activated only when you select the **Point Relative Thickness** option from the **Point Field Distance** drop-down list. It is dependent on the values of **Point Field Distance** and **Point Field Magnitude** attributes. The options in this area are, **Selected Position**, **Selected Value**, **Interpolation**, **Point Field Scale Input**, and **Input Max**. These options have already been discussed. The **Point Field Scale Input** option is explained next.

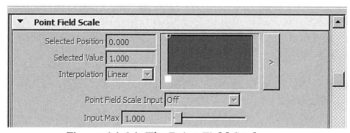

*Figure 14-14 The **Point Field Scale** area*

Point Field Scale Input: This attribute is used to determine per-particle Point Field Scale values. You can select the **Off**, **Age**, **Normalized Age**, **Speed**, **Acceleration**, **Particle ID**, **Randomization ID**, or **Radius** option from this drop-down list. By default, this attribute is set to Off.

Point Field Dropoff Area
This area is used to determine the value of Point Field Magnitude dropping off. The attributes in this area are shown in Figure 14-15. These attributes have already been discussed in the **Radius Scale Input** attribute section.

*Figure 14-15 The **Point Field Dropoff** area*

Rotation Area

Rotation is initiated by the friction generated between particles and collision objects. In the **Rotation** area, the **Compute Rotation** check box is cleared by default. On selecting this check box, the **Rotation Friction** and **Rotation Damp** attributes will be enabled, refer to Figure 14-16. These options are discussed next.

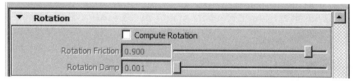

*Figure 14-16 The **Rotation** area*

Rotation Friction

This attribute is used to specify the amount of friction that is applied when nParticles collide with each other or with other nParticle objects. The default value of this attribute is 0.900. The value 0 means no rotation.

Rotation Damp

This attribute is used to specify the amount of damping applied to the nParticle's rotational velocity. On increasing the **Rotation Damp** value, nParticles rotation slows down after collision or self-collision.

Wind Field Generation Area

This area is used to define the properties of wind field that produces movement in the nParticles object. Various attributes in this area are shown in the Figure 14-17. These attributes are discussed next.

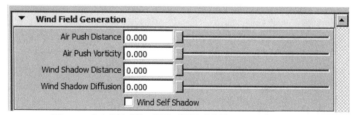

*Figure 14-17 The **Wind Field Generation** area*

Air Push Distance

The **Air Push Distance** attribute directly influences the nParticle system. The default value of this attribute is 0. It means no wind is produced by the motion of the selected nParticles.

Air Push Vorticity

This attribute is used to change the direction of wind created by the motion of the current nParticle object. It is used to specify the number of rotations or curls in the flow of wind caused by the current nParticle objects. By default, the value of this attribute is 0. The change in the **Air Push Vorticity** value affects the nParticle only when the value of the **Air Push Distance** attribute is greater than 0.

Wind Shadow Distance

This attribute is used to obstruct the wind of the nucleus system from other nParticle system. The default value of this attribute is 0, which ensures that no wind is obstructed from the nucleus system of the selected nParticle objects.

 Note

*The **Wind Shadow Distance** attribute should not be used in combination with the **Air Push Distance** attribute.*

Wind Shadow Diffusion

The **Wind Shadow Diffusion** attribute is used to specify the number of curls formed by the wind around the current nParticle object. The default value of this attribute is 0.

Wind Self Shadow

By default, this check box is clear. On selecting this check box, the current nParticle object blocks the dynamic wind of its nucleus system from affecting itself.

Liquid Simulation Area

The **Liquid Simulation** area is used to generate realistic liquid simulations. It helps nParticles in simulating the behavior of fluids. The attributes in the **Liquid Simulation** area are discussed next.

Enable Liquid Simulation

The **Enable Liquid simulation** check box is cleared by default. If you select this check box, then all liquid simulation properties will be added to the nParticle objects, refer to Figure 14-18.

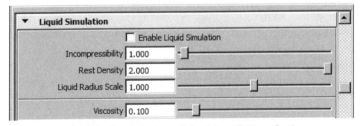

*Figure 14-18 Partial view of the **Liquid Simulation** area*

Incompressibility

It is used to specify the amount of nParticles that are impossible to compress. Its default value is 0.

Rest Density

This attribute is used to determine the amount of nParticles in the liquid overlapping with each other in the process of settling down when an nParticle object is at rest. The default value of this attribute is 2 implying that only two nParticles will overlap at any point while settling down.

Liquid Radius Scale

This area determines the amount of overlapping between nParticles. The default value of this attribute is 1.

Viscosity

The value of this attribute determines the resistance of the fluid to flow. For example, the thin fluids such as water have lower viscosity and thick fluids such as honey have higher viscosity. The default value assigned to this attribute is 0.100.

Viscosity Scale Area

The options in this area are used to determine the viscosity per nParticle. Figure 14-19 displays the **Viscosity Scale** area. Most of these options have already been discussed. The **Surface Tension** attribute is discussed next.

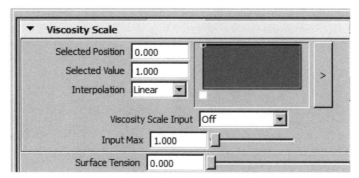

Figure 14-19 The **Viscosity Scale** *area*

Surface Tension

This attribute is used to add realism to the liquid simulation. The water molecules attract each other due to the force known as surface tension. The default value assigned to the **Surface Tension** attribute is 1. Increasing the value of surface tension increases the attracting power of molecules towards each other.

Surface Tension Scale Area

The **Surface Tension Scale** area sets the ramp for per-nParticle surface tension values. Figure 14-20 shows various attributes in this area and these options are discussed next.

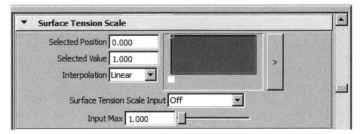

Figure 14-20   *Partial view of the **Surface Tension Scale** area*

Surface Tension Scale Input: This attribute is used to determine per nParticle surface tension scale values. You can select **Off**, **Age**, **Normalized Age**, **Speed**, **Acceleration**, **Particle ID**, **Randomization ID**, or **Radius** option from this drop-down list. By default this attribute editor is set to Off.

Input Max: It displays the maximum value of the range of **Surface Tension Scale** values.

Output Mesh Area

This attribute lets you control the charactersticts of nParticle objects such as size, smoothness, and so on after they are converted into polygon meshes. To convert nParticle objects into polygon meshes, choose **Modify > Convert > nParticles to Polygon** from the main menubar, as shown in Figure 14-21. Once the particles are converted into polygons, they automatically change into mesh and can be seen in the viewport. The other options in this area are shown in Figure 14-22.

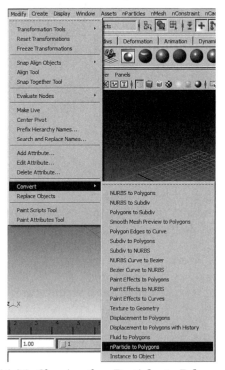

Figure 14-21   *Choosing the **nParticles to Polygons** option*

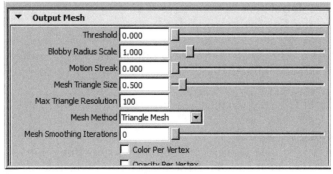

*Figure 14-22 The **Output Mesh** area*

Threshold

It is used to determine the smoothness of surface created by overlapping of nParticles and controls the blending of nParticle surfaces created by overlapping of nParticles. The default value of this attribute is 0.

Blobby Radius Scale

This attribute is used to specify the extent by which nParticle radius will be scaled to create continuous blobby surface nParticles. The default value of this attribute is 1.

Motion Streak

As the name suggests,this option is used to elongate individual nParticles based on its direction and to create motion blur effects. Its default value is 0 which specifies that nParticles will be round in shape.

 Note

Motion streaks can only be used when nParticles are converted into polygons.

Mesh Triangle Size

This attribute is used to specify the size of triangles that helps in creating output mesh. The size of triangle is inversely proportional to the resolution of mesh which means a small mesh triangle size will take more time to render as it has high resolution.

Max Triangle Resolution

This attribute is used to specify the resolution of volume pixel (voxel) of nParticles. Its default value is 100.

Mesh Method

This drop-down list is used to specify different types of polygon mesh that will be used in producing output mesh. By default, **Triangle Mesh** option is set in this drop-down list. The options in this drop-down list are discussed next.

Triangle Mesh: The **Triangle Mesh** option converts an nParticle to a cube polygon using a high resolution 3d surface algorithm (marching cubes) method. This option is selected by default.

Tetrahedra: The **Tetrahedra** option converts an nParticle into a triangle polygon mesh using the marching Tetrahedra method.

Acute Tetrahedra: The **Acute Tetrahedra** option converts an nParticle into a triangle polygon mesh with a slightly higher resolution as compared to the **Tetrahedra** method.

Quad Poly Mesh: It is used to convert nParticles into quad poly mesh.

Mesh Smoothing Iterations
This attribute is used to determine the amount of smoothing applied to smoothen the mesh. As a result, smooth topology is created which is uniform in shape. Its default value is 0.

Color Per Vertex
Select this check box to generate per-particle color value. This color value can only be generated when nParticle objects are converted to output mesh.

Opacity Per Vertex
Select this check box to generate opacity per vertex data.

Incandescence Per Vertex
Select the **Incandescence Per Vertex** check box to produce incandescence per vertex data.

Velocity Per Vertex
The **Velocity Per Vertex** attribute is used to produce velocity per vertex data. This helps in producing motion blur when rendering with mental ray.

UVW Per Vertex
The **UVW Per Vertex** attribute is used to produce UVW per vertex data of those nParticles which are converted into polygon mesh.

Use Gradient Normals
The **Use Gradient Normals** check box is used to improve the appearance and smoothness of nParticle output mesh. By default, this check box is clear.

Caching Area
Caching is used to cache the simulation data which will be cached or saved to local server or hard drive. The options in this area are shown in Figure 14-23 and are discussed next.

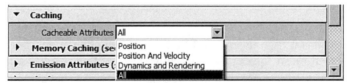

Figure 14-23 The Caching area

Position

This attribute is used to cache only **Particle ID**, **Age**, **Position**, and **Rotation Per-particle**.

Position And Velocity

This attribute is used to cache the **Particle ID**, **Age**, **Position**, **Rotation Per-particle**, **Velocity**, Angular Per-particle, and **Lifespan Per-particle** of nParticle.

Dynamics and Rendering

This attribute is used to cache only the **Mass**, **Radius Per-particle**, **Opacity Per-particle**, **RGB Per-particle**, and **Incandescence Per-particle**.

All

By default, the **All** option is selected in the drop-down list. It is used to cache all the nParticle attribute data.

Memory Caching Area

This area is used to specify whether the cache data is to be saved to the memory rather than to the hard disk or local drive. This check box is selected by default.

Emission Attributes Area

This attribute is similar to the **Emit from Object** attribute discussed in Chapter 13, refer to the Figure 14-24.

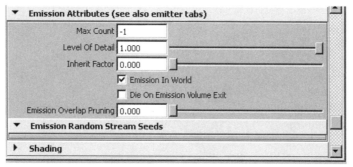

*Figure 14-24 The **Emission Attributes** area*

Max Count

This edit box is used to determine the number of nParticles emitted by the selected object. Its default value is -1.

Level Of Detail

This attribute affects only emitted particles. It scales the amount of emission to be used without altering the values of emitter. The default value of this attribute is 1.

Inherit Factor

This attribute is used to define the fraction velocity inherited by emitted nParticles. Its default value is 0. The velocity increases with the increase in its value.

Emission In World

By default, this check box is selected. As a result, nParticle objects are emitted from World space. It causes the particle object emission in the same way as done in the emitter.

Die On Emission Volume Exit

This check box is selected to specify that if nParticles are emitted from a volume, they will die when they exit that volume.

Emission Overlap Pruning

This attribute is used to determine that new nParticles will be eliminated before they are displayed in the simulation depending on collision with each other or with other nParticle objects.

Emission Random Stream Seeds Area

This attribute is used to create particle systems which operate in the same way with similar kind of forces but will look different in terms of placement.

Shading Area

This area is used to specify the appearance of nParticle objects in the viewport. It also displays the default form of nParticle object in the viewport which can be modified depending on the nParticle styles. Figure 14-25 shows various options in this area. These options are discussed next.

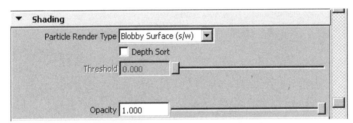

*Figure 14-25 Partial view of the **Shading** area*

Particle Render Type

This attribute displays various types of nParticle render types such as **Multipoint**, **Multistreak**, **Numeric**, **Points**, **Spheres**, and so on. By default, the nParticle objects are in the form of **Cloud (s/w)**.

Note
(s/w) indicates that this form of nParticle will be rendered in Maya software only.

Depth Sort

Select this check box to allow depth sorting of particles.

Threshold

This attribute is used to control the smoothness of the surface created due to overlapping of nParticles.

Opacity

It is used to specify the opacity of the nParticle object. The default value of this attribute is 1.

Opacity Scale Area

The **Opacity Scale** area is used to set the per-particle opacity scale value. Various attributes in this area are shown in Figure 14-26. These attributes are used to determine opacity scale values per nParticle.

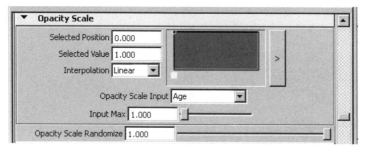

*Figure 14-26 The **Opacity Scale** area*

Opacity Scale Input: You can select the **Off**, **Age**, or **Normalized Age**, **Speed** from this drop-down list. By default, this attribute is set to Off.

Input Max: It is used to display the maximum range of **Opacity scale** values.

Opacity Scale Randomize: It is used to set a random multiplier for per-particle opacity value.

Color Area

The **Color** area is used to determine the variety of colors that can be applied to nParticles. The selected color corresponds to the values found on the ramp. The attributes under this area are shown in Figure 14-27.

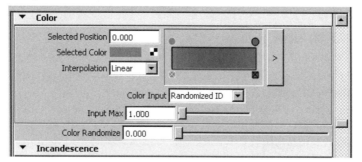

*Figure 14-27 The **Color** area*

Color Input

The options in this drop-down list are used to determine the color scale values per nParticle. You can select the **Off**, **Age**, **Normalized Age**, **Speed**, **Acceleration**, **Particle ID**, **Randomization ID**, or **Radius** option from this list. By default, Off option is selected in this list.

Input Max

The **Input Max** attribute is used to specify the maximum range of **Color** values.

Color Randomize

This attribute is used to set a random multiplier for per-particle value.

Incandescence Area

This attribute is used to control the intensity of the color of light emitted from the nParticle object due to self-illumination. The **Incandescence** area is shown in Figure 14-28. The options in this area are discussed next.

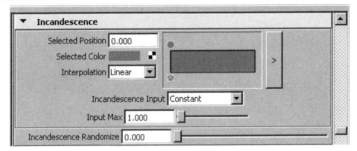

*Figure 14-28 The **Incandescence** area*

Incandescence Input

This drop-down list is used to determine per nParticle color values by selecting the **Off, Age, Normalized Age, Speed, Acceleration, Particle ID, Randomization ID**, or **Radius** option. By default, the Off option is selected in this drop-down list.

Input Max

This attribute is used to display the maximum range of **Incandescence** values.

Incandescence Randomize

This attribute is used to set a random multiplier for each nParticle value.

Per-particle Attributes Area

This area is used to set attributes on a per-particle basis, as shown in Figure 14-29.

Add Dynamic Attributes

This area is used to add custom attributes to an nParticle object. These attributes can be based on per-particle or per-object basis and are generally used to create complex particle effects. Choose the **General** button from this area; the **Add Attribute: nParticleshape1** dialog box will be displayed, as shown in Figure 14-30. Now, you can create custom attribute by using this dialog box.

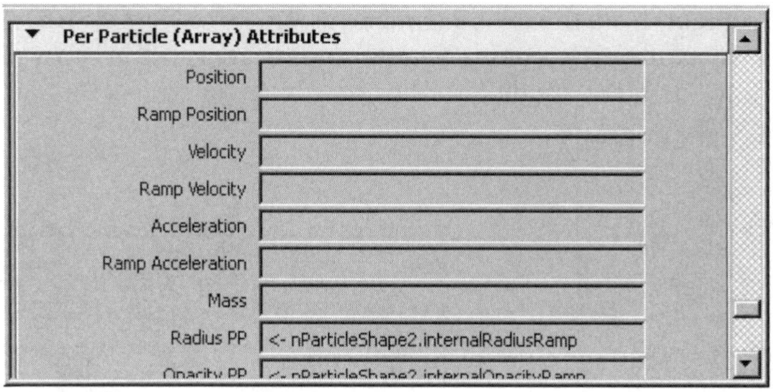

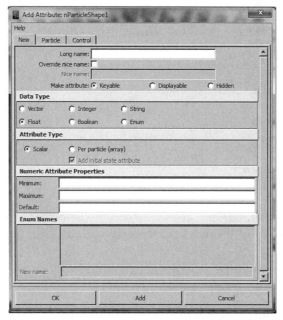

*Figure 14-29 The **Per Particle (Array) Attributes** area*

*Figure 14-30 **Add Attribute nParticle Shape1** dialog box*

Goal Weights and Objects Area

This area is used to determine the properties of goal objects whose attributes are used to control each nParticle simulation.

Goal Smoothness

The **Goal Smoothness** attribute is used to control the smoothness of goal forces as the weight ranges from 0.0 to 1. By default, the value of this attribute is 3. The higher the value of nParticle, the smoother will be the goal forces even if the weight changes.

Instancer (Geometry Replacement) Area

The attributes value in the **Instancer (Geometry Replacement)** area will not be activated till the selected nParticles are converted into Instancer. This can be done by choosing **nParticles >**

Instance (Replacement) from the main menubar, as shown in Figure 14-31. On doing so, the attributes in the **Instancer (Geometry Replacement)** area will be activated, as shown in Figure 14-32. These attributes are discussed next.

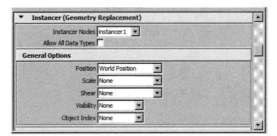

Figure 14-31 Converting
nParticle to Instancer

Figure 14-32 Partial view of the **Instancer**
(Geometry Replacement) area

Instancer Nodes
This attribute is used to select the instancer which is connected to selected instanced objects.

Allow All Data Types
On selecting this check box, all options that can be chosen to the inputs will be displayed.

General Options Area
The attributes in this area are discussed next.

Position: The **Position** attribute is used to specify the position of instanced objects. By default, it is set to World Position, regardless of local spacer in the instancer.

Scale: The **Scale** attribute is used to specify the scale of the instanced objects. This attribute is set to None (1,1,1) by default.

Shear: The **Shear** attribute is used to specify the shear of the instanced objects. This attribute is set to **None** (0,0,0) by default.

Visibility: The **Visibility** attribute is used to determine the visibility of the instanced objects. By default, it is set to None.

Object Index: The **Object Index** attribute is used to specify which object from the constrained object list is instanced for each particle. By default, it is set to None.

Rotation Options Area
The attributes in this area are used to determine the orientation of the currently instanced objects, refer to Figure 14-33.

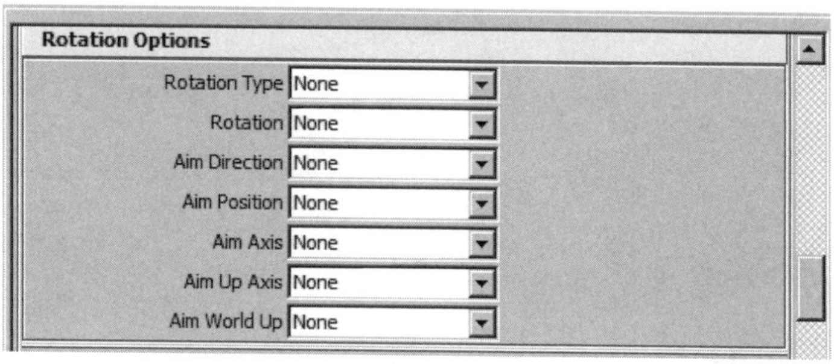

Figure 14-33 The Rotation Options area

Rotation Type: This attribute allows the user to choose between different types of rotation based on **Age**, **Birth Time**, **Mass**, **Particle ID**, **Acceleration**, **Force**, and so on. By default, this attribute is set to None.

Rotation: The options in the **Rotation** drop-down list are used to set the orientation of the instanced objects. The default value set in this drop-down list is None. Selected instanced objects can be rotated on the basis of **Acceleration, Force**, **Position**, **Ramp Acceleration**, and so on.

Aim Direction: In this drop-down list, the instanced object orientation is set along the direction of each instanced object in its local space. It ensures that particles face a general direction. You can specify other directions by selecting the options in this drop-down list.

Aim Position: The **Aim Position** attribute is used to set the orientation of the instanced object by specifying its loaction. By default, None is selected in the drop-down list.

Aim Axis: This attribute is used to specify the object axis that points directly at the **Aim Direction** or **Aim Position.** By default, this attribute settings is also set to None.

Aim Up Axis: This attribute is used to set the object axis. Its value is relative to how **Aim Axis** points at **Aim Direction** and **Aim Position**.

Aim World Up: This attribute is used to set the world coordinate axis that displays the Up direction used by **Aim Up Axis**.

Cycle Options Area

This attribute ensures that particles cycle in a sequential order. To instance the objects, choose **nParticles > Instancer (Replacement) > Option Box** from main menubar; The **Particle Instancer Options** dialog box will be displayed, as shown in Figure 14-34. Next, select **Sequential** from the **Cycle** drop-down list in this dialog box. Choose **Apply** and then the **Close** button to close the dialog box.

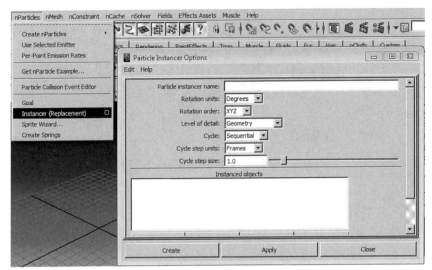

*Figure 14-34 The **Particle Instancer Options** dialog box*

Cycle Start Objects

The **Cycle Object Start** attribute is used to specify that the cycle's starting object from the list of instance object's given. The options in the drop-down list are **Age**, **Birth Time**, **Mass**, **Particle ID**, **Lifespan Per-particle**, and so on. The default option selected in this drop-down list is None.

Age

This attribute is used to determine how often Maya changes from one object to another.

Sprite Attributes Area

By default, the attributes in this area are inactive, as shown in Figure 14-35. To activate this attribute, choose **nParticle > Attribute Editor > Shading > Particle Render Type > Sprites** from the attribute editor. The options in this area are discussed next.

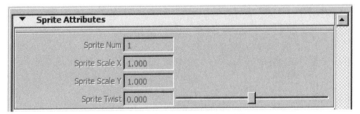

*Figure 14-35 The **Sprites Attributes** area*

Sprite Num

The **Sprite Num** attribute is an index number. It helps in identifying any file from stack of files. By default, its value is 1.

Sprite Scale X

The **Sprite Scale X** attribute scales the Sprite on the **X** axis or horizontal line. The default value assigned to this attribute is 1.

Sprite Scale Y

The **Sprite Scale Y** attribute scales the Sprite on the **Y** axis or vertical line. The default value assigned to this attribute is 1.

Sprite Twist

As the name suggests, this attribute is used to twist the Sprite in X or Y direction. The default value assigned to this attribute is 0.

NUCLEUS1 TAB

This tab is used to specify gravity wind, ground plane attributes, time scale attributes, and so on. These attributes are discussed next.

Enable

By default, this check box is selected. It enables nucleus solver to calculate simulation data which are part of its nucleus system.

Visibility

By default, this check box is selected. As a result, the location and direction of gravity and wind is displayed as arrows in the scene.

Gravity And Wind Area

In this area, nParticles are controlled by the Maya Nucleus solver. The options in this area are discussed next.

Gravity

This attribute is used to specify the amount of gravity applied to **Maya®Nucleus®** solver. The default value of this attribute is 9.8. A value of 0 means no gravity.

Gravity Direction

This attribute is used to specify the direction of gravity applied. By default, the value of this attribute is (0, -1, 0). This indicates that the gravity is applied in downward direction on Y-axis.

Air Density

This attribute is used to specify the air density applied to the nucleus solver. The default value of this attribute is 1. Higher the value, less will be the speed of the nParticle objects falling into the space.

Wind Speed

This attribute is used to determine the force and intensity of the wind. A higher value of this attribute indicates a faster wind speed.

Wind Direction

This attribute is used to indicate the direction of the wind. The default value of this attribute is (1,0,0), which means that the wind will move from left to right, along the X-axis.

Wind Noise

This attribute is used to specify the level of noise that affects the random falling of nParticle objects on the plane.

Ground Plane Area

The options in this area are used to create an imaginary ground plane which acts as a collision object for nParticle. The options in this area are discussed next.

Use Plane

Select this check box to use the plane as an object, which is not visible in the viewport.

Plane Origin

This attribute is used to specify the X, Y, and Z coordinates of the ground plane. The default coordinates of the plane are (0,0,0) which is same as grid origin.

Plane Normal

This attribute is used to specify the orientation of the ground plane. The default value of this attribute is (0,1,0).

Plane Bounce

This attribute is used to specify the intensity of the bounce of nParticle objects on the plane. The higher the value, the greater will be the amount of deflective force.

Plane Friction

This attribute is used to specify the amount of friction that is applied when nParticles collide with other nParticle objects. The strength of plane friction is determined by the type of surface it represents.

Plane Stickiness

This attribute is used to determine the degree to which the nParticles will stick to the ground plane when they collide with it.

Solver Attributes Area

The attributes in the **Solver Attributes** area are discussed next.

Substeps

This attribute is used to specify number of times the **Maya Nucleus** solver calculates an object's collision per frame. By default, the value assigned to this attribute is 3.

Max Collision Iterations

The iterations are used to determine the maximum number of collision iterations taken by nucleus objects on collisions with nParticles. By default, the value of this attribute is 4. The greater the number of iterations, better will be the accuracy, but it will tend to slow down the value of simulation.

Collision Layer Range

The **Collision Layer Range** attribute is used to specify the closeness of two objects so that they can intercollide. The objects can collide only if the differential value of collision layers is less than the **Collision Layer Range** value. The default value of this attribute is 4.

Note

*Collision layers can be used to organise collision between two or more nParticle objects that share the same **Maya Nucleus** solver.*

Timing Output

This attribute is used for editing the time of keyframe animation. The three options in this drop-down list are **None**, **Frame**, and **Sub frame**. By default, the timing output is set to None. As a result, no timing output is displayed in the **Script Editor** while the animation is being played. On selecting **Frame**, the evaluation time in seconds will be displayed at every frame on the **Script Editor**. On selecting **Subframe**, the time for evaluation will be displayed at every substep on the **Script Editor**.

Time Attributes Area

This area is used to edit the timing of the dynamic keyframe animation. There are three attributes in this area and they are discussed next.

Current Time

This attribute is used to specify the speed of per-nParticle at current time that can be edited independently. It indicates an incoming connection with the **Nucleus1** node. This connection can be broken by right-clicking on it and then choosing **Break Connection** from the shortcut menu displayed, as shown in Figure 14-36.

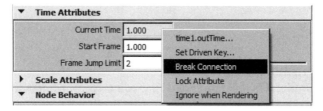

*Figure 14-36 The **Time Attributes** area*

Start Frame

The **Start Frame** option is used to indicate the starting frame at which **Maya Nucleus** Solver starts calculating. This attribute can be modified as per the requirement to start simulation from a specific frame.

Frame Jump Limit

This attribute is used to specify the maximum number of frames that can combined together to make one solver step. The default value of this attribute is 1.

Scale Attributes Area

This area has two options: **Time Scale** and **Space Scale**. The **Time Scale** attribute is used to specify the rate at which the simulation will occur.

Node Behavior Area

This area helps you in saving simulation data to a server or a local hard drive by caching your nParticle objects or effects.

Effects Assets

Autodesk Maya 2012 comes up with a number of preset effects in the Visor window.
They are known as Effects Assets. The effects are made up of 3D Fluid containers, nParticles, nParticle Emitters, and so on. These effects can be imported in your scene and their attributes can be edited by changing values in the **Attribute Editor.**

TUTORIALS

Tutorial 1

In this tutorial, you will simulate liquids using nParticles.   **(Expected time: 45 min)**

The following steps are required to complete this tutorial:

a. Create a project folder.
b. Create two glasses of similar type using the **EP Curve** tool.
c. Create nParticles.
d. Simulate nParticles.
e. Cache the scene.
f. Render the scene.
g. Save the file.

Creating the Project Folder

Before starting a new file, it is recommended that you create a project folder.

1. Create the project with the name *c14_tut1* in the folder *Maya_Tutorials*.

Creating Two Glasses

In this section, you will create two glasses on which the nParticles will collide.

1. Activate the Front viewport. Next, choose **Create > EP Curve Tool > Option Box** from the main menubar; the **EP Curve Tool** window is displayed. Select the **5** radio button in this window.

   Next, create a profile curve in the viewport, as shown in Figure 14-37.

2. Activate the Perspective viewport. Next, choose the **Surfaces** module from the **module** drop-down list in the status line.

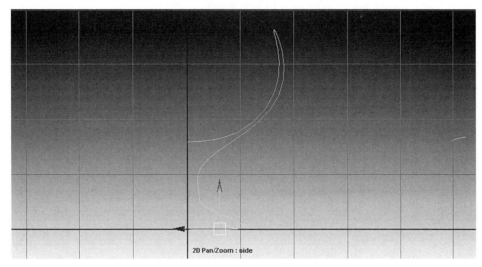

Figure 14-37 *The profile curve created*

3. Choose **Surfaces > Revolve** from the main menubar; the profile curve rotates at 360 degrees and a glass is created. Figure 14-38 shows the glass created. Press 6 to view the surface of the glass.

Figure 14-38 *The glass created*

4. Select the glass and then press CTRL+D; a duplicate of glass is created. Move the duplicate glass away from the original one, as shown in Figure 14-39.

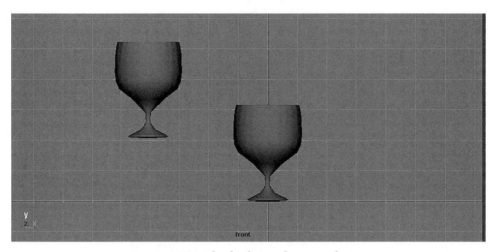

Figure 14-39 *The duplicate glass moved away*

Creating nParticles

In this section, you need to convert the glasses into polygons before filling nParticles in it.

1. You need to convert both the glasses into polygons. To do so, select one of the glasses and then choose **Modify > Convert > NURBS to Polygons** from the main menubar; the glass is converted into polygon. Repeat the process for another glass. Next, select and delete the original NURBS glasses from the scene.

2. Select the glass to be filled and then fill it with nParticles. Next, choose the **nDynamics** module from the module drop-down list in the status line.

3. Now, you need to change the nParticle style to water. To do so, choose **nParticles > Create nParticles >Water** from the main menubar.

4. Choose **nParticles > Create nParticles > Fill Object > Option Box** from the main menubar; the **Particle Fill Options** dialog box is displayed. In this dialog box, set the following parameters:

   Resolution: **30**   Min Y: **0.5000**   Max Y: **1.000**.

   Select the **Double Walled** check box.

5. Choose the **Particle Fill** button and then choose the **Close** button to close the dialog box; the particles are filled with nParticles.

Simulating nParticles

In this section, you need to simulate nParticles with the geometry.

1. Select both glasses. Choose **nMesh > Create Passive Collider** from the main menubar, as shown in Figure 14-40; two rigid bodies **nRigid 1** and **nRigid 2** are created. These bodies can be seen in the **Outliner** window.

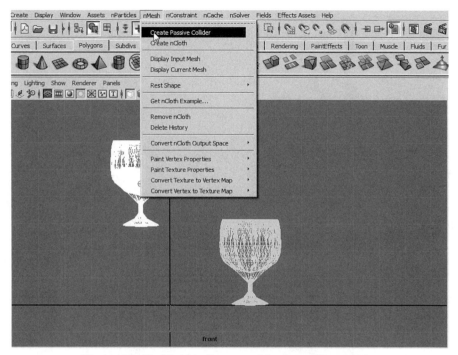

Figure 14-40 *Rigid bodies created in the outliner window*

2. Play the simulation till all nParticles settle down. Now, stop the simulation.

3. Select the nParticles in the viewport. Next, select **nSolver > Intial State > Set From Current** from the main menubar. Next, rewind and play the simulation.

4. Select nParticles in the viewport. Open the **Attribute Editor** and edit the values as given below:

Particle Size area
Radius: **0.050**

Radius Scale area
Radius Scale Input: **Randomized ID**
Radius Scale Randomized: **0.100**

Collisions area
Collide Width Scale: **0.50**

Liquid Simulation area
Liquid Radius Scale: **0.650**

5. Select nParticles and choose **nucleus1** tab in the **Attribute Editor**. Next, in the **Ground Plane** area, select the **Use Plane** check box. Set the value of **Plane Friction** to **0.506**.

6. Select the glass, place the cursor on first frame, and press the S key. Next, place the cursor on frame 30 and then rotate and move the glass, as shown in Figure 14-41. Again press the S key to set the keyframe.

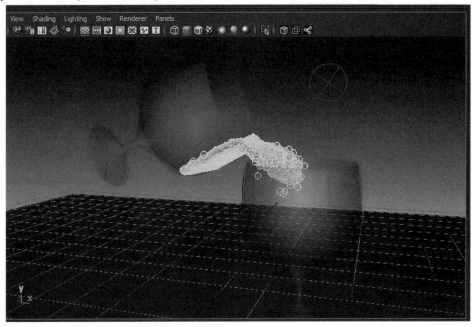

Figure 14-41 Pouring the nParticles into the glass

Caching the Scene

In this section, you need to cache the scene.

1. Increase the frames to 120 in the timeline. Select the nParticles. Choose **nCache > Create new cache** from the main menubar. Some of the nParticles will flow out of the glass, refer to Figure 14-41.

2. Select the **nParticleshape1** tab from the **Attribute Editor**. In the **Force Field Generation** area, select **ThicknessRelative** from the **Point Force Field** drop-down list. Next, set the values as follows:

    Point Field Magnitude: **-4.00**   Point Field Distance: **5**

3. Select nParticles. Choose **nParticles > nCache > Create new cache** from the main menubar to re-cache the scene.

Rendering the Scene

In this section, you will render the scene using **mental ray**.

1. Create a spot light in the viewport. Next, set the **Intensity** value to **0.50**. Next, select the spot light, open the **Channel Box\Layer Editor**, and then set the parameters as follows.

   Translate X: **1.939**   Translate Y: **5.689**   Translate Z: **-15.226**
   Rotate X: **-179.867**   Rotate Y: **-5.035**   Rotate Z: **145.591**

2. In the **Spot Light Attribute Editor**, open **Spot Light** attributes area and then set the parameters as follows:

   Cone angle: **69.232**   Penumbra angle: **5.747**

3. In the **Shadow** area, select the **Use Raytrace shadows** check box. Set the parameters as follows:

   Light Radius: **0.843**   Shadow Rays: **15**   Ray Depth Limit: **6**

4. In the mental ray **(Caustic and Global Illumination)** area, select the **Emit Photons** and set the parameters as follows:

   Photon Intensity: **5000.0**   Caustics: **500000**

5. Select the glasses, apply the **blinn** shader using the **Hypershade** window, and rename it as **Glass**. Open the **Attribute Editor** of spot light. Next, move the **Transparency** slider to the right in the **Common Materials Attribute** area.

6. In the **Specular Shading** area, set the parameters as follows:

   Ecentricity: **0.350**   Specular Roll offset: **0.350**

7. In the **Raytrace Option** area, select the **Refractions** check box and set the remaining parameters as follows:

   Refraction levels: **1.3**   Refractive limit: **6**

8. In the spot light settings, go to the **Caustics and Global Illumination** area, select the **Emit Photons** check box and change the parameters as follows:

   Photo Intensity: **5000.0**   Caustic Photons: **500000**

9. Select nParticles in the viewoprt. Apply the **Blinn** shader using the **Hypershade** window and rename it as **Water**. Set the values of color in the **Color History Palette** as follows: **Common Material Attributes** area

    Color: **0,0,0**   Transparency: **0.95, 0.95, 0.95**

    Specular Shading area

    Eccentricity: **0.080**   Specular Roll Off: **0.165**
    Reflectivity: **0.720**

    In the **Raytracing** area, select the **Refractions** options and then set the following values for the remaining parameters:

    Refractive Index: **1.250**   Refraction Limit: **8**
    Shadow Attenuation: **0.02**   Reflection Limit: **3**

Note

*By default, nParticles are invisible in the render view. To make them visible, select nParticle in the **Attribute Editor** under the **Render Stats** area. Next, select the **Visible in Refraction** check box.*

10. Select nParticles in the viewport. Choose **Modify > Convert > nParticles to Polygons** from the main menubar.

11. Select nParticles in the viewport. In the **Output Mesh** area of the **Attribute Editor** area, set the **nParticles** to **Blobby (s/w)** in the **Particle Render Type** drop-down list. Next, set the parameters as follows:

    Threshold: **0.850**   Blobby Radius Scale: **1.7**
    Motion Streak: **0.300**   Mesh Triangle Size: **0.050**
    Mesh Method: **Quads**   Mesh Smoothing Iterations: **3**

    After setting the parameters, nParticles are converted into a mesh displaying a smoother result.

12. Open the **Render Settings** window. Select the **Production** from the **Quality** drop-down list.

13. In the **Render Settings** window. Choose **Indirect Lighting** tab, open **Caustics** area, and then set the parameters as follows:

    Accuracy: **200**

14. Render the scene. The final output after rendering is shown in Figure 14-42.

Saving the File

In this section, you need to save the scene that you have created.

1. Choose **File > Save Scene** from the main menubar; the **Save As** dialog box is displayed.

    As the project folder is already set, by default the path *Documents\Maya_Tutorials\c14_tut1* scenes is displayed in **Look In** text box of the dialog box.

2. Enter **c14_tut1** in the **File name** text box and then select **Maya Binary** from the **Files of type** drop-down list. Next, choose the **Save As** button.

You can view the final rendered image of this model by downloading the *c14_maya_2012_render.zip* file from *http://www.cadcim.com*.

Figure 14-42 The final output

Tutorial 2

In this tutorial, you will create smoke by using an emitter object.   **(Expected time: 30 min)**

The following steps are required to complete this tutorial:

a.   Set a project folder.
b.   Download the texture file.
c.   Create nParticles, an emitter object, and volume axis field.
d.   Save the scene.

Setting the Project Folder

Before starting a new file, it is recommended that you set a project folder.

1.   Set a project with the name *c14_tut2* in the folder *Maya_Tutorials*.

Downloading the Texture File

1.   Download the *c14_maya_2012_tut.zip* file from *http://www.cadcim.com*. The path of the file
      is as follows:

      *Textbooks > Animation and Visual Effects > Maya > Autodesk Maya 2012: A Comprehensive
      Guide*

      Extract the contents of the zipped file and save them in the *\Documents* folder.

2.   Choose **Scene** from the **File** menu; the **Open File** dialog box is displayed. In this dialog
      box, browse to *\Documents\ c14_Maya_2012_tut* and select *c14_tut2_start.mb* file. Next,
      choose the **Open** button.

3.   Now, choose **Save As** from the main menubar; the **Save As** dialog box is displayed. Browse
      to the *\Documents\Maya\c14_tut2\scenes* folder. Save the file with the name *c14tut2.mb* in
      this folder.

Creating an Emitter

In this section, you need to create an emitter.

1.   Select **nDynamics** module from the drop-down list in the main menubar. Then, choose
      nParticles > Create nParticles > Create Emitter > Option Box from the main menubar;
      the **Emitter Options (Create)** dialog box is displayed, as shown in the Figure 14-43.

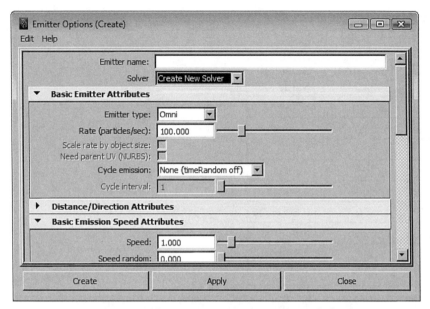

*Figure 14-43 The **Emitter Options (Create)** dialog box*

2. Type **Emitter_sm** in the **Emitter name** edit box. Next, select the **Create New Solver** option from the **Solver** drop-down list.

3. In the **Basic Emitter Attributes** area, set the following parameters:

   Emitter type: **Directional**   Rate (particles/sec): **128.0**

   In the **Distance/Direction Attributes** area, enter the value **1** in the **Direction X** edit box.

   In the **Basic Emission Speed Attributes** area, set the following parameters:

   Speed: **2.5**   Speed Random: **5**

   After setting the parameters, choose the **Create** button; an emitter is displayed in the viewport.

4. Select nParticles in the viewport. Choose the **nParticleshape1** tab in the **Attribute Editor** and set the parameters given below in the **Lifespan** area:

   Lifespan Mode: **Random Range**   Lifespan: **45**
   Lifespan Random: **5**

   In the **Particle size** area, enter the value **0.450** in the **Radius** edit box.

5. In the **Radius scale** area, add markers on different points by clicking on the left mouse button and adding value for each marker. The values for different markers are given next:

Marker	Selected Position	Selected Value
First	0	0.160
Second	0.470	0.120
Third	0.652	0.940
Fourth	0.765	0.600
Fifth	0.800	0.940
Sixth	0.870	0.600
Seventh	0.896	0.940
Eighth	0.965	0.840
Nine	0.995	1.000

Enter the value **0.250** in the **Radius Scale Randomize** edit box.

6. Clear the **Self Collide** check box in the **Collisions** area.

7. In the **Dynamics Properties** area, set the following parameters:

Conserve: **0.050**   Substeps: **0.145**

8. Choose the **Nucleus1** tab from the **emitter.sm Attribute Editor**. Set the following parameters in the **Gravity and Wind** area:

Gravity Direction: **(0,1,0)**

In the **Solver Attributes** area, set the following parameters:

Substeps: **50**   Max Collisions Iterations: **10**

9. Place the emitter on the ash tray. Play the simulation.

10. Choose **Fields > Volume Axis > Option Box** from the main menubar; the **Volume Axis** dialog box is displayed. In this dialog box, set the parameters as follows:

Magnitude: **100.0**   Attenuation: **5**

Choose the **Create** button. Now, choose the **Close** button to close the dialog box.

11. Select the **VolumeAxisField1** in the viewport. Next, in the **Volume Control Attributes** area, set the **Volume Shape** to **Cube** from the drop-down list. As a result, a cube is displayed in the viewport. Place the cube on the ash tray.

    In **Volume Speed Attributes** area, set the parameters as follows:

    Away From Center: **2**   Directional Speed: **1.5**
    Direction: **0,1,0**   Turbulence: **0.665**
    Turbulence speed: **0.150**

12. Set the timeline to **200** frames to increase the animation.

13. Select the nParticles in the viewport and choose the **nParticlesShape1** tab. In the **Force Field Generation** area, choose the **Thickness Relative** option from the **Point Force Field** drop-down list.

14. In the **Shading** area, choose **Cloud (s/w)** from the **Particle Render Type** drop-down list and set the following parameters:

    Threshold: **0.100**   Opacity: **0.100**

    In the **Opacity Scale** area, set the markers at different points. The values of different markers are given in the table below:

Marker	Selected Position	Selected Value
First	0.299	0.980
Second	0.563	0.915
Third	0.709	0.900
Fourth	0.913	0.720
Fifth	0.984	0.0

    Set the following parameters in **Opacity scale** area:

    Interpolation: **Spline**   Opacity Scale: **Normalized Age**
    Opacity Scale Randomize: **0.172**

15. In the **Color** area, set the color **black** in **Selected color** and for the three markers set the following values:

Marker	Selected Position
First	0.100
Second	0.522
Third	1.00

Enter the value **0.850** in the **Color Randomize** edit box.

16. Play the simulation and render the scene using the **mental ray** renderer. The final output after rendering is shown in Figure 14-44.

Figure 14-44 *The final output*

Saving the File

In this section, you need to save the scene that you have created.

1. Choose **File > Save Scene** from the main menubar; the **Save As** dialog box is displayed.

   As the project folder is already set, by default the path *\Documents\Maya_Tutorials\c014_tut2* scenes is displayed in the **Look In** text box of the **Save As** dialog box.

2. Save the file with the name **c14tut2.mb** and choose the **Save As** button.

You can view the final rendered image of this model by downloading the *c14_maya_2012_render. zip* file from *http://www.cadcim.com*.

Self-Evaluation Test

Answer the following questions and then compare them to those given at the end of this chapter:

1. Which of the following is a particle generation system that uses **Maya®nucleus** technology?

   (a) Nucleus 1   (b) nParticles
   (c) Particles   (d) nDynamics

2. Which of the following is the default value of the **Gravity Direction** attribute?

   (a) 1,0,0   (b) 0,0,1
   (c) -1,1,0   (d) 0,-1,0

3. The _____ is a linked particle system that simulates wide range of dynamic entities within a unified framework.

4. The default value of the gravity attribute is _____.

5. The _____ attribute is used to add realism to the Liquid Simulation.

6. The _____ attribute is used to specify total number of particles in an nParticles object.

7. The _____ area is used to define the life of the selected nParticle objects in the viewport.

8. The **Wind Direction** attribute is used to determine the direction of wind. (T/F)

9. There are three types of nParticle styles. (T/F)

10. The **Goal Smoothness** attribute is used to control the smoothness of goal forces. (T/F)

Review Questions

Answer the following questions:

1. What is the default value of Interpolation in the **Radius scale** area?

    (a) **None**   (b) **Linear**
    (c) **Spline**   (d) **Smooth**

2. The _____ attribute is used to define the life of selected nParticle object in the system.

3. nParticle system was introduced in Maya _____ .

4. The _____ is used to define the adhering of nParticle objects on self-collision or on colliding with other nParticle objects.

5. The **Bounce Scale** attribute is used to control _____ scale.

6. The default value of **Drag** is _____.

7. The _____ attributes define the properties of wind fields.

8. The **Air Push Distance** attribute is used to indirectly influence the nParticle system. (T/F)

9. **Goal Weights and Objects** attribute is used to determine properties of goal objects. (T/F)

10. The **Shading** attribute is used to specify the appearance of an nParticle object. (T/F)

Exercises

Exercise 1

Create hail snow in a scene by using the nParticles, as shown in Figure 14-45. Apply textures to the snow and then render the scene using mental ray. You can view the final rendered image of this scene by downloading the file *c14_maya_2012_render.zip* from *http://www.cadcim.com*. The path of file is as follows:

Textbooks > Animation and Visual Effects > Maya > Autodesk Maya 2012: A Comprehensive Guide
(Expected time: 30 min)

Figure 14-45 The snow effect

Exercise 2

Create constellation in a scene using the nParticles, as shown in Figure 14-46 and then render the scene. You can view the final rendered image of this scene by downloading the *c14_maya_2012_render.zip* file from *http://www.cadcim.com*. The path of the file is mentioned in Exercise 1.   **(Expected time: 30 min)**

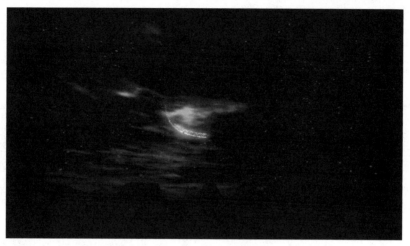

Figure 14-46 The constellation

Answers to Self-Evaluation Test
1. b, **2.** d, **3. Nucleus**, **4.** 9.8, **5. Surface Tension**, **6.** Count, **7. Lifespan**, **8.** T, **9.** F, **10.** T

Chapter 15

Fluids

Learning Objectives

After completing this chapter, you will be able to:
- *Learn about various types of fluids in Maya*
- *Apply the dynamic and non-dynamic fluid effects*
- *Modify fluid components*
- *Paint fluid containers*
- *Add ocean and pond effects to your scene*
- *Connect Maya fields to a container*

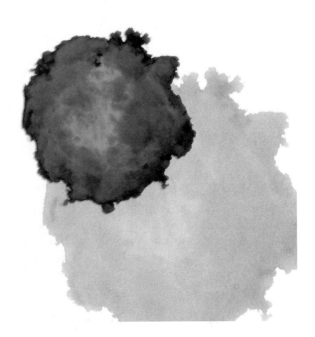

INTRODUCTION

In this chapter, you will learn about the fluid effects in Maya. Fluid effects help you add various stunning effects to your scene such as that of running water, explosion, smoke, realistic looking clouds, and many more. Maya's fluid effects simulation engine is based on Navier Strokes mathematical equations. It is the most complex engine in Maya. In this chapter, different fluid effects, which are used to create stunning effects in Maya, are discussed in detail.

CLASSIFICATION OF FLUID EFFECTS

There are three different types of fluid effects in Maya: open water, dynamic, and non-dynamic. These effects are discussed next.

Open Water Fluid Effects

The open water fluid effect is used to make open water fluid surfaces such as ocean, pond, river, and other watery scenes. The ocean surfaces are formed using NURBS planes with ocean shader applied to them. To create an ocean, select the **Dynamics** menuset from the menu set drop-down list in the status line. Next, choose **Fluid Effects > Ocean > Create Ocean > Option Box** from the main menubar; the **Create Ocean** dialog box will be displayed, as shown in Figure 15-1.

Figure 15-1 The **Create Ocean** *dialog box*

In this dialog box, the **Preview plane size** option is used to set the size of the plane that will be used for creating an ocean in the scene. Set the desired value either by entering a value or by using the slider bar on the right of the **Preview plane size** attribute in the **Create Ocean** dialog box. The default value for this option is 10. After setting all values as per your requirement, choose the **Apply** button to create the ocean in the viewport. Next, choose **Render the current frame (Maya Software)** from the status line to render the scene. After rendering, the realistic view of the ocean will be displayed, as shown in Figure 15-2.

Dynamic Fluid Effects

The dynamic fluid effect simulates the fluids based on the natural law of physics that describes how objects move. In this process, the simulation of the dynamic fluid is calculated on the basis of the Navier-Stokes fluid dynamic equation. To create a dynamic fluid effect, first you need to create a fluid container in which the fluid exists. In Maya, a fluid container is a rectangular boundary that defines space in the viewport, where the fluid simulation will be performed.

The fluid container is the main component for any dynamic or non-dynamic fluid effect. When you first create a container, it is empty. To create a fluid effect, you need to modify the container attributes.

Note
For open water effects, you do not require fluid containers.

Figure 15-2 *The ocean fluid type*

In Maya, there are two types of fluid containers, 3D and 2D. To create a 3D fluid container, choose **Fluid Effects > Create 3D Container** from the main menubar; a 3D container will be created in the viewport, as shown in Figure 15-3. Similarly, you can create the 2D container, as shown in Figure 15-4. The fluid containers are formed of grids. Each grid patch in a fluid container is known as voxel (volumetric pixel). Voxel density of the container determines the final output of the fluid particles to be created.

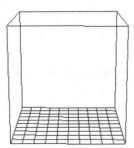

Figure 15-3 *The 3D fluid container*

Figure 15-4 *The 2D fluid container*

You can use the dynamic fluid effect to create stunning cloudy effects, fires, and so on. Figure 15-5 displays the fire created using the dynamic fluid effect.

Figure 15-5 *Fire or flames created using the dynamic fluid effect*

Non-Dynamic Fluid Effects

The non-dynamic fluid effects do not behave according to the natural law of fluid dynamics. Instead they use textures and animations to simulate the fluid and its motion. In this type of fluid effect, the fluid motion is created by keyframing the texture attributes. Moreover, in Non-Dynamic fluid effect, fluid solvers are not used to simulate the fluid motion. As a result, the rendering of the non-dynamic fluid effect is much faster than that of the dynamic fluid effect.

WORKING WITH FLUID CONTAINERS

The fluid simulation in Maya is governed by certain fluid components. The fluid always resides within a container (2D or 3D). Each fluid container is formed of three-dimensional grids, and each unit of a grid comprises of voxels. In other words, a group of voxels combines to form a fluid container. Voxels play a major role in defining the content method of the fluid property. There are two basic ways to define the fluid property in a fluid container: as a preset gradient or as a grid. By specifying the content method to gradient preset, the fluid property can be maintained as constant throughout the container. The gradient preset sets a ramp value between 1 and 0 in a particular axis. By setting the content method to grid, you can place an individual value in each voxel. The grid method provides a more precise control over the fluid property. Therefore, the grid preset can either be defined as static or dynamic. To modify the content method, choose the fluid container in the viewport and open the **Attribute Editor**; the **Contents Method** attribute area will be displayed, as shown in Figure 15-6.

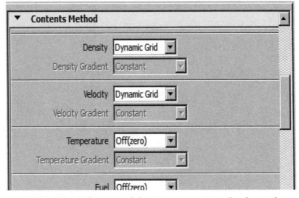

*Figure 15-6 Partial view of the **Contents Method** attribute area*

During animation, the fluid property value does not change in the static grid, whereas it changes in the case of dynamic grid. This is because the values in each voxel are recalculated at each frame. You can also resize the container and set its resolution. The resolution of the fluid is defined in voxels. Higher resolution produces finer details but increases simulation and rendering time. If you scale the container, the voxels in the container also get scaled without changing their contents. To make the container dense and add a finer detail to the fluid simulation, you need to increase its resolution. To do so, select the fluid container. Choose **Fluid Effects > Edit Fluid Resolution > Option Box** from the main menubar; the **Edit Fluid Resolution Options** dialog box will be displayed, as shown in Figure 15-7. Increase the resolution of the container using the options in this dialog box and then choose the **Apply** button. Note that increasing the fluid resolution increases the number of voxels in the fluid container, thus increasing the rendering time.

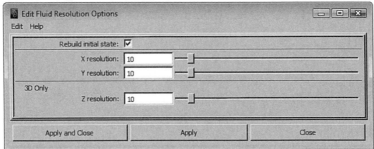

*Figure 15-7 The **Edit Fluid Resolution Options** dialog box*

Attributes of Fluid Shape

You can also edit the properties of a 2D or 3D container. To do so, choose **Fluid Effects > Create a 3D container** from the main menubar; a 3D container is displayed in the viewport. Press CTRL + a to open the **Attribute Editor** of the selected 3D container, as shown in Figure 15-8. By default, the **fluidshape1** tab is selected. The commonly used attributes in this tab are discussed next.

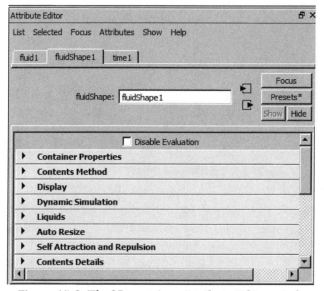

*Figure 15-8 The 3D container **Attribute Editor** window*

Container Properties

This area is used to edit the properties of the 2D or 3D container created. The attributes in this area are discussed next.

Keep Voxels Square

This attribute is used to set the container's resolution in such a way that the square voxels are maintained or arranged on the basis of the size of the container. By default, this attribute is selected.

Base Resolution

This attribute is used to set the resolution value of the current 2D or 3D container.

Resolution

It is used to set the resolution of the fluid containers manually. Increasing the resolution will increase the render time.

Size

This attribute is used to set the size of the fluid container. To get a good quality resolution, the size of container should be proportional to the **Base** resolution.

Boundary X, Boundary Y and Boundary Z

This attribute is used to control the behavior of the fluid when it comes in contact with the boundaries of the container.

Use Height Field

This option is available in 2D containers only.

Contents Method

Voxels play a major role in defining the content method of the fluid property. There are four ways of defining the fluid property in a fluid container. They are **Off (Zero), Static Grid, Dynamic Grid**, and **Gradient**. The attributes in this area are discussed next.

Display

This attribute is used to set the way fluids appear in the scene. They do not affect the final rendered image.

Shaded Display

This attribute is used to define which fluid property will be displayed in the container when the viewport is in the **Shaded Display** mode.

Opacity Preview Gain

This attribute is used to adjust the opacity of hardware display when the shaded display is not set to **As Render**.

Slices Per Voxel

This attribute is used only when Maya is in the **Shaded Display** mode. This mode defines the number of slices displayed per voxel.

Voxel Quality

This attribute is used to define the **Voxel Quality** of the 3D or 2D container. It can be set in two ways: **Better** and **Faster**.

Boundary Draw

This attribute is used to define the way the fluid container is displayed in the viewport. It can be displayed in various ways: **Bottom, Reduced, Outline**, and so on.

Numeric Display

It is used to define numeric values for the selected property.

Wireframe Display

This attribute is used to define the way the opacity of a property is represented when Maya is in the **wireframe display** mode.

Velocity Draw

This attribute is not selected by default. It is used to display the velocity vector in the fluid container.

Draw Arrowheads

This attribute is selected to display the arrowheads of the velocity vectors.

Velocity Draw Skip

By default, the value of this attribute is 1. Increasing its value will decrease the number of arrow-heads drawn.

Draw Length

This attribute is used to define the length of the arrow-heads.

Dynamic Simulation

This area is used to simulate the flow of the fluid. The attributes in this area are discussed next.

Gravity

This attribute is relative to the world coordinate system. By default, its value is set to 9.8.

Viscosity

This attribute is used to define the flow of the fluid. Increasing the value of this attribute makes the liquid thicker. Alternatively, decreasing its value makes the fluid to act similar to water.

Friction

This attribute is used to define the amount of friction used by the solver in the velocity solving.

Damp

This attribute is used to apply the damping to the velocity solving.

Solver

This attribute is used to select the solver used in the fluid simulation. There are three types of solvers: **None**, **Navier Stokes**, and **Spring Mesh**.

High Detail Solve

This attribute is used to add detailing to the solver without increasing the resolution, density, or velocity.

Substeps

This attribute is used to define the amount of calculations done in simulating fluids per frame.

Solver Quality

This attribute is used to determine the quality of the simulation taking place. Its value can be increased by increasing the number of steps taken by the solver.

Grid Interpolater

This attribute is used to select the type of interpolation grid to be used to recover values within the voxel grid.

Start Frame

This attribute is used to set the frame from which the simulation will begin. By default, it is set to 1.

Simulation Rate Scale

This attribute is used to scale the value of time step used in simulation.

Forward Advection

By default, this option is not selected. On selecting this option, it uses forward prorogation techniques.

Conserve Mass

This attribute is selected by default. It is used to conserve mass when values are updated.

Use Collisions

By default, this option is selected. It is used to collide the fluid in the container with the geometry.

Use Emissions

By default, this option is selected. It does not ignore all the connected fluid emitters during simulation.

Use Fields

When this option is selected, Maya ignores all commuted fluid emitters during simulation.

Emit In Substeps

By default, this option is not selected. It is used to calculate the fluid emission on every substep. It is useful for effects that have high emmision speed.

Liquids

This area is used to specify the simulation method used to generate Maya fluid. The default method used for all the non-liquid simulations is **Single Fluid**. The attributes in this area are discussed next.

Liquid Method

The two methods under this attribute are **Liquid and Air** and **Density Based Mass**. Both these methods are used to create liquid effects.

Density Tension

This attribute is used to add smooth details to fluid density without affecting the velocity in voxels.

Mass Range

This attribute is used to define the relation between mass and fluid density only when **Density Based Mass** simulation method is used.

Creating Fluid Containers with Emitter

You can also create a fluid container with an emitter to simulate the fluid in the container. To do so, choose **Fluid Effects > Create 3D Container with Emitter > Option Box** from the main menubar; the **Create 3D Container with Emitter Options** dialog box will be displayed, as shown in Figure 15-9.

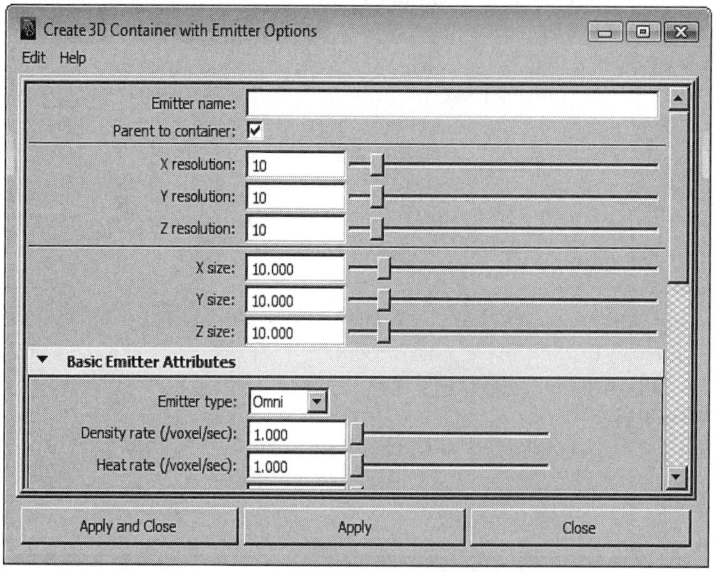

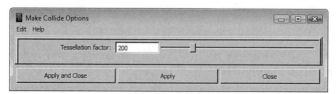

*Figure 15-9 The **Create 3D Container with Emitter Options** dialog box*

Set the required values in the dialog box and then choose the **Apply and Close** button. Similarly, you can create a 2D fluid container with an emitter. You can also make a surface collide with fluids. To do so, choose **Fluid Effects > Create 3D Container with Emitter** option from the main menubar; a 3D container with an emitter will be created in the viewport. Now, create a plane and move it inside the container just above the emitter. Select the plane and the fluid container, and then choose **Fluid Effects > Make Collide > Option Box** from the main menubar; the **Make Collide Options** dialog box will be displayed in the viewport, as shown in Figure 15-10. Increase the value in the **Tessellation factor** edit box and then choose the **Apply and Close** button. The default tessellation factor value is **200**. Maya internally converts a NURBS object to polygon before it animates the simulation. The tessellation factor sets the number of polygons created during the conversion. Less tessellation value means that more fluid will appear passing through the geometry. You can increase this value to get the desired smoothness, but it will also increase the simulation time. Now, preview the animation to see the effect of the collision. Figures 15-11 and 15-12 show the difference in the simulation after and before a surface collides with the fluid.

*Figure 15-10 The **Make Collide Options** dialog box*

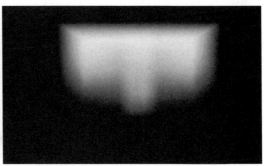

Figure 15-11 *Fluid simulation after colliding with a geometry*

Figure 15-12 *Fluid simulation without colliding with a geometry*

Painting the Fluid Effects into Containers

You can also paint the fluid effect into a fluid container. To do so, first create a 3D fluid container in the viewport. Next, choose **Fluid Effects > Add/Edit Contents > Paints Fluid Tool > Option Box** from the main menubar, the **Paint Fluids Tool** property window will be displayed on the left of the viewport, as shown in Figure 15-13. The attributes of the **Paint Fluids Tool** property window are similar to those of the **Sculpt Geometry Tool** property window. You can adjust the diameter of the paint brush by setting values in the **Radius(U)** and **Radius(L)** edit boxes. To set the radius of the paint fluids tool brush, press and hold the b key, press the middle mouse button, and then drag it in the viewport.

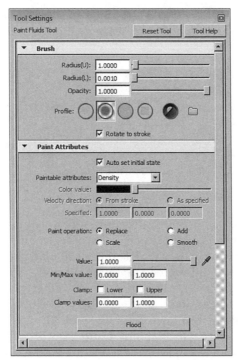

Figure 15-13 *Partial view of the **Paint Fluids Tool** property window*

FLUID COMPONENTS

The Maya fluid components are used to simulate and render the realistic fluid effects. In Maya, there are some pre-defined fluid components, which are discussed next.

Ocean

In Maya, the ocean effect is in-built. However, you can also create an ocean on your own. To create an ocean, choose **Fluid Effects > Ocean > Create Ocean > Option Box** from the main menubar; the **Create Ocean** dialog box will be displayed, as shown in Figure 15-14. Set a value for the ocean plane size in the **Preview plane size** edit box and then choose the **Create Ocean** button in the dialog box; an ocean will be created in the viewport. You can also add wakes to an ocean. Wakes are fluid containers having a spring mesh solver, which adds additional turbulence to the ocean by generating waves and ripples.

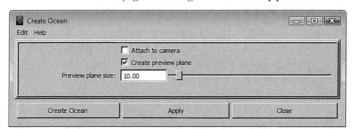

*Figure 15-14 The **Create Ocean** dialog box*

To add wakes to an ocean, choose **Fluid Effects > Ocean > Create Wake > Option Box** from the main menubar; the **Create Ocean Wake** dialog box will be displayed, as shown in Figure 15-15.

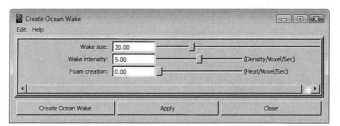

*Figure 15-15 The **Create Ocean Wake** dialog box*

Choose the **Apply** button from this dialog box; wakes will be created in the ocean, as shown in Figure 15-16. You can also adjust color, wavelength, foam creation, and other attributes related to the ocean. To do so, select the ocean plane in the viewport and open the **Attribute Editor**. In **Attribute Editor**, choose the **oceanshader1** tab; all attributes related to ocean will be displayed. Change the attributes as per your requirement. You can also make the objects float on the surface of an ocean. On doing so, the objects appear to be floating on the surface of the ocean along with the waves and ripples formed. To float the object, select the object on the ocean surface. Next, choose **Fluid Effects > Ocean > Make Boats** from the main menubar; the object will appear to be floating on the ocean when the animation is played, as shown in Figure 15-17.

Figure 15-16 *Wakes added to an ocean*

Figure 15-17 *An object floating on the surface of the ocean*

Pond

The pond fluid effect is also in-built in Maya. The pond effect is used to create surfaces using a height field and a spring mesh solver so that the resulting surface looks like a pond. To create a pond, choose **Fluid Effects > Pond > Create Pond > Option Box** from the main menubar; the **Create Pond** dialog box will be displayed, as shown in Figure 15-18. The rest of the process of creating a pond is similar to that of the ocean. You can create wakes in the pond similar to the way you did in the ocean, as shown in Figure 15-19.

Figure 15-18 *The* ***Create Pond*** *dialog box*

Figure 15-19 *The wakes applied to the pond*

FLUID EXAMPLES

In Maya, there are some in-built fluid effects that are stored in a library. You can select an effect from the default effect library of Maya whenever required. To apply an effect, choose **Windows > General Editors > Visor** from the main menubar; the **Visor** window will be displayed, as shown in Figure 15-20. Choose the **Fluid Examples** tab from the **Visor** window. Next, select the type of fluid example group from the left of the **Visor** window; the fluid examples will be displayed on the right of the **Visor** window. Press and hold the middle mouse button over the required fluid example and drag it in the viewport; the fluid example will be created in the viewport. Render the scene to see the final output. Some of the rendered fluid effects are shown in Figures 15-21 to 15-26.

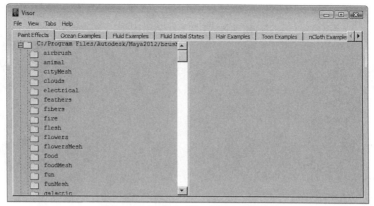

Figure 15-20 The **Visor** *window*

Figure 15-21 The cigarette smoke effect

Figure 15-22 The eagle nebula effect

Figure 15-23 The cloudsSun effect

Figure 15-24 The terrain effect

Figure 15-25 *The underwater caustics effect*

Figure 15-26 *The giantstorm scene effect*

TUTORIALS

Tutorial 1

In this tutorial, you will create the effect of a puffy fire explosion, as shown in Figure 15-26, using the 3D fluid containers in Maya.   **(Expected time: 30 min)**

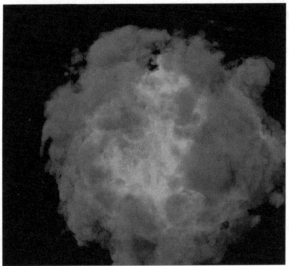

Figure 15-27 *The puffy fire explosion*

The following steps are required to complete this tutorial:

a.   Create a project folder.
b.   Create a 3D fluid container.
c.   Set the attributes of the container.
d.   Set the scene for animation.
e.   Render the scene.
f.   Save the file.

Creating the Project Folder

Before starting a new file, it is recommended that you create the project folder.

1.   Create a project with the name *c15_tut1* in the folder *Maya_Tutorials*.

Creating the 3D Fluid Container

In this section, you will create a 3D fluid container in which the explosion effect will be generated.

1.   Open a new Maya scene and select the **Dynamics** from the module drop-down list in the status line.

2.   Choose **Fluid Effects > Create 3D Container** from the main menubar; a 3D container is created in the viewport, as shown in Figure 15-28.

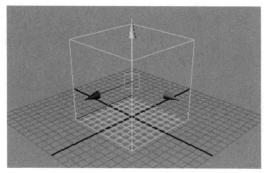

Figure 15-28 The 3D fluid container

3.   Invoke the **Move** tool from the toolbox and align the fluid container to the center of the viewport, if it is not already there.

Setting the Attributes of the Container

In this section, you need to set the attributes of the container to get the explosion effect, refer to Figure 15-26.

1.   Select the 3D fluid container from the viewport and choose **Display > UI Elements > Attribute Editor** from the main menubar; the Attribute Editor is displayed with the attributes of the fluid container.

2.   Expand the **Shading** attributes area in **Attribute Editor**. Now, in the **Color** attributes area, set the **Selected Color** attribute to dark grey color, as shown in Figure 15-29; the dark area is added to the explosion.

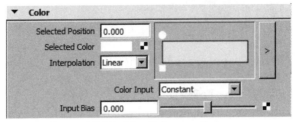

*Figure 15-29 The **Color** attributes area*

3. Expand the **Opacity** attribute area and set the opacity graph of explosion based on your requirement, as shown in Figure 15-30. Next, select the **Center Gradient** option from the **Opacity Input** attribute drop-down list and set the **Input Bias** attribute value to **-0.3** in the **Attribute Editor**; the fluid container appears, as shown in Figure 15-31.

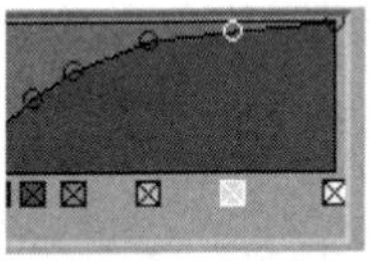

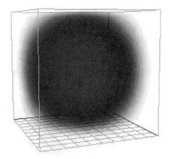

Figure 15-30 The
opacity value graph

Figure 15-31 The fluid container
after setting the attributes

4. Next, in the **Incandescence** attribute area, select **Center Gradient** from the **Incandescence Input** attribute drop-down list, refer to Figure 15-32. Incandescence controls the amount and color of light emitted from regions of density due to self illumination.

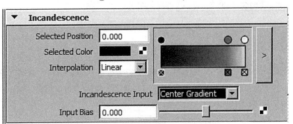

*Figure 15-32 The **Incandescence** attribute area*

5. Expand the **Textures** attributes area and then select the **Texture Color**, **Texture Incandescence**, and **Texture Opacity** check boxes in this area. Next, set the following values in the **Attribute Editor**:

Color Tex Gain: **0.6**   Incand Tex Gain: **0.8**   Depth Max: **4**
Frequency: **1.5**   Implode: **4**

6. Click in the viewport and press the numeric key 6 to see the effect in the viewport; the fluid container appears, as shown in Figure 15-33.

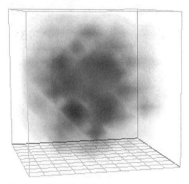

Figure 15-33 The 3d container on pressing the numeric key 6

7. Choose **Render the Current Frame (Maya Software)** from the status line to see the rendered view of explosion. Figure 15-34 shows the rendered output.

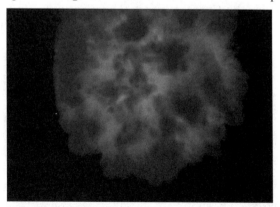

Figure 15-34 The rendered view of explosion

8. The rendered image shows some jittering. To fix it, expand the **Incandescence** attribute area in the **Attribute Editor** and set various attributes in it, refer to Figure 15-32. The fluid container after setting the attributes is shown in Figure 15-35.

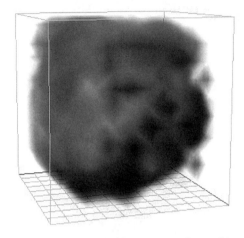

Figure 15-35 The fluid container after making changes

9. Expand the **Shading Quality** attribute area in the **Attribute Editor** and set the following values in it:

    Quality: **3**   Contrast Tolerance: **0.10**

10. Again, choose **Render the Current Frame (Maya Software)** from the status line to see the rendered effect. The rendered view of explosion after fixing the jittering is shown in Figure 15-36.

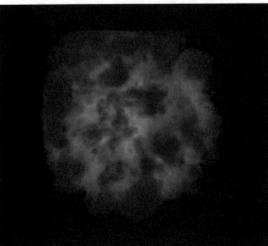

Figure 15-36 The rendered output of explosion

Setting the Scene for Animation

In this section, you need to animate the explosion.

1. Choose **Window > Setting/Preferences > Preferences** from the main menubar; the **Preferences** dialog box is displayed. Now, select the **Time Slider** category from the **Categories** area; the **Time Slider: Animation Time Slider and Playback Preferences** attributes are displayed on the right of the **Preferences** dialog box.

2. In this dialog box, set the **Playback start/end** and **Animation start/end** attributes to **1** to **200** frames and then choose the **Save** button; the active time segment is set from frames **1** to **200**. Close the **Preferences** dialog box.

3. Move the time indicator on the time slider to frame **1**. Expand the **Incandescence** attribute area and then set the **Input Bias** to **-0.2** in this area. Next, press the ENTER key. Press and hold the right mouse button over the **Input Bias** attribute; a flyout is displayed. Choose the **Set Key** option from the flyout, as shown in Figure 15-37; the key is set at frame **1**.

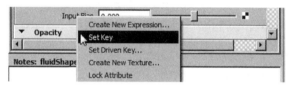

Figure 15-37 *Choosing* **Set Key** *from the* **Input Bias** *attribute*

4. Move to frame **200** and set the **Input Bias** attribute to **0.5** and press the ENTER key. Press and hold the right mouse button over the **Input Bias** attribute; a flyout is displayed. Again, choose the **Set Key** option from the flyout to set the key at frame **200**.

5. Move to frame **1** and expand the **Opacity** attribute area. In this area, set the **Input Bias** attribute to **-0.676** and press the ENTER key. Press and hold the right mouse button over the **Input Bias** attribute; a flyout is displayed. Now, choose the **Set Key** option from this flyout to set the key at frame **1**.

6. Move to frame **72**, set the **Input Bias** attribute to **-0.26**, and then press the ENTER key. Press and hold the right mouse button over the **Input Bias** attribute; a flyout is displayed. Choose the **Set Key** option from the flyout to set the key at frame **72**. Similarly, set the **Input Bias** attribute to **0.081** at frame **200**.

Rendering and Saving the Scene

In this section, you will render the scene and save it for further reference.

1. Select the **Rendering** menuset from the menuset drop-down list in the status line. Next, choose **Window > Rendering Editors > Render Settings** from the main menubar; the **Render Settings** window is displayed.

2. In this window, the **Maya Software** option is active by default. Set the render format to **AVI (avi)** from the **Image Format** drop-down list in the **Render Settings** window.

3. Expand the **Frame Range** attribute area and set the **End Frame** option to **200**. Next, choose the **Maya Software** tab from the **Render Settings** window, set the render quality to **Production Quality** from the **Quality** drop-down list, and then choose the **Close** button.

4. Now, set the final angle of the scene in the viewport for rendering. Choose **Render > Batch Render** from the main menubar; the rendering of 200 frames starts. The *.avi* file is saved with the name as *c15_tut1* in *images* folder.

 Note
The scene may take time to render, depending on the configuration of your system.

Saving the File

In this section you need to save the file.

1. Choose **File > Save Scene** from the main menubar; the **Save As** dialog box is displayed.

    As the project folder is already set, by default the path *\Documents\Maya_Tutorials\c15_tut1\ scenes* is displayed in **Look In** text box of the dialog box.

2. Enter **c15_tut1** in the **File name** text box and then select **Maya Binary** from the **Files of type** drop-down list. Next, choose the **Save As** button.

You can view the final rendered image of the model of the tutorial by downloading the *c15_Maya_2012_render.zip* file from *http://www.cadcim.com*.

Tutorial 2

In this tutorial, you will create the effect of melting text, as shown in Figure 15-38, using the fluid containers in Maya.   **(Expected time: 30 min)**

The following steps are required to complete this tutorial:

a. Set a project folder.
b. Create a 2D fluid container.
c. Set attributes and import the text into the container.
d. Set the scene for animation.
e. Save the file.

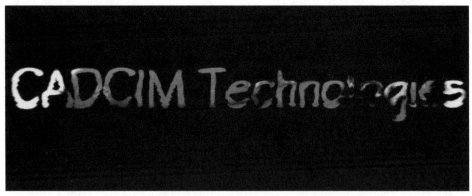

Figure 15-38 *The melting text*

Setting the Project Folder

Before starting a new file, it is recommended that you set the project folder.

1. Set the project with the name *c15_tut2* in the folder *Maya_Tutorials*.

Creating a 2D Fluid Container

In this section, you need to create a 2D fluid container in which the melting text effect will be generated.

1. Select the **Dynamics** menuset from the menuset drop-down list in the status line.

2. Choose **Fluid Effects > Create 2D Container** from the main menubar and click in the viewport; a 2D container is created in the viewport. Scale the fluid container to the shape shown in Figure 15-39.

Figure 15-39 *The scaled 2D fluid container*

3. Invoke the **Move** tool in the toolbox and align the fluid container to the center of the viewport, if it is not in the center. Now, select the 2D container and choose **Display > UI Elements > Attribute Editor** from the main menubar; the **Attribute Editor** is displayed.

4. Choose the **fluidShape1** attribute tab in the **Attribute Editor**. Expand the **Container Properties** attribute area and set the base resolution to **100** in both the edit boxes. You can start with low resolution for testing purpose; for final simulation set this value to **400**. Next, select the **None** option from the **Boundary X** and **Boundary Y** drop-down lists to set the boundaries of the fluid container to **None**.

Setting the Attributes and Importing the Text into Container

In this section, you need to set the attributes of the fluid container and apply the text image to the container.

1. Select the container from the viewport and choose **Fluid Effects > Add/Edit Contents > Paint Fluids Tool> Option Box** from the main menubar; the **Paint Fluids Tool** property window is displayed.

2. Expand the **Import** attribute area in the **Attribute Maps** area of the **Paint Fluid Tool** property window and choose the **Import...** button from the **Paint Fluids Tool** property window; the **Import** window is displayed.

3. Choose **text.png** from the **Import** window and then choose the **Open** button; the text becomes visible in the fluid container, as shown in Figure 15-40.

Figure 15-40 *The text visible in the fluid container*

4. Preview the animation; the text in the fluid container goes straight in the upward direction. Now, select the fluid container from the viewport and choose **Display > UI Elements > Attribute Editor** from the main menubar; the **Attribute Editor** is displayed.

5. Expand the **Dynamic Simulation** attribute area in the **Attribute Editor**, set the **Gravity** attribute to **-10.00**, and press the ENTER key. The gravity attribute defines the movement of the fluid while it is being animated. Setting a positive value makes the fluid move upward, whereas a negative value makes the fluid move in the downward direction, as shown in Figure 15-41. Preview the animation again to see the effect.

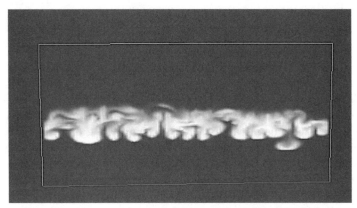

Figure 15-41 *Downward movement of the fluid as the* **Gravity** *value is set to* **-10**

6. Select the fluid container from the viewport and choose **Fluid Effects > Add/Edit Contents > Paint Fluids Tool> Option Box** from the main menubar; the **Paint Attributes Tool** property window is displayed.

7. Expand the **Paint Attributes** attribute area in the **Attribute Editor**. Now, select the **Color** option from the **Paintable attributes** drop-down list to add color to the text in the fluid container; the **Cannot paint 'color' on fluidShape1** dialog box is displayed, as shown in Figure 15-42. Choose the **Set to Dynamic** button to paint this attribute on the text in the fluid container.

Figure 15-42 *The* **Cannot paint 'color' on fluidShape1** *dialog box*

8. Expand the **Import** attribute area and choose the **Import...** button; the **Import** window is displayed.

9. Choose **Documents > melting_text > texture.png** from the **Import** window and then choose the **Open** button from the **Import** window; the texture map adds color to the text in the fluid container, as shown in Figure 15-43.

Figure 15-43 *The colored text in the fluid container*

10. Preview the animation; the colored text appears to be melting.

Setting the Scene for Animation

In this section, you will set the scene for animation.

1. Choose **Window > Setting/Preferences > Preferences** from the main menubar; the **Preferences** dialog box is displayed. Choose the **Time Slider** category in the **Categories** area of the dialog box; the **Time Slider: Animation Time Slider and Playback Preferences** attributes are displayed on the right of the **Preferences** dialog box.

2. Set the **Playback start/end** and **Animation start/end** attributes from frame **1** to **100** respectively, and choose the **Save** button; the active time segment changes from **1** to **100**. Preview the animation.

 Note
*In this tutorial, you learned to a create melting text. Similarly, you can create an evaporating text by changing the settings of the **Gravity** attribute of the fluid container.*

Saving the File

In this section you need to save the file.

1. Choose **File > Save Scene** from the main menubar; the **Save As** dialog box is displayed.

   As the project folder is already set, by default the path *Documents\Maya_Tutorials\c15_tut2\ scenes* is displayed in **Look In** text box of the dialog box.

2. Enter **c15_tut2** in the **File name** text box and then select **Maya Binary** from the **Files of type** drop-down list. Next, choose the **Save As** button.

You can view the final rendered image of the model of the tutorial by downloading the *c15_maya_2012_render.zip* file from *http://www.cadcim.com*.

Tutorial 3

In this tutorial, you will create cloud time lapse effect using non-dynamic fluid effect in Maya.   **(Expected time: 40 min)**

The following steps are required to complete this tutorial:

a. Create a project folder.
b. Create a 3D fluid container.
c. Set the container attributes.
d. Set the scene for animation.
e. Save the file.

Creating the Project Folder

Before starting a new file, it is recommended that you set the project folder.

1. Create a project with the name *c15_tut3* in the folder *Maya_Tutorials*.

Creating a 3D Fluid Container

In this section, you need to create a 3D fluid container in the viewport.

1. Open a new Maya scene. Select the **Dynamics** menuset from the menuset drop-down list in the status line.

2. Choose **Fluid Effects > Create 3D Container** from the main menubar and click in the viewport; a 3D container is created in the viewport. Invoke the **Move** tool in the toolbox and align the fluid container to the center of the viewport. Now, select the container and choose **Display > UI Elements > Attribute Editor** from the main menubar; the **Attribute Editor** is displayed.

3. Choose the **fluidShape1** attribute tab in the **Attribute Editor**. Expand the **Container Properties** attribute area and set the attributes, as shown in Figure 15-44.

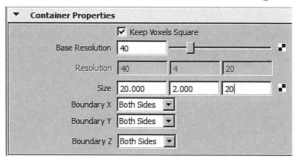

*Figure 15-44 Setting the attributes for **Resolution** of the container*

4. Expand the **Shading Attribute** area in **fluidshape1** tab. Next, expand the **Opacity** attribute area and set the opacity curve, as shown in Figure 15-45. Now, in the **Color** attributes area, set the selected color by specifying HSV values as **360**, **0.063**, and **0.937**. Next, in the **Incandescence** attributes area, set **Selected Color** to blue shades; it will give nice blue tint to clouds. Also, set **Incandescence Input** and **Opacity Input** to **Y Gradient**.

5. Click in the viewport and press the numeric key 6 to see the effect in the viewport; a fluid shape appears in the viewport.

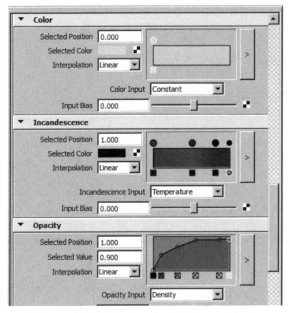

Figure 15-45 *Setting the shading attributes*

6. Expand the **Textures** attributes area and then select the **Texture Opacity** and **Texture Incandescence** check boxes. Next, set the following values in the **Attribute Editor**:

Texture Type: **Space Time**   Amplitude: **0.901**   Ratio: **0.560**
Frequency Ratio: **3.475**   Depth Max: **4**   Frequency: **0.1454**
Implode: **0.362**   Implode Center: **0, 0, -0.6**
Inflection: **On**

7. Choose **Render the Current Frame (Maya Software)** from the status line to see the rendered view of the clouds, see Figure 15-46.

Figure 15-46 *The rendered view of clouds*

8. To remove the jitter, expand the **Shading Quality** attributes area; set **Quality** to **3** and then select **smooth** in the **Render Interpolator** drop-down list. Re-render the scene. Note that now the render is smooth.

9. Now, to create a time lapse effect, you need to create an expression. In the **Textures** attributes area, press and hold the right mouse button over the **Texture Time** attribute; a flyout is displayed. Choose the **Create New Expression** from the flyout; the **Expression Editor** dialog box will open. Next, write the expression (**fluidShape1.textureTime=time*0.4**) in the **Expression** edit box and choose the **Create** button, as shown in Figure 15-47.

10. Choose the **Close** button from the **Expression Editor** dialog box, the required expression is created and displayed in the **Expression Edior**.

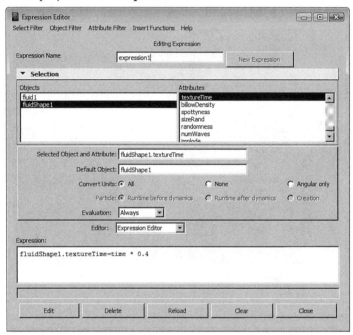

*Figure 15-47 The **Expression Editor** dialog box*

Setting the Scene for Animation

In this section, you need to set the scene for animation.

1. Choose **Window > Setting/Preferences > Preferences** from the main menubar; the **Preferences** dialog box is displayed. Choose the **Time Slider** category in the **Categories** area of the dialog box; the **Time Slider: Animation Time Slider and Playback Preferences** attributes are displayed on the right of the **Preferences** dialog box.

2. Set the **Playback start/end** and **Animation start/end** attributes from frame **1** to **200** respectively, and choose the **Save** button; the active time segment changes from **1** to **200**. Preview the animation.

Saving the File

In this section you need to save the file.

1. Choose **File > Save Scene** from the main menubar; the **Save As** dialog box is displayed.

    As the project folder is already set, by default the path *\Documents\Maya_Tutorials\c15_tut3\
    scenes* is displayed in **Look In** text box of the dialog box.

2. Enter **c15_tut3** in the **File name** text box and then select **Maya Binary** from the **Files of
    type** drop-down list. Next, choose the **Save As** button.

You can view the final rendered image of the model of the tutorial by downloading the
c15_Maya_2012_render.zip file from *http://www.cadcim.com*.

Tutorial 4

In this tutorial, you will learn how to use fields with fluids. The output of this tutorial is shown
in Figure 15-48.   **(Expected time: 30 min)**

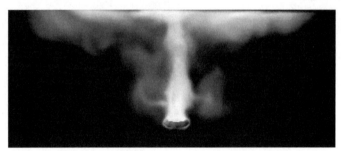

*Figure 15-48 The effect of the **Radial** field*

The following steps are required to complete this tutorial:

a. Create a project folder.
b. Create a 3D Fluid Container.
c. Set attributes of the fluid emitter and container.
d. Connect the field to the container.
e. Set the scene for animation.
f. Save the file.

Creating the Project Folder

Before starting a new file, it is recommended that you set the project folder.

1. Set a project with the name *c15_tut4* in the folder *Maya_Tutorials*.

Creating a 3D Fluid Container

In this section, you need to create a 3D fluid container in the viewport.

1. Open a new **Maya** scene. Select the **Dynamics** menuset from the menuset drop-down list in the status line.

2. Choose **Fluid Effects > Create 3D Container > Option Box** from the main menubar and click in the viewport; a 3D container is created in the viewport.

3. Choose **Fluid Effects > Extend Fluid > Option Box** from the main menubar; the **Extend Fluid Options** dialog box is displayed. Change the values in **Extend X** and **Extend Y** edit boxes to **10** to extend the fluid container. Next, choose **Apply and Close** button to close the dialog box.

4. Open **Attribute Editor** for the **fluidshape1** tab. Next, expand the **Container Properties** attribute area and set the **Base Resolution** to **100**.

5. Choose **Create > Polygon Primitives > Torus** from the main menubar and place it inside the container, as shown in Figure 15-49.

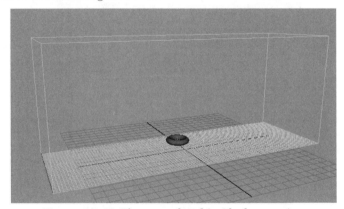

Figure 15-49 *The torus placed inside the container*

6. Select the container in the viewport. Next, press and hold SHIFT and then select the torus. Next, choose **Fluid Effects > Add Edit Contents > Emit From Object > Option Box**; set the following values in the **Emit From Object** options dialog box:

Density Rate: **5**	Heat Rate: **0**	Fuel Rate: **0**
(voxel/sec)	(voxel/sec)	(voxel/sec)

The above settings will only emit density values in the container and you will get a smoky fluid. Now, choose the **Apply and Close** button.

7. Select the fluid container and scroll down to the **Content Details** attribute area. Next, expand the **Density** attribute area and set the following values in it:

    Density Scale: **1.2**   Buoyancy: **10**   Dissipation: **0.01**

8. Expand the **Velocity** attribute in **Content Details** attribute area and set the **Swirl** value to **10**. It will give fluid some random motion.

9. Select the **fluid1** container and then choose **Fields > Radial** from the main menubar. By selecting the fluid container before creating a field, the field and fluid are automatically connected. Choose the **radialField1** tab and expand the **Volume Control Attribute** area in the **Attribute Editor**. Then, select **Sphere** from the **Volume Shape** drop-down list.

10. Scale the field icon in the viewport and place it at the center of the container, as shown in Figure 15-50.

Figure 15-50 The radial field in the viewport

11. Next, expand the **Radial Field** attribute area and set the following parameters:

    Magnitude = **1000**   Attenuation = **0**

12. Expand the **Volume Control** attribute and set **Volume Shape** to **Sphere**.

Setting the Scene for Animation
In this section, you need to set the scene for animation.

1. Choose **Window > Setting/Preferences > Preferences** from the main menubar; the **Preferences** dialog box is displayed. Choose the **Time Slider** category in the **Categories** area of the dialog box; the **Time Slider: Animation Time Slider and Playback Preferences** attributes are displayed on the right of the **Preferences** dialog box.

2. Set the **Playback start/end** and **Animation start/end** attributes from frame **1** to **200** respectively, and choose the **Save** button; the active time segment changes from **1** to **200**. Preview the animation.

Saving the File

In this section, you need to save the file.

1. Choose **File > Save Scene** from the main menubar; the **Save As** dialog box is displayed.

   As the project folder is already set, by default the path *\Documents\Maya_Tutorials\c15_tut4\ scenes* is displayed in **Look In** text box of the dialog box.

2. Enter **c15_tut4** in the **File name** text box and then select **Maya Binary** from the **Files of type** drop-down list. Next, choose the **Save As** button.

You can view the final rendered image of the model of this tutorial by downloading the *c15_Maya_2012_render.zip* file from *http://www.cadcim.com*.

Self-Evaluation Test

Answer the following questions and then compare them to those given at the end of this chapter:

1. Which of the following mathematical equations is used to simulate the fluid effects in Maya?

   (a) Differential equation   (b) Algebraic equation
   (c) Functional equation   (d) Navier-Stoke equation

2. Which of the following laws is applied to simulate the dynamic fluid effect in Maya?

   (a) Newton's law   (b) Physical law
   (c) Natural law of forces   (d) None of these

3. The _____ fluid effect does not behave according to the natural law of fluid dynamics.

4. Each fluid container is divided into three-dimensional grids, and each unit of a grid is known as _____.

5. The _____ **Tool** property window is similar to the **Sculpt Geometry Tool** property window.

6. The _____ effect is used to create a surface using a height field and a spring mesh solver.

7. The rendering of a scene with non-dynamic fluid effect is much faster than a scene with dynamic fluid effect. (T/F)

8. You can neither resize nor set the resolution of the fluid containers. (T/F)

9. The dynamic fluid effect simulates the fluids based on the natural law of physics. (T/F)

10. You cannot paint the fluid effect into a fluid container. (T/F)

Review Questions

Answer the following questions:

1. Which of the following is the most complex engines in Maya?

    (a) Fluids   (b) Particle
    (c) Hair and fur   (d) None of these

2. Which of the following effects is in-built in Maya?

    (a) Ponds   (b) Ocean
    (c) Terrain   (d) All the above

3. The _____ effect helps you create various stunning effects such as running water, explosion, cigarette smoke, and clouds.

4. The _____ grid does not make changes in fluid property values.

5. _____ are fluid containers having a spring mesh solver, which adds additional turbulence to the ocean by generating bubbles and ripples.

6. You can use an emitter to create a fluid container that will simulate fluid in the container. (T/F)

7. You can add wakes only to oceans, and not to ponds. (T/F)

8. Increasing the fluid resolution increases the number of voxels in the fluid container, thus increasing the rendering time. (T/F)

9. The content method gradient preset is used to maintain the fluid property as constant throughout the container. (T/F)

10. You cannot make the objects float on the surface of fluids in Maya. (T/F)

Exercises

Exercise 1

Create a fluid effect, as shown in Figure 15-51, by using the default effects given in Maya's **Visor** library. You can view the final rendered image of this model by downloading the *c15_maya_2012_render.zip* file from *http://www.cadcim.com*. The path of the file is as follows:

Textbooks > Animation and Visual Effects > Maya > Autodesk Maya 2012: A Comprehensive Guide
(Expected time: 30 min)

Figure 15-51 Fluid Effect

Exercise 2

Create 3D models of wood and stone, as shown in Figure 15-52. Next, apply texture to them and add a fluid container to the models to get the fire effect, as shown in Figure 15-53. You can view the final rendered image of this model by downloading the *c15_maya_2012_render.zip* file from *http://www.cadcim.com*. The path of file is mentioned in Exercise 1.

(Expected time: 30 min)

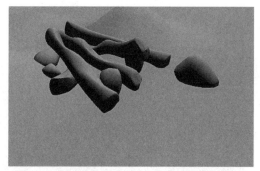

Figure 15-52 3D models of wood and stone

Figure 15-53 3D models of wood and stone

Answers to Self-Evaluation Test
1. d, **2.** c, **3.** non-dynamic, **4.** voxel, **5. Paint Attributes**, **6.** pond, **7.** T, **8.** F, **9.** T, **10.** F

Chapter 16

Hair and Fur

Learning Objectives

After completing this chapter, you will be able to:

• *Apply hair and fur to objects*
• *Understand hair simulation*
• *Make collision between hairs*
• *Paint textures on hair*
• *Modify fur attributes*
• *Use fur presets and animate them*

INTRODUCTION

In Autodesk Maya, you can create realistic hair and fur. Maya hair and fur are two powerful features of Maya. Maya hair lets you create complex hair motions and other dynamic hair systems.

Maya Hair

In Maya, hair can be created by using NURBS, polygonal surfaces, or paint effects. Paint effects provide a realistic look to hair strands. Before you create a hair system, you need to determine which renderer has to be used for rendering a scene. For example, if you create hair using paint effects, you cannot use the mental ray renderer. In this case, you need to convert paint effects into polygons and then render the hair created.

A hair follicle created in the viewport can be classified on the basis of three different positions: **start**, **current**, and **rest**. Throughout the workflow, you need to constantly switch between these positions. To do so, select the **Dynamics** module from the menu selector drop-down list in the status line and then choose **Hair > Display** from the main menubar; a flyout will be displayed. In the flyout, choose the position of hair to which you want to switch. Different positions of hair are discussed next.

Start Position

Menu bar:	Hair > Display > Start Position

The **Start Position** defines the hair curve at the frame one. To set the hair at the start position, choose **Hair > Display > Start Position** from the main menubar; the current position of the hair in the timeline will be set as the start position.

Rest Position

Menu bar:	Hair > Display > Rest Position

The **Rest Position** of the hair curve is on the position on which the hair simulation stops. In this position, none of the forces can act on the hair. The **Rest Position** option is used to influence the shape of the hair or to apply various styles on them. To set hair at the rest position, choose **Hair > Display > Rest Position** from the main menubar.

Current Position

Menu bar:	Hair > Display > Current Position

The **Current Position** is the position of the hair at any given frame. The **Current Position** option reflects hair behavior on playing the simulation. To set the hair at the current position, choose **Hair > Display > Current Position** from the main menubar.

Creating Hair

You can create hair on a NURBS or polygonal surface in Maya. To do so, create a surface in the viewport. Next, select the surface and choose **Hair > Create Hair** from the main menubar; the hair will be created on the selected surface, as shown in Figure 16-1.

Figure 16-1 *The default hair created on a sphere*

Creating hair on a surface solely depends on the UV coordinates of the selected surface. Maya software allows the user to specify the number of hair follicles that a user wants to generate in the U and V directions. The UV coordinates, thus, help the user to apply hair uniformly over the surface.

You can also define the hair attributes using the **Create Hair Options** dialog box. To do so, choose **Hair > Create Hair > Option Box** from the main menubar; the **Create Hair Options** dialog box will be displayed, as shown in Figure 16-2. The options in the **Create Hair Options** dialog box are discussed next.

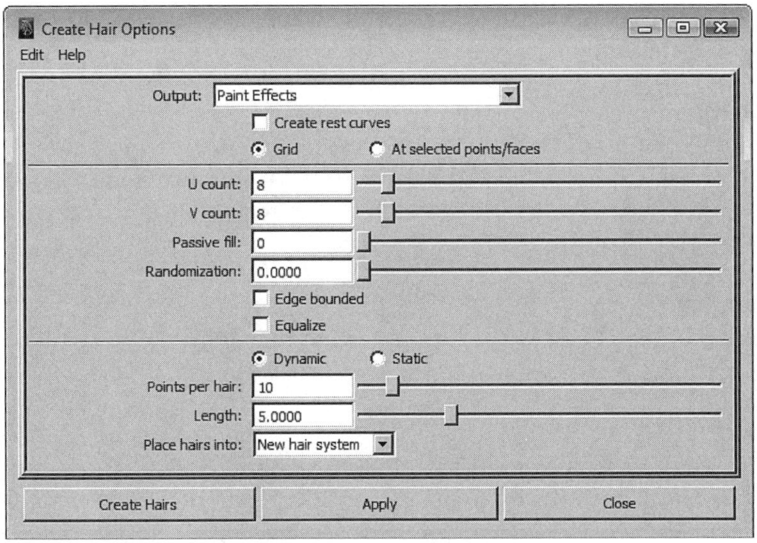

Figure 16-2 *The **Create Hair Options** dialog box*

Output

The **Output** drop-down list is used to define the output of the hair structure created in the viewport. You can select the **Paint Effects**, **NURBS curves**, or **Paint Effects and NURBS curves** option from this drop-down list. By default, the **Paint Effects** option is selected in this drop-down list. This option is used to set the attributes such as color, shading, and positioning of individual hair strands. The **NURBS curves** option is used to create hair follicles such that each hair follicle contains one NURBS curve defining the position of hair in that follicle. If you need to show the effect of the **Paint Effects** and **NURBS curves** options together, select the **Paint Effects and NURBS curves** option from this drop-down list.

Create rest curves

The **Create rest curves** check box is used to create a set of rest curves that are straight and normal to the surface. Select the **Grid** radio button located below this check box to create hair on the grid of the selected surface. Similarly, select the **At selected points/faces** radio button to create hair only on the selected vertex or faces.

U count

The **U count** edit box is used to specify the number of follicles to be created along the U direction. To do so, you can either enter a value in this edit box or move the slider on its right. The default value in this edit box is 8.

V count

The **V count** edit box is used to specify the number of follicles to be created along the V direction. To do so, you can either enter a value in this edit box or move the slider on its right. The default value in this edit box is 8.

Passive fill

The **Passive fill** edit box is used to specify the number of passive hair curves to be changed into active hair curves. To do so, you can enter a value in this edit box or move the slider on the right of this option.

Randomization

The **Randomization** edit box is used to specify the degree of randomization for the placement of hair in the U and V directions. The default value in this edit box is 0. You can set the randomization of follicles either by entering a value in the input box or by adjusting the slider bar.

Edge bounded

The **Edge bounded** check box is used to create hair follicles along the horizontal and vertical edges.

Equalize

The **Equalize** check box is used to equalize hair follicles on an uneven surface. On selecting this check box, the uneven mapping between the UV space and the world space is adjusted.

Static

The **Static** radio button is used to make hair follicles static. When we select this radio button, follicles stop responding to the dynamic forces. You can keyframe the static hair follicles to animate them.

Dynamic

The **Dynamic** radio button is used to make hair follicles dynamic. A dynamic hair follicle can respond to the dynamic forces. By default, this radio button is selected.

Points per hair

The **Points per hair** edit box is used to specify the number of points/segments of a follicle. Increasing the number of points in a hair follicle increases the smoothness of hair. For small and stiff hair, less number of points per hair is required. However, to apply styles to hair, the number of points per hair should be more. The default value is 10.

Length

The **Length** edit box is used to specify the length of hair follicles in world space units. To do so, enter a value in the **Length** edit box or move the slider on its right. The default value in this edit box is 5.

Place hairs into

The **Place hairs into** drop-down list is used to place hair into a new or existing hair system. By default, only the **New hair system** option is selected in this drop-down list. Once you create a hair system in the viewport and name it, it will be displayed in the drop-down list.

Simulating the Hair

Hair simulation is used to simulate the effect of dynamics and other gravitational forces over the hair follicles created. To view the complete simulation of hair, increase the number of frames in the timeline and then preview the animation. The hair system in the viewport simulates according to the default gravity applied to it. However, you can also simulate hair manually. To do so, choose **Window > Outliner** from the main menubar; the **Outliner** window will be displayed. Double-click on **hairSystem1** from the **Outliner** window; the **Attribute Editor** will be displayed on the right of the viewport. Choose the **hairSystemShape1** tab from the **Attribute Editor**; the **Dynamics** attributes area will be displayed, as shown in Figure 16-3.

Set the required values in the **Solve, Stiffness Scale,** and **Forces** areas of the **Dynamics** attribute to modify hair simulation. The options in the **Stiffness Scale** area are used to set stiffness in hair follicles. The **Damp** option in the **Forces** area is used to minimize the oscillation of hair follicles.

To select a hair system, select the hair system node from the **Outliner** window. To select all follicles in a hair system, select **hairSystem1Follicles** from the **Outliner** window. Alternatively, select **hairSystem1Follicles** by selecting hair or object on which the hair is applied. Next, choose **Hair > Convert Selection > To Follicles** from the main menubar to convert the hair selection to follicles. Now, you can select individual hair follicles from the hair system. To do so, first deselect **Strokes** and **NURBS Curves** from the **Show** menu of the **Panel menu**. Also, make sure that the **Follicles** option is selected in the **Show** menu. Next, you can select individual follicles from the viewport and modify them as per your need.

Hair Simulation

To simulate hair, select a hair system from the viewport. Choose **Hair > Display > Current position** from the main menubar. This will update the simulation of hair curves to dynamics with the change in the timeline. Set the timeline to **1000** in the timeline area. Next, select the surface from the viewport on which the hair is applied. Choose **Solvers > Interactive Playback** from the main menubar; the hair will simulate with the change in the shape, size, or rotation of the selected object. Move the surface to observe the change in the behavior of hair in response to the default dynamic forces applied to hair follicles.

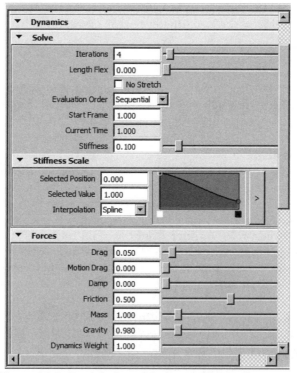

*Figure 16-3 Partial view of the **Dynamics** attributes area*

Colliding the Hair

You can collide hair system with any object in the viewport. To do so, create an object to collide with hair system. For example, create a sphere in the viewport and choose **Hair > Create Hair** from the main menubar; a hair system will be created on the sphere. Next, create a plane just below the sphere in the viewport and select the hair system node from the **Outliner** window.

Next, press and hold the SHIFT key and select the plane created. Then, choose **Hair > Make Collide** from the main menubar. Play the simulation to see the collision between the hair and the plane. Figures 16-4 and 16-5 show the hair before and after colliding with the plane. You can also collide one set of hairs with the other in a hair system. To do so, double-click on the hair system node in the **Outliner** window. Next, choose the **hairSystemShape1** tab from the **Attribute Editor** and expand the **Collisions** attribute area; all collision attributes will be displayed, as shown in Figure 16-6. Select the **Collide Ground** and **Self Collide** check boxes from the **Collisions** attribute area and play the simulation; the two sets of hair follicles will collide with each other in the hair system.

Figure 16-4 Hair simulation before colliding with the plane

Figure 16-5 Hair simulation after colliding with the plane

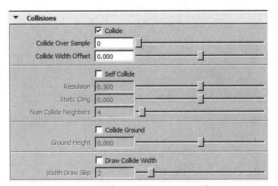

Figure 16-6 The **Collisions** attribute area

Painting the Texture on the Hair

You can paint textures on a hair system created in the viewport. To do so, select a hair system from the **Outliner** window. Next, choose **Hair > Paint Hair Textures > Hair Color** from the main menubar to color hair follicles. Next, choose the **Show or hide the tool settings** button from the status line; the **Tool Settings (3D Paint Tool)** property window will be displayed, as shown in Figure 16-7. Set the radius of the brush by using the **Radius(U)** and **Radius(L)** attributes in the **Brush** attributes area. Alternatively, set the radius of the brush by pressing and holding the b key and dragging the mouse by pressing the middle mouse button in the viewport. Next, set the color of hair by choosing the **Color** attribute box in the **Color** area.

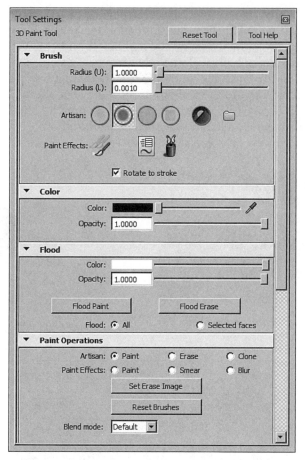

Figure 16-7 *Partial view of the **Tool Settings (3D**
***Paint Tool)** property window*

Painting the Hair on the Surface

You can paint hair on a NURBS or polygonal surface manually. To do so, choose
Hair > Paint Hair Follicles from the main menubar; the **Paint Hair Follicles Settings**
window will be displayed, as shown in Figure 16-8. Set the attributes in this window and then
paint the hair on the selected object. You can change the radius of the brush as discussed in
the previous topic.

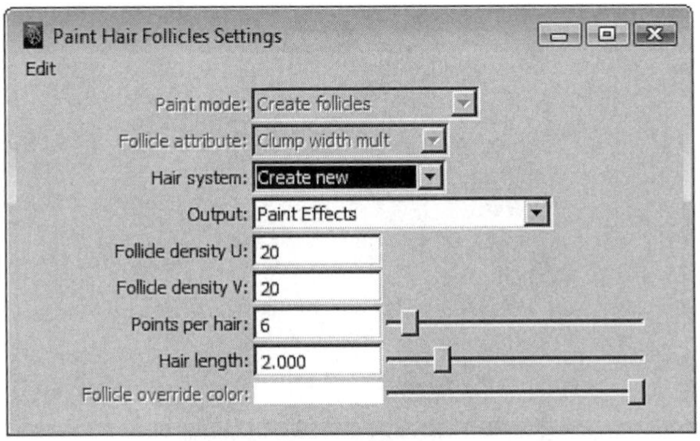

*Figure 16-8 The **Paint Hair Follicles Settings** window*

You can set hair in different styles using the attributes in the hair system **Attribute Editor** or in the **Channel box**. For creating a braid from a hair system, you can either use an individual follicle or the entire hair system. To create a braid, play the simulation and then stop it on the frame on which the hair stops simulating.

To set the current position of the hair as the start position, set the timeline to 1000 frames and choose **Hair > Set Start Position > From Current** from the main menubar. Now, select all hair follicles from the viewport and choose **Hair >Convert Selection > To Follicles** from the main menubar. Next, select the hair system node from the **Outliner** window and open the **Channel box**. Turn on the **Braid** option in this box; the straight hair will convert into braids. Next, choose the hair system node from the **Outliner** window. In the **Channel box**, set **Clump Width** to **0.6**, **Clump twist** to **0.5**, **Hair Per Clump** to **30**, **Thinning** to **0.5**, and **Multi Streaks** to **1** (setting these values will help in converting the selected hair to a perfect hair braid on rendering). Next, render the hair system; the braid will be created, as shown in Figure 16-9.

You can also apply various styles to hair such as to make them curly, wavy, and so on. To do so, select hair system and choose **Hair > Modify Curves** from the main menubar; a flyout will be displayed. You can choose different options from this flyout to set the hair styles.

Figure 16-9 The braid

Applying Shadow to the Hair

You can apply shadow to hair to give them a realistic effect. To do so, first create a spotlight in the viewport. Then, select the spotlight and open the **Attribute Editor**. Expand the **Shadows** attribute in the **Attribute Editor** and select the **Use Depth Map Shadows** check box. Next, clear the **Use Mid Dist** and **Use Auto Focus** check boxes in the **Depth Map Shadow Attributes** area. Set the value of **Focus** to **150**, **Filter Size** to **2**, and **Bias** to **0.006**. The **Bias** value determines how far the light will filter through the hair. Next, select the hair system node from the **Outliner** window. Open the **Attribute Editor** and expand the **Shading** attribute tab. Next, select the **Cast Shadows** check box in the **Shading** area. Render the scene to view the final result, as shown in Figure 16-10.

Figure 16-10 Braid after applying the shadow

Rendering the Hair

In Maya, you can render hair by using either the software renderer or by using the mental ray renderer. The software renderer is used only if you have selected paint effects as output while creating hair. But, if you want to use the mental ray renderer, then convert the paint effects strokes into polygons. Next, choose **Window > Rendering Editors > Render Settings** from the main menubar; the **Render Settings** window will be displayed. Set the mental ray as the active render from the **Render Settings** window. Next, choose the **Features** tab and expand the **Extra Features** attribute area in it, if it has not been already expanded; the **Extra Features** attribute area will be displayed, as shown in Figure 16-11. Also, ensure that the **Render Fur/Hair** check box is selected. Set **Quality Presets** to **Production: Rapid Hair** in the **Quality** tab of the **Render Settings** window.

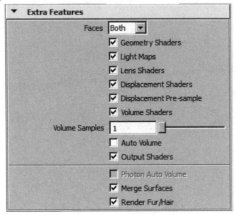

Figure 16-11 The **Extra Features** attribute area in the **Render Settings** window

Maya Fur

Maya fur is used to create the fur effect on the surfaces created in the software. You can apply fur on all types of surfaces: NURBS, polygonal, and subdivision. The method of applying fur on a 3D model is similar to applying hair. The placement of fur also depends on the UV coordinates of the surface on which it is being applied.

You can apply the fur effect to all 3D models in the viewport, except in the case of a trimmed area where rendering takes more time. In such a case, you first need to convert the trimmed area into polygons and then apply fur on them. As discussed earlier, the complete application of fur depends on the placement of UVs. So, the UVs must be laid out such that they do not overlap in the texture space. To avoid overlapping, apply automatic mapping on the surface on which you want to apply the fur effect. You can also set UVs using the **UV Texture Editor** (refer to Chapter 6 for details on the **UV Texture Editor**).

Creating Fur in Maya

In Maya, you can apply fur on an object by first creating its description. To create the fur description, select an object in the viewport and activate the rendering module from the status line. Next, choose **Fur > Attach Fur Description > New** from the main menubar; the fur will be applied to the selected object in the viewport, based on the default settings. Then, select fur in the viewport and open the **Attribute Editor**. Choose the **FurDescription1** attribute tab from this editor; the options related to this attribute will be displayed, as shown in Figure 16-12. The attributes required for setting the fur are discussed next.

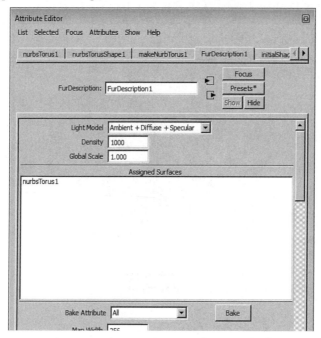

*Figure 16-12 Partial view of the **FurDescription1** attribute tab*

Light Model

The **Light Model** drop-down list is used to change the render type of the fur according to the base color and the tip color of hair in the scene. If you select the **Ambient Only** option in this drop-down list, then the attribute set in **Base Ambient Color** and **Tip Ambient Color** options will be applied to the fur, as shown in Figure 16-13. If you select the **Ambient + Diffuse** option in the **Light Model** drop-down list, the colors set in the **Base Ambient Color** and the **Tip Ambient Color** will be added to the colors specified in the **Base Color** and **Tip Color** and then applied to the fur, as shown in Figure 16-14. Similarly, if you select the **Ambient + Diffuse + Specular** option in the drop-down list, you need to specify the specular color in addition to the parameters that were specified in previous option. The color of the fur on selecting the **Ambient + Diffuse + Specular** option is shown in Figure 16-15. Select the **Specular Only** option from the drop-down list to render the hair by specifying only the **Specular Color** option for the fur, as shown in Figure 16-16.

Figure 16-13 Fur created using the **Ambient Only** option

Figure 16-14 Fur created using the **Ambient+Diffuse** option

Figure 16-15 Fur created using the **Ambient + Diffuse + Specular** option

Figure 16-16 Fur created using the **Specular Only** option

Density

The **Density** attribute is used to define the total number of hair on the selected surface. Higher the density of the fur, longer it will take to render the scene. The default value for this attribute is 1000.

Global Scale

The **Global Scale** attribute is used to scale the hair fur uniformly, as shown in Figures 16-17 and 16-18. Enter a suitable value in the **Global Scale** input box to scale the fur uniformly along the base width, tip width, length, and offset values. The default value for this attribute is 1.

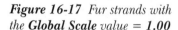

Figure 16-17 Fur strands with
the **Global Scale** value = **1.00**

Figure 16-18 Fur strands with
the **Global Scale** value = **3.00**

Assigned Surfaces

This area displays the names of the surfaces on which the fur is applied.

Base Color

The **Base Color** option is used to set the base color of the fur. You can set the color by using the color swatch or by moving the slider to the right. Alternatively, you can also apply texture to the base color of fur by choosing the checker box on the right of this attribute.

Tip Color

The **Tip Color** attribute is used to define the color of the tip of the fur. You can apply a textured map on the tip of the fur by choosing the checker box on the right of this attribute. The default tip color is white.

Base Ambient Color

The **Base Ambient Color** attribute is used to define the ambient color channel for the base of the fur.

Tip Ambient Color

The **Tip Ambient Color** attribute is used to define the ambient color channel for the base of the tip.

Specular Color

The **Specular Color** attribute is used to define the specular color channels of shiny highlights on the surface of the fur.

Specular Sharpness

The **Specular Sharpness** attribute is used to define the overall specularity across the whole fur description. Higher the specular sharpness value, sharper will be the specular highlight created on the fur description.

Length

The **Length** attribute is used to define the length of each fur hair. The default value of this attribute is 1.

Baldness

The **Baldness** attribute is used to define the amount of fur on a selected surface, as shown in Figures 16-19 and 16-20. This attribute is typically used with a map. The baldness value **1** indicates full fur and **0** indicates no fur on the surface. The default value for this attribute is 1.

Figure 16-19 *Fur with the* ***Baldness*** *value:* ***0.1***

Figure 16-20 *Fur with the* ***Baldness*** *value:* ***1.0***

Inclination

The **Inclination** attribute is used to determine the angle at which the fur will be inclined to the surface, as shown in Figures 16-21 and 16-22. If you set 0 as the attribute value, the fur will be perpendicular to the surface, and if you set 1 as the attribute value, the fur will be set flat to the surface.

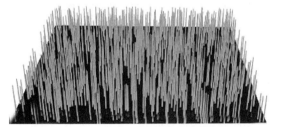

Figure 16-21 *Fur with the* ***Inclination*** *value:* ***0.0*** *Figure 16-22* *Fur with the* ***Inclination*** *value:* ***0.5***

Roll

The **Roll** attribute is used to rotate the fur about the surface in V axis, as shown in Figures 16-23 and 16-24. Set the **Roll** value to **0** to set the fur hair to **-90** or set the **Roll** value to **1** to set the fur hair to 90 degrees. The default value for this attribute is 0.5.

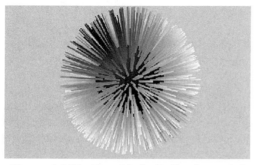

Figure 16-23 *Fur with the* **Roll** *value = 0.5*   *Figure 16-24* *Fur with the* **Roll** *value = 1.0*

Polar

The **Polar** attribute is used to rotate the fur normal to the surface. Enter **0** as the polar value to set the fur hair to -180 and enter **1** to set the fur hair to 180 degrees. The default value of this attribute is 0.

Base Opacity

The **Base Opacity** attribute is used to define the opacity of the base of the fur. Set the **Base Opacity** value to **0** to make the fur base completely transparent, and setting the value **1** to create a completely opaque fur base. The default value of this attribute is 1.

Tip Opacity

The **Tip Opacity** attribute is used to define the opacity of the fur tip. Set the **Tip Opacity** value to **0** to make the fur tip completely transparent. Set the value to **1** will create a completely opaque fur tip. The default value for this attribute is also 1.

Base Width

The **Base Width** attribute is used to define the base of each fur in the world coordinate axes. The default value of this attribute is 0.050.

Tip Width

The **Tip Width** attribute is used to define the tip of each fur in the world coordinate axes. The default value of this attribute is 0.030.

Base Curl

The **Base Curl** attribute is used to define the amount of curl at the base of the fur, as shown in Figures 16-25 and 16-26. This attribute will have no effect on the tip of the fur. Set the base curl value to **0.5** to create fur without curls. Set this value to less than **0.5** to have a half-circled curl on one side of the base. The default value of this attribute is 0.5.

*Figure 16-25 Fur with the **Base Curl** value = 0.5*

*Figure 16-26 Fur with the **Base Curl** value = 1.0*

Tip Curl

The **Tip Curl** attribute is used to define the amount of curl at the tip of the fur, as shown in Figures 16-27 and 16-28. This attribute does not have any effect on the base of the fur. Set the **Tip curl** value to **0.5** to create fur without curls. Set the value to less than **0.5** to have a half-circled curl on one side of the tip and set a value more than **0.5** to have a half-circled curl on another side. The default value of this attribute is 0.5.

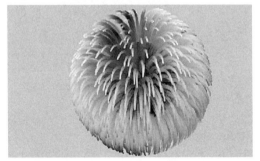

*Figure 16-27 Fur with the **Tip Curl** value = 0.5*

*Figure 16-28 Fur with the **Tip Curl** value = 1.0*

Scraggle

The **Scraggle** attribute is used to add randomness to the orientation of fur. This attribute adds kinks to individual hair and thus gives it a meshy appearance, as shown in Figures 16-29 and 16-30. The default value of this attribute is 0.

Scraggle Frequency

The **Scraggle Frequency** attribute is used to define deformation in fur, as shown in Figures 16-31 and 16-32. Higher the **Scraggle Frequency** value, more will be the deformation along each hair follicle. This attribute also governs the frequency at which the scraggle kinks occur. The default value of this attribute is 5.

Figure 16-29 *Fur with the* **Scraggle** *value = 0.0*

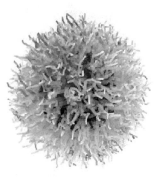

Figure 16-30 *Fur with the* **Scraggle** *value = 0.5*

Figure 16-31 *Fur with the* **Scraggle Frequency** *value=1.0*

Figure 16-32 *Fur with the* **Scraggle Frequency** *value=0.0*

Scraggle Correlation

The **Scraggle Correlation** attribute is used to define how the scraggling of one hair affects the other in a fur system. At the 0 value, each hair has a unique scraggle, which means there is no correlation between hair of a hair system. At the value **1**, all hair start scraggling in a similar manner, thus resulting in a complete scraggle correlation. The default value for this attribute is 0.

Clumping

The **Clumping** attribute is used to clump the fur hair together in a group, as shown in Figures 16-33 and 16-34. You can increase the value of this attribute to pull the hair to the center of the clump. By default, there is no clumping in the fur. The default value of this attribute is 0.

Clumping Frequency

The **Clumping Frequency** attribute is used to define the number of clumps on a surface, as shown in Figures 16-35 and 16-36. To set the value of this attribute, first you need to set the Clumping value on the fur. Higher the value of **Clumping Frequency**, more will be the number of clumps formed on the surface. Thus, thinner the clumps are formed and more will be the time taken by it to render. The **Clumping Frequency** value ranges from 0 to 100. The default value of this attribute is 5.

Figure 16-33 Fur with the **Clumping** value = **0.0**

Figure 16-34 Fur with the **Clumping** value = **1.0**

Figure 16-35 Fur with the Clumping Frequency value = 5.0

Figure 16-36 Fur with the Clumping Frequency value = 15.0

Clump Shape

The **Clump Shape** attribute is used to determine the shape of the clump formed on a surface, as shown in Figures 16-37 and 16-38. Set this value to -10 to get a concave shape or set the value to 10 to get a convex shape. The default value of this attribute is 0.

Figure 16-37 Fur with the
Clump Shape value= -10.0

Figure 16-38 Fur with the
Clump Shape value= 10.0

Segments

The **Segments** attribute is used to define the number of segments in the fur. More the number of segments, more will be the smoothness in the fur, and thus higher will be the reactivity of the fur to the forces applied on it while animating. The default value of this attribute is 10.

Attraction

The **Attraction** attribute is used to define the amount of attraction of the fur for attractors. The attractors in Maya fur are similar to the joint chains used to affect the movement of hair using dynamic forces.

Offset

The **Offset** attribute is used to define the distance of fur from the surface on which it is created in the world coordinate system. By default, the value of this attribute is set to 0. As a result, hair starts growing from the surface. Set a value less than 0 for this attribute to grow the fur from the surface. Similarly, set a value more than 0 for this attribute to grow the hair outside the surface.

Fur Presets

Maya has various default fur presets that can be applied on an object. To apply fur presets, choose the **Fur** shelf tab from the shelf bar; all default presets will be visible in the shelf area, as shown in Figure 16-39. Select a surface on which you want to apply fur from the viewport and choose the required fur preset from the **Fur** shelf tab in the shelf bar. Alternatively, apply any fur on the object in the viewport. Next, select the fur on the object and open the **Attribute Editor**. Next, choose the tab of the selected fur and press and hold the right mouse button over the **Presets*** button in the **Attribute Editor**; a flyout will be displayed. Next, you can choose the desired type of fur preset from the flyout menu. You can also blend one fur preset with another fur preset from the **Attribute Editor**, as shown in Figure 16-40. To completely replace a fur preset with another preset, choose **Replace** from the flyout menu. Various types of fur preset are given in Figures 16-41 through 16-58.

Figure 16-39 *The fur presets in the shelf area*

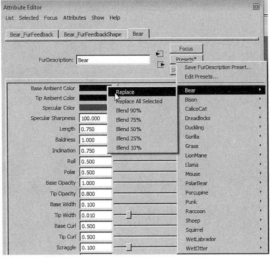

Figure 16-40 *Types of fur presets in the* **Attribute Editor**

Figure 16-41 *The* **Bear type** *fur preset*

Figure 16-42 *The* **Bison type** *fur preset*

Figure 16-43 *The* **CalicoCat** *type fur preset*

Figure 16-44 *The* **Dreadlocks** *type fur preset*

Figure 16-45 *The* **Duckling** *type fur preset*

Figure 16-46 *The* **Gorilla** *type fur preset*

Figure 16-47 *The* **Grass** *type fur preset*

Figure 16-48 *The* **LionMane** *type fur preset*

Figure 16-49 *The* **Llama** *type fur preset*

Figure 16-50 *The* **Mouse** *type fur preset*

Figure 16-51 *The **PolarBear** type fur preset*

Figure 16-52 *The **Porcupine** type fur preset*

Figure 16-53 *The **Punk** type fur preset*

Figure 16-54 *The **Raccoon** type fur preset*

Figure 16-55 *The **Sheep** type fur preset*

Figure 16-56 *The **Squirrel** type fur preset*

Figure 16-57 *The **WetLabrador** type fur preset*   **Figure 16-58** *The **WetOtter** type fur preset*

Animating Fur Presets

You can animate the fur presets by setting keys on the attributes of fur presets in the **Attribute Editor** or in the **Channel box**. To do so, first apply fur on the surface of an object and choose **Fur > Edit Fur Description > FurDescriptionName** from the main menubar; the **Attribute Editor** will be displayed. Next, press and hold the right mouse button over the attribute that you want to animate; a flyout will be displayed. Choose the **Set Key** option from the flyout to set the key, as shown in Figure 16-59. You can also set the key using the **Channel box**. To do so, choose **Key Selected** from the flyout menu to set the key on the current frame. Similarly, you can set the key for any attribute in the **Attribute Editor**. To do so, select any attribute in the **Attribute Editor** and press and hold the right mouse button over it; a flyout will be displayed. Similarly, set the keys at different frames in the timeline and preview the fur animation. Note that the **Density** attribute in the **Attribute Editor** is the only attribute that cannot be animated.

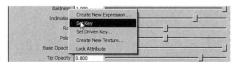

Figure 16-59 *Choosing the **Set Key** attribute from the flyout menu*

Fur Shading

In Maya, you can apply different shades to fur, depending upon the type of renderer used in project. For **Maya fur**, you can use two types of renderer: **Maya software renderer** and mental ray renderer. To shade Maya fur using the Maya software renderer, first you need to set the light attributes to get a realistic fur effect. To do so, create a light in the scene. Next, select the light and choose **Fur > Fur Shadowing Attributes > Add to Selected Light** from the main menubar to connect the light to the fur. Next, select the light again and open the **Attribute Editor** of that particular light. Next, expand the **Fur Shading/Shadowing** attribute in the **Attribute Editor**, as shown in Figure 16-60, and set various attributes as per your requirement. Figures 16-61 and 16-62 display the difference in the fur attribute with and without using the **Fur Shading** attribute.

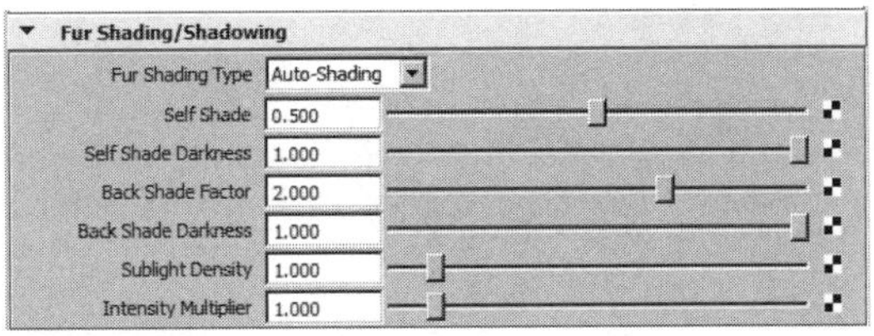

Figure 16-60 The **Fur Shading/Shadowing** *attributes area*

Figure 16-61 The object before
applying shades

Figure 16-62 The object after applying
shades using the Maya software renderer

To render a fur using the Maya mental ray renderer, create a spotlight in the viewport. Adjust the spotlight such that it is focused on the fur ball. Select the light and choose **Display > UI Elements > Attribute Editor** from the main menubar; the **Attribute Editor** will be displayed on the right of the viewport. In the **Attribute Editor**, expand the **mental ray** attribute tab. In the **Shadows** attribute node, select the **Use mental ray shadow map overrides** checker box. In the **Shadow Map Overrides** attribute section, choose the **Take Settings from Maya** button. Next, open the **Render Settings** window by choosing **Window > Rendering Editors > Render Settings** from the main menubar. Select the **mental ray** renderer from the **Render Using** drop-down list in the **Render Settings** window. Choose the **Quality** tab and set **Quality Presets** to **Production: Rapid Fur**. Render the fur ball to get the final output, as shown in Figure 16-63.

Figure 16-63 Shading fur using the mental ray renderer

TUTORIALS
Tutorial 1

In this tutorial, you will create jellyfish, as shown in Figure 16-64, by using the Maya hair.
(Expected time: 30 min)

The following steps are required to complete this tutorial:

a. Set a project folder.
b. Create the top part of the jellyfish.
c. Create tentacles of jellyfish.
d. Create a plane and apply the light to the scene.
e. Save the scene.

Figure 16-64 The jellyfish

Setting the Project Folder
Before starting a new file, it is recommended that you set the project folder.

1. Set a project with the name *c16_tut1* in the folder *Maya_Tutorials*.

Creating the Top Part of Jellyfish
In this section, you need to create the top part of jellyfish.

1. Create a new Maya file. Choose **Create > Polygon Primitives > Sphere** from the main menubar and click on the screen; a sphere is created in the viewport.

2. Press and hold the right mouse button over the sphere; a marking menu is displayed. Choose the Vertex option from the marking menu; the vertex component gets activated on the sphere.

3. Activate the Front viewport and select the bottom half vertices of the sphere, as shown in Figure 16-65. Next, choose **Edit Mesh > Merge To Center** from the main menubar; the selected vertices merge together at the center, as shown in Figure 16-66.

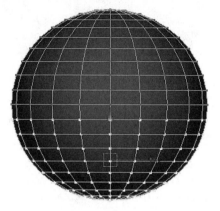

Figure 16-65 Bottom half vertices selected

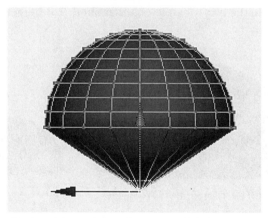

Figure 16-66 Selected vertices merged at center

4. Move the selected vertices along the Y-axis, refer to Figure 16-66. Next, activate the Perspective viewport, if it has not already been activated. Set the bottom of the sphere flat. Choose **Edit Mesh > Split Polygon Tool** from the main menubar and create the segments, as shown in Figure 16-67.

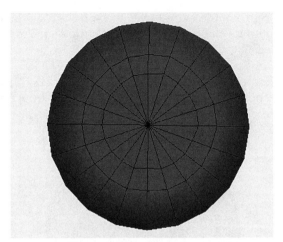

*Figure 16-67 Segments created using the **Split Polygon** Tool*

5. Select the sphere from the viewport and choose **Edit > Duplicate** from the main menubar; a duplicate of the selected part is created. Next, invoke the **Move Tool** from the toolbox and move the duplicate part away from the original sphere.

6. Name one sphere as **shell_1** and another sphere as **shell_2**. Invoke the **Scale Tool** from the toolbox and scale the two spheres such that **shell_1** is bigger than **shell_2**, as shown in Figure 16-68.

*Figure 16-68 Scaling of the **shell_1** and **shell_2** spheres*

7. Press and hold the right mouse button over **shell_1**; a marking menu is displayed. Choose **Assign New Material > Lambert** from the marking menu; the lambert attributes are displayed in the **Attribute Editor**.

8. Rename the lambert shader to **shell_1_color**. Next, in the **Common Material Attributes** area of the **Attribute Editor**, set the **Color HSV** value to **212**, **0.7**, and **0.7**, and set the **Transparency HSV** value to **212**, **0**, and **0.3**. Also, set the **Glow Intensity** value to **0.3** in the **Special Effects** attribute area.

9. Select **shell_2** from the viewport and press and hold the right mouse button over it; a marking menu is displayed. Choose **Assign New Material > Lambert** from the marking menu; the lambert attributes are displayed in the **Attribute Editor**.

10. Rename the lambert shader to **shell_2_color**. Next, set the **Color HSV** value to **58**, **0.8**, and **0.5** and the **Transparency HSV** value to **58**, **0.8**, and **0.17**. Also, set the **Glow Intensity** to **0.2** in the **Special Effects** attribute area.

11. Select the **shell_2** model from the viewport and move it into the center of **shell_1**, as shown in Figure 16-69.

Figure 16-69 Alignment of both shells

Creating the Tentacles of the Jellyfish

In this section, you need to create the tentacles for jellyfish.

1   Choose **View > Predefined Bookmarks > Bottom** from the panel menu; the active viewport changes to the bottom viewport.

2. Select **shell_1** and press and hold the right mouse button over it; a marking menu is displayed. Choose **Face** from the marking menu; the **Face** component gets highlighted. Select the faces on **shell_1**, as shown in Figure 16-70.

3. Choose **Create UVs > Planar Mapping** from the main menubar; the planar map appears on the selected faces.

4. Select the faces on the object, refer to Figure 16-70. Select the **Dynamics** module from the menu set drop-down list in the status line. Choose **Hair > Create Hair > Option Box** from the main menubar; the **Create Hair Options** dialog box is displayed.

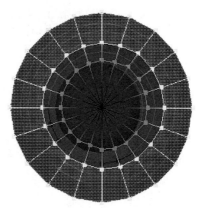

*Figure 16-70 The faces selected on **shell_1***

5. Select the **At selected points/faces** radio button and set **Length** to **10** in the **Create Hair Options** dialog box. Next, choose the **Create Hairs** button from the dialog box; hair is created on the selected faces.

6. Set the timeline to **1000** frames and play the animation. Stop the animation at frame **50**. Next, select the hair from the viewport and choose **Hair > Set Start Position > From Current** from the main menubar; the position of the hair at the current frame is set to **1**. Figure 16-71 displays the appearance of hair after making the modifications.

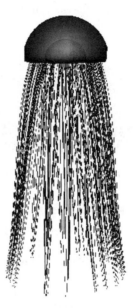

Figure 16-71 *The appearance of hair*

7. First, select **shell_2** and then **shell_1**. Next, press P on the keyboard to make **shell_1** the parent of **shell_2**. Select **shell_1** from the viewport. Next, choose **Solvers > Interactive Playback** from the main menubar and move **shell_1** in the viewport; As a result, hair start behaving interactively with the sphere.

8. Stop the animation and select the hair. Next, choose **Modify > Convert > Paint Effects to Polygons** from the main menubar; the hair change to polygons.

9. Press and hold the right mouse button over the hair and choose **Material Attributes...** from the marking menu; the hair attributes are displayed in the **Attribute Editor**. Select **Lambert** from the **Type** drop-down list in the **Attribute Editor**; the default shader changes to the **Lambert** shader.

10. Choose the checker button on the right of the **Color** attribute area in the **Attribute Editor**; the **Create Render Node** window is displayed. Select the **Ramp** texture from the **2D Textures** area; the ramp attributes are displayed in the **Attribute Editor**.

11. Create four nodes on the ramp and align them, as shown in Figure 16-72. Set the **HSV** values of these nodes as follows:

Node 1: **218, 0.9, 0.7**   Node 2: **200, 0.7, 1**
Node 3: **195, 0.2, 1**   Node 4: **0, 0, 1**

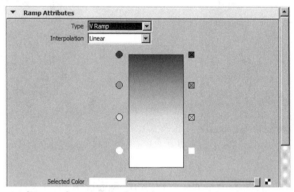

*Figure 16-72 Nodes arranged on the ramp in the **Attribute Editor***

12. Select the hair in the Perspective viewport, and press and hold the right mouse button over them; a marking menu is displayed. Choose **Material Attributes...** from the marking menu; the **Attribute Editor** is displayed.

13. Expand the **Special Effects** attribute tab in the **Attribute Editor** and set the **Glow Intensity** value to **0.5** to add glow to the hair on rendering.

14. Choose **Render the current frame (Maya Software)** from the status line to render the jellyfish created in the viewport, as shown in Figure 16-73.

    Next, you need to add more hair to the jellyfish to make it more realistic.

15. Select the hair in the Perspective viewport and choose **Display > Hide > Hide Selection** from the main menubar to hide the hair. Choose **View > Predefined Bookmarks > Bottom** from the panel menu; the active viewport changes to bottom viewport.

16. Press and hold the right mouse button over **shell_1** and choose **Face** from the marking menu; the face component of the object becomes active. Select the faces at the center, as shown in Figure 16-74.

Figure 16-73 *The rendered view of jellyfish*

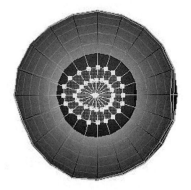

Figure 16-74 *The faces at the center*

17. Repeat steps 3, 4, and 5; hair is created on the selected faces. Select the new hair created and choose **Modify > Convert > Paint Effects to Polygons** from the main menubar; the hair change to polygons.

18. Repeat steps 9, 10, 11, 12, and 13, and then set **Glow Intensity** under the **Special Effects** attribute area to **0.5**.

19. Choose **Render the current frame (Maya Software)** from the status line to render the jellyfish created in the viewport.

Creating a Plane and Applying Light to the Scene

In this section, you need to create a plane and set the spot light and directional light in the scene.

1. Create a polygonal plane in the viewport with the following attributes:

    Width: **65**   Height: **60**
    Subdivisions Width: **40**   Subdivisions Height: **40**

2. Invoke the **Soft Modification Tool** from the toolbox and modify the plane to create bumps on it, as shown in Figure 16-75.

3. Press and hold the right mouse button over the plane and choose **Assign New Material > Lambert** from the marking menu; the **Attribute Editor** displaying the properties of the **Lambert** shader is displayed.

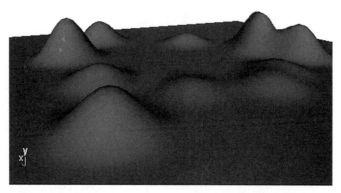

Figure 16-75 *The plane after using the **Soft Modification Tool***

4. Choose the **Open** button on the right of the **Image Name** attribute from the **File Attributes** area in the **Attribute Editor**; the **Open** dialog box is displayed. Next, select the *land.jpg* and then choose the **Open** button; the texture is applied on the plane, as shown in Figure 16-76.

Figure 16-76 *Texture applied on the plane*

5. Choose **Create > Lights > SpotLight** from the main menubar to create a spot light in the viewport.

6. Activate the Front viewport; the light is placed in the viewport, as shown in Figure 16-77. Invoke the **Rotate** and **Move** tools to adjust the spot light, as shown in Figure 16-78.

Figure 16-77 *The placement of spot light*

Figure 16-78 *The adjusted spot light*

7. Choose **Display > Show > Light Manipulators** from the main menubar; the light manipulators are displayed in the viewport, as shown in Figure 16-79. Select the manipulator ring 10. Next, press and hold the left mouse button over this manipulator ring and move it downward until the ring has passed through the polygonal plane in the viewport.

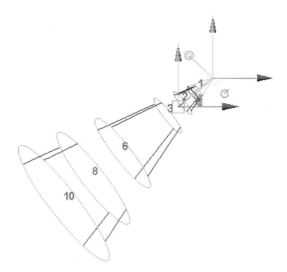

Figure 16-79 *The light manipulators*

8. Choose **Display > Hide > Light Manipulators** from the main menubar to hide the manipulators. Next, select the light and choose **Display > UI Elements > Channel Box/Layer Editor** from the main menubar; the **Channel box** is displayed. Enter the following values in the channel box:

    TranslateX: **1.5**   TranslateY: **20**   TranslateZ: **26**
    RotateX: **-45**   RotateY: **-4**

 Note
You can also set the position of the spot light with respect to the position of jellyfish in the viewport.

9. Select the spotlight and choose **Window > Attribute Editor** from the main menubar; the **Attribute Editor** is displayed. Next, choose the checker button on the right of the **Color** attribute; the **Create Render Node** window is displayed. Next, choose the **File** button in the **Create Render Node** area; the **File Attributes** are displayed in the **Attribute Editor**.

10. Choose the **Open** button on the right of the **Image Name** attribute from the **File Attributes** area in the **Attribute Editor**; the **Open** dialog box is displayed. Next, select the *texture_light.jpg* and then choose the **open** button.

11. Select the spotlight and then set the **Cone Angle** value to **60** in the **Attribute Editor**. Expand the **Light Effects** attribute tab in the **Attribute Editor**. Choose the checker button on the right of the **Light Fog** attribute to apply the fog effect to the spot light.

12. Choose **Create > Lights > Directional Light** from the main menubar; a directional light is created in the viewport.

13. Choose **Display > Hide > Light Manipulators** from the main menubar to hide the manipulators, if they are not already hidden. Next, select the light from the viewport and choose **Display > UI Elements > Channel Box/Layer Editor** from the main menubar; the **Channel box** is displayed. Enter the following values in the **Channel box**:

    TranslateX: **0**   TranslateY: **9**   TranslateZ: **1**
    RotateX: **-90**   RotateY: **-10**   RotateZ: **58**

14. Select the directional light from the viewport and choose **Window > Attribute Editor** from the main menubar; the **Attribute Editor** is displayed. Set the **HSV** value for the **Color** attribute to **55, 0.15**, and **1**. Also, set the value **0.5** in the **Intensity** edit box.

15. Create multiple copies of jellyfish. Invoke the **Move Tool** and then the **Scale Tool** from the toolbox. Scale the jellyfish randomly.

Saving the File

In this section, you need to save the file.

1. Choose **File > Save Scene** from the main menubar; the **Save As** dialog box is displayed.

    As the project folder is already set, by default the path *\Documents\Maya_Tutorials\c16_tut1\ scenes* is displayed in the **Look In** text box of the dialog box.

2. Enter **c16_tut1** in the **File name** text box and then select **Maya Binary** from the **Files of type** drop-down list. Next, choose the **Save As** button.

You can view the final rendered image of the model of the tutorial by downloading the file *c16_Maya_2012_render.zip* file from *http://www.cadcim.com*.

> **Tip**. *You can also enhance your scene by applying paint strokes in it. To do so, open the **Visor** window, expand the **underwater** paint strokes and then apply the **bubbles.mel** paint stroke in the scene to give it a realistic look. Similarly, apply other paint strokes in the scene to get the output, as shown in Figure 16-80.*

Figure 16-80   *The final rendered scene*

Tutorial 2

In this tutorial, you will add fur preset to a plane, as shown in Figure 16-81, using the Maya
Fur.   **(Expected Time: 20 min)**

The following steps are required to complete this tutorial:

a.   Create a project.
b.   Create a plane and apply the Lion Mane fur preset to it.
c.   Adjust **Fur Description** node parameters.
d.   Create texture for the **Polar** attribute.
e.   Bake the texture.
f.   Save the file.

Figure 16-81 Fur preset applied to a plane

Creating the Project Folder

Before starting a new file, it is recommended that you set the project folder.

1.   Set a project with the name *c16_tut2* in the folder *Maya_Tutorials*.

Creating the Plane

In this section, you need to create a plane and apply fur preset to it.

1. Open a new Maya scene and then choose **Create > Polygon Primitive > Option Box from the main menubar**. Set the **Width** and **Height** divisions values to **10**. Next, choose the **Create** button; a plane is created in the viewport.

2. Activate the **Fur Shelf** and click on the **Lion Mane** preset button; Maya applies the Lion Mane fur preset to the plane.

3. Select the **LionMane_FurFeedback** node in the **Outliner** window. Press CTRL+a; the **Attribute Editor** window is displayed. Set the **U** and **V** samples to **128** each; Maya updates the fur density in the viewport without affecting the render time, as shown in Figure 16-82.

Figure 16-82 Fur density updated in the viewport

4. Select the **LionMane** node in the **Attribute Editor** and set the following values:

    Density: **20,000**   Length: **1.5**

5. Press and hold the right mouse button over the **Polar** attribute; a flyout is displayed, as shown in Figure 16-83. Choose the **Create New Texture** option from the flyout to create a new texture; the **Hypershade** window is displayed.

6. Choose **Create > 2D Texture > Ramp** from the **Hypershade** menu bar. Now, adjust the ramp parameters, as shown in Figure 16-84.

Figure 16-83 *Choosing* **the Create New Feature** *option from the flyout*

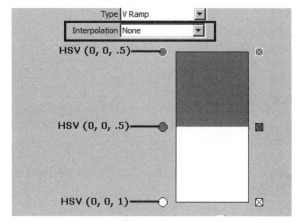

Figure 16-84 *Resolution settings*

7. Select the **LionMane** node in the **Outliner** window. Open the **Attribute Editor** and select the **Polar** option from the **Bake Attribute** drop-down list. Choose the **Bake** button. Figure 16-85 shows the fur after the bake operation.

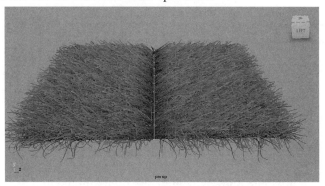

Figure 16-85 *The fur after the bake operation*

8. Click on the **Render Current Frame** button from the status line to view the rendered output.

Saving the File

In this section, you need to save the file.

1. Choose **File > Save Scene** from the main menubar; the **Save As** dialog box is displayed.

   As the project folder is already set, by default the path *\Documents\Maya_Tutorials\c16_tut2\ scenes* is displayed in the **Look In** text box of the dialog box.

2. Enter **c16_tut2** in the **File name** text box and then select **Maya Binary** from the **Files of type** drop-down list. Next, choose the **Save As** button.

You can view the final rendered image of the model of the tutorial by downloading the *c16_Maya_2012_render.zip* file from *http://www.cadcim.com*.

Self-Evaluation Test

Answer the following questions and then compare them to those given at the end of this chapter:

1. Which of the following is used to simulate the effect of dynamics and other gravitational forces over the hair follicles created?

   (a) Randomization   (b) Simulation
   (c) Hair Simulation   (d) Maya Hair

2. Which of the following attributes is used to define overall specularity across the whole fur description?

   (a) **Inclination**   (b) **Specular color**
   (c) **Specular sharpness**   (d) None of these

3. The _____ attribute is used to rotate the fur normal to the surface.

4. The _____ attribute is used to define the distance of the fur from the surface.

5. The _____ drop-down list is used to change the render type of the fur according to the base color and tip color of the hair in the scene.

6. The _____ attribute is used to define the total number of hair on a selected surface.

7. The **Global Scale** attribute is used to scale the hair fur uniformly. (T/F)

8. The **Scraggle Correlation** is used to clump the fur hair together in a group. (T/F)

9. The **Equalize** check box is used to adjust uneven mapping between the UV space and the world space. (T/F)

10. The **Clump Shape** attribute is used to define the number of segments in the fur. (T/F)

Review Questions

Answer the following questions:

1. Which of the following attributes is used to define the total number of hair fur on a surface in the viewport?

   (a) **Global Scale**   (b) **Length**
   (c) **Density**   (d) None of these

2. Which of the following attributes is used to rotate the fur normal to the surface?

   (a) **Scraggle**   (b) **Clumping**
   (c) **Attraction**   (d) **Polar**

3. The _____ area displays the names of the surfaces on which the fur attributes are applied.

4. The _____ attribute is used to define the color of the tip of the fur.

5. The _____ attribute is used to define the length of each hair fur.

6. The **Base Ambient Color** attribute is used to define the base color of fur. (T/F)

7. The **Clumping** attribute is used to add kinks to individual hair to give it a meshy appearance. (T/F)

8. The **Scraggle Frequency** attribute is used to define how the scraggling of one hair affects the other in the fur system. (T/F)

9. The **Attractors** in Maya fur are similar to the joint chains used to affect the movement of hair using dynamic forces. (T/F)

10. The **Inclination** attribute is used to determine the angle at which the fur will be inclined to the surface. (T/F)

Exercise

Exercise 1

Create the model of a tennis ball, as shown in Figure 16-86. Next, apply the fur preset on it to get the output, as shown in Figure 16-87. You can view the final rendered image of this model by downloading the *c16_maya_2012_render.zip* file from *http://www.cadcim.com*. The path of the file is as follows:

Textbooks > Animation and Visual Effects > Maya > Autodesk Maya 2012: A Comprehensive Guide
(Expected time: 30 min)

Figure 16-86 The tennis ball

Figure 16-87 The tennis ball after applying the fur preset

Answers to Self-Evaluation Test
1. c, **2.** c, **3. Polar**, **4. Offset**, **5. Light Model**, **6. Density**, **7.** T, **8.** F, **9.** T, **10.** F

Index

Other Publications by CADCIM Technologies

The following is the list of some of the publications by CADCIM Technologies. Please visit www.cadcim.com for the complete listing.

Autodesk 3ds Max Design Textbooks
- Autodesk 3ds Max Design 2012: A Tutorial Approach
- Autodesk 3ds Max Design 2011: A Tutorial Approach
- Autodesk 3ds Max Design 2010: A Tutorial Approach

Autodesk 3ds Max Textbooks
- Autodesk 3ds Max 2012: A Comprehensive Guide
- Autodesk 3ds Max 2011: A Comprehensive Guide
- Autodesk 3ds Max 2010: A Comprehensive Guide

Autodesk Maya Textbooks
- Autodesk Maya 2011: A Comprehensive Guide
- Autodesk Maya 2010: A Comprehensive Guide
- Character Animation: A Tutorial Approach

AutoCAD LT Textbooks
- AutoCAD LT 2012 for Designers
- AutoCAD LT 2011 for Designers
- AutoCAD LT 2010 for Designers

Autodesk Revit Architecture Textbooks
- Autodesk Revit Architecture 2012 for Architects and Designers
- Autodesk Revit Architecture 2011 for Architects & Designers
- Autodesk Revit Architecture 2010 for Architects & Designers

Autodesk Revit Structure Textbook
- Exploring Autodesk Revit Structure 2011

AutoCAD Civil 3D Textbooks
- Exploring AutoCAD Civil 3D, 2012
- AutoCAD Civil 3D 2009 for Engineers

AutoCAD Map 3D Textbooks
- Exploring AutoCAD Map 3D, 2012
- Exploring AutoCAD Map 3D 2011

Autodesk Inventor Textbooks
- Autodesk Inventor 2012 for Designers
- Autodesk Inventor 2011 for Designers
- Autodesk Inventor 2010 for Designers

Solid Edge Textbooks

- Solid Edge ST3 for Designers
- Solid Edge ST2 for Designers

NX Textbooks

- NX 7 for Designers
- NX 6 for Designers
- NX 5 for Designers

Autodesk Alias Textbooks

- Learning Autodesk Alias Design 2010
- Autodesk AliasStudio 2009 for Designers

SolidWorks Textbooks

- SolidWorks 2011 for Designers
- SolidWorks 2010 for Designers

CATIA Textbooks

- CATIA V5R20 for Designers
- CATIA V5R19 for Designers
- CATIA V5R18 for Designers

EdgeCAM Textbooks

- EdgeCAM 11.0 for Manufacturers
- EdgeCAM 10.0 for Manufacturers

ANSYS Textbook

- ANSYS 11.0 for Designers

Pro/ENGINEER Textbooks

- Pro/ENGINEER Wildfire 5.0 for Designers
- Pro/ENGINEER Wildfire 4.0 for Designers
- Pro/ENGINEER Wildfire 3.0 for Designers

Coming Soon from CADCIM Technologies

- The Eyeon Fusion 6: A Tutorial Approach
- Adobe Flash Professional CS5: A Tutorial Approach
- Adobe Premiere Pro CS5: A Tutorial Approach
- The Foundry NukeX: A Tutorial Approach
- Autodesk Softimage 2012: A Tutorial Approach
- ANSYS Workbench 13.0 for Designers

Online Training Program Offered by CADCIM Technologies

CADCIM Technologies provides effective and affordable virtual online training on various software packages such as CAD/CAM/CAE, Animation, Civil, GIS, and computer programming languages. The training will be delivered 'live' via Internet at any time, any place, and at any pace to individuals, students of colleges, universities, and training centers. For more information, please visit the following link:
http://www.cadcim.com